ENCOUNTER
WITH
FAMILY REALITIES

*

ENCOUNTER WITH WITH FAMILY REALITIES

Edward A. Powers
Mary W. Lees
Iowa State University

WEST PUBLISHING COMPANY
St. Paul • New York • Boston • Los Angeles • San Francisco

CREDITS

Photography by Susan Nicholson from her private collection of paper memorabilia; additional photos by H. Armstrong Roberts.

Library of Congress Cataloging in Publication Data

Main entry under title:

Encounter with family realities.

    Includes index
    1. Marriage—Addresses, essays, lectures.
    2. Family—Addresses, essays, lectures.
I. Powers, Edward A. II. Lees, Mary W.
HQ734.E64   301.42   76–58337
ISBN 0-8299-0051-9

To our families with whom we have shared these realities

EAP
MWL

*

Contents

✝

Introduction

For years intrepid scholars have studied the family. Still, the complexity of family life almost defies analysis. The picture is compounded further by the variety of theoretical orientations from which one can approach the family: symbolic interactionism, structural functionalism, developmental cycles, cross-cultural comparisons, etc. It has been difficult to develop a total perspective on the family, as the various approaches tend to isolate or segmentalize certain ages, inclusive processes or common events. In any of these perspectives, we come away with a somewhat myopic or tunnel view of the family. We are not suggesting there is no value in these approaches, but we do feel the need for a more holistic view of the family. If family life could be depicted as on a continuum from infancy through death, we propose to cut vertically through that continuum to examine the crucial issues in certain periods—in Kirkpatrick's terminology, "family dramas."[1] This vertical view could be likened to still shots of people and families at certain times in the life experience during which critical issues must be faced and resolved.

In cutting vertically through the family experience the areas are not discrete. Dating for some begins in preadolescence and extends through those years when others are already married. For a number, the parenting of preadolescents may occur when others are involved in grandparent roles. Thus, a holistic view of family life disregards age and instead presents the variety of interrelated factors operating at various stages—even as a drama portrays the interaction of persons, their past experiences, present events, the cultural setting and a myriad of other factors. There is a commonness to these experiences that permits generalizations to be made. Although the degree, form or time may vary, these experiences constitute the realities of family life.

Decisions at one stage may be extremely functional for that period of life but certainly will have repercussions for a later stage also. Some of these represent cultural values while others suggest lack of awareness. For example, in our socialization of children, we encourage boys to develop independence and value indications of that independence. Within mature family life, that independence can be dysfunctional to the marriage relationship. Men are trained subtly and openly to make decisions on the basis of their knowledge and insight and then to act on those decisions. The husband/wife relationship needs a different interactive pattern. Similarly, girls are socialized to be dependent and not to be decisive. Women are to derive affirmation of self-worth, not from who they are or what they do, but from their relationship to others. This may raise the middle-age question of "Who am I?" when the mother-child relationship is no longer a crucial issue.

Neuhaus and Neuhaus portray these family developmental periods as occurring for most people (wedding, birth of the first child, children entering school, adolescence, middle years . . . . and the years of retirement and later life), yet they use the term "crises".[2] We do not see these realities as crises with the usual understanding of the term, nor are they necessarily traumatic, although they may become so through the interrelatedness of internal and/or external factors. Significant change and learning are occurring—change being a reality of life for all people at all times. We propose to examine these times of change and learning for a more complete view of family life when critical issues are to be resolved. This is reality to a family.

Although most of the articles selected are contemporary, the photos chosen illustrate the timelessness of these experiences in family life. The details of the dramas change over time, but the underlying issues have constituted reality for generations and will continue to do so in the foreseeable future.

The selections encompass two approaches to family reality. Within each section are substantive articles related to the issues. We are sociologists and believe the sociological perspective on family life to be valid and worth consideration. Also within each section we present personal accounts illustrating or dramatizing family realities at each stage. Certainly a reader is more interesting that includes personal accounts, and we want this book to be read.

Vicarious experience, however, is no adequate substitute for working through a situation. Reading about family dramas is not the same as encountering those realities. Although no substitute, reading about and study of family realities can provide understanding of the past and facilitate preparation for the future. This has been our hope for *Encounter with Family Realities*.

References

1.   C. Kirkpatrick, *The Family as Process & Institution* (New York: Ronald Press, 1963).
2.   R. Neuhaus & R. Neuhaus, *Family Crisis* Columbus: Charles Merrill Publishing Company, 1974).

*

1

BEGINNINGS

It seemed reasonable to divide our study into broad periods to encompass the major realities. In Section 1, "Beginnings," we suggest that reality for young children includes their need for security, ego struggle, development of their own logic of learning, play as work, and sex role learning. Admittedly, food, shelter and clothing are basic necessities. But beyond these, every child needs a sense of security. Similarly, ego struggle is a critical issue for children. This struggle occurs with the first awareness of "Who am I?" Ego struggle may be a gentle process or a difficult one if mixed signals are received from parents and other significant persons. However gentle or difficult, the issue arises.

A third reality of this early period occurs because the logic and reasoning of childhood differs from that of adulthood. Parents often are perplexed about their children in the typical, "I'll never understand why he/she did that!" or "Why in the world did you do *that*?" We assume that children think and reason as adults do although on a more elementary level. What seem as wild flights of fancy to adults may to children make the most sense. A particular example of this is the role of play. Adults see play as random activity or as exploration of the visible universe. From the perspective of children, it is their work and they work hard at it. If we can understand this, we are more likely to be supportive and affirming of children with their view of the world.

The last issue with which we deal is sex-appropriate behavior. Sex roles are culturally prescribed and even preschoolers have clear perceptions of what the expectations will be for them as adults. These expectations are conveyed by parents, other adults, school experiences, the media, and in a host of other subtle and not-so-subtle ways.

We make no pretense of saying these issues are the only ones important to children in their first years. Different family situations, other siblings and subcultural norms may emphasize other issues as well. What we are suggesting is that these concerns have a commonality that make them at least a part of reality for all children in all families.

CONTENTS: SECTION 1

SOMETHING HAPPENED AT SCHOOL*

Adele Schwarz

I must tell someone about my first day at school.
I woke up and I began to dress.
None of the socks in my drawer matched.
My dress ripped under the arm.
I had to wear my sweater. It itches.
The hem was hanging from my skirt.
I had to hunt for a safety pin.
In the mirror I saw my hair curling up instead of under.
My sister was in the bathroom with the door locked.
I had a stomachache.
At breakfast my brother grabbed my Snoopy place mat.
I dribbled milk on my sweater. The spot got bigger as I rubbed.
My mom said I had to carry an umbrella to school.
I was the only kid with an umbrella.
There are two teachers in the second grade.
I got the one who puts kids in the closet. Everybody says so.
My seat is in the back of the room behind the tallest boy in the class.
It is next to the window and in front of the radiator.
The sun was in my eyes. I was broiling.
The girl next to me said mind your own business when she opened her desk.
The teacher told *me* to stop talking when the boy in front asked for a pencil. My face turned scarlet. Everyone noticed.
The teacher handed out new reading books. There were not enough to go around. I had to share with the girl next to me, the one who said I was nosy. She kept pulling the book closer.
She sneezed all over the page. I held my breath so I would not get the flu.
At lunch my sandwich was soggy from the smashed tomato.
The teacher saw me throw out my lunch.
In gym I had no sneakers. I had to watch.
In art we had to paint a picture of ourselves . . . with watercolors.
I look like I am melting.
The teacher did not hang it up. I will never be an artist.
On the way home Sammy pulled up my skirt. As I ran away from him, the button popped.
I fell on the sidewalk and got a bloody knee. I think the pebbles are still in it.

---

*By permission of the author, Adele Schwarz.

My sister called me crybaby.
My mother said it could not hurt that much.
She put *iodine* on it!
At dinner my dad said how was your first day at school.
I said it was okay. . . .

HOW CHILDREN LEARN ABOUT SEX & BIRTH*

Anne C. Bernstein

"To get a baby, go to the store and buy a duck."—Susan, a Four Year Old

Every day, thousands of parents sit down to tell their offspring about the birds and the bees. And the cows. And the chickens. And the ducks. Parental descriptions of sex and birth often sound like morning roll call on Noah's Ark. When it comes to people, the lecture suddenly takes on the clinical precision of an advanced anatomy course, as the anxious parent rushes through enough detail to confuse a medical student.

Children take this information, process it through mental Jungle gyms, and create their own versions of who comes from where, and how. The children seem content with their answers, and parents, having provided the answers, are not about to start following up with more questions. Chances are, therefore, that misunderstanding will persist.

The most effective way to tell children about sex is to provide information matched to their level of mental development. But because no one ever asks children what they really believe, as opposed to what they were told, we don't understand how their ability to analyze and assimilate information changes year by year.

As part of my research at the University of California, Berkeley, I decided to find out how children understood the explanations and gossip that form their early sex education. With Philip A. Cowan, I devised an interview plan that amounted to turning back on children their perennial question, "How do people get babies?"

It might seem as if the answer to that question will depend on what a child has been told, but that's not the case. Even when adults give children straight facts, the story of human reproduction often gets twisted into a remarkable version of creation.

Jane, aged four, told me: "To get a baby to grow in your tummy, you just make it first. You put some eyes on it. Put the head on, and hair, some hair, all curls. You make it with head stuff you find in the store that makes it for you. Well, the mommy and daddy make the baby and then they put it in the tummy and then it goes quickly out."

Jane had never been told, by parents, peers or sex-education books, that babies were manufactured, using parts purchased from the store. She put together the answer out of information gathered and given, and held together by a thread of childish logic that reflected her understanding of the physical world.

Jane's story comes from my interviews with 60 boys and girls, all of whom had younger brothers and sisters. They were all white, middle-and upper-middle-class children who lived in a university community. One third of the children were either three or four years old; one third were seven or eight; and one third were 11 or 12. The children's ages corresponded to certain developmental levels suggested by Swiss psychologist Jean Piaget.

Piaget regards each child as a philosopher who works at making his universe intelligible. As the child develops, he shapes the world in terms of his own level of understanding and then restructures his understanding when he gets new information that doesn't fit his old view of the universe.

Answers to my questions fell into six levels of maturity that show a consistent sequence of development. The differences between any two levels reflect a difference in problem-solving strategies. It's the structure of a child's answer, not its content, that distinguishes one level from another.

LEVEL ONE: GEOGRAPHY

The youngest children answered the question, "How do people get babies?" as if it were a question about geography. These children, usually three to four years old, told me:

"You go to a baby store and buy one."

"From tummies."

"From God's place."

"It just grows inside mommy's tummy. It's there all the time. Mommy doesn't have to do anything. She just waits until she feels it."

Antonia, who will soon be four, carried on the following conversation:

ME: How did your brother start to be in your mommy's tummy?

ANTONIA: Um, my baby just went in my mommy's tummy.

ME: How did he get in?

ANTONIA: He was just in my mommy's tummy.

ME: Before you said that he wasn't there when you were there. Was he?

ANTONIA: Yeah, and then he was in the other place . . . in America.

ME: In America?

ANTONIA: Yeah, in somebody else's tummy. And then he went through somebody's vagina, then he went in my mommy's tummy.

ME: In whose tummy was he before?

ANTONIA: Um, I don't know who his, her name is. It's a her.

This little girl, typical of level-one children, believes a baby that now exists has always existed. The only real question is where he was before he came to live at her house. She knows that her brother grew inside her mother's body. How and when he happened to grow there is beyond her grasp, but she extrapolates from the information she has: babies grow inside tummies and come out vaginas. Before her brother was in her mother's tummy, he must have been in somebody else's tummy, and that somebody must be female because only big girls can grow babies. Presumably this chain can go on indefinitely, with each mommy getting her baby in turn from another woman.

The level-one child does not understand the laws of cause and effect. His belief that babies have always existed is consistent with his conviction that he and all the people he knows have always existed. He cannot imagine a world without himself in it.

LEVEL TWO: MANUFACTURING

This is a level that Henry Ford would have recognized and admired, for these children believe that babies are manufactured by people as if they were refrigerators, TV sets or automobiles. A level-two child knows that babies have not always existed; they must be built.

According to four-year-old Laura, "When people are already made, they make some other people. They make the bones inside, and blood. They make skin. They make the skin first and then they make blood and bones. They paint the blood, paint the red blood and the blue blood." Asked how babies start to be in mommies' tummies, she replied: "Maybe from people. They just put them in the envelope and fold them up and mommy puts them in her 'gina and they just stay in there." Asked where the babies were before they were in the envelope, she answered, "They buy them at the store."

These children seem undeterred by the fact they've never seen a baby factory or a rack of diapered infants at the local supermarket. When provoked by curiosity or question, they simply make up answers, fitting what they have been told and what they have seen into their view of the world. Because children at this level believe that everything in the world has been made either by a magicianlike God or by people, they assume that babies are created in a similar way.

These children are still egocentric; they can interpret the world only in terms of events or processes they have experienced themselves. Therefore, they often fall into the "digestive fallacy," and believe that babies are conceived by swallowing and born by elimination. One four-year-old boy uses the digestive to explain how mommies and daddies get to be parents. He says that God makes mommies and daddies "with a little seed": "He puts it down on the table. Then it grows bigger. The people grow together. He makes them eat the seed and then they grow to be people from skel'tons at God's place. Then they stand up and go someplace else where they could live."

A few children at level two connect a father with the birth process, but fit what they have been told to a mechanical process. One girl said, "he puts his hand in his tummy and gets it (the seed) and puts it on the bottom of the mommy and the mommy gets the egg out of her tummy and puts the egg on top of the seed. And then they close their tummies and the baby is born." The child believes that the seed and the egg can come together only by manual means. She conscientiously tried to fit what she had been told about reproduction into physical processes, but she had a few doubts. She told me that "the daddy can't really open up all his tummies."

LEVEL THREE: TRANSITIONAL

Children at this level explain procreation as a mixture of physiology and technology, but they stick to operations that are technically feasible. A level-three child knows that mommy and daddy can't open and close their tummies, but he may assume that conception is impossible without marriage. He may also take quite literally his parents' explanation of conception as "planting a seed." Jack, aged four, told me: "The daddy plants the seed like a flower, I think, except you don't need dirt."

A child at this level of understanding still believes that the world of nature is alive; he talks about nonliving and living things as if they possessed will and acted purposefully. Jeanne, who is seven, said: "The sperm goes into the mommy to each egg and puts it, makes the egg safe. So if something bump comes along, it won't crack the egg. The sperm comes from the daddy. It swims into the penis, and I think it makes a little hole and then it swims into the vagina. It has a little mouth and it bites a hole."

Level-three children may know that three major ingredients go into making babies: social relationships such as love and marriage; sexual intercourse; and the union of sperm and ovum. However, their ability to combine these factors into a coherent whole is limited. These children are in a transitional period between the stages of development that Piaget calls preoperational and concrete operational.

A preoperational child builds mental maps based on his own experiences; he solves problems by intuition. He cannot assign objects to categories. Asked to define an apple, he's likely to say, "It's to eat." As he moves into the next stage, which can happen any time between seven and 10 years old, he learns to think systematically and generally about concrete objects. Ask him about an apple now, and he'll say, "It's a fruit."

During this transitional period, children are often aware that their explanations don't quite add up. Ursula, who is eight, describes the father's role in reproduction: "Well, he puts his penis right in the place where the baby comes out, and somehow it (sperm) comes out of there. It seems like magic sort of 'cause it just comes out."

Asked why the male contribution is necessary, Ursula, who has seen cartons of eggs in the refrigerator, replied: "Well, the father puts the shell. I forget what it's called, but he puts something in for the egg. If he didn't, then a baby couldn't come. Because it needs the stuff that the father gives. It helps it grow. I think that the stuff has the food part, maybe, and maybe it helps protect it. I think he gives the shell part, and the shell part, I think, is the skin."

Her description transforms the father's traditional social role as family protector into a literal protector of the growing baby. His genetic contribution is first a protective shell for the egg, and then the outer covering of the baby.

LEVEL FOUR: CONCRETE PHYSIOLOGY

At levels four through six, the eight-to 12-year-old children give primarily physiological explanations. They can think logically about objects and people and can consider past and future. They understand the idea of cause and effect.

Although level-four children may know the physical facts of life, they don't understand why genetic material must unite before new life can begin. One child thought that sperm existed primarily to provide an escort service; "The sperm reaches the eggs. It looses 'em and brings 'em down to the forming place, I think that's right, and it grows until it's ready to take out."

Karen, who is eight, explained: "The man and the woman get together, and then they put a speck, then the man has his seed and the woman has an egg. They have to come together or else the baby won't really get hatched very well. The seed makes the egg grow. It's just like plants. If you plant a seed, a flower will grow."

Karen knew that sexual intercourse provides a means for the seed and egg to come together. She knew that both are necessary to create new life, but she had no clear idea of why this was so. Nor did she attempt to reason her way to a solution.

Karen's return to the agricultural metaphor is a reminder that children's thought develops in a spiral, not a straight line. They circle back to the same issues, but deal with old information on a more sophisticated level.

Most of the level-four children I talked to were eight years old. At first, they were embarrassed by questions about sex. A typical response was, "I don't know much about it." Having disclaimed knowledge, these children would go on to say that the union of sperm and egg or sexual intercourse was the cause of procreation.

LEVEL FIVE: PREFORMATION

At level five, children at least attempt to explain the necessity for sperm and ovum to join, but most insist that the baby springs preformed from one of the sperm cells. These children, usually 11 or 12 years old, seem to repeat the history of the science of embryology. Like 17th century scientists, they believe that one germ cell carries a fully formed, miniature person who simply grows to full size in the uterus. They see no need for a final cause.

Some of these children believe that the baby is in the sperm, which is given food and shelter by the egg. As Patrick, who is nearly 13, explains it: "The lady has an egg and the man has a sperm and sort of he fertilizes the egg, and then the egg slowly grows. The serm grows into a baby inside the egg. Fertilize? It means it gets inside the egg, the sperm does. The egg before the sperm goes in it sort of like, well, I guess it doesn't have anything in it to grow. It just has food and I guess a shell on the outside. It's sort of the beginning of the baby. It has to happen, because otherwise the sperm would just die because it has no shelter on the outside to keep it alive, no food, nothing. And then the egg, there's nothing in it to grow. It has no . . . no . . . no living animal in there."

Twelve-year-old William, on the other hand, believes that the miniature person inhabits the ovum. He describes fertilization: "That's when the sperm enters the egg. I guess the egg just has sort of an undeveloped embryo and when the sperm enters it, it makes it come to life. It gives it energy and things like that."

The child's sex plays no part in choosing the key ingredient of a baby. As many boys as girls believed that the egg was fully responsible. Others of both sexes were convinced that the sperm carried the child. Unlike the three-and four-year-olds who believe that babies come preformed, level-five children embed this notion in a complex theory of causation.

All these children mentioned sexual intercourse or fertilizing the egg by their second sentence, but some seemed embarrassed by the whole topic. A few complained that it was hard to talk about the subject because it required unacceptable language. Another said, after mentioning marriage and affection, "Then . . . I guess uh, they uh, I guess they would . . . go to bed and do something there."

LEVEL SIX: PHYSICAL CAUSALITY

About the time they are 12, children begin to put it all together. They give exclusively physical explanations of conception and birth, and realize that both parents contribute genetic material to the embryo. They are aware of the moral and social aspects of reproduction, but they do not insist that marriage is necessary for conception.

Eleven-year-old Tina describes fertilization: "Well, it just starts it off, I guess. Mixes the genes or puts particles or something into the egg. Genes are the things from the father and the mother, you know, and they put a little bit of each into the baby so the baby turns out to be a little bit like the mother or father or something."

Children like Tina are beginning to move into what Piaget calls the stage of formal operations. They can develop theories and test them against reality; they can think about thinking. Twelve-year-old Michael's account is scientific: "The sperm encounter one ovum and one sperm breaks into the ovum, which produces like a cell, and the cell separates and divides. And so it's dividing, and the ovum goes through a tube and embeds itself in the wall of the, I think it's the fetus of the woman."

Michael's substitution of fetus for uterus leads to an important point. It is the sophistication of a child's reasoning, not simply whether his explanation is correct, that indicates the level of his understanding. Michael's verbal error is like the error of an algebra student who understands quadratic equations but makes a mistake in multiplication.

Not all level-six children gave as thorough an explanation of fertilization as Michael; some said simply, "the two cells meet and start growing."

When questioned, level-six children referred immediately to fertilization or sexual intercourse. None of them seemed embarrassed when I asked, "How do people get babies?"

Surprised Parents

Few of the parents of the children I questioned had accurate ideas about the extent of their children's sexual knowledge. Parents of children at levels one and six predicted their offsprings' answers with some accuracy; most others expected a greater degree of information than the children possessed. All the parents of level-three children expected that their children knew "the truth," and none anticipated the distortions that turned up. Not a single parent anticipated the level-five child's belief in the existence of a preformed person.

As I talked to children of various ages, it seemed apparent that our present efforts at sex education often confuse children. A four-year-old boy, trying to explain where babies come from, told me, "First they were little, a duck, then they grow older, into a baby." His solution seemed peculiar, but his source became clear when a level-two girl repeated it. This four-year-old was explicit.

ME: How would a lady get a baby to grow in her tummy?

SUSAN: Get a duck. 'Cause one day I saw a book about them, and they just get a duck or a goose and they get a little more growned and then they turn into a baby.

ME: A duck will turn into a baby?

SUSAN: They give them some food, people food, and they grow like a baby.

To get a baby, go to a store and buy a duck.

ME: How did you find that out?

SUSAN: I just saw, find out from this book.

One widely distributed book, which is recommended for children as young as three, starts with a pencil dot (to represent an ovum), then proceeds through the sex lives of flowers, bees, rabbits, giraffes, chickens and dogs before it reaches the human level. Few young children can encounter this kind of explanation without complete confusion.

Daddy as Cannibal

Another writer, Selma Fraiberg, encountered a four-year-old boy who knew a sex-education book by heart, but insisted that some of the mother's eggs never become babies because the daddy eats them up. "It says so in my book," he claimed, and indeed, it did—in a discussion of reproduction in fish.

Other research suggests a way out of confusion. Lawrence Kohlberg, of Harvard and Elliot Turiel, of the University of California, have studied the development of morality in children. They have found that children can expand their understanding to include concepts that are one level beyond their own.

Using these findings as a guide, we can reduce sex misinformation to a minimum. The level-one preschooler who thinks that babies just grow in mommy's tummy can move up to the manufacturing stage by learning that mommy and daddy make babies. The level-two child, who thinks that babies are manufactured, is ready to learn about the meeting of sperm and ovum. He is not ready for information about dividing cells and the genetic contribution of both parents.

Parents can use their child's curiosity as a guide to the amount of detail he is ready to absorb. By asking the kinds of questions I used, they can find out the level of their child's understanding and begin to provide information geared to the next level. Specific suggestions are listed in the accompanying box.

Children are not miniature adults, and will not think like adults until they grow up. My talks with children have shown that educators need to find out just how children adopt, adapt, and distort information, and then talk to children about sex in new ways. Until they do, our young philosophers will keep on creating unnecessarily confused accounts of the beginnings of life.

Talking to Your Child About Sex and Birth

Never inundate a child with information, but tell him what he wants to know in terms he can understand. The child's own curiosity should be a guide to the explicitness of your explanation. Begin by asking questions that will elicit the child's beliefs without leading his reply. In that way, his level of understanding will become apparent. Some of the questions I asked were: How do people get babies? How do mommies get to be mommies? How did your daddy get to be your daddy?

Children usually are ready to hear explanations of sex in terms that are one level beyond their present understanding. If parents communicate their own comfort, the child will feel he has permission to ask what he wants to know.

Never make a child feel stupid or foolish because he looks at reproduction in a fanciful way. It is important to support the child's problem-solving effort without confirming his erroneous information.

Level-One Child

This child believes that babies have always existed. Speaking in level-two terms, a parent might tell him: "Only people can make other people. To make a baby person, you need two grown-up people, a woman and a man, to be the baby's mommy and daddy. The mommy and daddy make the baby from an egg in the mommy's body and a sperm from the daddy's body."

Level-Two Child

This child believes that babies are manufactured. The parent could say, "That's an interesting way of looking at things. That's the way you'd make a doll. You would buy a head and some hair and put it all together. But making a real live baby is different from making a doll or a cake or an airplane."

This child can be led to understand that while a factory may have a wide range of components at its disposal, babymakers have only certain ingredients from their own bodies as materials. The parent might continue: "Mommies and daddies have special things in their bodies that they use to make babies. Mommies have tiny eggs and daddies have tiny sperms. When an egg from a mommy and a sperm from a daddy join together, they grow into a baby. The baby grows inside the mommy's body."

The level-two child who speaks of opening tummies might be told: "Can you put your hand inside your tummy? Then do you think the mommy and daddy can really put their hands in their tummies? There must be another way. Do you want to know how they get the egg and the seed together? The daddy's sperm are in his testicles and they come out through his penis. The mommy's vagina is a tunnel to where her eggs are. So if the daddy put his penis into her vagina, the sperm could go through the tunnel to the egg."

Level-Three Child

This child already restricts himself to reproductive processes that are technically possible. The task of the level-three's parents is to clear up misapprehensions, explain why some of his beliefs are mistaken, and provide other physiological explanations.

The child who described the sperm biting a hole with its little mouth to gain access to the vagina can be led to understand that while sperm move in a way that resembles swimming, the sperm is not a whole animal. Unlike a fish, it has no mouth with which to bite. She can be told why a sperm doesn't need a mouth to get into the vagina, which is like a tunnel.

One level-three child described conception in the following manner: "I guess it's like mothers and fathers are related, and their loving each other forms a baby. I don't know how it really comes just by loving and stuff. I guess the love forms the beans and I guess the beans hatches the egg."

This child's parents should agree with him, that loving is an important part of making babies. His statement shows that they have already given him an integral part of their value system. They could say, "It's really important for a baby that mothers and fathers love each other and love the baby, so that when the baby is born they can take good care of it. But loving is a feeling and can't start the baby all by itself. A baby is a living creature and it starts growing from living material. When the mother and the father make love, a sperm from the father goes through his penis into the mother's vagina. When the sperm joins with an egg from the mother, the sperm and the egg form one new thing, which grows into a baby."

Levels Four and Five

In talking to level-four and level-five children, the objective is the same, although the level-four child may take longer to understand why genetic material must unite to produce a baby. The level-five child believes that the whole baby exists in either the sperm or the egg, needing the other only to promote its growth. Children at levels four and five need to learn that the baby has not begun to exist until the sperm and egg meet and fuse. They can learn that the seeds of life come from both parents, from whom the baby inherits its physical characteristics.

A useful way to explain genetic contributions is to talk in terms of information. A parent might say that both sperm and egg contain coded information about the baby they will grow to be. He can go on to talk about facial features, color of eyes, hair and skin. It is important to stress that neither the sperm nor the egg has the entire code until they unite. Together, they complete the message to develop into a baby that is the child of a particular set of parents.

THE WORK OF LITTLE CHILDREN*

Norman K. Denzin

Societies and people organize themselves into interacting moral orders: families and schools, rich people and poor people, the educated and the uneducated, the child and the adult. Relationships between them are grounded in assumptions which justify the various social evaluations. Thus, it is taken as right and proper that the rich should have more privileges than the poor, or that children cannot engage in adult activities. These assumptions are institutionalized and routinely enforced, so that those people who are judged to be less competent are kept in their place. In this article, I want to look at some of the ideologies that surround the adult-child relationship. I shall present data from an ongoing field study of young children in "preschools," in recreational areas and in families, which challenge the view of children that is taken for granted, at least in America.

Childhood is conventionally seen as a time of carefree, disorganized bliss. Children find themselves under constant surveillance. They are rewarded and punished so that proper standards of conduct can be instilled in their emergent selves. The belief goes that they enjoy nonserious, play-directed activities. They avoid work and serious pursuits at all costs. It is the adult's assignment to make these nonserious selves over into serious actors. In America, this belief lasts at least until the child enters the world of marriage and gainful employment.

There is a paradox in these assumptions. Even if a child or adolescent wants to take part in serious concerns, he may find himself excluded. Thus, when the state of California recently passed a law, along the lines already adopted in Britain, giving the vote to 18-year-olds, members of the assembly refused to accord them drinking privileges, and one argument held that 18-year-olds were not yet competent enough to incur debts and assume other adult responsibilities (like signing contracts).

The paradox extends beyond exclusion. Even when children go so far as to act in adultlike ways, these actions are usually defined as unique, and not likely to occur again unless an adult is there to give guidance and direction. This assumption serves to justify the position of the educator. If children could make it on their own, there would be no place for the teacher. This fact is best seen in American preschools, where instructors assume that little children have short attention or concentration spans. The belief is quite simple. If left to their own ingenuity, little children become bored. Therefore, time structures must

*This article first appeared in *New Society*, London, The Weekly Magazine of the Social Sciences.

be developed, so that the child does not become bored. In California, these timetables typically go as follows:

9–9:15: Hang up coats and say "Good morning" to other children.

9:15–10: Play inside on solitary activities (painting, puzzles, toys).

10–10:30: Go outside for group activities on swings, in sandbox, dancing, making things.

10:30–11: Juice and biscuit time in small groups around tables.

11–11:20: Quiet time; small groups around instructors where instructor reads a story.

11:20–11:30: Get coats and jackets and prepare to be picked up by parents.

11:30: Session over; instructors relax and have coffee and cigarettes.

When there are clashes over timetables—if, for example, a child refuses to come in for juice and biscuits—an instructor will be dispatched to inform him that it is time to come in.

These timetables are revealing and serve several functions. They tell the instructor what he will be doing at any given moment. They give instructors control over the children. They state that children, if left on their own, could not organize their own actions for two and one-half hours.

Another paradox is evident. Although children are systematically informed of their incompetence, and rewarded for the quality of their nonserious conduct, adults appear to assume that something important is happening at these early ages. In fact, it is something so serious that normal, everyday adults cannot assume responsibility for what occurs. As rapidly as possible, the child is taken from the family setting and placed in any number of child-care educational and babysitting facilities.

My interviews with, and observation of, 100 American parents, who delivered their children to a cooperative and experimental preschool, revealed two assumptions. First, the school was a cheap and effective babysitter. The parents had no fears for their child's safety when he was there. Second, if the child was an only child, or if the parents lived in a neighborhood where there were no other playmates, the preschool would expand and cultivate the child's skill at getting on with other children. These parents fear that their child would appear later in kindergarten, and not know how to interact with other children. Because preschools do not formally assess how a child is doing, the parent felt fairly safe. They transferred the function of looking after their child's sociability from themselves to a neutral party—the preschool instructor.

The school, then, gave the parents a year to get the child ready for his first encounter with formal education. The task of the preschool was to shape up the child's speech, teach him or her how to be polite and considerate of others. A side function was to give the child different toys and play experiences—finger painting, say, which many parents defined as too messy for their homes. Economically stable families with several children were less likely to send their child to the preschool. The child's brothers and sisters performed the sociability function of the preschool.

Let me now note a final paradox. Observers like Iona and Peter Opie—in their *Lore and Language of Schoolchildren* and their *Children's Games in Street and Playground* have found that, when left on their own, children produce complex societies and social orders. The fact that children's games are often spontaneously produced, yet are passed on from generation to generation, and that their songs and stories are made to fit special selves, must indicate the child's ability to be a serious, accountable actor.

An example from the Opies' study of children's games reveals the serious character of play. Here the game is "playing school":

"The most favorite game played in school is 'Schools,' " says an Edinburgh 9-year-old.

> Tommy is the headmaster, Robin is the school-teacher, and I am the naughty boy. Robin asks us what are two and two. We say they are six. He gives us the belt. Sometimes we run away from school and what a commotion! Tommy and Robin run after us. When we are caught we are taken back and everyone is sorry.

In their analysis of this game, the Opies observe:

> Clearly, playing "Schools" is a way to turn the tables on real school: a child can become a teacher, pupils can be naughty, and fun can be made of punishments. It is noticeable, too, that the most demure child in the real classroom is liable to become the most talkative when the canes are make-believe.

Urie Bronfenbrenner's recent study of child-rearing practices in the Soviet Union shows, too, that Russians take the games of their young children quite seriously. Such games are used to instill self-reliance and collective respect on the part of the child. Here is one instance:

> Kolya started to pull at the ball Mitya was holding. The action was spotted by a junior staff member who quickly scanned the room and then called out gaily: "Children, come look! See how Vasya and Marusya are swinging their teddy bear together. They are

*good comrades." The two offenders quickly dropped
the ball to join the others in observing the praised
couple, who now swung harder than ever.*

Bronfenbrenner notes that such cooperation is not left to chance. From
preschool on, Soviet children are encouraged to play cooperatively. Group
games and special toys are designed to heighten this side of self-development.

The point I want to make is that when they are left on their own, young
children do not play, they work at constructing social orders. "Play" is a fiction from the adult world. Child's work involves such serious matters as developing languages for communication; presenting and defending their social
selves in difficult situations; defining and processing deviance; and constructing rules of entry and exit into emergent social groups. Children see these as
serious concerns and often make a clear distinction between their play and
their work. This fact is best grasped by entering those situations where children are naturally thrown together and forced to take account of one another.

Many specialists have assumed that young children lack well-developed
self-conceptions. My observations show, on the contrary, that as early as four,
a child can stand outside his own behavior and see himself from another's perspective. I carried out intensive interviews with 15 four-year-olds. These revealed support for the general hypothesis that a person's self-concept reflects
the number of people he interacts with. The more friends a child had, or the
larger his network of brothers and sisters, the more elaborate his self-concep-
tion.

Keith, who was four years seven months old at the time of the interview, described himself as follows:

1.   My name is Keith—.
2.   I am a boy who plays at a nursery school.
3.   If I was asked, "What do you like to play best?" I would say: "I like to dance to my favorite records." [What are your favorite records?] *"Yummy, Yummy; Bonnie and Clyde."*
4.   If someone asked me, "Where do you live?" I'd say, [Name of street]."
5.   If someone said, "Do you know how to do cartwheels?" I'd say "No!"
6.   If someone said, "What kind of picture can you draw?" I'd say, "I can draw my favorite things. I like to draw a man's head." [Why?] "Because so much can be added to it. I'd put hair, a chin, eyes, a forehead, a nose, a mouth, and a chin on it."

Keith was a leader of the boys' group at the preschool, had nine good friends, and was one of the family that had two other children. Nancy, on the other hand, was an isolate, having only four acquaintances at the school. However, her family also had two other children. Her low integration in the social network of the school is reflected in the fact that she could only give two self-descriptions:

1.   I'm at school.
2.   I live in [name of city].

As extremes, Keith and Nancy point to a basic feature of life at the preschool. Insofar as a child is a member of the social life of the preschool, the more adultlike will be his, or her, behavior. The social life of the school, then, makes the child into a small adult.

Name games take many forms, and they reveal another side of the child's serious self. Children may reverse or switch names. On a Halloween afternoon, I saw three girls, all aged four, who were sitting around a table mixing pumpkin muffins, systematically assign to themselves and all newcomers the name of the child next to them. The rule was quite simple. Each child was assigned every name in the group but their own. One girl resisted and said: "That's a mistake! My name isn't Kathy, I'm Susan." Kathy replied: "We know your name isn't mine, silly; we're just pretending. We don't mean it."

There was a clear separation of play, fantasy, and serious activity in this episode. Each girl knew her name. The sequence merely solidified their self-identity. Martha Wolfenstein, in a study of children's humor, has observed that inevitably some child will find these games disturbing, refusing to accept the identity that goes with the new name. Probably such children are not yet firmly committed to the identity designated by their proper name.

Name calling is another game. Here, the child's proper name is dropped and replaced by either a variation on that name, or by an approving/disapproving term. Martha Wolfenstein noted names like "Heinie," "Tits," "Freeshow," "Fuckerfaster," and "None-of-your-business." In name-calling games the child's real identity is challenged. He or she is signed out of the group and made a special object of abuse or respect. (Parenthetically, it must be noted that adults also engage in such games. Special names for sports and political figures are examples.)

A more severe game is where the child has his name taken away. The other children simply refuse to interact with him. By taking away his name, they effectively make him a nonperson, or nonself. In name-loss games the child may be referred to as a member of a social category (young child, honkie, brat, dwarf). In those moments his essential self, as a distinct person, is denied.

The Opies have described another name game, called "Names," "Letters in Your Name," or "Alphabet." Here, a child calls out letters in the alphabet, and contestants come forward every time a letter contained in their name is called. All of these name games reflect the importance children assign to their social selves. A name is a person's most important possession simply because it serves to give a special identity.

In preschools, children are continually constructing rules to designate group boundaries. In those schools where sexual lines are publicly drawn, boys and girls may go so far as to set off private territories where members of the opposite sex are excluded. One observer working with me noted boys and girls in a four-year-old group carrying posters stating that they were "Boys" or "Girls." On another occasion I observed the creation of a "Pirate Club" which denied entry to all females and all males who did not have the proper combination of play money for paying the membership dues. This group lasted for one hour. At juice and biscuit time, it was disbanded by the instructor and the boys were made to sweep out their tree house. Adult entry into the club seemed to reduce its interest for the boys.

The study of early childhood conversations reveals several similarities to adult speech. Like adults, young children build up special languages. These languages are silent and gestural. What a child says with his eyes or hands may reveal more than his broken speech. As children develop friendships, "private" terms and meanings will be employed. To grasp the conversations of young children, it is necessary to enter their language communities and learn the network of social relationships that bind them together. Single words have multiple meanings ("baby" can cover a younger brother or sister, all small children, or contemporaries who act inappropriately). To understand what the word "baby" means for the child, it is necessary to (a) understand his relationship to the person called a baby, (b) the situation where he uses the word, and (c) the activity he is engaging in at the moment.

Neologisms are especially crucial in the development of new relationships. The involved children attempt to produce a word that outsiders cannot understand. Its use sets them off from the other children; it serves to give a special designation to the newly formed relationship. I observed two girls, aged three, who had suddenly discovered one another. Within an hour they had developed the word "Buckmanu." With smiles on their faces they came running inside the preschool holding hands and singing the new word. After several repetitions of "Buckmanu," they came over for juice, and a mother asked them what they were saying. They ignored her and suddenly switched the word to "Manubuck." And then, with precision and correct enunciation, they said, "Manuel bucked us off!" Manuel was the name of a preschool instructor. They had taken one of his actions (playing horseback) and his name, and forged the two into a new word. Once they revealed the name to the mothers, they ceased using it.

IT'S A CRAZY GIFT...*

Barry Stevens

It's a crazy gift we have, this trickery. My inside knowing of it is remembered only as far back as my own third year when:

My mother and father laugh at me because I am enchanted by a hole in the ground. The hole is being dug on the next street so I cannot go there alone. I wait with excitement for my father to take me. When he does, I look into that everdeepening hole with the same fascination that I watch my mother peel potatoes, noticing the changing form, the changing color, the changing texture, and the changing fragrance of both holes in the ground and potatoes.

My father tells my mother, "A hole in the ground!" (The way that he says it, I know this is not much.) "You'd think there was a magnet at the bottom. If I didn't hold her hand, she'd tumble right in," (I don't catch all those words at the time. There are too many that I don't know. I hear them later on, when my father tells someone, and I remember my pain, and what I did about it.)

My mother and father laugh together and are tender with me and love me, but they do not understand. I feel alone, and my enchantment is bleeding around the edges. I am the angry which is hurt. Being at the moment true to me, I scowl at my parents.

They jolly me then, because children must be kept happy. And then I am not true to me. I laugh, because in that grownup world of which I would like to be a part, that is the thing to do. (A few years later, when I am attracted by a hole in the ground, I drop a marble into it, so that if anyone comes along I can say that I am looking for my marble, not that I am enjoying the hole, which would be ridiculed.)

There are times when I scowl at my parents not because I am misunderstood, or not understood, but because I have discovered that that is a way to get their attention. And then, when they have brought me around from scowls to laughter they are very pleased with both themselves and me.

And I am pleased with myself for having figured this out.

That's a long way from being happy with a hole in the ground.

Less than three years in this world, and I have got involved in cleverness. I didn't develop that all by myself. Already my parents have been tricking *me*, and I have watched other trickery go on with aunts and uncles, grandpa....

My parents and I love each other and enjoy each other. Most of the time we are sensitive to each other at some level. We don't know that increasingly we are being superficial, that there is a dimension missing, and that their lack of respect for me is developing in me a lack of respect for them. They respect

---

*From *Person To Person* by Carl R. Rogers and Barry Stevens © 1967. Real People Press.

me in the outside things, like letting me paint the railings on the porch and carry things that would break if I dropped them, but they don't respect my insides because they think I haven't any

When I am playing on the floor, they talk together or with other people about things I am "too little to understand" and so it is all right to say them. But they don't know what my understanding is, and I have no way to tell them. So it goes round and round inside my head. Sometimes I understand some things, and I am hurt. Other times, I do not understand and I try to put things together, with not enough information in my head to arrive at making sense. So what I make of it is nonsense, but I don't know that. And sometimes what I make of it won't stay put. I think of it one way and I hurt, so I think of it another way so I'll feel comfortable. But it slips around, and I don't know which way it *is*. I am too young to know that the word for my trouble is confusion.

To my parents, aunts and uncles, my life is good: I have loving parents, aunts and uncles, and "How blessed it is to be a child and have no worries."

To me, it often seems that I must have been born to the wrong parents, or that these are not my parents, because my *real* parents would know *me*.

My sister, six years older than I, bewilders me, because sometimes she is a child with me, and then suddenly she switches and talks like a grownup. She tells me what to think and feel. What *I* think and feel she says is silly. A moment ago, she was agreeing with me. Sometimes I fight my sister about this. But sometimes I say that I think and feel what she does, and then I feel BIG.

But then I get all mixed up and I am crying " Who am I?"

And no one helps me with that because it is a silly question. I'm me. Who else could I be? This seems so to me, too, so why is it that I don't know? There must be something so wrong with me that no one will tell me about it.

I talk to my puppy and my dolls, and to the trees. They don't confuse me because they listen, and I can say *anything* I want and they don't talk back. They go on listening. And then I begin to hear myself and know it's me.

EGO STRUGGLE OF CHILDHOOD*

Clifford Kirkpatrick

It is convenient for certain purposes to think of children as organisms striving for power, for control of environment, for freedom, and for self-realization. To put the matter more simply, children want what they want when they want it in their own way and with reference to their own essential uniqueness of personality. Comments may be made upon this tendency.

There is an early struggle for physical satisfactions. The child wants to eat, drink, sleep, manipulate, and play to his own satisfaction. In Freudian terms, he is guided by the pleasure rather than the reality principle. Observation of children and their elders reveals a more or less open warfare in which children grab or demand whatever they want and challenge the restrictions of their elders. They put up a good fight to have their way and few holds are barred. They may kick their heels, hold their breath, outshout their opponents, wear down opposition, and outdo a totalitarian country in demanding appeasement. Having little else to think about, they can concentrate upon getting their way, and they reveal, by their persistence, a vague awareness that a parent who is permitted to get out of hand will be harder to dominate in the future. Yet children are smaller and weaker organisms, and hence the mother can outrun the adventurous toddler and the writhing child can be picked up bodily and thrust into bed. In a tug of war an able-bodied parent can generally wrest a butcher knife from an energetic child. Defeat is frustrating and therefore certain consequences can be expected.

The child, in contrast to the infant, develops a fantasy world and dreams his way out of conflicts and defeats. Imagination can create a useful play companion, a more loving parent, or transform the child wishfully to a personality of power. Identification with power explains the sale of countless millions of comic books and the bang-bang activities of miniature cowboys. It is amusing to note the avid reaction of a child to an imaginary reversal of the child-parent role. Children react, for example, with awed delight to the tale of a child who upon eating magic candy assumed parental power and parental roles. The thought of putting a father out of the way upon a shelf is delightful, and the prospect of plumping a mother into a bathtub for a good scrubbing behind her ears produces peals of laughter. Children object not so much to domination as to being the person dominated.

Uniqueness of personality is a goal in the ego struggle of childhood. Countless children struggle against being treated like their siblings who are differ-

ent, and there is a defiant refusal to introject roles which are not congenial. A small boy will fight to the last ditch to avoid wearing a girlish costume, or perhaps insist that his own kind of work be assigned to him. One small girl brought up in a musical family docilely accepted for years the assumption that she likewise should be musical. After a recital in which she hammered out—mechanically no doubt—such pieces as the "Barcarolle" and "Country Gardens," she anounced that never again would she touch a piano except to dust it. That vow was kept. This comment upon the urge for uniqueness should not obscure the paradox of human nature provided by the fact that children likewise seek conformity and evenhanded justice.

Ambivalence and aggression are common by-products of the ego struggle of childhood. It is rare to find even loving children who have not expressed at some time hatred of their parents. Reverence for the Fifth Commandment should not prompt parents to take seriously such childish outbursts.

To wish a parent dead lacks the meaning for a child which it has for an adult, and aggression directed against the parent may mean need for love rather than lack of love. Since aggression is not really approved even by the most tolerant parents, it may be repressed or directed against some non-parental object such as a political leader, a social class, a teacher, a minority group, or in fact any convenient out-group. This possibility is not unrelated to uprisings, revolutions, wars, and political movements.

PARENTAL OBSTACLES TO EGO EXPRESSION IN CHILDHOOD

It takes two sides to make a struggle, and hence parents and parental roles are intimately interwoven with the ego demands of children. Both parties may resist and demand too much.

Exploitative attitudes on the part of parents constitute one type of obstacle to the child's ego expression. The term "exploitative" means the inclination of the parent to use the child for parental purposes.

Formerly there was exploitation in the sense of seeking economic or personal convenience from the child. The mechanical revolution in its early stages introduced the problem of child labor, and even today in rural areas a child may be regarded as an increment to the labor supply to be utilized as soon as possible. A more restrained exploitation of this type exists when children are regarded as little servants to fetch and carry and later are expected to repay in full, and perhaps with interest, the cost of their rearing. One father denied his small son the pleasure of companionship on a fishing trip, yet roused him at midnight to clean the fish which the father had caught.

Domination of children is a more subtle form of exploitation. Children may be ordered about not so much for the value of their services as for pleasure in the authoritarian role. Not uncommonly such a dominating parent acts in accordance with the basic postulate by reversing the roles which defined him as exploitable by his own parents.

Excessive demands for satisfaction of parental pride in children may be a form of exploitation. The pride in such cases is not so much a matter of being proud of the child as of being proud of oneself as parent to the child. The expectation is that the child should make the parent proud. Mothers dress up their little girls as symbols of themselves, and fathers demand strength and fortitude from their sons to the greater glory of the parental ego. Such parents often delude themselves that they are giving to the child when they are really receiving, and they may be pressing for familial maturation beyond the capacity of the child, with possible negativistic familial regression as the outcome.

A martyrdom motivation yields an extremely subtle form of exploitation which is not uncommon. The parent, in effect, demands from the child justification for parental self-pity. The parents seeking martyrdom have more than a desire that the child remove the grounds for self-pity, for the self-pity is often maintained in spite of the best efforts of the child to give love and sympathy. For the parent taking pride in his or her monstrous burden of suffering there is always a way of showing that the child is responsible. Obviously this craving for martyrdom, with the child as a convenient justification, merges with domination. The infantile parent says, in effect, "You must let me control you by the pity which I arouse and the obligations which I make you feel." The mother may control a child by an imaginary headache, or actually exert so much unnecessary effort for the child that a real headache results.

A devoted attitude of parents is the counterpart of an exploitative attitude, yet such opposites may have similar long-run effects. Devotion and responsibility toward children is a characteristic of the American family as "child-centered." However, social critics are quick to sense cultural contradictions and question our mature love for children because of social conditions which are permitted to exist. The oncoming generation of children is offered a world containing slums, death-dealing motorists, neglected health, civic corruption, outmoded educational methods, and above all the threat of the thermonuclear war.

Regardless of the balance between devotion and indifference in American culture, there are tremendous variations from family to family in regard to devotion. There are countless mothers who show neurotic overresponsibility for their children and seek to wrap them eternally in protective cotton. There are morbid fears of germs and accidents, in fact of anything which might remove a child from the protective parental clutch. Overconcern of course could mean overcompensation for unconscious rejection and balm for guilt feelings with respect to children.

The devoted attitude implies familial regression and an excess of that brand of affection aptly called "smother" love. Much has been written of the silver cord by which mothers selfishly bind children to them. Wylie has made the term "Mom" into a satirical epithet. The psychiatrist Strecker has bemoaned in more sober psychiatric language the hold mothers have upon their sons which hampers mature adjustment to military life and fills the hospitals with grown-up little boys who reveal by complicated symptoms that they cannot live without their mothers.[1]

Naïve projective expectation that parental attitudes will be introjected is a third obstacle to ego impulses of childhood and more specifically to those indicating a striving toward maturity.[2] The projection of sex aversion begun in infancy may continue into childhood. Preferences as to sex may be projected with such vigor that a child introjects profound distaste for his or her own sex type. For example, a girl may twist her own personality and complicate her unfolding life pattern by striving to be the boy that her father wanted. Again, there are countless examples in which the moral standards of the parent are projected upon the child, not only in the realm of sex but in regard to other aspects of morality. A morbid respect for cleanliness, a fantastic ideal of honesty, a miserly attitude, a glorification of hard work, or a rigorous conception of piety may be imposed upon the child. The simple, hackneyed phrase "Mother knows best" symbolizes the grim process by which a host of personal prejudices are imposed with self-righteous fervor upon helpless offspring. Totalitarian thought control occurs in the family as in the state, and the one perhaps paves the way for the other. Often parents are blissfully unconscious that their compacent sense of duty may verge upon tyranny over the human mind.

Special mention should be made of the projection of ambitions either personal or reflecting the family culture. The frustrated artist may impose artistic ambitions upon a child without talent, and a weakling may insist that his son be strong. There is a powerful desire for vicarious satisfaction of defeated ambitions. In other cases there is projection of ambition in the sense of vicarious continuation of fulfilled aspirations. A father, for example, wants to see his son continue the thriving business which he has built. Often it is not individual parental pressure but collective pressure which is exerted upon the child. There may be a family tradition in regard to law, medicine, or the ministry which entraps the child. With great self-righteousness powerful economic sanctions may be applied to enforce the family will. Even enlightened parents who pride themselves upon their tolerance and their restraint as to projective expectations deceive themselves. A professor, for example, insists that he does not urge scholarship upon his daughter and naïvely comments, "All I expect of her is a B average." His attentive colleague in the campus club has the daughter as a student and knows full well her anguished effort to make a grade of C.

References

1. E. Strecker, *Their Mothers' Sons* (Philadelphia: J. B. Lippincott Co., 1946); see also E. Ginzberg, J. K. Anderson, S. W. Ginsburg and J. L. Herma, *The Ineffective Soldier* (New York: Columbia University Press, 1959) see vol. 1, *The Lost Divisions*.
2. W. McCord, J. McCord and A. Howard, "Early Familial Experiences and Bigotry" *American Sociological Review*, XXV (1960), 717–22.

A VISIT FROM UNCLE MACHO*

Brian Allen

"Wake up, boy, the early bird gets the worm, you know!"

Mark rolled over and rubbed the sleep from his eyes, then he squinted up through the semi-darkness of the early morning at the figure standing beside the bed. Towering over Mark was a large man with a red face, a crew cut, and a thick neck that bulged over his shirt collar.

"Strong silent type, eh?" the man observed, "A real chip off the old block!"

Suddenly, Mark became frightened by this strange man in his bedroom and he began to cry.

"Hey, cut that out, young fellow!" the man said, leaning over and snapping his fingers in front of Mark's face, "Big boys don't cry."

Mark noticed for the first time that the man had a brown leather briefcase in his hand, one just like his father carried to work in the morning and brought home at night. The man spoke again, this time in a very business-like tone of voice.

"I'm your fairy godfather, but you can call me Uncle Macho. We have some very important business to discuss, you and I, man to man." Mark swallowed hard and blinked.

"But I'm not a man yet. I'm just a little boy."

"But you will be a man before long," Uncle Macho replied, "and you must begin preparing as soon as possible. You are five years old today and it's high time you began thinking about how to get a jump on the other guy and get ahead in this dog-eat-dog world."

Mark became confused and a bit frightened once again. A tear crept to the corner of his eye, climbed over a long, dark lash, and spilled onto his cheek, but the big man continued, seeming not to notice.

"Mark, I have a present for you here, the most important birthday present you will ever receive. What I have here will tell you what you need to know to become a man."

What Uncle Macho withdrew from the briefcase didn't look like any birthday present Mark had ever seen. It was nothing but a plain cardboard folder with some sheets of paper inside. Uncle Macho continued, speaking rapidly, like the used-car salesman on T.V.

"This is your script, Mark, and each of the great men in history has followed one like it, just as you will follow this one."

"Is it O.K. if my parents help me," Mark asked, still puzzled, "I'm only in kindergarten and I don't read too well yet."

"Of course they will help you," Unchle Macho replied, but added quickly, "however, you must never *ask* them for help. In fact, you must never ask *anyone* for help, or even let anyone know that you are confused or frightened. That's part of learning to be a man. But all that is in the script. And don't worry about the words too much: there are plenty of pictures."

Mark opened the script in the middle and sure enough, there was a picture of a muscular-looking man in swim trunks carrying a pretty girl along a beach. Below the picture it said, "Dominate women." Mark wasn't sure what "dominate" meant, but he decided it had something to do with swimming. He looked up at Uncle Macho and smiled knowingly.

"Getting the idea already I see," said Macho with a wink, as he fastened the clasp on the briefcase. "Bright boy. You'll go far . . . in more ways than one." Then he buckled the straps and rose to his feet. Mark saw through the window behind his rocking horse that the sun was just beginning to come up.

"I've got to be going now," the fairy godfather said, "but I'll be seeing you again when you're about thirteen. That's when young men begin to have a lot of trouble with their scripts."

Mark looked up from the page with a puzzled expression on his face.

"What will you do then?" he asked.

"I'll ride your ass," said Uncle Macho, as he strode out the door, "that's what I'll do!"

THE EYE OF THE BEHOLDER: PARENTS' VIEWS ON SEX OF NEWBORNS*

Jeffrey Z. Rubin, Frank J. Provenzano, and Zella Luria

As Schaffer has observed, the infant at birth is essentially an asocial, largely undifferentiated creature.[1] It appears to be little more than a tiny ball of hair, fingers, toes, cries, gasps, and gurgles. However, while it may seem that "if you've seen one, you've seen them all," babies are *not* all alike—a fact that is of special importance to their parents, who want, and appear to need, to view their newborn child as a creature that is special. Hence, much of early parental interaction with the infant may be focused on a search for distinctive features. Once the fact that the baby is normal has been established, questions such as, "Who does the baby look like?" and "How much does it weigh?" are asked.

Of all the questions parents ask themselves and each other about their infant, one seems to have priority: "Is it a boy or a girl?" The reasons for and consequences of posing this simple question are by no means trivial. The answer, "boy" or "girl," may result in the parents' organizing their perception of the infant with respect to a wide variety of attributes—ranging from its size to its activity, attractiveness, even its future potential. It is the purpose of the present study to examine the kind of verbal picture parents form of the newborn infant, as a function both of their own and their infant's gender.

As Asch observed years ago, in forming our impressions of others, we each tend to develop a *Gestalt*—a global picture of what others are like, which permits us to organize our perceptions of the often discrepant, contradictory aspects of their behavior and manner into a unified whole.[2] The awareness of another's status,[3] the belief that he is "warm" or "cold,"[4,5] "extroverted" or "introverted,"[6] even the apparently trivial knowledge of another's name[7]—each of these cues predisposes us to develop a stereotypic view of that other, his underlying nature, and how he is likely to behave. How much more profound, then, may be the consequences of a cue as prominent in parents' minds as the gender of their own precious, newborn infant.

The study reported here is addressed to parental perceptions of their infants at the point when these infants first emerge into the world. If it can be demonstrated that parental sex-typing has already begun its course at this earliest of moments in the life of the child, it may be possible to understand bet-

*Terry Rubin, Frank Provenzano and Zella Luria, *American Journal of Orthopsychiatry*, vol. 44, no. 4. Coypright © 1974 the American Orthopsychiatric Association, Inc. Reproduced by permission.

ter one of the important antecedents of the complex process by which the growing child comes to view itself as boy-ish or girl-ish.

Based on our review of the literature, two forms of parental sextyping may be expected to occur at the time of the infant's birth. First, it appears likely that parents will view and label their newborn child differentially, as a simple function of the infant's gender. Aberle and Naegele[8] and Tasch,[9] using only fathers as subjects, found that they had different expectations for sons and daughters: sons were expected to be aggressive and athletic, daughters were expected to be pretty, sweet, fragile, and delicate. Rebelsky and Hanks found that fathers spent more time talking to their daughters than their sons during the first three months of life.[10] While the sample size was too small for the finding to be significant, they suggest that the role of father-of-daughter may be perceived as requiring greater nurturance. Similarly, Pedersen and Robson reported that the fathers of infant daughters exhibited more behavior labeled (by the authors) as "apprehension over well being" than did the fathers of sons.[11]

A comparable pattern emerges in research using mothers as subjects. Sears, Maccoby and Levin for example, found that the mothers of kindergartners reported tolerating more aggression from sons than daughters, when it was directed toward parents and peers.[12] In addition, maternal nurturance was seen as more important for the daughter's than the son's development. Taken together, the findings in this body of research lead us to expect parents (regardless of their gender) to view their newborn infants differentially—labeling daughters as weaker, softer, and therefore in greater need of nurturance, than sons.

The second form of parental sex-typing we expect to occur at birth is a function both of the infant's gender *and* the parent's own gender. Goodenough interviewed the parents of nursery school children, and found that mothers were less concerned with sex-typing their child's behavior than were fathers.[13] More recently, Meyer and Sobieszek presented adults with videotapes of two seventeen-month-old children (each of whom was sometimes described as a boy and sometimes a girl), and asked their subjects to describe and interpret the children's behavior.[14] They found that male subjects, as well as those having little contact with small children, were more likely (although not always significantly so) to rate the children in sex-stereotypic fashion—attributing "male qualities" such as independence, aggressiveness, activity, and alertness to the child presented as a boy, and qualities such as cuddliness, passivity, and delicacy to the "girl." We expect, therefore, that sex of infant and sex of parent will interact, such that it is fathers, rather than mothers, who emerge as the greater sex-typers of their newborn.

In order to investigate parental sextyping of their newborn infants, and in order, more specifically, to test the predictions that sex-typing is a function of the infant's gender, as well as the gender of both infant and parent, parents of newborn boys and girls were studied in the maternity ward of a hospital, within the first 24 hours postpartum, to uncover their perceptions of the characteristics of their newborn infants.

METHOD

Subjects

The subjects consisted of 30 pairs of primiparous parents, fifteen of whom had sons, and fifteen of whom had daughters. The subjects were drawn from the available population of expecting parents at a suburban Boston hospital serving local, predominantly lower-middle-class families. Using a list of primiparous expectant mothers obtained from the hospital, the experimenter made contact with families by mail several months prior to delivery, and requested the subjects' assistance in "a study of social relations among parents and their first child." Approximately one week after the initial contact by mail, the experimenter telephoned each family, in order to answer any questions the prospective parents might have about the study, and to obtain their consent. Of the 43 families reached by phone, eleven refused to take part in the study. In addition, one consenting mother subsequently gave birth to a low birth weight infant (a 74-ounce girl), while another delivered an unusually large son (166 ounces). Because these two infants were at the two ends of the distribution of birth weights, and because they might have biased the data in support of our hypotheses, the responses of their parents were eliminated from the sample.

All subjects participated in the study within the first 24 hours postpartum—the fathers almost immediately after delivery, and the mothers (who were often under sedation at the time of delivery) up to but not later than 24 hours later. The mothers typically had spoken with their husbands at least once during this 24 hour period.

There were no reports of medical problems during any of the pregnancies or deliveries, and all infants in the sample were full-term at time of birth. Deliveries were made under general anesthesia, and the fathers were not allowed in the delivery room. The fathers were not permitted to handle their babies during the first 24 hours, but could view them through display windows in the hospital nursery. The mothers, on the other hand, were allowed to hold and feed their infants. The subjects participated individually in the study. The fathers were met in a small, quiet waiting room used exclusively by the maternity ward, while the mothers were met in their hospital rooms. Every precaution was taken not to upset the parents or interfere with hospital procedure.

Procedure

After introducing himself to the subjects, and after congratulatory amenities, the experimenter (FJP) asked the parents: "Describe your baby as you would to a close friend or relative." The responses were tape-recorded and subsequently coded.

The experimenter then asked the subjects to take a few minutes to complete a short questionnaire. The instructions for completion of the questionnaire were as follows:

> *On the following page there are 18 pairs of opposite words. You are asked to rate your baby in relation to these words, placing an "x" or a checkmark in the space that best describes your baby. The more a word describes your baby, the closer your "x" should be to that word.*

> *Example: Imagine you were asked to rate Trees.*
> *Good* :__:__:__:__:__:__:__:__:__: *Bad*
> *Strong* :__:__:__:__:__:__:__:__:__: *Weak*

> *If you cannot decide or your feelings are mixed, place your "x" in the center space. Remember, the more you think a word is a good description of your baby, the closer you should place your "x" to that word. If there are no questions, please begin. Remember, you are rating your baby. Don't spend too much time thinking about your answers. First impressions are usually the best.*

Having been presented with these instructions, the subjects then proceeded to rate their baby on each of the eighteen following, eleven-point, bipolar adjective scales: firm-soft; large featured-fine featured; big-little; relaxed-nervous; cuddly-not cuddly; easy going-fussy; cheerful-cranky; good eater-poor eater; excitable-calm; active-inactive; beautiful-plain; sociable-unsociable; well coordinated-awkward; noisy-quiet; alert-inattentive; strong-weak; friendly-unfriendly; hardy-delicate.

Upon completion of the questionnaire, the subjects were thanked individually, and when both parents of an infant had completed their participation, the underlying purposes of the study were fully explained.

Hospital Data

In order to acquire a more objective picture of the infants whose characteristics were being judged by the subjects, data were obtained from hospital records concerning each infant's birth weight, birth length, and Apgar scores. Apgar scores are typically assigned at five and ten minutes postpartum, and represent the physician's ratings of the infant's color, muscle tonicity, reflex irritability, and heart and respiratory rates. No significant differences between the male and female infants were found for birth weight, birth length, or Apgar scores at five and ten minutes postpartum. . . . .

Discussion

The data indicate that parents—especially fathers—differentially label

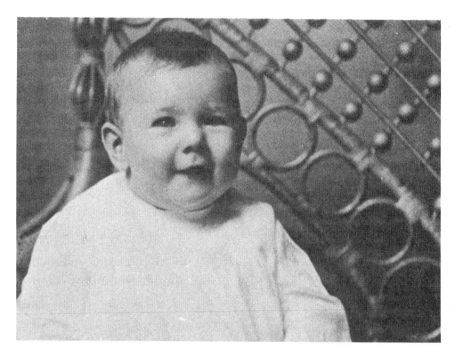

their infants, as a function of the infant's gender. These results are particularly striking in light of the fact that our sample of male and female infants did *not* differ in birth length, weight, or Apgar scores. Thus, the results appear to be a pure case of parental labeling—what a colleague has described as "nature's first projective test" (personal communication, Leon Eisenberg). Given the importance parents attach to the birth of their first child, it is not surprising that such ascriptions are made.

But why should posing the simple question, "Is it a boy or a girl?", be so salient in parents' minds, and have such important consequences? For one thing, an infant's gender represents a truly *distinctive* characteristic. The baby is either a boy or a girl—there are no ifs, ands, or buts about it. A baby may be active sometimes, and quiet at others, for example, but it can always be assigned to one of two distinct classes: boy or girl. Secondly, an infant's gender tends to assume the properties of a *definitive* characteristic. It permits parents to organize their questions and answers about the infant's appearance and behavior into an integrated *Gestalt*. Finally, an infant's gender is often a *normative* characteristic. It is a property that seems to be of special importance not only to the infant's parents, but to relatives, friends, neighbors, and even casual passersby in the street. For each of these reasons, an infant's gender is a property of considerable importance to its parents, and is therefore one that is likely to lead to labeling and the investment of surplus meaning.

The results of the present study are, of course, not unequivocal. Although it was found, as expected, that the sex-typing of infants varied as a function of the infant's gender, as well as the gender of both infant and parent, significant differences did not emerge for all eighteen of the adjective scales employed. Two explanations for this suggest themselves. First, it may simply be that we have overestimated the importance of sex-typing at birth. A second possibility, however, is that sex-typing is more likely to emerge with respect to certain classes of attributes—namely, those which denote physical or constitutional, rather than "internal," dispositional factors. Of the eight different adjective pairs for which significant main or interaction effects emerged, six (75%) clearly refer to external attributes of the infant. Conversely, of the ten adjective pairs for which no significant differences were found, only three (30%) clearly denote external attributes. This suggests that it is physical and constitutional factors that specially lend themselves to sex-typing at birth, at least in our culture.

Another finding of interest is the lack of significant effects, as a simple function of sex of parent. Although we predicted no such effects, and were therefore not particularly surprised by the emergence of "non-findings," the implication of these results is by no means trivial. If we had omitted the sex of the infant as a factor in the present study, we might have been led to conclude (on the basis of simply varying the sex of the parent) that *no* differences exist in parental descriptions of newborn infants—a patently erroneous conclusion! It is only when the infant's and the parent's gender are considered together, in interaction, that the lack of differences between overall parental mean ratings can be seen to reflect the true differences between the parents. Mothers rate both sexes closer together on the adjective pairs than do fathers (who are the stronger sex-typers), but *both* parents agree on the direction of sex differences.

An issue of considerable concern, in interpreting the findings of the present study appropriately, stems from the fact that fathers were not permitted to handle their babies, while mothers were. The question then becomes: Is it possible that the greater sex-typing by fathers is simply attributable to their lesser exposure to their infants? This, indeed, may have been the case. However it seems worthwhile to consider some of the alternative possibilities. Might not the lesser exposure of fathers to their infants have led not to greater sex-typing, but to a data "wash out"—with no differences emerging in paternal ratings? After all, given no opportunity to handle their babies, and therefore deprived of the opportunity to obtain certain first-hand information about them, the fathers might have been expected to make a series of neutral ratings—hovering around the middle of each adjective scale. The fact that they did not do this suggests that they brought with them a variety of sex-stereotypes that they then imposed upon their infant. Moreover, the fact that mothers, who were allowed to hold and feed their babies, made distinctions between males and females that were in keeping with cultural sex-stereotypes suggests that even if fathers had had the opportunity of holding their infants, similar results might have been obtained. We should also not lose sight of the fact that father-mother differences in exposure to infants continue well into later years. Finally, one must question the very importance of the subjects' differential exposure on the grounds that none of the typical "exposure" effects reported in the social psychological literature[14] were observed. In particular, one might have expected mothers to have come to rate their infants more favorably than fathers, simply as a result of greater exposure. Yet such was not the case.

The central implication of the study, then, is that sex-typing and sex-role socialization appear to have already begun their course at the time of the infant's birth, when information about the infant is minimal. The *Gestalt* parents develop, and the labels they ascribe to their newborn infant, may well affect subsequent expectations about the manner in which their infant ought to behave, as well as parental behavior itself. This parental behavior, moreover, when considered in conjunction with the rapid unfolding of the infant's own behavioral repertoire, may well lead to a modification of the very labeling that affected parental behavior in the first place. What began as a one-way street now bears traffic in two directions. In order to understand the full importance and implications of our findings, therefore, research clearly needs to be conducted in which delivery room stereotypes are traced in the family during the first several months after birth, and their impact upon parental behavior is considered. In addition, further research is clearly in order if we are to understand fully the importance of early paternal sex-typing in the socialization of sex-roles.

References

1. H. Schaffer, *The Growth of Sociability* (Baltimore: Penguin Books, 1971).
2. S. Asch, "Forming Impressions of Personality" *Journal of Abnormal Social Psychology*, XLI (1946), 258–90.
3. P. Wilson, "The Perceptual Distortion of Heights as a Function of Ascribed Academic Status" *Journal of Social Psychology*, LXXIV (1968), 97–102.
4. R. Zajoni, "Attitudinal Effects of Mere Exposure" *Journal of Personal Social Psychology Monograph Supplement*, IX (1968), 1–27.
5. H. Kelley, "The Warm-Cold Variable in First Impressions of Persons" *Journal of Personality*, XVIII (1950), 431–39.
6. A. Luchins, "Experimental Attempts to Minimize the Impact of First Impressions" in *The Order of Presentation in Persuasion*, C. Hovland, ed. (New Haven: Yale University Press, 1957).
7. H. Harari and J. McDavid, "Name Stereotypes and Teachers' Expectations" *Journal of Educational Psychology* (in press).
8. D. Aberle and K. Naegele, "Middle-Class Fathers' Occupational Role and Attitudes Toward Children" *American Journal of Orthopsychiatry*, XXII (1952), 366–78.
9. R. Tasch, "The Role of the Father in the Family" *Journal of Experimental Education*, XX (1952), 319–61.

10. F. Rebelsky and C. Hanks, "Fathers' Verbal Interaction With Infants in the First Three Months of Life" *Child Development*, XLII (1971), 63–68.
11. F. Petersen and K. Robson, "Father Participation in Infancy" *American Journal of Orthopsychiatry*, XXXIX (1969), 466–72.
12. R. Sears, E. Maccoby and H. Levin, *Patterns of Child Rearing* (Evanston, Illinois: Row, Peterson, 1957).
13. E. Goodenough, "Interest in Persons as an Aspect of Sex Differences in the Early Years" *Genetic Psychological Monographs*, LV (1957), 287–323.
14. J. Meyer and B. Sobieszek, "Effect of a Child's Sex on Adult Interpretation of Its Behavior" *Developmental Psychology*, XI (1972), 42–8.

BELIEFS ABOUT SEX DIFFERENCES*

Eleanor Maccoby and Carol Jacklin

UNFOUNDED BELIEFS ABOUT SEX DIFFERENCES

That Girls are More "Social" Than Boys

The findings: First, the two sexes are equally interested in social (as compared with nonsocial) stimuli, and are equally proficient at learning through imitation of models. Second, in childhood, girls are no more dependent than boys on their caretakers, and boys are no more willing to remain alone. Furthermore, girls are not more motivated to achieve for social rewards. The two sexes are equally responsive to social reinforcement, and neither sex consistently learns better for this form of reward than for other forms. Third, girls do not spend more time interacting with playmates; in fact, the opposite is true, at least at certain ages. Fourth, the two sexes appear to be equally "empathic," in the sense of understanding the emotional reactions of others; however, the measures of this ability have so far been narrow.

Any differences that exist in the "sociability" of the two sexes are more of kind than of degree. Boys are highly oriented toward a peer group and congregate in larger groups; girls associate in pairs or small groups of age-mates, and may be somewhat more oriented toward adults, although the evidence for this is weak.

That Girls are More "Suggestible" Than Boys

The findings: First, boys and girls are equally likely to imitate others spontaneously. Second, the two sexes are equally susceptible to persuasive communications, and in face-to-face social-influence situations (Asch-type experiments), sex differences are usually not found. When they are, girls are somewhat more likely to adapt their own judgments to those of the group, although there are studies with reverse findings. Boys, on the other hand, appear to be more likely to accept peer-group values when these conflict with their own.

That Girls Have Lower Self-esteem

The findings: The sexes are highly similar in their overall self-satisfaction and self-confidence throughout childhood and adolescence; there is little infor-

*Reprinted from *The Psychology of Sex Differences* by Eleanor Emmons Maccoby and Carol Nagy Jacklin with the permission of the publishers, Stanford University Press. Copyright © 1974 by the Board of Trustees of the Leland Stanford Junior University.

mation about adulthood, but what exists does not show a sex difference. However, there are some qualitative differences in the areas of functioning where the two sexes have greatest self-confidence: girls rate themselves higher in the area of social competence; boys more often see themselves as strong, powerful, dominant, "potent."

Through most of the school years, the two sexes are equally likely to believe they can influence their own fates, rather than being the victims of chance or fate. During the college years (but not earlier or later), men have a greater sense of control over their own fate, and greater confidence in their probable performance on a variety of school-related tasks that they undertake. However, this does not imply a generally lower level of self-esteem among women of this age.

That Girls are Better at Rote Learning and Simple Repetitive Tasks, Boys at Tasks That Require Higher-level Cognitive Processing and the Inhibition of Previously Learned Responses

The findings: Neither sex is more susceptible to simple conditioning, or excels in simple paired-associates or other forms of "rote" learning. Boys and girls are equally proficient at discrimination learning, reversal shifts, and probability learning, all of which have been interpreted as calling for some inhibition of "available" responses. Boys are somewhat more impulsive (that is, lacking in inhibition) during the preschool years, but the sexes do not differ thereafter in the ability to wait for a delayed reward, to inhibit early (wrong) responses on the Matching Familiar Figures test (MFF) or on other measures of impulsivity.

That Boys are More "Analytic"

The findings: The sexes do not differ on tests of analytic cognitive style. Boys do not excel at tasks that call for "decontextualization," or disembedding, except when the task is visual-spatial ability (see below), and no sex differences in analytic ability are implied. Boys and girls are equally likely to respond to task-irrelevant aspects of a situation, so that neither sex excels in analyzing and selecting only those elements needed for the task.

That Girls are More Affected by Heredity, Boys by Environment

The findings: Male identical twins are more alike than female identical twins, but the two sexes show equivalent amount of resemblance to their parents.

Boys are more susceptible to damage by a variety of noxious environmental agents, both prenatally and postnatally, but this does not imply that they are generally more influenced by environmental factors. The correlations between parental socialization techniques and child behavior are higher for boys in some studies, higher for girls in others. Furthermore, the two sexes learn with equal facility in a wide variety of learning situations; if learning is the primary means whereby environmental effects come about, sex equivalence is indicated.

That Girls Lack Achievement Motivation

The findings: In the pioneering studies of achievement motivation, girls scored higher than boys in achievement imagery under "neutral" conditions. Boys need to be challenged by appeals to ego or competitive motivation to bring their achievement imagery up to the level of girls'. Boys' achievement motivation does appear to be more responsive to competitive arousal than girls', but this does not imply a generally higher level. In fact, observational studies of achievement strivings either have found no sex difference or have found girls to be superior.

That Girls are Auditory, Boys Visual

The findings: The majority of studies report no differences in response to sounds by infants of the two sexes. At most ages boys and girls are equally adept at discriminating speech sounds. No sex difference is found in memory for sounds previously heard.

Among newborn infants, no study shows a sex difference in fixation to visual stimuli. During the first year of life, results are variable, but neither sex emerges as more responsive to visual stimuli. From infancy to adulthood, the sexes are highly similar in interest in visual stimuli, ability to discriminate among them, identification of shapes, distance perception, and a variety of other measures of visual perception.

SEX DIFFERENCES THAT ARE FAIRLY WELL ESTABLISHED

That Girls Have Greater Verbal Ability Than Boys

It is probably true that girls' verbal abilities mature somewhat more rapidly in early life, although there are a number of recent studies in which no sex difference has been found. During the period from preschool to early adolescence, the sexes are very similar in their verbal abilities. At about age 11, the sexes begin to diverge, with female superiority increasing through high school and possibly beyond. Girls score higher on tasks involving both receptive and productive language, and on "high-level" verbal tasks (analogies, comprehension of difficult written material, creative writing) as well as upon the "lower-level" measures (fluency). The magnitude of the female advantage varies, being most commonly about one-quarter of a standard deviation.

That Boys Excel in Visual-Spatial Ability

Male superiority on visual-spatial tasks is fairly consistently found in adolescence and adulthood, but not in childhood. The male advantage on spatial tests increases through the high school years up to a level of about .40 of a standard deviation. The sex difference is approximately equal on analytic and nonanalytic spatial measures.

That Boys Excel in Mathematical Ability

The two sexes are similar in their early acquisition of quantitative concepts, and their mastery of arithmetic during the grade-school years. Beginning at about age 12–13, boys' mathematical skills increase faster than girls'. The greater rate of improvement appears to be not entirely a function of the number of math courses taken, although the question has not been extensively studied. The magnitude of the sex differences varies greatly from one population to another, and is probably not so great as the difference in spatial ability. Both visual-spatial and verbal processes are sometimes involved in the solution of mathematical problems; some math problems can probably be solved in either way, while others cannot, a fact that may help to explain the variation in degree of sex difference from one measure to another.

That Males are More Aggressive

The sex difference in aggression has been observed in all cultures in which the relevant behavior has been observed. Boys are more aggressive both physically and verbally. They show the attenuated forms of aggression (mock-fighting, aggressive fantasies) as well as the direct forms more frequently than girls. The sex difference is found as early as social play begins—at age 2 or 2½. Although the aggressiveness of both sexes declines with age, boys and men remain more aggressive through the college years. Little information is available for older adults. The primary victims of male aggression are other males—from early ages, girls are chosen less often as victims.

OPEN QUESTIONS: TOO LITTLE EVIDENCE, OR FINDINGS AMBIGUOUS

Tactile Sensitivity

Most studies of tactile sensitivity in infancy, and of the ability to perceive by touch at later ages, do not find sex differences. When differences are found, girls are more sensitive, but such findings are rare enough that we cannot have confidence that the difference is a meaningful one. Additional work is needed with some of the standard psychophysical measurements of tactile sensitivity, over a range of ages. Most of the existing studies in which the data are analyzed by sex have been done with newborns.

Fear, Timidity, and Anxiety

Observational studies of fearful behavior usually do not find sex differences. Teacher ratings and self-reports, however, usually find girls to be more timid or more anxious. In the case of self-reports, the problem is to know whether the results reflect "real" differences or only differences in the willingness to report anxious feelings. Of course, the very willingness to assert that one is afraid may lead to fearful behavior, so the distinction may not turn out to be important. However, it would be desirable to have measures other than self-report (which make up the great bulk of the data from early school age on) as a way of clarifying the meaning of the girls' greater self-attribution of fears and anxiety.

Activity Level

Sex differences in activity level do not appear in infancy. They begin to be seen when children reach the age of social play. During the preschool years, when sex differences are found they are in the direction of boys' being more active. However, there are many instances in which sex differences have not been found. Some, but not all, of the variance among studies can be accounted for by whether the measurement situation was social. That is, boys appear to be especially stimulated to bursts of high activity by the presence of other boys. But the exact nature of the situational control over activity level remains to be established. Activity level is responsive to a number of motivational states—fear, anger curiosity—and is therefore not a promising variable for identifying stable individual or group differences. More detailed observations are needed on the vigor and qualitative nature of play.

Competitiveness

When sex differences are found, they usually show boys to be more competitive, but there are many studies finding sex similarity. Madsen and his colleagues find sex differences to be considerably weaker than differences between cultures and, in a number of studies, entirely absent. Almost all the research on competition has involved situations in which competition is maladaptive. In the Prisoner's Dilemma game, for example, the sexes are equally cooperative, but this is in a situation in which cooperation is to the long-run advantage of both players and the issue is one of developing mutual trust. It appears probable that in situations in which competitiveness produces increased individual rewards, males would be more competitive, but this is a guess based on commonsense considerations, such as the male interest in competitive sports, not upon research in controlled settings. The age of the subject and the identity of the opponent no doubt make a difference—there is evidence that young women hesitate to compete against their boyfriends.

Dominance

Dominance appears to be more of an issue within boys' groups than girls' groups. Boys make more dominance attempts (both successful and unsuccessful) toward one another than do girls. They also more often attempt to dominate adults. The dominance relations between the sexes are complex: in childhood, the sex segregation of play groups means that neither sex frequently attempts to dominate the other. In experimental situations in which the sexes are combined, the evidence is ambiguous on whether either sex is more successful in influencing the behavior of the other. Among adult mixed pairs or groups, formal leadership tends to go to males in the initial phases of interaction, but the direction of influence becomes more sex-equal the longer the relationship lasts, with "division of authority" occurring along lines of individual competencies and division of labor.

Compliance

In childhood, girls tend to be more compliant to the demands and directions of adults. This compliance does not extend, however, to willingness to accept directions from, or be influenced by, age-mates. Boys are especially concerned with maintaining their status in the peer group, and are probably therefore more vulnerable to pressures and challenges from this group, although this has not been well established. As we have seen in the discussion of dominance, it is not clear that in mixed-sex interactions either sex is consistently more willing to comply with the wishes of the other.

Nurturance and "Maternal" Behavior

There is very little evidence concerning the tendencies of boys and girls to be nurturant or helpful toward younger children or animals. Cross-cultural work does indicate that girls between the ages of 6 and 10 are more often seen behaving nurturantly. Within our own society, the rare studies that report nurturant behavior are observational studies of free play among nursery school children; sex differences are not found in these studies, but the setting normally does not include children much younger than the subjects being observed, and it may be that the relevant elicitors are simply not present. Female hor-

mones play a role in maternal behavior in lower animals, and the same may be true in human beings, but there is no direct evidence that this is the case. There is very little information on the responses of adult men to infants and children, so it is not possible to say whether adult women are more disposed to behave maternally than men are to behave paternally. If there is a sex difference in the tendency to behave nurturantly, it does not generalize to a greater female tendency to behave altruistically over varying situations. The studies of people's willingness to help others in distress have sometimes shown men more helpful, sometimes women, depending on the identity of the person needing help and the kind of help that is needed. The overall finding on altruism is one of sex similarity.

. . . On . . . the question of whether the female is more passive than the male, the answer is complex, but mainly negative. The two sexes are highly similar in their willingness to explore a novel environment, when they are both given freedom to do so. Both are highly responsive to social situations of all kinds, and although some individuals tend to withdraw from social interaction and simply watch from the sidelines, such persons are no more likely to be female than male. Girls' greater compliance with adult demands is just as likely to take an active as a passive form; running errands and performing services for others are active processes. Young boys seem more likely than girls to put out energy in the form of bursts of strenuous physical activity, but the girls are not sitting idly by while the boys act; they are simply playing more quietly. And their play is fully as organized and planful (possibly more so), and has as much the quality of actively imposing their own design upon their surroundings as does boys' play. It is true that boys and men are more aggressive, but this does not mean that females are the passive victims of aggression—they do not yield or withdraw when aggressed against any more frequently than males do, at least during the phases of childhood for which observations are available. With respect to dominance, we have noted the curious fact that while males are more dominant, females are not especially submissive, at least not to the dominance attempts of boys and girls their own age. In sum, the term "passive" does not accurately describe the most common female personality attributes.

Returning to one of the major conclusions of our survey of sex differences, there are many popular beliefs about the psychological characteristics of the two sexes that have proved to have little or no basis in fact. How is it possible that people continue to believe, for example, that girls are more "social" than boys, when careful observation and measurement in a variety of situations show no sex difference? Of course it is possible that we have not studied those particular situations that contribute most to the popular beliefs. But if this is the problem, it means that the alleged sex difference exists only in a limited range of situations, and the sweeping generalizations embodied in popular beliefs are not warranted.

However, a more likely explanation for the perpetuation of "myths," we believe, is the fact that stereotypes are such powerful things. An ancient truth is worth restating here: if a generalization about a group of people is believed, whenever a member of that group behaves in the expected way the observer notes it and his belief is confirmed and strengthened; when a member of the group behaves in a way that is not consistent with the observer's expectations, the instance is likely to pass unnoticed, and the observer's generalized belief is protected from disconfirmation. We believe that this well-documented process occurs continually in relation to the expected and perceived behavior of males and females, and results in the perpetuation of myths that would otherwise die out under the impact of negative evidence. However, not all unconfirmed beliefs about the two sexes are of this sort. It is necessary to reconsider the nature of the evidence that permits us to conclude what is myth and what is (at least potentially) reality.

section

2

BECOMINGS

Section 2, "Becomings," deals with the realities of life for preteens and early adolescents. There will be some carry-over from the first section, as certain questions must be further resolved, albeit on a deeper level. Ego struggle is one such issue. With several more years of experience, of questioning and of peer and cultural expectations, the identity of the self must be clarified and sharpened. When we are reminded that these are important school years, it is easier to understand the stresses placed upon the individual. What is the school experience for the young person? Does it increase self-doubts, or is it an affirming experience?

Complicating the situation for the early adolescent is the uneven development of physical growth and emotional maturing. Some have mature bodies with emotional and psychological insights lagging, while for others, development is reversed. Males suddenly are all hands and feet with fuzzy cheeks or upper lips and oddly cracking voices. Girls are no less affected by the onset of puberty with menstruation and the first appearance of roundnesses here and there. These physical changes may be disturbing to young persons whose emotional maturity is still that of the little boy or girl. When there is a wide disparity between these forms of growth, questions and anxiety result.

Even when physical and emotional development occurs at a similar rate, the first awareness of sexual feelings may be overwhelming. Improved health and nutritional standards have lowered the age for the physical onset of puberty, and there is increasing sexual activity at ever earlier ages. Older adults are often startled at the sexual precocity of their grandchildren. Special boy/girl friends are named earlier than they were three or four generations ago, and our society assumes a sexual component to these relationships, whether expressed or not. The acceptance of one's sexuality in these years is thus obviously a crucial issue of growth within family life.

Perception of the appropriate sex roles was begun in preschool years. The degree to which preteens accept these cultural definitions is now an important issue. In the adolescent world, how are masculinity and femininity defined? Is academic excellence equally as masculine as superior athletic performance? How does the tomboy affirm her femininity? What family, peer and cultural support is there for the behavior pattern chosen by the young person? What happens to the person whose choices are perceived as inappropriate?

With the exuberance and exaggeration not uncommon to youth, "I love . . . ." is often heard. There are few of us for whom the first love is the one and only love—the lasting love. The American custom of dating begins in this period and is seldom free of near crises, heartbreak, and frustration. Yet, the importance of dating can scarcely be overestimated. Our culture posits the dating relationship as the prescribed method of male-female interaction leading to later mate selection. The nature of adolescence almost guarantees there *will* be conflict as a reality of family life at this period.

Ego struggle, parent-peer conflict, uneven physical and emotional growth rates, sexual awakening, sex appropriate behavior and early dating—adults who work with preteens and adolescents will recognize the importance of these issues. Not all of them will be of the first magnitude but neither can their significance be ignored. They constitute a large portion of life for families which include adolescents and certainly a large portion of the major concerns of adolescents themselves.

CONTENTS: SECTION 2

MY LIFE WITH WOMEN*

Richard Armour

Then I fell in love with Miss Webster, and everything changed.

Miss Webster was my third-grade teacher and all I had ever hoped for in a woman. She had a soft, sweet voice. Her eyes crinkled when she smiled. She smelled good. And she could write on the board without making the chalk squeak.

One day when I came home from school, I broke the news to my mother, who was in the kitchen making cookies.

"I'm going to marry Miss Webster," I said.

"That's nice," my mother said, not the least surprised. It was almost as if she already knew. Could Miss Webster have told her? And yet I hadn't told Miss Webster myself.

"And we're going to have two children, both boys," I said.

"That's fine," my mother said. "Now you can scrape the bowl and lick the spoon.

All the time I was scraping the bowl and licking thee spoon, I was thinking of Miss Webster. We were going to be very happy together. I would look after her and give her everything she wanted, and she could just stay home and make cookies.

A short time afterward, I disclosed my plans to one of my friends during recess while we were swinging on the monkey bars.

"I'm going to marry Miss Webster," I said.

"So am I," he said.

This came as a surprise to me. I was even more surprised to learn, after a little asking around, that every boy in the class planned to marry Miss Webster. I was not greatly disturbed, however, since I had an advantage over most of the others. We were seated alphabetically, and I sat in the front row. I was much closer to Miss Webster than boys like Jack Williams and Eddy Zorn. Besides, Miss Webster obviously liked me. Who else got to clap erasers twice a week?

But I had competition more serious than my classmates. One day I saw Miss Webster go by in a sporty car with the top down. She smiled and waved at me. I waved back but I couldn't smile. A man was driving the car, and he had one hand on the steering wheel and the other around Miss Webster. After waving at me, Miss Webster said something to the man, and he turned and looked back at me and laughed.

As the car drove on and disappeared around a corner, I had a feeling that

58

I was losing Miss Webster. For the first time it occurred to me that she might marry someone else, someone who owned a car and was old enough to drive it.

I was right about Miss Webster. Just before the end of the school year, when I should have been excited about summer vacation and being promoted to fourth grade, I got the bad news. Though I had rather expected it, I was pretty depressed for several days.

"I am not going to teach after this year," Miss Webster told our class. "I am getting married." The girls cried, they were so happy, and the boys would have cried too, if they had not been boys. As it was, they just looked miserable.

It was the first time I had ever been beaten out by a rival, and I took it hard. Miss Webster had led me on and then let me down. But she wasn't as much to blame as the man in the car. I hated him. A couple of times I imagined myself fighting a duel with him, the winner to get Miss Webster. One time it was with swords and one time it was with pistols, and I won both times. But I couldn't go on imagining forever, and when I wasn't imagining I knew I had lost Miss Webster for good.

When I came home from school and told my mother Miss Webster was getting married, she sympathized with me.

"I know how you feel," she said. "But I've always thought she was a little old for you."

Then she told me that Miss Webster was twenty-two, and by the time I was twenty-two she would be thirty-six. By the time I was thirty-six she would be fifty.

"A woman can be older than her husband," she said, "but she shouldn't be too much older. I'm three years older than your father, and that's about enough.

"Why?" I asked.

"Well, it just is," she said, and seemed to think this is a satisfactory answer. It was all I could get out of her.

By the time I was eight years old, I had learned a good deal about women. From the girl next door I learned that the ones who are always after you are the ones you don't want. From Miss Webster I learned that the ones you want are always the wrong age or something, and then somebody comes and carries them off anyhow.

WHEN I WAS ABOUT FOURTEEN . . .*

Peter Candell

When I was about fourteen I slapped this kid Jeff Cook across the face right in the middle of a football huddle. I was boiling inside because he wasn't playing seriously. (I think it was the summer after I bit Barry Paley in the stomach after I tackled him, also during a football game. I remember being really embarrassed when his father came up to me later and bawled the hell out of me in front of other people. He couldn't understand why I wanted to bite his son and leave those ugly teeth marks. I didn't like Barry Paley.) Jeff Cook was a nice kid.

He was just goofing at a time when I was most serious and I slapped him out of pure rage. In fact I used to get pissed off a lot when we played ball whenever someone showed any signs of having fun, if that seemed more important to the kid than winning.

A softball or football game to me was deadly serious: if we won, the day was fine; if we lost, everything would be a little bitter for a while. If we won, I'd try to figure out how much I contributed to the victory. If we lost, I mulled over my mistakes, real and imagined, for hours. If I made a good play, I was a hero. An error, and I was a total failure. I still don't take my mistakes very lightly, even when they're trivial. And I remember my own greatest moments in sports vividly.

Jeff Cook probably felt that day, before I slapped him, anyway, the way that I wanted to feel today when I played football, only I couldn't. He must've been really bored durng that game, because he wasn't getting much of a chance to do anything except stand on the line and "block" every play. Anybody who plays touch football knows that the most boring position is on the line blocking somebody play after play. And in most games, the guys who are the worst players get the job as linemen, while two or three "stars" do all of the running, passing and catching.

Anyway Jeff Cook was one of these linemen and was undoubtedly bored stiff, for good reason, so he was goofing off, which seems to me now to be the best way to deal with the situation. Because he was entertaining himself and the other linemen, and also, although he may not have known it, he was goofing on us "stars" who were so serious. And I must have known somehow that he was goofing on me especially and I couldn't take it so I gave it to him.

Today I was treated like Jeff Cook on the football field. I was chosen last in

*A selection from _brother: a forum for men against sexism_; POB #4387, Berkeley, California 94704. This single selection does not reflect the overall content or political orientation of _brother_. Its inclusion in this collection does not reflect _brother_'s endorsement of this anthology.

two different games and I was pretty much ignored the whole day when plays were called in the huddle.

I guess it happened because I'm small and I didn't know anyone else playing. It was obvious early in the day there was a pecking order of "stars" based on who knew who and also on how tough a guy talked and acted. Since I didn't know anyone, the only way for me to break through that pecking order and get into the game was to start acting really tough. But I can't do that, it's just not my style. So I just kept my mouth shut and went through the motions sulking to myself, dragging my ass and my sense of pride through the mud on that wet field. It would have done me good to goof on the whole thing the way Jeff Cook did, but I couldn't do that either. I was too hurt.

But the thing is I really understood male chauvinism during those games today, and I felt it. I felt pushed around, ignored, used, and worst of all, powerless to do anything about it, except to leave. I felt like a little girl surrounded by all the older boys on the block.

My brother Steve used to lose his temper with me, just the way I did with Jeff Cook, except with Steve it was usually a punch in the arm. I loved my brother and his punches and noogies told me he loved me too. And I feel sad now to think how far away I am from my brother, because I have been searching for new brothers ever since he went away to summer camp when he was about thirteen and I was about nine, but it's never been the same.

I think I learned a lot of the jock mentality from my brother. He was always serious during a game, too. I guess he learned from my father, who probably learned it from his father. I knew I was admired for having such good "spirit." Incredible.

The summer I was 15 I got to play softball with the men's teams which is like being called up to the majors after years of playing Class C ball. It was a rite of passage. My manhood was on the line. They put me in right field which is usually where the worst player on the team was put and I knew that I had to prove myself and it wouldn't be easy in right field because you were lucky to get one chance a game out there.

There I was in right field spiritually urging the pitcher on with such gems as "no batta, baby, no batta," "right pastim," "lettim hitit, letim hitit," and the like, the visor of my baseball cap pulled down tight on my crew cut and over my eyes and there it was: A high foul ball behind first base, normally an easy play for the first or second baseman, but way out of reach of the old men with no legs playing these position on OUR TEAM.

I take off at full speed not knowing whether I would reach it but knowing very clearly that this is *my chance*. My cap flies off my head, which must have been pre-ordained, and a second later I one-hand it as cool as can be, still moving at top speed. I glance to the left as I hear the applause from the thirty or so fans and there's MOM kvelling, beaming, in a lounge chair she brought from the bungalow. My catch is the third out so I continue on to the sidelines and I hear voices congratulating my mother for having such a good athlete for a son:

"Quite a kid you've got there, Netti." Everybody on the team pounds my back as they come in from the field, letting me know that I've MADE IT.

But I know enough not to blow my cool so all I do is mumble thanks under a slightly trembling upper lip which is fighting the rest of my face, the rest of my being, from exploding with laughter and tears of joy. I don't even allow myself to smile because I know that it won't be just a smile, that if I let go even a quarter of an inch it will get beyond control and at the very least I'll giggle, which is unheard of on the ballfield.

I learned to be so cool partly from watching baseball stars on TV. The stars were always super-modest: they were responsible only for their failure, successes being due to Divine Intervention or Luck. My star, super-modest super-hero, was Mickey Mantle. What a name—Mickey Mantle—a born hero to millions of war babies who were freaking out on Bill Haley and the Comets the same year Mickey was on the way to the Triple Crown.

Mickey Mantle was far and away my most important person during those years. I lived through him, through his performance on the baseball field. Blond, crew-cut, strong, very strong, handsome and innocent—downright dumb in fact. He had a certain way of running after he hit a homerun, hunching his shoulders and clinking his arms, bent sharply at the elbow, up and down, but not backwards and forwards the way most other people do, which made him look even stronger; and so I started to run like him going to position or coming back in and very soon I was doing it without realizing I was doing it. In fact, I'm not even sure I ever was actually *aware* I was doing it but I was sure as hell doing it.

The whole vicarious masculinity thing went on for a long time, and when Mickey started fading out in the early sixties, I was still hooked on New York teams, which amounted to almost the same thing.

I rooted passionately for all the New York teams, getting most involved with the ones that were winning, and to *this day*, fans, to this day, I occasionally follow Giants football and Knicks basketball in the *Chronicle* sports pages, and *it still matters* whether they win or lose.

MARCELLA (EXCERPT)*

Marilyn Coffey

She had to face it, that's all. She could no longer postpone buying Marcella—a brassiere. She had been hoping that the matter could rest until fall, become part of going-back-to-school clothes, but there could be no more waiting. Marcella's breasts were definitely showing: this morning, at breakfast, her nipples sticking right out over her dish of Corn Flakes, looking like buttons on her T-shirt! Positively disconcerting. And rippling away under her shirt when she ran, just like a chippy's! That undershirt wasn't enough to hold them down. Of course (and Mrs. Colby had to chuckle), Marcella wasn't really *developed* yet, her bust more like the superfluous flesh of a fat boy than like a woman's chest. Still.

She called her daughter in from the yard—probably up in that treehouse again, whatever did she find to do up there?

"Go upstairs and get undressed," Mrs. Colby told her. "I need to take some measurements."

"I'll get Lucille," Marcella said. "She's over at the Cronins'."

"Never mind Lucille. This is for something you need. Go along. I'll be right up, as soon as I get the tape measure."

When Mrs. Colby entered the bedroom, minutes later, quilted sewing box in hand, she found Marcella still standing there, in her shirt and blue jeans.

"You're not even undressed! What were you doing, daydreaming again?"

Marcella hung her head and wiggled a foot around, disgusting habit, made her look so sullen. She finally asked:

"In front of you?"

"Goodness, yes, in front of me. I'm not your father."

Mrs. Colby watched Marcella turn her back. So sensitive, all of a sudden. Like that day in the bedroom, Marcella standing with robe half unbuttoned, stuttering and stammering like a three-year-old with wet pants. What did she have to hide? Nothing yet, that's for sure. Who did she think changed her diapers for her anyway? Hers, and Lucille's, and, God willing, no more!

Mrs. Colby took the tape from a side pocket of the sewing box, and looked up to see Marcella's undershirt going over her head.

"No, no! Not your undershirt. I'm only going to take measurements."

"Oh," Marcella's voice half-smothered as she pulled the shirt down again. "I thought you meant . . ." Turning around. Standing once more in undershirt and cotton briefs. Mrs. Colby shook her head.

---

*Reprinted with permission of Marilyn Coffey from her novel *Marcella*. Charterhouse/New York, 1973.

"Here. Come over here . . . That's right. Now lift your arms." What a piece of wood, this child! "No, no. Lift them. Up, up, up. High! In the air!" Marcella inched them up a bit farther, then stopped, her elbows protruding like chicken wings.

"I've got hair under there," she whispered.

So that's what was bothering her.

"Of course you have hair under there." Mrs. Colby flipped the tape under the girl's arms—"Now lift!"—and pulled it around to the back. "Do you think you're the only person in the world to grow hair? Turn around."

Marcella turned, silently. Mrs. Colby matched the tape in the middle of her back and noted it: only thirty-one. Strange. Smaller than she'd expected. She leaned forward. Of course! The tape wasn't even across the "full part of the bosom," as they say. She reached to adjust it. Marcella jerked away.

"Stand still, won't you!" Mrs. Colby's voice began to rasp.

"But it tickles!"

"Oh, don't be so silly. Here, turn and face me, then. I have to get the measurement across your chest. It does no good if the tape is lying across your belly."

Mrs. Colby pulled the tape around, or tried to. Marcella kept squirming, jerking each time her mother's hand grazed her breast.

"My! Aren't you something! How do you expect me to get an accurate measurement, if you keep shifting around all the time? You must stay still, Marcella. And stand up straight. How can I tell a thing with your shoulders all hunched over like that?"

"Let me do it. Here." Marcella grabbed the tape. "Where does it go?"

"That's right," watching her lay the yellow and red tape gently, first across one undershirted nipple, then across the other "Now let me have it," Mrs. Colby pulled the tape together in front of Marcella's armpit, so she could see the "full parts" without accidentally touching them. "Now put your arms down. Stand nice and straight." She squinted front and back: tape across nipples, tape in flat line across shoulder blades, not riding too high, nor too low. "Stand still."

"You're pulling it too tight."

"Nonsense." But she released the tape a little. "Mmmmmm. Thirty-two and a half. Call it thirty-two." She flipped the tape away.

"But it wasn't comfortable."

"You're not used to the way it feels, that's all," with a deft flick calculating the five and a half inches below the waist to get a perfect hip measurement, the tape down and around the tiny buttocks, above their swelling, across the widespread pelvic bones. Thirty-four.

So her measurements hadn't changed that much at all, must be the shifting in shape that made her seem different.

"You can get dressed now," Mrs. Colby said. . . .

It took a while for Mrs. Colby to figure out how to introduce the clothes to

Marcella. For that was her idea, to introduce them, to make them seem important. It could be a critical step in the process of transforming her daughter into
a lady. To woo her away from any ideas she might have of becoming a hussy, a
common pickup. Oh, girls! She knew how their minds ran with pretty things,
lacy things. These matters were so delicate . . . how to create the proper atmosphere, make the privilege of wearing grown-up things acquire its own code,
its duties. For she would have to direct Marcella, somehow, that was clear. But
not too bluntly. No, not outright. If there was one thing she understood about
her daughter, it was Marcella's stubbornness. Tell her she had to do something, and she'd end up doing the opposite. Oh, a delicate matter indeed.

She waited until after lunch, having made arrangements for Lucille to visit
a friend. That way, she and Marcella wouldn't be interrupted. She called her
daughter into the bedroom.

"What's this?" Marcella wanted to know, as Mrs. Colby gave her the
store-wrapped packages.

"The clothes I measured you for. Go ahead. Open them up."

Marcella pulled a tangle of elastic and ribbon out of the first package. The
ribbons were attached to a piece of smooth white satin, a rose embroidered in
one corner.

"Oh," she cried, "for me?" As silky as Rosemary's slip?

"Yes, but here. Try this one first," and Mrs. Colby set the flat hose box
aside, to hand her daughter the third box. Inside, under folds of tissue, Mar-

cella found another scramble of straps, hooks and eyes, and delicate edgings. These weren't silky though. Just cotton. Quilted cotton.

"Is it . . ." Marcella couldn't bring herself to say the word in front of her mother.

"A brassiere," Mrs. Colby replied as matter of factly as she could, unscrambling the straps. "Two of them. Here. Let me help you." She stripped Marcella's T-shirt and undershirt off in one swift motion, before the girl had time to be shy.

"Mother! Really! I can take off my own clothes."

"Did I catch your nose? Sorry."

Mrs. Colby picked up the brassiere.

"No! Here. Let me!" Marcella insisted. She took the brassiere and stuck her arms through the strap holes, as though she were donning a coat. Then, reconsidering, she turned it around so the breast pieces were in front.

"Not that way. You've got it upside down." Mrs. Colby deftly retrieved the brassiere, circled it around Marcella, pulled the elastic taut, and fastened the hooks in the last row of eyes. Snug! That was strange. She was certain the measurement had been only thirty-two and a half, and Marcella with such little breasts . . . She twisted the circle of cotton around the girl's body. "There. Now you can put your arms through."

Marcella began wiggling into the cups.

"No, not like that. Bend over." She helped her daughter jiggle her breasts into the quilted containers.

The straps hung in long ribbons off Marcella's shoulders. Mrs. Colby adjusted the bands, pushing the metal clips along. "Move around a bit and see how it feels."

It felt awkward. The elastic dug into Marcella's chest; the padded cups pushed her breasts flat against her body.

"I don't know," said Marcella. "I can barely move."

"Well, there's no call to move. It's not good for your bosom to jiggle all over the place."

"It's pretty tight."

"Why don't you wear it awhile, and see. We can always exchange it. But better too small than too big—that elastic stretches with washing, anyway. Besides, I think you'll be more comfortable with a snug fit, once you get used to it. When you run, especially. Come. Let's see how it looks under your T-shirt."

"Shouldn't I put my undershirt on first?" She'd been wearing them all summer long, even on the hottest days—ever since her breasts became noticeable.

"Oh, no. You wear this instead of an undershirt."

"Every day?" Marcella was incredulous. She had thought maybe on Sundays, maybe with dresses . . .

"Yes, every day. Of course. That's why I bought two. Here. Put your T-shirt on."

Marcella's voice came muffled through her shirt:

"You mean Rosemary wears a bra every day?"

"Well, if she doesn't, she should," Mrs. Colby sniffed, watching the cups ride up on Marcella's breasts as she wriggled into the shirt. "And say 'brassiere,' Marcella. 'Bra' is vulgar. Here. Don't wiggle so much." She helped her daughter jounce her breasts back into the cups again. The brassiere was too tight, there was no mistaking it. Cups too small! But how could she return it, after . . .

"There. Let's see how you look." Oh, Gladys was right! No sign of nipple marks, only the cross-stitching at the tip of the cup. Although the bosom, well, actually the breasts did protrude, but they seemed . . . "Move around a bit, Marcella, and let me have a look." Excellent! Her breasts remained as static as marble ones. With a larger T-shirt, maybe striped . . . infinitely better.

Marcella stood staring at her breasts. They seemed so gigantic. She seemed all breasts, nothing but these huge lumps slapped on her chest, oh! Every day! She would surely get teased. How awful Rosemary must feel, with hers so big. You had to peek over the points to see your own feet! No longer flat, like a child, and wearing undershirts, but stuck with this contraption all the time, ugh! How could she even run, any more, the elastic cutting in every which way, and hot! Whew! All this quilting, hotter than her undershirt had been, and pushing her breasts so tightly against her, they felt like an enormous ledge, a slab of flesh and cotton bound to her chest.

"And you let the other one air out the next day," her mother was explaining. "That way, they don't get smelly."

"Don't you wash them?"

"On Saturdays, with the rest of the clothes. Not by hand, that's too much bother. See what else I got you?"

Mrs. Colby held up the garter belt. Marcella was alarmed.

"Do I have to wear that every day, too?"

"Goodness, no. This is only for Sundays. To hold up your hose."

Marcella knew what the belt was for, but it looked suspiciously confining . . . though it was pretty. She took it, and began smoothing the satin part. So grown-up. As pretty as that slip had been. Maybe it wouldn't be so bad, and only for dress-up . . .

". . . like a lady," her mother was saying. "Don't ever let me catch you sitting like this." Marcella looked. Mrs. Colby sat on the edge of her bed, knees flung apart, toes turned in. "Anybody can see right up your skirt if you sit like this." The thought was startling. Then Mrs. Colby crossed her legs, letting one foot dangle in the air. "And don't sit this way, either.

"Crossing legs is okay for older women, like myself," she explained, "but not for young girls. They just look fast. Besides, it's a good way to snag your hose with the heel of your shoe. You can cross your ankles, if you must. But here's how a nice girl sits."

So strange to have to show Marcella all this. Lucille just seemed to know—or was it that she was a better mimic?

ADOLESCENCE:
A TIME FOR "ADJUSTMENT"*

Janet Chafetz

In analyzing the impact of the media and schools on sex role learning, it should be recalled that the media directed to adolescents, whether popular songs, magazines and underground papers, TV, or school texts, have been found to strongly reinforce sex role sterotypes. In addition, junior and senior high school curricula counseling, and extracurricular activities tend to segregate the genders and encourage them to think, behave, and plan in different (stereotyped ways. . . .

In any consideration of adolescents, two related concepts appear repeatedly: "identity crisis" and "anxiety." From puberty until they complete school and enter their adult statuses both males and females in contemporary American society are thought to undergo more or less severe emotional crises centered around questions of who they are and what they will become. Questions concerning sex role identities contribute mightily to such problems, although they are broader than this alone. It is during the years following the onset of puberty that both males and females are faced with making major decisions that will usually influence the manner in which they live the rest of their lives. Such decisions are most often made within the boundaries of sex role stereotypes. Boys are generally urged into courses of action preparatory to some occupational commitment, girls into behaviors designed to ultimately attract a suitable mate.

The impact of peers on behavior and thought is probably never greater than at this period of life when, as young adults, they strive to establish their independence by breaking ties with their parents. The strong gender segregation characteristic of younger peer groups begins to break down somewhat during adolescence, with dating. However, all-male and all-female friendship groups or cliques persist, as indeed they do in adulthood. Moreover, peer groups become relatively more important in influencing the behaviors and attitudes of young adults. They also play a major role in determining the chances of their members for success with the opposite sex.

As a general rule, all-male groups determine the relative status and prestige of the various individual males within them. Such prestige is a function of how well the adolescent boy fulfills the norms of the group. Thus, in middle

---

*Reproduced by permission of the publisher, F.E. Peacock Publishers, Inc., Itasca, Illinois. From Janet Saltzman Chafetz, *Masculine/Feminine or Human?* An overview of the Sociology of Sex Roles. 1974 copyright, pp. 90—95.

class peer groups boys are often expected to be good (but not *too* good) students and active in a number of extracurriclar activities, which function as modes of preparation for college and a high-status career. They are also expected to maintain athletic competence and achieve considerable independence from their families. Working and lower-class peer groups usually place heaviest emphasis on independence, physical courage, and adventuresomeness, sometimes as tested in illegal ventures. These groups generally deemphasize and even denigrate school success. Those who manage to achieve high status within such all-male groups attract the most numerous and attractive females from among class and ethnic equals. In turn, status within all-female groups is largely contingent upon the status of the males the girl is able to attract as dates or "steadies." In other words, female peer groups at this stage of the life cycle (and probably thereafter) base their internal prestige structure on their members' relative abilities to do best that which society commands: attract (potential) outstanding mates.

Note that in the case of female groups there are no differences by socioeconomic class. Male groups also base their internal structure on that which society suggests is appropriate to the gender, but class variations do exist. Females of all classes are enjoined to find mates as their primary responsibility. Males of all classes are enjoined to be physically coordinated and aggressive, and to acquire an occupation. However, the occupational roles anticipated by working- and lower-class youths are generally not of a nature where school performance will be very relevant. Thus, in these peer groups, other aspects of the stereotype become overwhelmingly dominant. Middle-class males, for whom school performance is relevant to future occupational expectations, develop norms by which these other characteristics share importance with academic success.

In examining the pressures exerted on adolescents and the ways in which they contribute to "anxieties" arising from "identity crises," it should be noted that whether or not the female has conformed previously to sterotypical notions of femininity (and substantial numbers of "tomboys" have not), the pressure by peers and parents to do so in adolescense becomes substantial.[1] At this point in her life, preparation for the search for a "mate" and the search itself begin in earnest, and that is presumably the one crucial fact of her entire future existence and identity. Girls perform substantially better than boys in the earlier years of school, probably out of a "feminine" desire to please the teacher. Suddenly in high school and, especially, college their performance declines noticeably, while that of males, particularly those in middle class, improves markedly in preparation for a career. Adolescent girls are enjoined to "play dumb and weak" in order to "boost male egos" and thereby attract and hold a suitable mate whose identity they can then assume. In a now-famous series of experiments conducted among female college students, Matina Horner demonstrated that females actually fear achievement and success.[2]*

---

*See Maccoby and Jacklin.

The bright, dynamic, adolescent Jane, the one who is planning a career, or the good athlete either "plays dumb and weak" and lives a frustrating lie, or she pursues her interests as a relative outcast, dateless and low in prestige among her peers, wondering bitterly and anxiously why she isn't more "feminine." This will continue and increase in college, in graduate school, and even throughout life. Many finally conclude that they cannot have both a fulfilling life in terms of their own interests and aspirations and a satisfactory relationship with a male. Whichever goes by the wayside, life will be less rich as a result of the phony choice offered by society and beginning most notably in adolescence.

Nor is the girl who opts for "femininity" at the expense of her individual needs and inclinations any better off later. . . . In their quest for identity through an attachment to a male, many adolescent females find themselves pressured into sexual relationships in an attempt to attract, please, or "hold" boyfriends. This may be particularly true for less attractive girls. Such relationships often result in out-of-wedlock pregnancies, "shotgun" marriages, adjudication as "delinquent," or serious emotional problems for those who have been trained to consider sex outside of marriage as "evil" or "sinful." In any case, such sexual experiences, *when engaged in for those kinds of reasons,* often develop into unpleasant situations, fraught with problems of every variety and hardly beneficial to the development of a positive identity. In this context I am not addressing myself to all premarital sexual relations but only those engaged in out of a desire on the part of the female to please the male, regardless of her own personal needs and feelings at the time. In their quest for identity through attachment to a male, all too many young women leave themselves open to crass sexual exploitation and, as we shall see, most males are pressured into taking advantage of such situations.

Dick, too, is facing his share of problems at this stage. Where Jane at least has the option, however unpleasant the consequences may eventually become, of taking a future mate's identity as her own with no further ado, Dick must work out his own in an increasingly complex and incomprehensible world. First and foremost, especially if Dick is middle class, that identity will be in terms of his occupation, and beginning in high school he must seriously begin to decide what he "wants to be when he grows up." The decision to become a minister rather than a professional soldier, for instance, is based on rather different notions about oneself and the world, and these must first be sorted out. In addition, if his potential occupational talents and personal predilections run in certain tabooed directions, such as art, literature, or music, he will face ridicule from his peers for being something less than "masculine"; likewise, in many cases, if he takes his studies "too seriously."

While engaged in these decisions, he must nonetheless maintain some demonstration of his "physical prowess" and "bravery." That may not present too much of a problem if he happens to be 6' tall, 180 pounds, and coordinated, but what of all those who are 5'6" and 115 pounds? Those who, in the old Charles Atlas ads, got sand kicked in their faces, the sensitive souls who cannot bear to inflict pain in others, the boys who lack coordination, are all subject to severe doubts about their masculine identity. Such "shortcomings" can be particularly anxiety-producing for working- and lower-class youth, although they will obviously affect the middle-class male as well.

Equally important to adolescent boys is the need for independence, sometimes financial and almost always in terms of freedom from adult supervision. However, in a society where, increasingly, males remain in school under adult supervision and out of the labor force well into their twenties, such independence becomes problematic. Told to "act like a man" but often constrained to "beg" his parents for money, use of the car, and other "necessities," adolescent males sometimes find it difficult to live up to the social prescriptions and so begin to doubt their very "masculinity." Dick finds himself in need of emotional support from people who accept him as he is, with all his weaknesses, shortcomings, and insecurities. Yet he is trying to break away from emotional dependence on his family, about the only people who might accept him unconditionally. The world of adolescent males has little mercy on the boy who never managed to make the break from a too close identification with and attachment to mother.

Left with residual doubts about his masculinity from childhood, faced with making important career decisions, encouraged to be independent and physically and emotionally strong while also constrained from these things by his inexperience, student status, and need for emotional support, the adolescent male faces a tough time in developing a sense of himself. Finally, while he is not pressured into seeking a mate at this point (except by adolescent females), he is expected by his peers to "prove his masculinity" by revealing his "prowess" with the girls. As they brag to one another about their sexual exploits, some unfortunate lads actually believe what they hear (or say). A vicious cycle of anxiety and lies is often the result. The inexperienced (namely, most boys) lie about their conquests to cover their felt inferiority, listen to others do the same, believe them, and feel yet more anxiety about their masculinity. At its worst, this eventuates in sexual exploitation of girls who allow themselves to be used in an attempt to establish their own feminine identity.

This brings us finally to the subject of the nature of the relationship between adolescent males and females. It is, first and foremost, broadly sexual in nature and based around "dating." For the boy or girl who is not interested in this or who matures late physically, relationships with the opposite sex are almost nonexistent, and prestige with the same sex is low. We are all quite familiar with the pattern: the female more or less passively awaits an invitation from a male, after taking the greatest pains to appear "attractive" by whatever are the standards of the day; the boy will usually try to "get as much" as he can from her sexually; she, as repository of "sexual morality," is responsible for not allowing sexual play to "get out of hand." She has been fed (and believes) a diet of "romantic" notions about love and sex which puts her at a disadvantage in relationship to boys, who are usually substantially less devoted to the ideal of romance. While she bases her existence on his attentions, he has a variety of other, often more important, matters to attend to. The game that ensues makes honest communication and affection between two human beings difficult, if not impossible. Moreover, in many ways this process comprises the worst possible preparation for a satisfactory marriage for either. Indeed, as Margaret Mead first pointed out nearly three decades ago, dating is really oriented toward gaining prestige among the peers of one's own gender, and it is thus quite impersonal.[3] More recently the process has been viewed as a failure "because it does not assist couples in learning how to develop and maintain vital and meaningful relationships.[4]

References

1. J. Freeman, "Growing Up Girlish" *Trans-Action*, VIII (1970), 36–43.
2. M. Horner, "Fail: Bright Women" *Psychology Today*, III (1969), 36.
3. M. Mead, *Male and Female* (New York: Dell Publishing Co., 1970).
4. D. Olson, "Marriage of the Future" in *Non-Traditional Family Forms in the 1970's* M. Sussman, ed. (Minneapolis: National Council on Family Relations, 1972).

THE AMERICAN DATING GAME:
THE HETEROSEXUAL STAGE*

Frank Cox

The normal heterosexual stage in our culture begins with puberty. The onset of puberty occurs, on the average, at about 12 years of age for the female and about 14 years of age in the male. At this time the child becomes adult biologically (able to reproduce the species) and for the first time the male-female relationship takes on an overtly sexual . . . nature. This stage, under normal conditions will last throughout adulthood until sexual potency begins to decline in the later years. The early years of dating and mate selection are a sub-stage of full adulthood. . . .

It is a stress period because biology has prepared the child for normal adult sexual behavior (intercourse) and yet our society traditionally denies and tries to repress this readiness by placing restrictive rules and taboos on early sexual behavior. . . .

There are two logical methods by which to reduce the length of this stress period. Either the average age of marriage can be reduced still further or the gang stage can be prolonged. Many of the more primitive societies as well as some of the eastern societies practice child marriage which completely eradicates the American sexual stress period. In addition, some cultures, such as the Polynesians, are highly permissive in allowing early sexual experimentation, thus also avoiding a prolonged period of conflict and restrictive social folkways. In fact, an anthropological study by Murdock found that of 250 societies throughout the world, some 70% permit sexual experimentation before marriage.[2] In the nuclear western type family, the first solution, reducing the average age of marriage, has many things against it. . . .

The second method, prolonging the gang stage, can only reduce the stress period by at most a few years since one cannot postpone or reverse the biological process of puberty. One can, however, slow down the rate of male-female interaction. This is the system used by the middle and upper classes of most western European countries. The girls and boys are kept more segregated than in the United States. Many more of the schools are segregated according to sex. Early adult behavior, such as the use of make-up, dating, etc., is strongly discouraged. The middle class European girl of 15 or 16 is, on the average, most similar to the American girl of 11 or 12. She still participates mainly with her gang of girlfriends. Her behavior toward boys is one of early teasing and flirtation with little if any prolonged contact. What dating there is will usually be on

---

*From: Cox, Frank D., *Youth, Marriage and the Seductive Society*, revised edition, 1968 Dubuque, Iowa, Wm. C. Brown Company Publishers.

a group basis. It should be noted, however, that the system of being influenced by the American culture and this description of the European middle class girl is gradually being modified with time.

The American system, unfortunately, does nothing to slow the early heterosexual contact of its youth. In fact, just the opposite is the case. The society works to encourage early heterosexual contact. Many elementary schools promote coeducational dances and parties. Often parents worry that their child will not become popular and so pressure their children into developing an early interest in the opposite sex. Make-up, more adult fashions including bras for 10 years olds (size AAA, termed "air cups" by the author), increased sophistication through close contact with mass media, etc., all tend to speed the transition from the gang stage to the adult heterosexual stage.[3]. . .

Compounding still more the conflict over emerging sexuality during the stress period is the extended opportunity that a young couple in modern society has to be alone together. The automobile has not only revolutionized transportation and contributed to the highly mobile American way of life but it has also revolutionized early sexual experimentation for the youth. The automobile for the teen-age boy is more than mere transportation, it is an extension of his ego. It becomes as much a part of himself as his physical stature. He will be known and admired, or not, by the car he drives. His ability to attract girls will be greatly influenced by his auto. And most pertinent to this discussion, the mobile bedroom characteristic of his automobile will increase greatly the pressure of the stress period. He can be alone with his girl at almost any time and in almost any place he chooses. By escaping the company of others, group control and influence is lessened. There is no one that might report a breach of the established social mores. The feeling of anonymity and distance from the social system is increased. In essence, the young couple are thrown completely onto their own resources in determining just what their behavior will be. In the end, they alone will make the decision as to the type of sexual behavior in which they will engage before marriage. The auto, probably more than any other single influence, has wrought a change in premarital sexual behavior among the young.* One researcher terms this change, "The glandular crisis of a parked car."[4]

Let us follow a young American couple through an extended period of dating and observe how the American dating game is played. Remember the weakness of generality when it is applied to actual rather than ideal behavior and do not consider the actions about to be described as descriptive of any particular young couple. The couple we will observe is a nice, well-reared, clean-cut pair of American youth. Everything about their relationship has been done in the socially prescribed manner. They are in no way bad or promiscuous or delinquent. They are simply good middle class, young American teenagers. We

---

*An Idaho study reported in *Life* magazine some years ago showed that not a single straight A student owned a car and only 15% of the B students owned one. But 41% of the C students had cars and 71% of the D students. And among the flunkers, a spectacular 83% owned cars.

will take a developmental approach to their dating behavior. Let us start, then, when they were first allowed to begin dating. This age will vary greatly with each family but, in general, it has gradually become younger so that dating at 11 and 12, especially for the girl, is not as unusual as it once was. Let us further assume that the boy has just reached the age of legal driving and is able to talk his father out of the family auto for his date.

The young man has known the girl superficially for some time since they both attend the same school and have met previously at various school functions. Although it requires courage, he finally asks if she can accompany him to a movie on the coming Saturday night. A movie is usually a safe first date for the young adolescent since it requires so little interaction with one's date. Both the boy and girl receive an O.K. from their own parents. It may even be that the parents contact one another although this is increasingly unusual. At the appointed time on Saturday night, the young man proudly arrives at the wheel of the family auto. Although she has been ready for some time, she is discreetly "not ready." This serves a two-fold purpose: she does not appear over-eager (her mother has told her to play hard-to-get) and secondly, it gives the parents a few moments in which to look over the boy and discuss the evening's rules with him; mainly the proposed time of return. At the psychologically correct moment she makes her entry and together they depart.

The darkened theatre actually becomes the location of the first confrontation. The young man strongly feels the pressure of his friends, and the anonymous larger group of peers loosely defined as "the boys." According to the mores, enough of the double standard remains so that it is he who must take the initiative. And, indeed, to feel masculine and proud among "the boys," the young man is obligated to at least try some type of physical contact with the girl. Thus, as he sits watching the movie, the first of many conflicts concerning sexuality begins to take form. He notices that her hands are lying one inch in his direction upon her lap. Perhaps this is a clue. Should he attempt to hold her hand? If she vigorously rejects this advance everyone in the row might notice and his embarrassment will be acute. If, on the other hand, she accepts, how will he be able to withdraw his hand from hers when it becomes sweaty and begins to cramp without her taking it as some kind of rejection? This little game is obviously at a very early and naive level.

The fascinating and unique characteristic of the American dating game is what one may term "escalation." In other words, dissolution of this first level minor conflict does not end the problem. If the girl accepts his first advance, then the pressure he feels to prove himself to "the boys" actually increases since the whole procedure is designed to test just how far he can go toward overt sexuality with the girl. Granted, much of this pressure may be unconscious for the boy, yet he feels the need to prove himself. Naturally, the further the boy moves, the more pride he will feel when bragging to his friends of his prowess with the girls. Thus, once he has taken her hand he must now look to the slightly greater problem of attempting to place his arm around her. The rewards are obviously greater but so are the risks. If she vigorously rejects his

attempt, the whole movie house will notice (at least it will seem this way to him). If she accepts, there is always the ensuing cramped shoulder to look forward to as well as the necessity of facing the new escalation level and all of its ensuing conflicts and insecurities. The girl is having conflicts too because she does not want to lose her reputation and yet at the same time she does like the boy and thus does not want him to think her a prude in which case he may not ask her for another date.

The American dating game evolves into a game of offense versus defense, and in the course of history, a defense has never won a war. With each step toward sexual intercourse taken by the boy, the girl will have to retreat and reintegrate her new behavior into her value system. Since her value system will in all probability already be vague and nebulous because of the swift changing and pragmatic character of the American society, the continuing pressure upon her will cause great confusion and insecurity.* By this age, it will be the

---

*One of the most susceptible periods for the girl insofar as premarital sex is concerned is after she and her steady boy friend have broken up over sexual problems and then go back together again. Her fear of losing him makes her acquiesce to his demands as a way of holding him.

peer group that wields the greatest influence and both she and the boy will be highly susceptible to the argument that everyone else engages in such behavior. Her own insecurity will be her worst enemy.

Thus escalation brings physical relations from the naive level described to necking, petting, petting to orgasm, and finally to intercourse in an increasing number of cases. The rapidity of the escalation depends upon the inner security of each member of the couple and the length of time and exclusiveness with which they date one another. The more insecure the young person the more they will seek security in conforming to what they believe the peer group is doing. Time is obviously an important factor. To place highly vigorous young adults who like one another together for long periods of time without supervision is obviously going to lead to sexual activity.

In the last analysis, as stated before, it is the couple alone that is forced to make the decision as to how far they will go. At this point there begins a strange (almost schizophrenic like) unrealistic game called "sex-not-sex" and it is usually the girl who makes up the rules. Since she must control how far the boys goes, she must have some operational definition of what sexaul behavior is. She knows that actual intercourse is sex but she is unsure of how to categorize all the other behavior; kissing, necking and various degrees of petting in which she gradually indulges. If she can categorize kissing as "non-sex" she can kiss as much as she likes and need feel no threat or guilt. If, on the other hand, because of upbringing, she categorizes it as "sex" she will then have conflict and guilt will arise when she engages in such behavior.

When one asks a cross-section of young American women what they define as sexual behavior there is no one agreed upon answer. One girl may become upset and in a state of conflict when she feels passion upon kissing. Another girl may be able to indulge in mutual masturbation with little if any conflict because she has defined all but actual intercourse as "non-sex." In reality, in the broadest sense, intimate physical contact of any kind between male and female is sexual behavior. It can be and indeed should be the foreplay to sexual intercourse.

The boy is not only pressured by his peers into making advances toward the girl but he also feels this necessity because he cannot judge where any one particular girl will draw the line. Thus, he is insecure in her presence until he knows the rules whereby she is willing to play the game.

Because of the type of dynamics herein described, the young adult stress period becomes centered on sex to the exclusion of most other things. Even a final solution to escalation problems, sexual intercourse, does not end the preoccupation with sex.* Indeed it often serves to exaggerate it even more . . . It might be noted that boy-girl relationships tend to be much more relaxed and comfortable in societies where the attitude toward sex is more realistic than in

---

*If one agrees with Terman that only 20% of the marital adjustment depends upon sexual compatibility, the American dating couple who preoccupy themselves with sex miss out on testing the other 80% of their future marital relationship.[5]

our own. Cultures that allow early sexual experimentation do not find the young people's relationships centered in sex. Sex is allowed to take a more natural place and the need to be preoccupied with it is absent. Many young American soldiers find themselves more comfortable with foreign girls where sex is more open and honest. If a girl looks inviting and acts the role, she is usually available. He need not continually concern himself with whether each girl he meets will play the game differently. In this context then, premarital sexual experimentation is more natural than prolonged and frustrating petting in which so many of our young American middle class couples indulge.

Further compounding the problems of this period has been the increasing tendency to pair off at an early age and "go steady." There is little doubt that this tendency has increased since World War II but the exact rules and manifestations of it vary greatly from one locale to another. The phenomenon tends to add pressure to the sexual conflicts experienced by the young couple. Their contact is much more frequent and because there is little distraction by dating others, their relationship becomes more quickly intimate. As a result, a great deal of possessiveness manifests itself in jealous behavior. The American boy tends to regard any attention or compliments paid to his steady as insulting and usually resricts her social interactions to himself. Actually in a more mature relationship, attention and compliments to one's girl or boy friend can be taken as a compliment to oneself. It is flattering to be out with a person whom others regard as attractive. This, of course, demands a certain amount of security in both partners as well as within the relationship itself.

For example, among most middle class European young adults, general social interaction with numerous persons of the opposite sex is preferred to tying oneself too tightly to just one. At a dance each male is expected to dance with at least every other female sitting at his table. It is regarded as highly impolite if he does not. This serves to reduce the level of emotional attachment to an easier level for the young adult to handle. . . .

In summary, the American Dating Game is generally characterized by an exaggerated emphasis on sex, a tendency to narrow one's field through the technique of "going steady," resulting in greater possessiveness and jealousy which serves to heighten even further the emotionality of the relationship. Because of these dynamics and the rapidly changing value structure of the modern American society, premarital intercourse is increasing.

References

1. *Demographic Yearbook,* United Nations, 1965.
2. G. Murdock, "Sexual Behavior: What is Acceptable" *Journal of Social Hygiene,* XXXVI (1950), 1–31.
3. M. McLuhan and A. Flore, *The Medium is the Message: An Inventory of Effects* (New York: Random House, 1967).

4. V. Eller, "Old Morality of MAD Magazine Praised" an interview article by J. Dart in the *Los Angeles Times*, January 1, 1968

5. L. Terman, *Psychological Factors in Marital Happiness* (New York: McGraw-Hill, 1938).

PSYCHOSEXUAL DEVELOPMENT*

William Simon and John Gagnon

Erik Erikson has observed that, prior to Sigmund Freud, "sexologists" tended to believe that sexual capacities appeared suddenly with the onset of adolescence. Sexuality followed those external evidences of physiological change that occurred concurrent with or just after puberty. Psychoanalysis changed all that. In Freud's view, libido—the generation of psychosexual energies—should be viewed as a fundamental element of human experience at least beginning with birth, and possibly before that. Libido, therefore, is essential, a biological constant to be coped with at all levels of individual, social, and cultural development. The truth of this received wisdom, that is, that sexual development is a continuous contest between biological drive and cultural restraint should be seriously questioned. Obviously sexuality has roots in biological processes, but so do many other capacities, including many that involve physical and mental competence and vigor. There is, however, abundant evidence that the final states which these capacities attain escape the rigid impress of biology. This independence of biological constraint is rarely claimed for the area of sexuality, but we would like to argue that the sexual is precisely that realm where the sociocultural forms most completely dominate biological influences.

It is difficult to get data that might shed much light on the earliest aspects of these questions: Adults are hardly equipped with total recall and the preverbal or primitively verbal child does not have ability to report accurately on his own internal state. But it seems obvious—and it is a basic assumption of this paper—that with the beginnings of adolescence many new factors come into play, and to emphasize a straight-line developmental continuity with infant and childhood experiences may be seriously misleading. In particular, it is dangerous to assume that because some childhood behavior appears sexual to adults, it must be sexual. An infant or a child engaged in genital play (even if orgasm is observed) can in no sense be seen as experiencing the complex set of feelings that accompanies adult or even adolescent masturbation.

Therefore, the authors reject the unproven assumption that "powerful" psychosexual drives are fixed biological attributes. More importantly, we reject the even more dubious assumption that sexual capacities or experiences tend to translate immediately into a kind of universal "knowing" or innate wisdom—that sexuality has a magical ability, possessed by no other capacity, that

---

allows biological drives to be expressed directly in psychosocial and social behaviors.

The prevailing image of sexuality—particularly that of the Freudian tradition—is that of an intense, high-pressure drive that forces a person to seek physical sexual gratification, a drive that expresses itself indirectly if it cannot be expressed directly. The available data suggest to us a different picture—one that shows either lower levels of intensity, or, at least, greater variability. We find that there are many social situations or life-roles in which reduced sex activity or even deliberate celibacy is undertaken with little evidence that the libido has shifted in compensation to some other sphere.

A part of the legacy of Freud is that we have all become remarkably adept at discovering "sexual" elements in nonsexual behavior and symbolism. What we suggest instead (following Kenneth Burke's three-decade-old insight) is the reverse—that sexual behavior can often express and serve nonsexual motives.

NO PLAY WITHOUT A SCRIPT

We see sexual behavior therefore as *scripted* behavior, not the masked expression of a primordial drive. The individual can learn sexual behavior as he or she learns other behavior—through scripts that in this case give the self, other persons, and situations erotic abilities or content. Desire, privacy, opportunity, and propinquity with an attractive member of the opposite sex are not, in themselves, enough; in ordinary circumstances, nothing sexual will occur unless one or both actors organize these elements into an appropriate script. The very concern with foreplay in sex suggests this. From one point of view, foreplay may be defined as merely progressive physical excitement generated by touching naturally erogenous zones. The authors have referred to this conception elsewhere as the "rubbing of two sticks together to make a fire" model. It would seem to be more valuable to see this activity as symbolically invested behavior through which the body is eroticized and through which mute, inarticulate motions and gestures are translated into a sociosexual drama.

A belief in the sociocultural dominance of sexual behavior finds support in cross-cultural research as well as in data restricted to the United States. Psychosexual development is universal—but it takes many forms and tempos. People in different cultures construct their scripts differently; and in our own society, different segments of the population act out different psychosexual dramas—something much less likely to occur if they were all reacting more or less blindly to the same superordinate urge. The most marked differences occur, of course, between male and female patterns of sexual behavior. Obviously, some of this is due to biological differences, including differences in hormonal functions at different ages. But the significance of social scripts predominates; the recent work of Masters and Johnson, for example, clearly points to far greater orgasmic capacities on the part of females than our culture would lead us to suspect. And within each sex—especially among men—different social and economic groups have different patterns.

Let us examine some of these variations, and see if we can decipher the scripts.

CHILDHOOD

Whether one agrees with Freud or not, it is obvious that we do not become sexual all at once. There is continuity with the past. Even infant experiences can strongly influence later sexual development.

But continuity is not causality. Childhood experiences (even those that appear sexual) will in all likelihood be influential not because they are intrinsically sexual, but because they can affect a number of developmental trends, *including* the sexual. What situations in infancy—or even early childhood—can be called psychosexual in any sense other than that of creating potentials?

The key term, therefore, must remain potentiation. In infancy, we can locate some of the experiences (or sensations) that will bring about a sense of the body and its capacities for pleasure and discomfort and those that will influence the child's ability to relate to others. It is possible, of course, that through these primitive experiences, ranges are being established—but they are very broad and overlapping. Moreover, if these are profound experiences to the child—and they may well be that—they are not expressions of biological necessity, but of the earliest forms of social learning.

In childhood, after infancy there is what appears to be some real sex play. About half of all adults report that they did engage in some form of sex play as children and the total who actually did may be half again as many. But, however the adult interprets it later, what did it mean to the child at the time? One suspects that, as in much of childhood role-playing, their sense of the adult meanings attributed to the behavior is fragmentary and ill-formed. Many of the adults recall that, at the time, they were concerned with being found out. But here, too, were they concerned because of the real content of sex play, or because of the mystery and the lure of the forbidden that so often enchant the child? The child may be assimilating outside information about sex for which, at the time, he has no real internal correlate or understanding.

A small number of persons do have sociosexual activity during preadolescence—most of it initiated by adults. But for the majority of these, little apparently follows from it. Without appropriate sexual scripts, the experience remains unassimilated—at least in adult terms. For some, it is clear, a severe reaction may follow from falling "victim" to the sexuality of an adult—but, again, does this reaction come from the sexual act itself or from the social response, the strong reactions of others? (There is some evidence that early sexual activity of this sort is associated with deviant adjustments in later life. But this, too, may not be the result of sexual experiences in themselves so much as the consequence of having fallen out of the social main stream and, therefore, of running greater risks of isolation and alienation.)

In short, relatively few become truly active sexually before adolescence. And when they do (for girls more often than boys), it is seldom immediately related to sexual feelings or gratifications but is a use of sex for nonsexual goals and purposes. The "seductive" Lolita is rare but she is significant: she illustrates a more general pattern of psychosexual development—a commitment to the social relationships linked to sex before one can really grasp the social meaning of the physical relationships.

Of great importance are the values (or feelings, or images) that children pick up as being related to sex. Although we talk a lot about sexuality, as though trying to exorcise the demon of shame, learning about sex in our society is in large part learning about guilt; and learning how to manage sexuality commonly involves learning how to manage guilt. An important source of guilt in children comes from the imputation to them by adults of sexual appetites or

abilities that they may not have but that they learn, however imperfectly, to pretend they have. The gestural concomitants of sexual modesty are learned early. For instance, when do girls learn to sit or pick up objects with their knees together? When do they learn that the bust must be covered? However, since this behavior is learned unlinked to later adult sexual performances, what children must make of all this is very mysterious.

The learning of sex roles, or sex identities, involves many things that are remote from actual sexual experience, or that become involved with sexuality only after puberty. Masculinity or femininity, their meaning and postures, are rehearsed before adolescence in many nonsexual ways.

A number of scholars have pointed, for instance, to the importance of aggressive, deference, dependency, and dominance behavior in childhood. Jerome Kagan and Howard Moss have found that aggressive behavior in males and dependence in females are relatively stable aspects of development. But what is social role, and what is biology? They found that when aggressive behavior occurred among girls, it tended to appear most often among those from well-educated families that were more tolerant of deviation. Curiously, they also reported that "it was impossible to predict the character of adult sexuality in women from their preadolescent and early adolescent behavior," and that "erotic activity is more anxiety-arousing for females than for males" because "the traditional ego ideal for women dictates inhibition of sexual impulses."

The belief in the importance of early sex-role learning for boys can be viewed in two ways. First, it may directly indicate an early sexual capacity in male children. Or, second, early masculine identification may merely be an appropriate framework within which the sexual impulse (salient with puberty) and the socially available sexual scripts (or accepted patterns of sexual behavior) can most conveniently find expression. Our bias, of course, is toward the second.

But, as Kagan and Moss noted, the sex role learned by the child does not reliably predict how he will act sexually as an adult. This finding also can be interpreted in the same two alternative ways. Where sexuality is viewed as a biological constant which struggles to express itself, the female sex role learning can be interpreted as the successful repression of sexual impulses. The other interpretation suggests that the difference lies not in learning how to handle a preexistent sexuality but in learning how to be sexual. Differences between men and women, therefore, will have consequences both for *what* is done sexually, as well as *when*.

Once again, we prefer the latter interpretation, and some recent work that we have done with lesbians supports it. We observed that many of the major elements of their sex lives—the start of actual genital sexual behavior, the onset and frequency of masturbation, the time of entry in sociosexual patterns, the number of partners, and the reports of feelings of sexual deprivation—were for these homosexual women almost identical with those of ordinary women. Since sexuality would seem to be more important for lesbians—after all, they sacrifice much in order to follow their own sexual pathways—this is surprising. We concluded that the primary factor was something both categories of women share—the sex-role learning that occurs before sexuality itself becomes significant.

Social class also appears significant, more for boys than girls. Sex-role learning may vary by class; lower-class boys are supposed to be more aggressive and put much greater emphasis on early heterosexuality. The middle and upper classes tend to tolerate more deviance from traditional attitudes regarding appropriate male sex-role performances.

Given all these circumstances, it seems rather naive to think of sexuality as a constant pressure, with a peculiar necessity all its own. For us, the crucial period of childhood has significance not because of sexual occurrences but because of nonsexual developments that will provide the names and judgments for later encounters with sexuality.

ADOLESCENCE

The actual beginnings and endings of adolescence are vague. Generally, the beginning marks the first time society, as such, acknowledges that the individual has sexual capacity. Training in the postures and rhetoric of the sexual experience is now accelerated. Most important, the adolescent begins to regard those about him (particularly his peers, but also adults) as sexual actors and finds confirmation from others for this view.

For some, as noted, adolescent sexual experience begins before they are considered adolescents. Kinsey reports that a tenth of his female sample and a fifth of his male sample had experienced orgasm through masturbation by age 12. But still, for the vast majority, despite some casual play and exploration that post-Freudians might view as masked sexuality, sexual experience begins with adolescence. Even those who have had prior experience find that it acquires new meanings with adolescence. They now relate such meanings to both larger spheres of social life and greater senses of self. For example, it is not uncommon during the transition between childhood and adolescence for boys and, more rarely, girls to report arousal and orgasm while doing things not manifestly sexual—climbing trees, sliding down bannisters, or other activities that involve genital contact—without defining them as sexual. Often they do not even take it seriously enough to try to explore or repeat what was, in all likelihood, a pleasurable experience.

Adolescent sexual development, therefore, really represents the beginning of adult sexuality. It marks a definite break with what went on before. Not only will future experiences occur in new and more complex contexts, but they will be conceived of as explicitly sexual and thereby begin to complicate social relationships. The need to manage sexuality will rise not only from physical needs and desires but also from the new implications of personal relationships. Playing, or associating, with members of the opposite sex now acquires different meanings.

At adolescence, changes in the developments of boys and girls diverge and must be considered separately. The one thing both share at this point is a reinforcement of their new status by a dramatic biological event—for girls, menstruation, and for the boys, the discovery of the ability to ejaculate. But here they part. For boys, the beginning of a commitment to sexuality is primarily genital; within two years of puberty all but a relatively few have had the experience of orgasm, almost universally brought about by masturbation. The corresponding organizing event for girls is not genitally sexual but social; they have arrived at an age where they will learn role performances linked with proximity to marriage. In contrast to boys, only two-thirds of girls will report ever having masturbated (and, characteristically, the frequency is much less). For women, it is not until the late twenties that the incidence of orgasm from any source reaches that of boys at age 16. In fact, significantly, about half of the females who masturbate do so only after having experienced orgasm in some situation involving others. This contrast points to a basic distinction between the developmental processes for males and females: males move from privatized personal sexuality to sociosexuality; females do the reverse and at a later stage in the life cycle.

THE TURNED-ON BOYS

We have worked hard to demonstrate the dominance of social, psychological, and cultural influences over the biological: now, dealing with adolescent boys, we must briefly reverse course. There is much evidence that the early male sexual impulses—again, initially through masturbation—are linked to physiological changes, to high hormonal inputs during puberty. This produces an organism that, to put it simply, is more easily turned on. Male adolescents report frequent erections, often without apparent stimulation of any kind. Even so, though there is greater biological sensitization and hence masturbation is more likely, the meaning, organization, and continuance of this activity still tends to be subordinate to social and psychological factors.

Masturbation provokes guilt and anxiety among most adolescent boys. This is not likely to change in spite of more "enlightened" rhetoric and discourse on the subject (generally, we have shifted from stark warnings of mental, moral, and physical damage to vague counsels against nonsocial or "inappropriate" behavior). However, it may be that this very guilt and anxiety gives the sexual experience an intensity of feeling that is often attributed to sex itself.

Such guilt and anxiety do not follow simply from social disapproval. Rather, they seem to come from several sources, including the difficulty the boy has in presenting himself as a sexual being to his immediate family, particularly his parents. Another source is the fantasies or plans associated with masturbation—fantasies about doing sexual "things" to others or having others do sexual "things" to oneself, or having to learn and rehearse available but proscribed sexual scripts or patterns of behavior. And, of course, some guilt and anxiety center around the general disapproval of masturbation. After the early period of adolescence, in fact, most youths will not admit to their peers that they did or do it.

Nevertheless, masturbation is for most adolescent boys the major sexual activity, and they engage in it fairly frequently. It is an extremely positive and gratifying experience to them. Such an introduction to sexuality can lead to a capacity for detached sex activity—activity whose only sustaining motive is sexual. This may be the hallmark of male sexuality in our society.

Of the three sources of guilt and anxiety mentioned, the first—how to manage both sexuality and an attachment to family members—probably cuts across class lines. But the others should show remarkable class differences. The second one, how to manage a fairly elaborate and exotic fantasy life during masturbation, should be confined most typically to the higher classes, who are more experienced and adept at dealing with symbols. (It is possible, in fact, that this behavior, which girls rarely engage in, plays a role in the processes by which middle-class boys catch up with girls in measures of achievement and creativity and, by the end of adolescence, move out in front. However, this is only a hypothesis.)

The ability to fantasize during masturbation implies certain broad consequences. One is a tendency to see large parts of the environment in an erotic light, as well as the ability to respond, sexually and perhaps poetically, to many visual and auditory stimuli. We might also expect both a capacity and need for fairly elaborate forms of sexual activity. Further, since masturbatory fantasies generally deal with relationships and acts leading to coitus, they should also reinforce a developing capacity for heterosociality.

The third source of guilt and anxiety—the alleged "unmanliness" of masturbation—should more directly concern the lower-class male adolescent. ("Manliness" has always been an important value for lower-class males.) In these groups, social life is more often segregated by sex, and there are, generally, fewer rewarding social experiences from other sources. The adolescent therefore moves into heterosexual—if not heterosocial—relationships sooner than his middle-class counterparts. Sexual segregation makes it easier for him than for the middle-class boy to learn that he does not have to love everything he desires and therefore to come more naturally to casual, if not exploitative, relationships. The second condition—fewer social rewards that his fellows would respect—should lead to an exaggerated concern for proving masculinity by direct displays of physical prowess, aggression, and visible sexual success. And these three, of course, may be mutually reinforcing.

In a sense, the lower-class male is the first to reach "sexual maturity" as defined by the Freudians. That is, he is generally the first to become aggressively heterosexual and exclusively genital. This characteristic, in fact, is a distinguishing difference between lower-class males and those above them socially.

But one consequence is that although their sex lives are almost exclusively heterosexual, they remain homosocial. They have intercourse with females, but the standards and the audience they refer to are those of their male fellows. Middle-class boys shift predominantly to coitus at a significantly later time. They, too, need and tend to have homosocial elements in their sexual lives. But their fantasies, their ability to symbolize, and their social training in a world in which distinctions between masculinity and femininity are less sharply drawn, allow them to withdraw more easily from an all-male world. The difference between social classes obviously has important consequences for stable adult relationships.

One thing common in male experience during adolescence is that while it provides much opportunity for sexual commitment in one form or another, there is little training in how to handle emotional relations with girls. The imagery and rhetoric of romantic love is all around us; we are immersed in it. But whereas much is undoubtedly absorbed by the adolescent, he is not likely to tie it closely to his sexuality. In fact, such a connection might be inhibiting, as indicated by the survival of the "bad-girl-who-does" and "good-girl-who-doesn't" distinction. This is important to keep in mind as we turn to the female side of the story.

WITH THE GIRLS

In contrast to males, female sexual development during adolescence is so similar in all classes that it is easy to suspect that it is solely determined by biology. But, while girls do not have the same level of hormonal sensitization to sexuality at puberty as adolescent boys, there is little evidence of a biological or social inhibitor either. The "equipment" for sexual pleasure is clearly present by puberty but tends not to be used by many females of any class. Masturbation rates are fairly low, and among those who do masturbate, fairly infrequent. Arousal from "sexual" materials or situations happens seldom, and exceedingly few girls report feeling sexually deprived during adolescence.

Basically, girls in our society are not encouraged to be sexual—and may be strongly discouraged from being so. Most of us accept the fact that while "bad boy" can mean many things, "bad girl" almost exclusively implies sexual delinquency. It is both difficult and dangerous for an adolescent girl to become too active sexually. As Joseph Rheingold puts it, where men need only fear sexual failure, women must fear both success and failure.

Does this long period of relative sexual inactivity among girls come from repression of an elemental drive or merely from a failure to learn how to be sexual? The answers have important implications for their later sexual development. If it is repression, the path to a fuller sexuality must pass through processes of loss of inhibitions, during which the girl unlearns, in varying degrees, attitudes and values that block the expression of natural internal feelings. It also implies that the quest for ways to express directly sexual behavior and feelings that had been expressed nonsexually is secondary and of considerably less significance.

On the other hand, the "learning" answer suggests that women create or invent a capacity for sexual behavior, learning how and when to be aroused and how and when to respond. This approach implies greater flexibility: unlike the repression view, it makes sexuality both more and less than a basic force that may break loose at any time in strange or costly ways. The learning approach also lessens the power of sexuality altogether; all at once, particular kinds of sex activities need no longer be defined as either "healthy" or "sick." Lastly, subjectively, this approach appeals to the authors because it describes female sexuality in terms that seem less like a mere projection of male sexuality.

If sexual activity by adolescent girls assumes less specific forms than with boys, that does not mean that sexual learning and training do not occur. Curiously, though girls are, as a group, far less active sexually than boys, they receive far more training in self-consciously viewing themselves—and in viewing boys—as desirable mates. This is particularly true in recent years. Females begin early in adolescence to define attractiveness, at least partially, in sexual terms. We suspect that the use of sexual attractiveness for nonsexual purposes that marked our preadolescent "seductress" now begins to characterize many girls. Talcott Parsons' description of how the wife "uses" sex to bind the husband to the family, although harsh, may be quite accurate. More generally, in keeping with the childbearing and child-raising function of women, the development of a sexual role seems to involve a need to include in that role more than pleasure.

To round out the picture of the difference between the sexes, girls appear to be well-trained precisely in that area in which boys are poorly trained—that is, a belief in and a capacity for intense, emotionally-charged relationships and the language of romantic love. When girls during this period describe having been aroused sexually, they more often report it as a response to romantic, rather than erotic, words and actions.

In later adolescence, as dates, parties, and other sociosexual activities increase, boys—committed to sexuality and relatively untrained in the language and actions of romantic love—interact with girls committed to romantic love and relatively untrained in sexuality. Dating and courtship may well be considered processes in which each sex trains the other in what each wants and expects. What data is available suggests that this exchange system does not always work very smoothly. Thus, ironically, it is not uncommon to find that the boy becomes emotionally involved with his partner and therefore lets up on trying to seduce her, at the same time that the girl comes to feel that the boy's affection is genuine and therefore that sexual intimacy is more permissible.

In our recent study of college students, we found that boys typically had intercourse with their first coital partners one to three times, while with girls it was ten or more. Clearly, for the majority of females first intercourse becomes possible only in stable relationships or in those with strong bonds.

section

3

TESTINGS

Section 3, *Testings,* examines the major decisions of the premarried years. During this time choices are clarified regarding the values on which adult life is to be based, career choices are made, sexual relations are explored and mate selection is completed.

One important issue is the extent to which parental values become one's own. Decisions that are contrary to parental expectations can be threatening to parents and young adults alike, but the issue must be resolved. It is also disconcerting when close friends go different ways. The first year out of high school can see graduates eager for the class reunion, but subsequent reunions emphasize diverse life-styles and the loss of the commonness of experiences. Values and standards are forged in the environment in which one finds oneself and are not identical for all persons.

"What are you going to do after graduation?" is a common question in this stage, whether graduation refers to high school, community college or four year college. In earlier generations, the question was primarily directed to males, although it was acknowledged that females might prepare for a career "just in case" or as "something to fall back on." Young women are increasingly opting for a career, so plans after graduation are relevant for both women and men. In addition, career fields formerly restricted or closed to women are now open. Competent career counseling is essential and helpful for both women and men, but knowledge of interests and abilities is still the critical element. Young adults and parents alike should be reassured that a change in career plans is common and does not necessarily represent insecurity. At one large midwestern university it was found recently that 60 percent of graduates had changed majors at least once during their college career. Whether the first career choice is final or whether changes are made, the importance of the decision and planning is questionable.

Realities of the family drama at this time of life must certainly include the concerns of sex, love and mate selection. Although part of the American ideal makes sex and love synonymous or simultaneous, pragmatically they are separate issues. Two questions related to sex in the early dating relationship are how much and how soon. The element of commitment must be examined by both women and men. Some will believe love and commitment a necessity before any sexual intercourse occurs. Others will see it as desirable but not essential. Still others may perceive it as irrelevant. Perhaps the need for, and the degree of, commitment differs for women and for men and thus must be negotiated. Although perhaps changing, the double standard for sexual behavior is generally operative, affecting both the quality and the interaction of relationships. By the end of this stage in family life, the first sexual experience undoubtedly will have been a reality for many. The context of the experience and its subsequent meaning are of great significance for men and women alike—given that the meaning and significance may differ for the two sexes.

"Falling in love" expresses a common understanding and a prevalent misunderstanding of what love is all about. It suggests a precipitous change in feelings toward another person; it hypothesizes an emotional response over which one has little or no control; and presumes a state of *being*, i.e., that one is either "in love" or not "in love." "Growing to love" might well represent a more realistic perspective on the process and contribute to a more stable experience. However it is described, love is a crucial issue. Our culture, with its romantic love complex, compounds the issue and undoubtedly contributes to the too common disenchantment which often develops in marriage. Yet, there are relatively few guidelines for understanding love in any context other than as romantic love.

Similarly, the cultural myth of some day meeting and marrying the "right" one makes life difficult for many young adults. Neither the family nor educational institutions do much to prepare young people for wise choices in the selection of a mate. Sexual attraction and interpersonal response are often assumed to be "love" which, in turn, is believed to be the only good basis for marriage. It is near heresy to suggest that "being in love" is an adequate basis for marriage, or that sexual attraction may have little or nothing to do with love.

The pattern for adult life is defined through the decisions made in the pre-married years. The structures determined here influence career options as well as the concerns of sex, love and mate selection: the realities for the years immediately prior to marriage.

CONTENTS: SECTION 3

THE OUTSIDER*

Cindy Wickersham

In early September St. Paul is beautiful. The grass is still green, the leaves are beginning their multi-hued fall transition, and the air feels soft and clean against your face. From high banks you can look upon the sparkle and might of the Mississippi River. It is a time and place to breathe deeply and feel alive with all around you.

St. Paul and Minneapolis contain, among other things, a large university and many, many small liberal arts colleges. So every September the Twin Cities fill with young people from around the country and around the world. But most of these young people come from the Midwest—from Minnesota, South Dakota, Wisconsin, Illinois, and Iowa. Their differences are obvious to one another; their common Midwest heritage less so perhaps. Except to the outsider.

No one really noticed one outsider when he first hit our campus that September. He didn't look terribly different. Perhaps a little neater in his dress—his shirts were ironed. And he didn't wear blue jeans. But otherwise, he looked normal enough. He was six feet tall, slim, and had fine cheek bones. His hair was light brown and waved about his ears. His eyes were light blue and peered at you somewhat from behind his black spectacles. He had a sweet, crooked smile which lit up his otherwise serious face.

He completely escaped my attention until second semester when we both took Modern Poetry from the campus genius. The Genius was inspirational; he lit up your soul. He must also have inspired terror, or awe, or something because this outsider and I were the only two out of 100 students who ever talked in that class. The outsider acquired a name, Robby Walters. Robby Walters, the Genius, and I had a great semester with Frost, Eliot, Pound, Robinson, and all the other modern poets. We became fast friends in our own intellectual utopia—crazed English majors! After a while Robby and I began to have coffee together in the Union. We'd play bridge and talk poetry. He discovered that I had had the Genius for a novel class and soon we were off on Sartre, Camus, Faulkner and Joyce. People began to avoid us. We were often alone and happy to be left to our own conversations. Meeting Robby in this way it took me quite a while to realize that he was an outsider. In finding him, I also found myself to be more outside than I had previously realized. But I wore Midwest coloring and passed.

He slowly would piece out his life to me. It came in bits here and remembrances there. "I have dual citizenship. My mother lives in a castle in Germany."

---

*By permission of the author, Cindy Wickersham.

"Sure she does, Robby."

"She really does, you know.'

"And your father?"

"He is an American. He lives in Rhode Island."

"Oh! I'm sorry. But you never speak of him, and I thought. . ."

"It's okay. They're divorced. She's remarried and has a new family. He's remarried, too. He has lots of kids. I guess I don't ever talk about him."

"Your mother still lives in Germany?"

"Yes, but she's coming over sometime soon. I should like very much for you to meet her."

"I'd like that, too."

One day I asked him what his father did for a living and was brusquely informed that he owned the largest advertising agency on the East coast!

"He's a very busy man." Robby didn't seem to want to say any more.

I found this somewhat odd as I was extremely proud and fond of my father and loved to talk with him and about him. I told Robby about him and he seemed very pleased that my father, too, was important.

"We're both in Who's Who." He seemed delighted. He seemed to feel closer.

He taught me how to test the wine when the waiter brings it to your table.

"For my eighteenth birthday I was taught about wine in the Rothschild's wine cellar."

"You did what?"

He repeated exactly what I had heard the first time. By this time I was beginning to believe almost anything. What did I know about people from Rhode Island whose fathers owned advertising agencies and whose mothers lived in castles in Germany. They probably did drink wine in famous cellars. He did not seem to think it was unusual. So neither would I.

"Are you close to your brothers and sisters, Robby?"

"No. I don't know them."

"How can you not know them?"

"They live with my mother or my father."

"Well didn't you, too?"

"No. I was sent away to school. To prep school, and all, you know."

"Oh." Sometimes I didn't have answers for Robby. We had in common famous fathers, trips to Europe, and highs on Twentieth Century writers and poets. We were friends. His life had been one I wouldn't have believed in Fitzgerald. But I believed it in Robby Walters.

He was very excited when he came back from Rhode Island the one vacation he went there. "While I was home, one of my father's friends came from Washington and when they were talking I heard your father's name. I just had to interrupt. I had to ask. He knows your father, too! He said that they are great friends! That he thinks the world of your father! That he knows him! One of my father's friends knows your father!"

"Isn't that nice? Who is it?"

Robby named a nice, old friend of my father's. I didn't see how he could be so exciting. I didn't see then how such a weak link could mean so much. But Robby was beside himself with happiness.

The school year wore on slowly. Robby seemed happy. He enjoyed his classes. He wrote poetry and played bridge in the Union. But he didn't seem to have friends. Kids gave him side glances and half smiles. They said he talked funny—like he was from the East. And he told absurd stories about his life and his family. They all know no one ever lived like that. No one from Minot, Fargo, Prarie du Chien, or Hibbing. And he talked in class! He asked questions! He even was seen reading books no one had asked him to read. He was very definitely an outsider and an outsider he should stay. Sure, he was nice; but how do you relate to someone like that?

One day Robby called me and asked me to come to see him.

"Sure, Robby. Where are you?"

"St. Luke's Hospital. Fourth floor. Please come alone. Please come."

"What's wrong, Robby?"

"Oh, please come. You'll see. You'll see."

"Okay, Robby. Hold on. I'll be there. It's okay." Famous last words. It's so easy to say, "Hold on. It's okay," when it's not yourself you're talking to. I hurried downtown on the bus searching a map for St. Luke's as I went. I wondered about the whole thing even more when I had to go through a big, heavy door midway on the Fourth floor and saw locked doors along the hallway.

"Pardon me, nurse. I'm looking for Robby Walters."

"Straight ahead and to your left. He's in the big, sunny room with the television."

I followed my orders and was soon in a big room full of milling people. Robby was sitting off by himself. As I approached, he got up and came forward. He seemed to be shaking and he looked scared.

"Robby? What's wrong?" I reached toward him as I spoke.

"Don't touch me! Don't touch me! Oh, please, don't touch me!" He didn't move away from me, but stood rooted to the spot. Quivering.

"Okay, Robby," I tried very hard to look and sound calm. "Would you like to sit down and talk?"

"Yes. Over there." He seemed to be shaking less, but still looked very afraid.

"Now what's wrong, Robby? Why are you in the hospital? Can I help?"

"I turned myself in."

"For what?" The first time around you can ask some pretty dumb questions.

"I turned myself in."

"Why?"

"It's a good sign. To know when you need help. I did. I turned myself in. That's a good sign, isn't it? He looked very pleased yet desperately in need of assurance.

"Yes, Robby. They say that's a very good sign."

"My doctor says you can come see me. Just don't touch me. He says I can come out sometime soon on Saturdays if you'll take me with you. He'd like to meet you."

"I'd like to meet him. Do you like him?"

"Oh yes. He talks and talks with me. He's nice to me. He'll let me stay. He'll help me. He talks to me."

"What can I do for you, Robby?"

"Come and see me. Please come and see me. And talk to the school. Please tell them I'll be back. Talk to my teachers. And tell me what they say."

"Sure, Robby. I'll be glad to."

We talked vaguely for about an hour and then it was time for him to go see his doctor again. I left promising to come again tomorrow. I went many tomorrows and he came with me many Saturdays. Very, very slowly he became less and less withdrawn. His father never came. His father never wrote. He paid the bills. I became bitterly angry with him and Robby made more sense than ever.

Not too long after he got out and was trying to come back to school, his mother came from the castle. She seemed very nice and we three had a pleasant lunch. Like you'd have with anybody's mother. She seemed to care about Robby. At lunch, anyway. Then she was gone. Robby lasted about one month in school. This time I could see him withdrawing—into a world he could relate to.

Again the phone call came. This time I knew the way to St. Luke's.

"Hi, Robby."

"Hi."

I knew he knew I was there. I knew he could see me. But there wasn't much more. This time he had retreated even further away from St. Paul and life as he knew it. How could they send a kid like this out to us—I asked myself that a thousand times. I still ask. I have always wanted to hit his father over the head with a two-by-four and shout at him. But I never got to meet him. Every day I went on the bus and it was a long, long time this time before Saturday ever came. We'd sit in silence or a remembrance would slip out. I would try to relate it to my life. To rebuild the feeble bridge he seemed to cross on. Such a weak link.

"I told my doctor that a good friend of my father's is a good friend of your father's. He was impressed. I knew he would be."

COUNSELING COLLEGE WOMEN ABOUT CAREERS*

Shirley S. Angrist

A longitudinal study of college women conducted between 1964 and 1968 was undertaken in order to discover (a) the ways in which educated young women choose and change their preferences for adult life, including advanced education, occupation, marriage, and children and (b) the factors which move college women toward career planning or away from it.

The data derives from longitudinal research on one class in the women's college of a small, coeducational, private, and technologically oriented university. The university is located in a large eastern city and is known for its professional-vocational orientation, especially in the sciences, engineering, and the arts. The curriculum and reputation of the university attract students seeking occupational preparation, and it was largely because of this feature that the study of women's career aspirations was undertaken there.

Questionnaires were administered every fall semester to the total class, and tape-recorded interviews were conducted among a sample of the class every spring over the four college years. The questionnaires dealt with adult role conceptions, occupational plans, work experience, classwork, school activities, dating, and marriage plans. The interviews probed deeply into these same areas and into occupational choice processes. In the senior year the entire class was interviewed. The class initially consisted of 188 freshman who began college in 1964; of these 58 percent were graduated together four years later. The results reported in this article stem mainly from the questionnaires for the entire class at each point in time and for the core group of 87 students who proceeded through college in phase, and provided four-wave panel data.

The article reports first on the findings concerning the process of developing career aspirations and then on the factors which foster career interests. The results are then interpreted with a view to counseling and advising college women. Ways of affecting the career decision process, of fostering career influences, of altering vocational counseling, and of utilizing role options are described.

DEVELOPING CAREER ASPIRATIONS

It was found that college women's decisions about graduate school, occupations, and working generally progress with each succeeding year, as their potential to pursue careers grows. These women vary and waver, however, in their ideas about adult life. Most of them seek an interesting life with room for advanced education, work, a husband and children, and perhaps leisure, travel, hobbies. But they pursue a contingency approach, remaining open and shifting—not ready to commit themselves to a binding blueprint. Work will play an important part in their lives. They hope to find an interesting job, preferably at a professional level. Mainly, however, they expect to tie work around family exigencies. Husband, children, economic pressures will dictate either the woman's need to work or her freedom to seek it. Thus, these women are rather conventional in building their lives around family. They are even conventional when they specify an occupation because they generally pursue typical women's fields; few gravitate toward medicine, law, journalism, or scientific research.[1]

A further finding concerns the amount and timing of change in these role aspirations. Great changeability is typical. The period of greatest change in occupational choice is unquestionably the freshman year. But the time between the junior and senior years is noteworthy for shifts made in career orientation. A great sport occurs at that time toward interest in combining work with family life. Between the freshman and junior years there are gradual rather than abrupt shifts in aspirations.[2]

From the patterns of women's choices for adult life over the four college years that emerged, five types of women were found: (a) *careerists*—the consistent career aspirers who want to combine career with family roles; (b) *noncareerists*—oriented primarily to family roles, with some work and leisure pursuits; (c) *converts* to career aspirations—beginning college without such interests but moving towards careers by the sophomore, junior, or senior years; (d) *defectors*—career oriented as freshmen and even after, but shifting to domestic concerns by senior year; and (e) *shifters*—changeable and inconsistent, whose aspirations vary from year to year and who lack clear-cut direction. Despite this variation the noncareerists predominate in the class studied; consistent careerists and converts to career comprise only 40 percent of the class. It is the noncareerists, defectors from career, and shifters who predominate.[3]

Both the preponderantly conventional aspirations and the great shifting suggest how rare and difficult career choices remain even for college-educated women.

FACTORS INFLUENCING CAREER ASPIRATIONS

A variety of factors seem to influence young women's career patterns, including experiences in the family, the work world, and college. The noncareer-oriented more often join a sorority and go steady by the senior year than do the other types; their mothers tend to pursue leisure activities and volunteer work.

Career-oriented women value work which allows them to use their special abilities and gives them freedom from supervision. They are more likely to choose male-dominated occupations. They more often have working mothers and themselves have more work experience. They feel their occupational choice has been influenced by people such as teachers, professors, counselors, and others rather than by family and peers.[4]

Two important influence processes appear to be at work. First, the career-oriented women are exposed to a wide variety of possible role models—their mothers, their male and female peers, and people in various occupations. Women can more readily perceive themselves in careers when those around them demonstrate that having an occupation is an important personal commitment. Others serve as reference groups by showing how to perform in a specific occupation. When these significant others are female, they explicate how a woman can play several central life roles. The role modeling process then goes beyond learning to be a teacher, librarian, or doctor. For women this process means learning how to play wife, mother, and worker and perhaps many other roles in close interdependence.[5] By contrast, for the non-career-oriented strong influences come from reference groups supporting traditional sex roles. Sorority membership is a striking example of such influence, but so are parents and boyfriends.[6]

The second important influence process is a more general environmental socialization. Career-oriented women have different experiences in growing up, experiences which stress solitary and nondomestic pursuits.[7] These women, while statistically unusual, are not behaviorally deviant or maladjusted.[8] Rather, they have experienced enriching environments at home, at school, and through jobs, environments that reveal multiple options for a woman's adult life. Through such broadening rather than conventional socialization, career becomes a viable commitment for a young woman.[9]

WHAT COUNSELORS CAN DO

These findings help to explain why the radical expansion of the female labor force is accompanied neither by women's increased career commitment nor by choosing "men's" work.[10] Counselors should be able to foster career aspirations through their impact on three crucial elements in women's role development: (a) process and timing of change, (b) influence sources, and (c) vocational guidance.

AFFECTING THE PROCESS

Students welcome the potential for self-development offered in the college context. The educational benefits proclaimed as the promise of university education are taken by all students as the student legacy, regardless of sex. But women have to unravel the contradiction (or perhaps merely contend with it) between the educational goal, with its centrality of personal-intellectual growth, and the instilled societal goal for the woman to be an activator of husband and children, but not of herself. Only the career-oriented can reconcile these two goals; the other types of college women simply accept the conventional roles. This prevails despite the current image of educated women as independent, sexually free, and participants in the labor force, and of marriage as democratic and equalitarian. Parelleling this emancipated view is the image of women as glamorous, leisure-oriented, and family-centered, an image emphasizing the need to please and guide others. How are these opposing views reconciled? They are not.

The sex role dilemmas girls heard about in high school hover around during college and re-emerge afterwards. Counselors can expose these dilemmas and help students surmount or alter such obstacles; they can evoke career pursuit as a special form of achievement It is during the freshman year that students are most affected by the college environment. While the senior year is also a time of marked change, it does not have nearly the impact of the first year. Many studies of college students corroborate this finding.[11] The freshman year involves the experiencing of newness, adjustment to college life, and some disillusionment in precollege expectations. Despite these disillusionments the first year is one of excitement. Senior year has the specialness of being a finale, a disengagement from the institution and very often from student status. Counselors should be particularly sensitive to freshman women concerned about choice of major and to beginning seniors groping to make after-college plans. Perhaps intervention at these two stages can be most influential in moving potential careerists towards their goals.

FOSTERING CAREER INFLUENCES

The role models for a girl include parents, friends, and teachers. All of these are important. The mother sets an example in her emphasis on leisure or work or both. If a mother works while the girl is growing up, she shows that jobholding is acceptable and manageable for a woman with family responsibilities. She may even show that work is stimulating and enjoyable. Women teachers in high school and college serve not only to show that work is feasible, but along with male colleagues they particularly demonstrate how the teacher's work is carried out. Regardless of their sex, teachers serve to reward the girl's ability, to encourage her inclinations and to shape her self-image as an able person.

The faculty power to elicit and encourage women in career pursuits, at least in academic fields, seems great.[12] The counselor can contribute by directing a young woman's attention to exemplary role models. Especially impressive might be the student's working mother and some of her female teachers, counselors, employers, or co-workers. When teachers and counselors are female, they can do more than merely praise a student for her academic achievement. As women, wives, and mothers, they can explicate how a professional career articulates with the woman's entire constellation of roles.

VOCATIONAL COUNSELING

In vocational counseling there is a dire need to clarify ossified notions about occupational choice. Myths about women's work, men's work, childraising, and leisure persist. Young women are heir to these societal stereotypes. For example, the idea that women's fields are secure or practical implies that a teacher, nurse, or librarian can "always find a job" and can re-enter her field after a 10 year lapse without finding her skills obsolete. No professional field can be safe in this unchanging way. This view is unprofessional and belittles the fields it describes.

The idea the "women's fields" permit working short hours or flexible, convenient schedules does not always hold up to fact. Nurses may work night shifts, and department store buyers have a six-day week. On the other hand, the physician or architect may work part time or even for only part of the year. Yet the entire work world is built around the concept of the 40-hour week, the full-time job, the permanent employee. The educational world imposes the same norm: that of a full-time student. The widespread occurrence of part-time and temporary jobs is viewed as unusual, an exceptional arrangement. Each woman who wants to avoid the standard work week is forced to carve out a schedule and negotiate to obtain it. The expanding emphasis on leisure and the shrinking demand for workers have already altered the work pattern in some skilled occupations. Some of the professions may follow suit, to women's benefit as well as to men's. But until the rigid time structure in most jobs is modified, women will continue to pay the penalties for convenience: lower wages, no retirement or medical benefits, no seniority or promotion. They may go on accepting the male myths and definitions pervasive in the work world.

The counselor can stress that occupational choice should be made in order to fulfill one's individual potential, not merely to earn a livelihood, or to be practical. Counselors also have to question and even abandon existing vocational preference tests that segregate male and female occupations by using different population norms and separate test forms. Such a practice perpetuates outdated and unacceptable sex role stereotypes in work choices. Counselors must help to end the circular process in which "women discover and assert their gender by their choices" of field, and then these fields "take on a feminine character because they are chosen by women or rejected by men.[13]

EXPANDED LIFESTYLES FOR WOMEN

If the economy continues to expand, the demand for women workers will continue. "More married women are working today than ever before in our history because there are economic opportunities for them to do so.[14] But an indicated decline in the fertility rate and a resulting slower population growth rate will yield fewer children to teach and less demand for workers of all kinds. Add to this the occasional economic recession and automation of many jobs (computerized instruction in teaching, diagnosis in nursing, and information retrieval in library work). With such job shrinkage, are women who are told to seek careers misled? No. They may be joined increasingly at home, in leisure activities, and in volunteer work by men. Both sexes may then be liberated from work. Men especially will need to know how to live meaningful lives without paid work. To be liberated will then mean to be free to choose from among many options, of which a gainful career is only one. Guidance counselors will have to sketch out such broad alternatives so that young people's future plans include a glimpse of the whole spectrum of possibilities. To live in a changing world, contingency planning will become the norm. Instead of letting young people fall into the hazards of life's stages by not planning, counselors will have to make the contingencies explicit and important rather than vague and trivial.[15]

The haphazard falling into graduate school or marriage or work which is common to women carries costs. The price paid is that women fail to plan for their adult lives; they ignore the long years in which childbearing and child-raising are over and family life contracts. This has created the re-entry or re-tread problem—women seeking further education or training after 40 to fill their lives. Preparation for a chosen occupation that is stimulating, challenging, and remunerative should be seen as explicit contingency planning. It should realistically take account of the high probability that a college graduate will work much of her life.[16]

If educated women cannot overcome stereotyped sex role thinking, no women can. But even educated women cannot surmount the sterotype alone. To do this, changes in existing patterns of socialization, education, and work are required. The challenge for counselors is to help young women change sex role conceptions by fulfilling their human potential. Counselors can encourage career aspirers and uncover career interests. Counselors can aid college women to prepare for multiple and changing roles in society.

References

1. S. Angrist, "Changes in Women's Work Aspirations During College" *International Journal of Sociology of the Family*, 11 (1972), 1–11.
2. *Ibid.*
3. S. Angrist, "Variations in Woman's Adult Aspirations During College" *Journal of Marriage and the Family*, XXXIV (1972), 465–68.
4. E. Almquist and S. Angrist, "Career Salience and Atypicality of Occupational Choice Among College Women" *Journal of Marriage and the Family*, XXXII (1970), 242–49.
5. T. Kemper, "Reference Groups, Socialization and Achievement" *American Sociological Review*, XXXIII (1968), 31–45.
6. E. Almquist and S. Angrist, "Role Model Influences on College Women's Career Aspirations" *Merrill-Palmer Quarterly of Behavior and Development*, XVII (1971), 263–79.
7. A. Rossi, "The Roots of Ambivalence in American Women" Paper presented at The Continuing Education Conference, Oakland University, Michigan, 1967.
8. S. Angrist, "Personality Maladjustment and Career Aspirations of College Women" *Sociological Symposium*, V (1970), 1–8.
9. Almquist and Angrist, 1970, *op. cit.*
10. J. Ridley, "The Changing Position of American Women: Education, Labor Force Participation and Fertility" Paper presented at the Conference on the Family in Transition, National Institute of Health, Bethesda, Maryland, 1969.
11. K. Feldman, and T. Newcomb, *The Impact of College on Students* (San Francisco: Jossey-Bass, 1969).
12. Almquist and Angrist, 1971, *op. cit.*
13. O. Hall, "Gender and the Division of Labour" Paper presented at the Conference on the Implications of Traditional Divisions Between Men's Work and Women's Work in Our Society, Ottawa, Canada, 1964.
14. Rossi, *op. cit.*
15. S. Angrist, "The Study of Sex Roles" *Journal of Social Issues*, XXV (1969), 215–32.
16. *Ibid.*

TEEN-AGE SEX:
LETTING THE PENDULUM SWING*

> *Girls can score just as many times as boys if they want to. I've gone to bed with nine boys in the past two years. It's a natural thing, a nice thing and a nice high. It sure can clear up the blues.*—MIMI, 18, a June graduate of Tenafly (N.J.) High School

> *I'm still a virgin. My friends last year blamed it on the fact that I was the youngest girl on campus. But I can't see having intercourse unless it's part of a tight emotional bond. My father has influenced me, but the fact that he is a minister has nothing to do with it. The church is not a stronghold against sex any more.*—AMANDA, 16, a junior at Shimer College, Mount Carroll, Ill.

They could hardly be more unlike, Mimi and Amanda.† Yet both are representative of American teen-agers. . . . Though Amandas predominate among the nation's boys and girls between 13 and 19, there are enough Mimi's so that many parents are alarmed. Even some of the teen-agers themselves, especially those in college, are uneasy about their almost unlimited new sexual license. Along with a heady sense of freedom, it causes, they find, a sometimes unwelcome sense of pressure to take advantage of it. "I'm starting to feel the same way about getting laid as I did about getting into college," Dustin Hoffman confessed in *The Graduate*. A Columbia University psychiatrist reports that students come to him to find out what is wrong with them if they are not having intercourse. "My virginity was such a burden to me that I just went out to get rid of it," a junior at the University of Vermont revealed to a Boston sex counselor. "On a trip to Greece, I found any old Greek and did it so it wouldn't be an issue any more."

Was her trip necessary? Is there really a notable increase in teen-age sex? Foolproof statistics about sexual habits are hard to come by, but a recent survey prepared for the Nixon-appointed commission on population seems to offer reasonably reliable figures. Of 4,611 unmarried black and white girls liv-

---

*Reprinted by permission from *Time*, The Weekly Newsmagazine; Copyright Time Inc.

†The names of the children and their parents in this story are fictitious.

ing at home or in dormitories in 1971, more than 46% had lost their virginity by age 20, according to Johns Hopkins Demographers Melvin Zelnik and John Kantner. Comparison with previous generations is difficult because earlier studies are incomplete; Alfred Kinsey, for example, author of the first large-scale studies of sexual behavior, did not include blacks in his statistics. However, Kinsey's 1953 survey of some 5,600 white women disclosed that 3% were nonvirgins at age 15, and 23% had had premarital intercourse by the time they were 21. By contrast, Zelnik and Kantner report that of the 3,132 whites in their sample, 11% of the 15-year-olds were nonvirgins, and 40% of all the girls had lost their virginity by the age of 20. In short, youth's sexual revolution is not just franker talk and greater openness; more teen-agers, and especially younger ones, are apparently having intercourse, at least occasionally.

Another indication of the reality of youthful sex is the rising incidence of VD, which has now reached epidemic proportions in high schools and colleges. After the ordinary cold, syphilis and gonorrhea are the most common infectious diseases among young people, outranking all cases of hepatitis, measles, mumps, scarlet fever, strep throat and tuberculosis put together. In 1970 there were at least 3,000 cases of syphilis among the 27 million U.S. teen-agers and 150,000 cases of gonorrhea, more than in any European country except Sweden and Denmark. From 1960 to 1970 the number of reported VD cases among girls 15 to 19 increased 144%, and that percentage does not begin to tell the story, because it is estimated that three out of four cases go unreported.

The spiraling rate of pregnancies among unmarried girls is yet another indicator of sexual activity by the young. Per thousand teen-agers, the number of illegitimate births has risen from 8.3 in 1940 to 19.8 in 1972. Of an estimated 1,500,000 abortions performed in the U.S. in 1971, it is believed that close to a third were performed on teen-agers. Last year women at one prominent Eastern university had 100 illegitimate pregnancies, while at another there were almost 400—a rate of one for every 15 students. Nationwide the college pregnancy rate runs from 6% to 15%.

IN PERSPECTIVE

"Anything that discourages heterosexuality encourages homosexuality," says Paul Gebhard, executive director of the Kinsey Institute for Sex Research. Is the opposite also true? Some psychiatrists speculate that the new sexual freedom enjoyed by teen-agers may lead to a decrease in homosexuality. "Because there are fewer sexual taboos in our society today, the adolescent is more likely to find a heterosexual pathway," says Dr. Judd Marmor of Los Angeles. Yet only a small number of adolescents are likely to be affected. Marmor contends, since generally "the origins of homosexuality derive from certain specific conditions in the home, and these conditions still exist." There are no recent statistical studies that show changes in the incidence of homosexuality among teen-agers. There are, however, some changes in attitudes. Just as there is a greater willingness to "come out of the closet" among their elders, younger men and women are more open about homosexuality, especially in cities and on campuses where there are organizations like the Gay Activist Alliance.

In heterosexual relationships, too, it is the teen-agers' attitudes that have probably changed more than the statistics. The different sexual experiences of two sisters, eight years apart in age, illustrate at least some of the changes that are taking place.

Sue Franklin, now 25, had a traditional middle-class Midwestern upbringing. In 1965, when she was 18 and a college freshman, her sorority sisters talked about their sexual feelings only with extremely close friends, and nearly all gossiped about girls they suspected of having affairs. "Virginity was all important," Sue remembers. Then her boy friend of five years' standing issued an ultimatum: "Either you go to bed with me or I'm leaving you." She gave in and was overcome with remorse. "My God," she thought, "what have I done? The more I learned about sex, the guiltier I felt, especially about enjoying it. I almost felt I had to deny myself any pleasure. My boy friend felt bad, too, because I was so hung up."

Sue's sister Pat, on the other hand was just 15 and in high school when she first went to bed with a boy. Only one thing bothered her: fear of getting pregnant. She appealed to Sue, who helped her get contraceptive advice from a doctor. Since then, Pat has had one additional serious relationship that included sex. Observes Sue: "Pat had as healthy an attitude as could be imagined, as healthy as I wish mine could have been. She and her friends are more open. They're not blasé; they don't talk about sex as they would about what they're going to have for dinner. But when they do discuss it, there's no hemming and hawing around. And boys don't exploit them. With Pat and her boy friends, sex isn't a motivating factor. It's not like the pressure that builds when sex is denied or you feel guilty about it. It's kept in perspective, not something they're especially preoccupied with. They don't see sex as something you can do with everyone; they're not promiscuous."

Nor are most teen-agers. Though the number of very youthful marriages appears to be declining, a fourth of all 18- and 19-year-old girls are married. More often than not, they had already had intercourse: more than half of them got married because they were pregnant. But on the whole, teen-agers actually are not very active sexually, in spite of the large number of nonvirgins. Of those questioned by the Johns Hopkins demographic team, 40% had not had intercourse at all in the month before the survey, and of the remainder 70% had done so only once or twice that month. About 60% had never had more than one partner, and in half the cases that one was the man they planned to marry. When promiscuity was reported, it was more often among whites: 16% admitted to four or more partners, while only 11% of blacks had had that many.

Teen-agers generally are woefully ignorant about sex. They may believe that "most teen-age boys can almost go crazy if they don't have intercourse," that "you can't get pregnant if he only comes one time," or that urination is impossible with a diaphragm in place. Other youths cherish the notion that withdrawal, douching, rhythm or luck will prevent conception. Overall, "the pervasiveness of risk taking" is appalling, Zelnik and Katner discovered. More than 75% of the girls they interviewed said they used contraceptives only occasionally or never.

To close the information gap, schools and colleges have begun to provide telephone hot lines, new courses, manuals of instruction and personal counseling. By dialing 933-5505, University of North Carolina students can get confidential information about pregnancy, abortion, contraception, sexual and marital relationships. More than 30 trained volunteer counselors answer 50 calls a week, with at least one man and one woman always on duty so that shy callers can consult someone of their own sex. Complex questions are referred to a dozen experts, mostly physicians, who have offered their help.

Away from the campus, counseling is hard to come by, but contraceptive advice is usually available, at least to urban teen-agers, from private social agencies and public health departments. This has not long been so. Birth Control Crusader Bill Baird was arrested in 1967 for giving out contraceptive devices to Boston University coeds. His conviction was overturned last March when the Supreme Court ruled that a state could not outlaw contraceptives for single people when they were legal for married couples. In most states the law is ambiguous about giving teen-agers birth control advice, particularly without parental consent. But nowadays many authorities interpret the law liberally, believing that since teen-age sex is a fact, it ought at least to be protected sex. In any court test, they believe, the trend toward recognizing the civil rights of minors would prevail.

The policy of Planned Parenthood in New York City is typical. Before 1968 it gave birth control information to unmarried teen-age girls only if they already had had a child. Observes Executive Vice President Alfred Moran: "We were saying, in effect: 'We'll be glad to provide protection if you buy the ticket of admission—one pregnancy.' " Realizing the illogic of that position and swept along with the "new ethos," the organization now serves almost everyone and estimates that nearly 40% of its new patients are 19 or under.

At Manhattan's Margaret Sanger Research Bureau, clinic workers include teen-agers like Kathy Hull, 17, who gets course credits at her Brooklyn high school for volunteering. Chocolate cookies are passed around at the rap sessions that patients attend before they are examined and given contraceptives; boy friends are invited to the meetings and may even be present at the pelvic examinations if their girl friends agree. Said one who did: "He held my hand, and I was glad he cared enough to be there."

DOLLS WITH BREASTS

What brought about the new sexual freedom among teen-agers? "Obviously," nine parents out of ten would probably say, "it's all this permissivness." But permissiveness is just a word that stands for many things, and as with most societal changes, it is often difficult to tell what is cause and what is effect. One major factor is the "erotization of the social backdrop," as Sociologists John Gagnon and William Simon express it. American society is committed to sexuality, and even children's dolls have breasts and provocative outfits nowadays. Another frequently cited factor is the weakening of religious strictures on sex. Observes social critic Michael Harrington: "One of the great facts about our culture is the breakdown of organized religion and the disappearance of the inhibitions that religion once placed around sexual relationships." Sociologists have found an inverse relationship between churchgoing and sexual experimentation: the less of the former, the more of the latter. In fact, suggests Sociologist Ira Reiss, today's teen-agers may have more influence on religion than the other way round. Among liberal clergymen, at least, there is something of a scramble to keep up with youthful ideas on sex. Permissive Catholic priests let their views become known and so in effect encourage liberated youngsters to seek them out for confession. Unitarian churches give courses for 12- to 14-year-olds "About Your Sexuality," complete with frank lectures and discussions, as well as films showing intercourse, masturbation and homosexuality.

Diminishing family influence has also shaken up the rules. The disillusionment of many youths with Viet Nam, pollution and corruption has sexual side effects, say Simon and Gagnon. It reinforces the idea of the older generation's moral inferiority. In fact, the two sociologists assert, many young people begin sexual activity in part as a "personal vendetta" against their parents. Nor does the older generation have a very good record of marital stability. Since there are now 357 divorces for every 1,000 marriages, it is little wonder that children do not necessarily heed their parents' advice or consider marriage their ultimate goal.* "There's a healthy disrespect for the facade of respectability behind which Albee-like emotional torrents roll on," says Yale Chaplain William Sloane Coffin Jr.

Parents are not necessarily straight-forward in their advice when they give it. Recalls Bob, a senior at the University of Pittsburgh: "When I was in high school, my father warned me about sex. It wasn't so much the moral part that bothered him; he was afraid I'd knock up a girl and have to get married and get a job. I think he knows I'm living with a girl now, but if it bothers him, he hasn't made any big deal about it. I guess he figures it will help keep me in college and away from someone who might have marriage in mind."

IN THE SACK

As with churches, some parents are following the lead of the children. One of these is a real estate executive in California, father of three sexually ac-

---

*Note! The divorce rate is higher now.

tive teen-age girls. "I see sex being treated by young people more casually, yet with more respect and trust. This has had an effect on me and my wife," he asserts. In fact, he claims that it has transformed their 20-year marriage into "a damned exciting relationship." It has also led to a startling willingness to forgo privacy. One of the children recently asked her father at dinner: "Dad, how often do you masturbate?" And the children's mother confides: "Once in a while at breakfast Jim'll say, 'Gosh, we had a good time in the sack last night, didn't we?' " According to her, the girls "get a kick" out of this sort of confidence.

Many sensitive teen-agers find such "liberated" parents worse than old-fashioned ones. "In an attempt to be hip," says a recent Bard graduate, "parents and teachers can often rob an adolescent of his own private times, his first secret expressions of love. Overliberal parents can make a child self-conscious and sexually conscious before he is ready. Sex cannot be isolated from the other mysteries of adolescence, which each person must explore for himself."

Disillusioned as they may be with their elders, teen-agers owe much of their sexual freedom to parental affluence. More of them than ever before can now afford the privacy of living away from home, either while holding jobs or going to college. The proliferation of coed dorms has eased the problem of where to make love; though such dorms are not the scenes of the orgies that adults conjure up, neither are they cloisters. A phenomenon that seemed shocking when it first appeared in the West and Midwest in the 1960s, two-sex housing is now found in 80% of the coed campuses across the country. At some colleges, boys and girls are segregated in separate wings of the same buildings; at other they live on separate floors; at still others, in adjacent rooms on the same floor.

Some behavioral experts claim that in these close quarters, brother-sister relationships develop, so that a kind of incest taboo curbs sex. Moreover, Sarah Warren, a June graduate of Yale, suggests that "if you've seen the girls with dirty hair, there's less pressure to take their clothes off." But Arizona Psychiatrist Donald Holmes insists that "where the sexual conjugation of man and woman is concerned, familiarity breeds consent." At a coed dorm at the University of Maryland recently, boys poured out of girls' rooms in droves when a fire alarm sounded in the middle of the night. At Bryn Mawr, one student explains: "When a boy and girl have been going together for a while, one of them drags his mattress into the other's room." A new kind of study problem has recently been brought to a college psychiatrist: what to do if your roommate's girl friend parades around your room nude. Ask her to get dressed? Or go elsewhere to study?

As for the Pill, nearly all laymen consider it a major cause of the new freedom, but a majority of professionals disagree. Because most girls dislike seeing themselves as on the lookout for sex, few go on the Pill until they are having intercourse regularly. Even then, because they are worried about its side effects, almost half choose other means, if indeed they use contraceptives at all. Just the same, Hartsdale, N.Y., Psychiatrist Laurence Loeb believes, the very existence of the Pill has important psychological effects because it means that pregnancy is avoidable.

Then why so many illegitimate births? A principal reason, say behavioral experts, is unconscious ambivalence about pregnancy—both wanting and not wanting it. According to Planned Parenthood, teen-agers may see pregnancy as a way of remaining childishly dependent on others or, conversely, as a step toward adulthood. Besides, adds Chicago Youth Counselor Merry Allen, "it's still a way to get married, if that's what you want.

According to popular opinion, the drug culture is yet another spur to sexual activity. "Once you've taken drugs and broken that rule, it is easier to break all the others," says a senior at the University of Pittsburgh. "Drugs and sexual exploration go hand in hand," insists Charlotte Richardson, a lay therapist in Atlanta. But many doctors doubt that drug use increases sexual experimentation (whether marijuana increases sexual pleasure is even a matter of some dispute). Stanford Psychiatrist Donald Lunde, among others, believes that drugs do not lead to sex but that depression causes many teen-agers to try both sex and drugs; each, he says, is a "temporary way of feeling good." Some kids actually use drugs to avoid sex. Says Daniel X. Freedman, University of Chicago professor of psychiatry and one of the most respected drug researchers: "You can't blame rising nonvirginity on drugs. A lot of adults do so, just as they blame pornography, when the real issue is how their children regulate themselves."

What about Women's Liberation? During the '20s, the feminist drive for

equal rights for women was partly responsible for an increase in premarital sex even greater than the present acceleration. Today's extreme militants, who believe that the new wave of permissiveness is a conspiracy to exploit them, want to put a damper on sex. But for the vast majority of women, the movement stands in part for a new freedom in sexual matters.

Over the past four years, Philip and Lorna Sarrel, sex counselors at Yale, have asked 10,000 students to fill out anonymous questionnaires on sexual knowledge and attitudes. Once it was easy to tell which answers came from males and which from females. No more. "At last, both young men and women are beginning to express their sexuality without regard to stereotypes," Sarrel declares with satisfaction. "We're getting rid of the idea that sex is something men do to women." As Jonathan Goodman, 17, of Newton High remarks, "I'd probably want to talk it over with a girl, rather than just let it happen. Her reasons for doing it or not doing it would be as important as mine."

Most observers think the equality movement has weakened, though not demolished, the double standard, and reduced, though not ended, male preoccupation with virility. There is somewhat less boasting about sexual conquest. Jonathan, for one, asserts that "I respect my girl friend and our relationship enough not to tell everyone what we're doing." Anyway reports recent Columbia Graduate Lou Dolinar, "Now that girls are living with their boy friends in the dorm, it's pretty hard to sit around with them and talk like a stud. Male bull sessions of sexual braggadocio have been replaced by coed bull sessions about sexual traumas."

IDENTITY CRISIS

Can teen sex be harmful, apart from causing such problems as illegitimate pregnancy and disease? Manhattan Psychoanalyst Peter Blos believes that the early adolescent, however physically developed, is psychologically a child and lacks the emotional maturity necessary to manage sexual relationships. If a child tries to grow up too fast, Blos says, he may never grow up at all. Says Catholic Author Sidney Cornelia Callahan: "Sexuality is very intimately related to your sense of self. It should not be taken too lightly. To become an individual, the adolescent has to master impulses, to be able to refuse as well as accept."

Even on campuses where sex is relaxed, says Sociologist Simon, "kids still experience losing their virginity as an identity crisis; a nonvirgin is something they did not expect to be." Sexually involved adolescents of all ages are sometimes beset by guilt feelings, though less often than were their elders. Admits Ellen Sims, a Tenafly girl of 15 who says she has turned celibate after sleeping with three boys when she was in the eighth grade: "I was ashamed of myself. Sometimes I wish I didn't even know what I've done." Similarly, University of Pittsburgh Junior Kathy Farnsworth confesses that "I know sex isn't dirty. It's fun. But I always have this nagging thing from my parents in my head. They'd kill me if they knew, and I've never been able to have an orgasm." Occasionally the pangs of old-fashioned conscience are so strong that a student drops out of school and requires months of therapy before he is able to resolve the conflict between his "liberated" behavior and the standards, acquired from his parents, that he still unconsciously accepts.

Experts also detect a frequent sense of shame and incompetence at not enjoying sex more. "A great many young people who come into the office these days are definitely doing it more and enjoying it less," says Psychiatrist Holmes. According to Simon and Gagnon, sexual puritanism has been replaced by sexual utopianism. "The kid who worries that he has debased himself is replaced by the kid who worries that he isn't making sex a spectacular event."

Infidelity creates additional problems, warns Columbia University Psychiatrist Joel Moskowitz. "A couple agree that each can go out with anyone. The girl says, 'So-and-so turns me on; I'm going to spend the night with him.' Despite the contract they've made the boy is inevitably enraged, because he feels it's understood that such things hurt him." When the hurt is great enough to end the affair, the trauma for both may approach that of a divorce, or worse. One college student asked his high school girl friend to live in his room with him, and then watched despairingly as she fell in love with his roommate, and, overcome with grief and confusion, tried to commit suicide.

COOL SEX

To lay and professional observers alike, one of the most distressing aspects of teen sex is its frequent shallowness, particularly when the participants are still in high school. At that stage, Simon and Gagnon report, it is often the least popular students who engage in sex—and who find, especially if they are girls, that their sexual behavior brings only a shady sort of popularity and more unhappiness. Wisconsin Psychiatrist Seymour Halleck ascribes a "bland, mechanistic quality" to some youthful relationships, and Beverly Hills Psychoanalyst Ralph Greenson observes that, "instant warmth and instant sex make for puny love, cool sex."

His words seem to fit the experience of Judy Wilson. Recalling the day she lost her virginity in her own bedroom at the age of 17, she says blithely: "One afternoon it just happened. Then we went downstairs and told my younger sister because we thought she'd be excited. We said, 'Guess what. We just made love.' And she said, 'Oh, wow. How was it?' And we said, 'Fine.' Then we went out on the roof and she took pictures of us."

But among more mature young people, shallowness is anything but the rule. "Our kids are actually retrieving sexuality from shallowness," insists Sex Counselor Mary Calderone. "They are moving away from the kind of trivialization we associated with the Harvard-Yale games in the '20s when the object was to get drunk and lay a lot of girls." Los Angeles Gynecologist J. Robert Bragonier agrees: "Kids aren't looking for the perfect marriage, but they're idealistic about finding a loving relationship." Sarrel adds that he finds most student liaisons "more meaningful than the typical marriage in sharing, trusting and sexual responsibility."

Epitomizing this free but deep relationship is the experience of Yale students Rachel Lieber and Jonathan Weltzer. Recently she wrote about it for a forthcoming book: "We had always assumed we'd marry eventually. We had lived together for two years and were growing closer . . . On our wedding night, Jonathan and I lay in bed, letting all the feelings well up around us and bathe our skins in warmth as the words we had said during the ceremony started coming back. We mixed our faces in each other's hair, and we looked at each other for a long time. So we spent our wedding night, not as virgins, but very close."

Informal liaisons often mature into marriage, and when they do, Yale's Coffin has found, many areas of the relationship are apt to be sounder than in less tested unions. This is especially true now that unmarried sex has largely lost its stigma. As Coffin explains, "The danger of premarital sex while it was *verboten* was that it covered up a multitude of gaps. A girl had to believe she was in love because, she told herself, she wouldn't otherwise go to bed. As a result, the real relationship never got fully explored."

Many psychiatrists have come to agree that the new openness has much to recommend it. One of these is Graham Blaine, until recently chief psychiatrist of the Harvard health services. In 1963, Blaine wrote that "college administrations should stand by the old morality" and decried relaxed dormitory rules that allowed girls to visit boys' rooms till 7 p.m. In 1971 he switched sides. "I have been convinced by the young that the new relationships are a noble experiment that should be allowed to run its course."

Today Blaine elaborates: "I thought we college psychiatrists would see a lot more emotional problems. I was wrong; most students are not being hurt. The pendulum should be allowed to swing." It will swing back—at least part way back—he predicts, as it did after the easygoing days of the English Restoration. "It's much more in keeping with human nature to make sex a private thing and to have some elements of exclusivity." Mrs. Callahan, speaking to student audiences, has found on campuses "a new puritanism or perhaps a lingering puritanism," and she usually gets a smiling response when she calls on her listeners to "join the chastity underground."

YES OR NO

Whether or not the chastity underground is the wave of the future, as Mrs. Callahan hopes, some youths, at least, appear to be searching for firmer guidelines. "Sometimes I wish I were a Victorian lady with everything laid out clearly for me," admits Sarah Warran. Warns Coffin: "It's much easier to make authority your truth than truth your authority."

At Yale, the Sarrels, who had dropped a lecture on morals, were asked by the students to add one on sexual values and decision-making. But to search for guidelines is not necessarily to find them. Most of the proliferating courses, clinics and handbooks detail, meticulously, the biology of intercourse, contraception, pregnancy and abortion, few do more than suggest the emotional complexities of sex. For instance, *The Student Guide to Sex on Campus* (New American Library; $1), written by Yale students with the help of the Sarrels, has this to say on the subject of "Intercourse—Deciding Yes or No":

"When a relationship is probably not permanent, but still very meaningful, it is more difficult to decide confidently . . . There is so much freedom . . . The decision is all yours, and can be very scary . . . No one should have intercourse just because they can't think of any reason *not* to. The first year in college can create confusion about sexual values. Your family seems very far away, and their ideas about almost everything are challenged by what you see and hear . . . Girls who have intercourse just to get rid of virginity usually seem to find it not a pleasurable or fulfilling experience."

SENSE OF TRUST

In personal counseling sessions, the Sarrels offer psychological support for students who would rather not rush things, telling them that "it's just as O.K. not to have sex as it is to have it." "People need to unfold sexually," Sarrel believes, and there is no way to speed the process. What is right may vary with a student's stage of emotional development. "A freshman may need to express rebellion and independence from his family and may use sex to do it." That is acceptable, Sarrel believes, as long as the student understands his motives: "We don't worry too much about the freshman who's going to bed with someone. We worry about the freshman who's going to bed and thinks it's love." For an older student, intercourse may be right only if the lovers are intimate emotionally. How to judge? One crucial sign of intimacy is "a sense of trust and comfort. If you find you're not telling each other certain kinds of things, it's not a very trusting relationship."

Apparently this kind of advice is what the students want. Sarrel has been dubbed "the Charlie Reich of sex counseling" by an irreverent observer, and like the author of *The Greening of America*, he is very popular: 300 men and women crowd into his weekly lectures at Yale, and more than 1,000 other colleges have asked for outlines of his course. For good reason. The Sarrels' careful counseling has cut the VD and unwanted pregnancy rate at Yale to nearly zero.

But what about ethical questions? For those who are not guided by their families or their religion, Sarrel's system—and the whole body of "situation ethics"—fails to offer much support for making a decision. Years ago William Butler Yeats wrote a poem about the problem:

> I whispered, "I am too young."
> And then, "I am old enough";
> Wherefore I threw a penny
> To find out if I might love.

How did the toss come out? Yeats, unsurprisingly, gave himself a clear go-ahead, ending his poem:

> Ah penny, brown penny, brown penny,
> One cannot begin it too soon.

Nowadays a great many adolescents, like Yeats, seem to be simply tossing a coin, and singing the same refrain.

ON LIVING TOGETHER
WITHOUT MARRIAGE*

Ibithaj Arafat and Betty Yorburg

Attitudes toward the living together pattern on the part of large numbers of young people who could potentially engage in this type of relationship have not been investigated. Motives, personality traits and the relative influence of parents, peers and the mass media on those who actually engage in living together without marriage are not well understood, nor do we have a clear picture of the relationship between class origins, degree of religiosity, sex, age and education, and attitudes and behavior in this area. Above all, we do not know whether the majority of young, well-educated men and women who set up housekeeping together without the legal sanction of marriage view their relationship as a transient stage in their life cycle, as a prelude to marriage or as a substitute for marriage.

To cast some light on these questions, the authors conducted a survey at a large, urban, Northeastern university in 1971. Nine hundred questionnaires were distributed, to a sample of students who were generally representative of the total student population with respect to age and year at college, major field of study, religion, sex, marital status and class origins (as indicated by father and mother's occupation). Of the 762 students who returned the questionnaire (approximately 85 per cent), about one-fifth (139) were engaged in a living together relationship with a member of the opposite sex.

In addition to demographic data, our questions centered on the relative influence of parents, peers and the mass media on the respondent's opinions and behavior, generally, and on the topic under investigation, their willingness to engage in the living together pattern, their willingness to do so despite parental or peer objections and their self-evaluation as shy, isolated, introspective; outgoing, aggressive, not particularly introspective; and independent or easily influenced.

We asked those who were favorably disposed toward entering a living together relationship and those who were actively participating in this kind of relationship to rank their reasons, in order to relative importance. The latter respondents were also asked to indicate their expectations with respect to the future of the relationship and to describe the attitudes and reactions of their parents and friends to their behavior.

Since recent evidence has indicated that parents continue to have more influence than peers upon adolescents in major decision-making areas such as

*Reprinted with permission of the Society for the Scientific Study of Sex from the *Journal of Sex Research*, Volume 9, No. 2, Feb. 1973.

career choice and education the authors expected that parental disapproval would be more important than peer disapproval in affecting attitudes and behavior.[1][2][3] It is well known that authority and influence over others is associated with resources—economic, intellectual, physical and emotional.[4] Parental resources (economic support, particularly), we felt would give them greater authority than peers in the decision of young men and women to cohabit without legal sanctions.

We expected also that the mass media would have the least effect upon the attitudes and behavior of our respondents, because citizens in democratic countries select what they will expose themselves to in the mass media and they tend to select messages that are consistent with their values. Furthermore, no investigator has been able to establish that the mass media do more than precipitate preexisting impulses. They cannot create impulses that are inconsistent with the personality and values of viewers and readers.

Since the vanguard of change in contemporary family life appears to be the urban, upper-middle class, we also anticipated that students of upper-middle class origins would be more accepting of the living together pattern and would be most apt to be engaged in it.[5][6] And since intensity of religious belief is known to have a strong effect on premarital sexual behavior particularly where sexual abstinence is emphasized by the church, we expected that this factor would also be strongly related to attitudes and behavior in this area.[7][8][9]

On the level of personality and emotional needs that are satisfied by adolescents in heterosexual love relationships, since expedient motives such as validating popularity and enhancing prestige appear to be declining in favor of needs to clarify identity through dating and love relationships[10][11] we anticipated that college students who regard themselves as dependent, shy, isolated and introspective would be more favorable to the pattern than those who view themselves as outgoing, aggressive, independent, and not particularly introspective. The former type of student, presumably, would have stronger dependency needs and would be more intensely involved in the search for identity and more in need of a close heterosexual relationship that does not at the same time involve the permanent commitment of marriage and the more crystallized identity that this implies.

FINDINGS

A large majority of the students (79.2 percent) indicated that they would live with a member of the opposite sex, without marriage, given the opportunity to do so. The remaining respondents (20.8 percent) would not do so, under any circumstances.

Neither social class origins nor major field of study and occupational goals were significantly related to attitudes toward this type of relationship or the fact of being actively in it. Males and females approved or disapproved about equally. Age and marital status did significantly affect attitudes: older, engaged and married students were less likely to approve of the pattern. Religiosity was also significantly related to unfavorable attitudes toward living together (P < .0001).

With respect to self-image, approximately three quarters of the male and female students who were living together unmarried characterized themselves as independent, outgoing and aggressive. Those who disapproved of the pattern were far less likely to characterize themselves in this way (60.77% of the males and 57.74% of the females). And while females were twice as likely to regard themselves as easily influenced, and those who disapproved of the living together pattern were also more apt to view themselves in this way, the great majority of all respondents did not regard themselves as easily influenced.

At the same time, our respondents judged peer group influence on their attitudes and behavior to be strongest, parental influence less strong and the effects of the mass media least strong. Female students were much more apt to attribute to their parents a moderate degree of influence rather than little influence over their attitudes and behavior. Table 1 indicates these very highly significant relationships.

When the respondents who were living together were asked about their reaction to parental or peer group disapproval of their behavior, more respondents reported themselves as willing to act in opposition to peer group disapproval (87.76%) than to parental disapproval (80.19%). This willingness was not put to the test for a majority of those who were engaged in this kind of rela-

tionship, however, since less than one half of the males had informed their parents and only approximately one fourth of the females had done so.

Those who would not engage in a living together relationship were far less apt to go against parental disapproval than peer disapproval: "My mother would have a neurosis." "My parents would cut me off." "My father would drag me home by my hair." In both cases, where students were actually living together and where they would not consider participating in such a relationship under any circumstances, parental disapproval was more important than peer disapproval.

Many students who approved of the living together relationship rejected the legal sanction of marriage: "A wedding license is just a scrap of paper." "Marriage is just one of society's definitions." "I feel that if two people want to live together unmarried, they should because all the legalities in the world won't keep them together if they want out. So to save time and energy, do whatever comes natural—not legal."

For the total sample, the most frequent first choice of possible motives for participating in a living together relationship for males was sexual gratification (35.90%): "It's less of a hassle to get laid." "Sex—when you want it, where you want it." For females, the most frequent first choice was marriage (29.10%): "It's a first step toward marriage and if I don't grab him, somebody else will." Males were half as likely to list future marriage rather than sexual gratification as a primary reason for engaging in a living together relationship and females were almost half as likely as males to list sexual gratification as a primary motive. And when males gave future marriage as a first response, their rationale was apt to be pragmatic rather than sentimental: "You wouldn't buy a new car without test driving it first!" For over 80 per cent of our male respondents and for over two thirds of our female respondents, however, future marriage would not be the most important reason for entering into a living together relationship.

Economic reasons came next on the list of choices for both sexes: "Two can live more cheaply than one—particularly if the rent is $250 a month!"

Almost one third of our respondents checked the category "Others, specify" as an additional response, the most frequent reasons specified coming under the categories of emotional gratification and support, companionship, and obtaining knowledge and understanding of each other: "A fantastic way to understand yourself, others and interpersonal relationships. Marriage sets up fixed roles and expectations which bear no true relationship to the people involved and are detrimental to individual growth and fulfillment. Living together is not as permeated with norms, rules, etc."

Of those who are actually living together, only 13.67% of the males and 15.11 percent of the females claimed eventual marriage as a reason for entering the relationship and approximately the same number were planning to get married in the future. About two thirds of those who were engaged in a living together relationship claimed that they were not sure of their original motives

Table 1

Influence of Parents, Peers and Mass Media on Opinion of Respondents by Sex

Degree of influence as perceived by respondent	Living together unmarried												Do not live together unmarried											
	Parents				Peers				Mass media				Parents				Peers				Mass media			
	Male		Female		Male		Female		Male		Female		Male		Female		Male		Female		Male		Female	
	N	%	N	%	N	%	N	%	N	%	N	%	N	%	N	%	N	%	N	%	N	%	N	%
Great, degree	5	6.17	3	5.17	10	12.35	6	10.34	2	2.47	1	1.72	38	10.92	35	12.73	46	13.23	51	18.55	13	3.74	19	6.91
Moderate degree	25	30.87	20	34.48	38	46.91	37	63.79	21	25.93	17	29.31	160	45.98	165	60.0	219	62.93	188	68.36	149	42.82	112	40.73
Little degree	51	62.96	35	60.35	33	40.74	15	25.87	58	71.68	40	68.97	150	43.10	75	27.27	83	23.85	36	13.09	186	53.44	144	52.36
Total	81	100.0	58	100.0	81	100.0	58	100.0	81	100.0	58	100.0	348	100.0	275	100.0	348	100.0	275	100.0	348	100.0	275	100.0
			$N_1 = 139$				$N_1 = 139$				$N_1 = 139$				$N_2 = 623$				$N_2 = 623$				$N_2 = 623$	

Grand Total = $N = 762$ = 100.00 percent = the sample. Living together unmarried = $N_1 = 139 = 18.24\%$ of the sample. Do not live together unmarried = $N_2 = 623 = 81.76\%$ of the Sample.

Table 2

Living Together Unmarried against Objection of Parents and Peers

Respondents' response to objection	Living together unmarried								Do not live together unmarried							
	Parents objected				Peers objected				Parents objected				Peers objected			
	Male		Female		Male		Female		Male		Female		Male		Female	
	N	%	N	%	N	%	N	%	N	%	N	%	N	%	N	%
Go ahead with plans	68	49.92	42	30.22	73	52.51	49	35.25	231	37.08	115	18.46	316	50.73	239	38.37
Yield to their wishes	2	1.44	4	2.88	3	2.16	5	3.60	41	6.58	76	12.22	9	1.44	9	1.44
Other	11	7.91	12	8.63	5	3.60	4	2.88	76	12.22	84	13.45	23	3.69	27	4.33
Total	81	58.27	58	41.73	81	58.27	58	41.73	348	55.85	275	44.14	348	55.85	275	44.14
	$N_1 = 139 = 100.00\%$				$N_1 = 139 = 100.00\%$				$N_2 = 623 = 100.00\%$				$N_2 = 623 = 100.00\%$			

Grand Total = $N = 762$ = 100.00 percent = the sample. Living together unmarried = $N_1 = 139 = 18.24$ percent of the sample. Do not live together unmarried = $N_2 = 623 = 81.76$ percent of the sample.

and slightly over half did not know if they would marry in the future. Females were more apt than males to have future marriage plans, but only a small minority had these plans.

In the instances where parents and peers had been informed, parental disapproval (53.24 percent) was higher than peer disapproval (25.90 percent) but parental neutrality was high (35.97 percent).

DISCUSSION

The strong relationship between strength of religious beliefs and negative attitudes toward the living together pattern confirmed the authors' expectations and is consistent with other data on the inhibiting effects of religious beliefs on premarital sexual liberalism. The fact that older students and those who were engaged or married were more apt to disapprove of the pattern probably reflects the newness of the phenomenon among college students and the stronger effects of the college subculture on younger students.

Despite greater concern with parental than peer disapproval by our respondents, only approximately 10 percent of the parents who had been informed that their children were participating in a living together relationship approved of their childrens' behavior. If the resource theory of social power is valid, one would expect parents to have more influence than they, in fact, had because of the economic sanctions they were in a position to exercise. What happens, apparently, is that parents do not exercise these sanctions (if they are informed)—very likely because they fear losing their children.

Another possibility is that the students who were living together and who informed their parents perceived parental neutrality as tacit approval or they perceived parental disapproval as more formal than real. This interpretation stems from Reiss' finding that two-thirds of a nationwide sample of high school and college students felt that their sexual standards were at least similar to those of their parents, despite the apparent greater conservatism of parents.[12] In the case of our respondents, presumably they would not have informed their parents unless they anticipated acceptance of their behavior, at some level. The fact that three quarters of the women and one half of the males did not inform their parents supports this interpretation: these respondents probably feared the sanctions that their parents would be likely to exercise, because their disapproval would have been real and unambiguous.

The fact that liberal behavior and attitudes toward the living together pattern were not significantly related to major fields of study (humanities, the arts, and the social sciences as opposed to natural sciences, business, architecture and engineering) would seem to indicate that the status of college student and the student subculture is more effective in determining attitude and behavior in this area than would be expected on the basis of previous studies linking major fields of study and occupation with conservatism and liberalism, generally on a number of other issues.[13] [14] Living together is apparently becoming a general pattern among college students and should not be regarded as exclusive to counter-culture members. The latter may have led the way, among college students, but at this point the living together relationship appears to be spreading to those students who do not necessarily embrace other aspects of the counterculture—political radicalism, for example.

A similar interpretation applies to the lack of relationship between class origins and attitudes and behavior in this area. Students of working class and lower middle class origins were as liberal as those of upper-middle class origins. The well-documented greater conformity of the stable working class and the lower-middle class in a number of areas, including the traditional morality, is apparently irrelevant to student attitude and behavior in living together without marriage.[15] The student subculture prevails, at least temporarily.

The authors' expectation that students engaged in a living together relationship would be more apt to characterize themselves as shy, introspective, isolated and dependent was also not borne out. Quite the contrary. Both males and females, equally, who were involved in living together relationships, were far more likely to characterize themselves as independent, aggressive and outgoing than respondents who disapproved of the relationship and would not engage in it. It would seem that in the mating game as well as in other areas of competition and attainment the meek are relegated to watching and waiting.

While female respondents were consistently more apt than males to give more traditional responses—future marriage as a reason for living together, for example—most female students did not give these responses and three quarters of those who were involved in living together relationships (the same percentage as their male counterparts) characterized themselves as aggressive, independent and outgoing. We see here, we believe, the emergence of the new woman—educated, liberated and increasingly like males in self-image, attitude and behavior. Pesumably, these women were reared in homes where sex typing of male and female children was less extreme. Interestingly, they were as likely to come from the working class as from the middle class—a surprising datum since child-rearing practices, generally, are more traditional in the working class. On the other hand, women students in our sample who came from the working class were in college—which is still atypical for females from working class homes. The very fact that they were in college reflects the fact of a less traditional upbringing.

Perhaps the most important finding of our study is that for the great majority of students who were involved in a living together relationship, future marriage was not a goal at the time when they first entered the relationship, nor did they have definite expectations of marrying their present partners in the future. The living together relationship may represent a pattern that is crystallizing as a universal stage in the life style of young adults or it may come to represent a universal substitute for marriage for adults of all ages. It certainly was not regarded as a prelude to a marriage or a trial marriage for most of our respondents—male and female—who were living together, nor was it defined as such by those who would potentially engage in this type of relationship.

The heterosexual pairing relationship that endures is likely to continue to be valued in human societies as long as the nuclear family with its exclusive parent-child relationship continues as the crucible of childbearing and child-rearing. The ritual of marriage, however, may disappear, in time. This has been the fate, historically, of other rituals that have marked important transitions in status—rituals such as puberty rites, and more recently, funeral rites.

References

1. E. Douvan and J. Adelson, *The Adolescent Experience* (New York: Wiley, 1966).
2. H. Sebald, *Adolescence: A Sociological Analysis* (New York: Appleton-Century Crofts, 1968).
3. D. Kandel and G. Lesser, "Parental and Peer Influences on Educational Plans of Adolescents" *American Sociological Review*, XXXIV (1969), 212–22.
4. J. French, Jr. and B. Raven, "The Bases of Social Power" in *Studies in Social Power*, (Ann Arbor: Institute for Social Research, 1959).
5. L. Burchinal, "The Rural Family of the Future" in *The Family and Change*, J. Edwards, ed. (New York: Alfred A. Knopf, 1969).
6. J. Cuber and P. Harroff, *The Significant Americans* (New York: Appleton-Century, 1966).
7. I. Reiss, *Premarital Sexual Standards in America* (New York: Free Press, 1960).
8. I. Arafat and B. Yorburg, "Drugs and the Sexual Behavior of College Women" *Journal of Sex Research*, IX (1973), 21–29.
9. M. Heltsley and C. Broderick, "Religiosity and Premarital Sexual Permissiveness: A Re-examination of Reiss' Traditionalism Proposition" *Journal of Marriage and the Family*, XXXII (1969), 441–43.
10. E. Erikson, *Childhood and Society* (New York: Norton, 1950).
11. D. Knox, Jr. and M. Sporakowski, "Attitudes of College Students Towards Love" *Journal of Marriage and the Family*, XXX (1968), 638–42.
12. I. Reiss, *The Social Context of Premarital Permissiveness* (New York: Holt, Rinehart and Winston, 1967).
13. M. Rosenberg, *Occupation and Values* (Glencoe, Ill: The Free Press, 1957).
14. L. Goodwin, "The Academic World and the Business World: A Comparison of Occupational Goals" *Sociology of Education*, XII (1969), 170–87.
15. M. Kohn, *Class and Conformity: A Study in Values* (Homewood, Ill: Dorsey, 1969).

AN ALTERNATIVE MODEL
OF THE WHEEL THEORY*

Delores M. Borland

THE WHEEL THEORY

Reiss proposed his Wheel Theory of the Development of Love by graphically representing it as a wheel with spokes.[1] This is a broad concept which can cover all primary relationships in all social classes including the development of the heterosexual love relationship. This theory does not depend on the truth or falsity of the two opposing views of mate selection—heterogamy, do opposites attract as proposed by Winch's Theory of Complementary Needs; versus homogamy, do likes attract as proposed by Burgess and Wallin and Strauss. Both views are compatible with this theory. The first stage of Reiss' theory is a mutual feeling of rapport—a feeling of ease with each other, a desire to know more about each other, and a willingness for each to reveal oneself to the other.

Rapport can be established between two individuals of homogamous or similar backgrounds. One or both believe they have so much in common that they feel a degree of mutual understanding and rapport. A common statement is, "I feel I have known you for a long time." Rapport can also be established between individuals of heterogamous or complementary backgrounds. Each individual believes the other person to be an interesting contrast to himself or he see qualities in this other person which he has always wanted to have in himself. Regardless of the cause of rapport, once it is established, the relationship follows the Wheel Theory cycle.

The feeling of rapport usually leads into the second stage of the social process, self-relevation. The more relaxed one is with another the more he will reveal about himself. He begins to disclose things about himself at a more intimate level. The way one is socialized will affect the quantity or level of self-relevation. Some people, for example, are raised to be wary of others until they "prove trustworthy;" true feelings or beliefs of a religious or sexual nature should not be revealed except to an intimate person; admission of personal problems or weaknesses should be discussed only among "family;" or men are innately superior while women's place is in the home thinking of only domestic things.

*From Delores M. Borland, M.A., Teaching Assistant, Department of Sociology & Social Work, Texas Women's University, "An Alternative Model of the Wheel Theory," *The Family Coordinator* 24, no. 3 (July 1975): 289–292. Copyright 1975 by National Council on Family Relations. Reprinted by permission.

Several studies have found additional information on self-relevation. Jourard defined self-disclosure as "the act of making yourself manifest, showing yourself so others can perceive you."[2] Self-disclosure follows an attitude of respect and trust which then leads to a type of love depending on the relationship involved. People are more likely to disclose themselves when they respect, trust, and like the other person and when that person is willing to disclose his experience to the same depth and breadth—disclosure begets disclosure. Jourard called this reciprocity the "dyadic effect." Gouldner in his Principle of Functional Reciprocity submitted that a relationship is more likely to persist if the functional interchange is reciprocal.[3] If not functionally reciprocal, compensatory mechanisms must be present to make up for the lack of reciprocity. A person, for example, may marry someone he does not love because of the status he will receive from this marriage. One receives love; the other does not receive love but status which in his eyes compensates for the lack of love. What is mutually exchanged, therefore, need not be identical but the net result or worth of what is received by the exchange must be perceived by the recipients as equal if the structure or relationship is to continue to exist. Worthy, Gary, and Kahn also found that this principle of reciprocity occurred in their experiment and that the more the people liked one another the more they would reveal or disclose about themselves.[4] This disclosing of information about oneself is rewarding to the listener as well as to the disclosing person in that the recipient's self-esteem is raised, i.e., one is worthy to be told this information and it allows him the freedom to disclose himself.

Self-disclosure and its satisfactions usually lead to the third stage of the social process. The two people desire to spend more time together and develop mutual dependencies or interdependent habit systems. These habits require the presence of the other person and, therefore, they begin to depend on one another. An example might be that evening television watching becomes a lonesome time without the other person as the enjoyment depends now not only on the television program but on the person being there to share it.

This dependency leads to the fourth part of the process, the fulfillment of their personality needs. Each individual has emotional needs such as someone to love, to be loved, to trust, to confide, to be supported, and to be encouraged among others. These two people begin to find these needs satisfied by the other person. As this personality need is fulfilled, more rapport is developed which leads to more self-revelation, more mutual habits, and deeper personality need fulfillment. Reiss indicated that the initial rapport between the two people really may be a vague feeling that this other person was someone who could fulfill these personality needs.

> These four processes are in a sense really one pro
> cess for when one feels rapport, he reveals himself
> and becomes dependent, thereby fulfilling his per
> sonality needs. The circularity is most clearly seen in

that the needs being fulfilled were the original rea-
son for feeling rapport.[5]

This four stage process can recur indefinitely in a lasting, deep relationship or it can occur only a few times in a passing friendship. The process also is reversible in that something can happen, be revealed, or another relationship can develop which is more meaningful and detracts from the first relationship and thus the first social process reverses and the relationship diminishes—the wheel reverses direction.

THE CLOCKSPRING ALTERNATIVE

It is the contention here that this social process could be represented more dynamically as a clockspring with the most intimate aspects or the "real self" of an individual at the center of the spring. The real self is defined here as the total self as the individual perceives himself. This self concept includes not only his ideal self—what he thinks he should be—but also such elements as what he would like to be, how he believes others perceive him, his aspirations and regrets, and his positive and negative attributes. In other words, all his inner thoughts concerning himself make up his real self.

This clockspring representation has several advantages. As these four processes occur and lead one into the other, they wind themselves toward a closer and more intimate relationship with an understanding of the real inner self of the other person. As this occurs, the individuals form an increasingly tighter bond to one another in much the same way as a clockspring tightens as it is wound.

Another advantage of the clockspring model is that it can exemplify the depth of a relationship as these four processes lead into one another toward a more intimate knowledge of the other person. A person allows others to know in varying degrees the unique and private view he has of himself. The more he allows another to know this private concept of himself, the more he lays himself open for attack, for this person then knows his so called vulnerable and sensitive spots. This progressive self-disclosure requires more and more trust and respect which are important ingredients for rapport.

In the classroom, a discussion of how a primary relationship develops might be introduced by asking students to list a number of their closest friends by name on a sheet of paper. They can then be asked to draw a diagram of the clockspring model and to appropriately place these names on the model according to the degree of knowledge they have of the student's real self. Students then ask themselves if they feel more rapport, have expressed more self relevation, have developed more mutual dependencies, and find more of their personality needs met by those persons closest to the center of the spring. This can lead into the discussion of how relationships develop, are maintained, or are terminated. In the Reiss model, the wheel turns at varying speeds and turns more often for deeper relationships. It does not, however, illustrate a comparative view of the depth of the many relationships an individual has with others.

The length of time required and the difficulty of "unwinding" a relationship can be visually represented with the clockspring model. The tighter or closer the relationship has progressed around the person's "real self" the more difficult it is and the longer it takes to "unwind" the relationship. Referring to their diagrams once again, students might be asked if those persons appearing closer to the center of the clockspring tend to be those people the individual has known for a longer period of time. In some instances, time does not increase understanding. Generally, however, the longer or more often people go through this cycle, the deeper the understanding they have of each other's real self. An example for discussion might be marriages based on a relationship on the periphery of the clockspring model which may not be able to withstand the sacrifices required for married life to the extent of relationships that have developed farther.

The clockspring model also illustrates the relationship which becomes so tightly overwound that the individuals cannot grow or the relationship in which one individual becomes so threatened by the other person being "too close" that he ends the relationship abruptly. This can be seen when a person "bares his soul" to someone in the time of emotional stress only to find himself desiring to avoid or withdraw from that person later when the crisis has passed.

Counselors may experience this withdrawal if a certain degree of respect, trust, and rapport has not been built up before this deep self-relevation. The cycle has been short circuited and goes directly from self-relevation to the real self. The importance of going through these four stages for a lasting relationship can thus be better exemplified with the clockspring model.

The clockspring model, additionally, indicates in a dynamic fashion similar to the winding of a clock, how a relationship can indefinitely wind and unwind, and then rewind again with a new incident, to a more positive intimate level than before or unwind to a more negative superficial level of intimacy and meaning. An argument, a new relationship, the birth of a child, or prolonged intermittent stress, such as occurs for married couples in graduate school, are examples of incidents which can "wind up" a relationship and lead to a tighter bond and increased understanding through communication and working together toward a common goal. Those same incidents can unwind a relationship to a lessened degree of rapport, self-relevation, mutual dependencies, and personality needs met, if, for example, the argument is destructive rather than constructive.

Reiss's Wheel Theory is a significant contribution to the understanding of the development of primary relationships—how they are begun, maintained, and/or terminated. With its illustrative advantages, the clockspring model, as a more dynamic visual aid, can add to the teaching and understanding of primary relationships as pulsating, demoralizing, or revitalizing interactions.

References

1. I. Reiss, "Toward a Sociology of the Heterosexual Love Relationship" *Journal of Marriage and Family Living*, XXII (1960), 139–45.
2. S. Jourard, *The Transparent Self* (New York: Van Nostrand Reinhold Co., 1971).
3. A. Gouldner, "Reciprocity and Autonomy in Functional Theory" in *Symposium on Sociological Theory*, L. Gross, ed. (Evanston: Row, Peterson, and Company, 1959).
4. M. Worthy, A. Gary, and G. Kahn, "Self-disclosure as an Exchange Process" *Journal of Personality and Social Psychology*, XIII (1969), 59–63.
5. Reiss, *op. cit.*

THE STYLES OF LOVING*

John Alan Lee

We will accept variety in almost anything, from roses and religions to politics and poetry. But when it comes to love, each of us believes we know the real thing, and we are reluctant to accept other notions. We disparage other people's experiences by calling them infatuations, mere sexual flings, unrealistic affairs.

For thousands of years writers and philosophers have debated the nature of love. Many recognized that there are different kinds of love, but few accepted them all as legitimate. Instead, each writer argues that his own concept of love is the best. C. S. Lewis thought that true love must be unselfish and altruistic, as did sociologist Pitirim Sorokin. Stendhal, by contrast, took the view that love is passionate and estatic. Others think that "real" love must be wedded to the Protestant ethic, forging a relationship that is mutually beneficial and productive. Definitions of love range from sexual lust to an excess of friendship.

The ancient Greeks and Romans were more tolerant. They had a variety of words for different and, to them, equally valid types of love. But today the concept has rigidified; most of us believe that there is only one true kind of love. We measure each relationship against this ideal in terms of degree or quantity. Does Tom love me more than Tim does? Do you love me as much as I love you? Do I love you enough? Such comparisons also assume that love comes in fixed amounts—the more I give to you, the less I have for anyone else; if you don't give me everything, you don't love me enough.

"There is hardly any activity, any enterprise, which is started with such tremendous hopes and expectations, and yet which fails so regularly, as love," wrote Erich Fromm. I think that part of the reason for this failure rate is that too often people are speaking different languages when they speak of love. The problem is not *how much* love they feel, but *which kind*. The way to have a mutually satisfying love affair is not to find a partner who loves "in the right amount," but one who shares the same approach to loving, the same definition of love.

THE STRUCTURE OF LOVE

My research explored the literature of love and the experiences of ordinary lovers in order to distinguish these approaches. Color served me as a use-

Copyright © 1974 Ziff-Davis Company. Reprinted by permission of *Psychology Today* magazine.

ful analogy in the process. There are three primary colors—red, yellow and blue—from which all other hues are composed. And empirically I found three primary types of love, none of which could be reduced to the others, and a variety of secondary types that proved to be combinations of the basic three. In love, as in color, "primary" does not mean superior; it simply refers to basic structure. Orange is no more or less a color than red, and no less worthy. In love, as in color, one can draw as many distinctions as one wishes; I have stopped, somewhat arbitrarily, with nine types.

EROS

Stendhal called love a "sudden sensation of recognition and hope." He was describing the most typical symptom of eros: an immediate, powerful attraction to the physical appearance of the beloved. "The first time I saw him was several weeks before we met," a typical erotic lover said in an interview, "but I can still remember exactly the way he looked, which was just the way I dreamed my ideal lover would look." Erotic lovers typically felt a chemical or gut reaction on meeting each other; heightened heartbeat is not just a figment of fiction, it seems, but the erotic lover's physiological response to meeting the dream.

Most of my erotic respondents went to bed with their lovers soon after meeting. This was the first test of whether the affair would continue, since erotic love demands that the partner live up to the lover's concept of bodily perfection. They may try to overlook what they consider a flaw, only to find that it undermines the intensity of their attraction. There is no use trying to persuade such a lover that personal or intellectual qualities are more lasting or more important. To do so is to argue for another approach to love.

My erotic respondents all spoke with delight of the lover's skin, fragrance, hair, musculature, body proportions, and so on. Of course, the specific body type that each lover considered ideal varied, but all erotics had such an ideal, which they could identify easily from a series of photographs. Erotic lovers actively and imaginatively cultivate many sexual techniques to preserve delight in the partner's body. Nothing is more deadly for a serious erotic lover than to fall in love with a prudish partner.

Modern usage tends to define *erotic* as *sexual*; we equate erotic art with pornography. But eros is not mere sexual attraction; it is a demanding search for the lover's ideal of beauty, a concept that is as old as Pygmalion. Eros involves mental as well as sexual attraction, which is faithful to the Platonic concept. Most dictionaries define Platonic love as "devoid of sensual feeling," which is certainly not what Plato had in mind. On the contrary, it was sensual feeling for the beautiful body of another person that evoked eros as the Greeks understood it.

The Dream of the Ideal

The fascination with beauty that marks eros is the basis for personal and psychological intimacy between the lovers. The erotic lover wants to know everything about the beloved, to become part of him or her. If an erotic relationship surpasses the initial hurdles of expectation and physical ideals, this desire for intimacy can sustain the relationship for years. (And this knowledge must be first-hand. The playful lover may ask a friend what so-and-so is like in bed. No erotic lover would dream of relying on such vicarious evidence.)

An essential component of successful erotic love is self-assurance. It takes confidence to reveal oneself intensely to another. A lover who doubts himself, who falls into self-recriminations if his love is not reciprocated, cannot sustain eros.

The typical erotic lovers in my sample avoided wallowing in extremes of emotion, especially the self-pity and hysteria that characterize mania. They recalled happy and secure childhoods, and reported satisfaction with work, family, and close friends. They were ready for love when it came along, but were not anxiously searching. They consider love to be important, but they do not become obsessive about it; when separated from the beloved, they do not lose their balance, become sick with desire, or turn moody. They prefer exclusive relationships but do not demand them, and they are rarely possessive or afraid of rivals. Erotic lovers seek a deep, pervasive rapport with their partners and share development and control of the relationship.

But because the erotic lover depends on an ideal concept of beauty, he is often disappointed. The failure rate of eros has littered our fiction with bitter and cynical stories of love, and caused conventional wisdom to be deeply suspicious of ideal beauty as a basis for relationships. Indeed, I found that the purer the erotic qualities of a respondent's love experience, the less his chances of a mutual, lasting relationship.

An erotic lover may eventually settle for less, but he or she never forgets the compromise, and rarely loses hope of realizing the dream. However, I found several cases of 'love at first sight'' in which initial rapture survived years of married life. The success of a few keeps the dream alive for many more.

LUDUS

About the year One A.D. the Roman poet Ovid came up with the term *amor ludens*, playful love, love as a game. Ovid advised lovers to enjoy love as a pleasant pasttime, but not to get too involved. The ludic lover refuses, then, to become dependent on any beloved, or to allow the partner to become overly attached to him or her, or too intimate.

Other types of lovers dismiss ludus as not a kind of love at all; erotic types disdain its lack of commitment, moralists condemn its promiscuity and hedonism. But to make a game of love does not diminish its value. No skilled player of bridge or tennis would excuse inept playing because "it's only a game," and ludus too has its rules, strategies, and points for skill. Ludus turns love into a series of challenges and puzzles to be solved.

Ludic Strategies

For example, ludus is most easily and most typically played with several partners at once, a guarantee against someone on either side getting too involved. "Love several persons," a 17-century manual advises, for three lovers are safer than two, and two much safer than one. A ludic lover will often invent another lover, even a spouse, to keep the partner from becoming too attached.

But most of my ludic respondents had other tactics. They were careful not to date a partner too often; they never hinted at including the partner in any long-range plans; they arranged encounters in a casual, even haphazard, way: "I'll give you a call"; "See you around sometime." Such indefiniteness is de-

signed to keep the partner from building up expectations or from becoming pre-occupied with the affair.

Of course, as in many games, one must be on guard against cheats. Cheats in ludic love are cynical players who don't care how deeply involved the partner becomes, who may even exploit such intensity. Such players scandalize ludic lovers who believe in fair play. Insincerity and lies may be part of the game, so long as both partners understand this.

The ludic lover notices differences between bodies, but thinks it is stupid to specialize. As the ludic man said in *Finian's Rainbow*, when he is not near the girl he loves, he loves the girl he's near. But ludus is not simply a series of sexual encounters. A lover could get sex without the rituals of conversation, candles and wine. In ludus, the pleasure comes from playing the game, not merely winning the prize.

Actually, sexual gratification is only a minor part of the time and effort involved in ludic love. Of any group, ludic respondents showed the least interest in the mutual improvement of sex techniques. Their attitude was that it is easier to find a new sex partner than to work out sexual problems and explore new sexual pleasures with the current one; this view contrasts sharply with that of erotic and storgic lovers. Ludic people want sex for fun, not emotional rapport.

Don Juans Aren't Always Doomed

Ludus has enjoyed recurring popularity through history. Montesquieu could write of 18th-century France: "A husband who wishes to be the only one to possess his wife would be regarded as a public killjoy." The first Don Juan emerged in Tirso de Molina's *The Trickster of Seville* in 1630, the diametric opposite of the erotic Tristan, the courtly ideal. Tirso's hero conquered only four women, but a century later Mozart's Don Giovanni won a thousand and three in España alone.

Of course the various fates of the legendary ludic lovers reflect society's ambivalence toward them. They usually go to hell, get old and impotent, or meet their match and surrender. Rarely is ludus tolerated, much less rewarded.

But I was struck by the fact that most of my ludic respondents neither suffered nor regretted their ways. Like successful erotics, they play from a base of self-confidence. They believe in their own assets so much that they do not "need" other people, like most mortals. These ludic lovers prefer to remain in perfect control of their feelings; they do not think that love is as important as work or other activities; they are thus never possessive or jealous (except as a teasing ploy in the game). They typically recall their childhoods as "average," and their current lives as "OK, but occasionally frustrating."

My ludic respondents seemed quite content with their detachment from intense feelings of love but most failed the acid test of ludus: the ability to break off with a partner with whom they were through. Their intentions were ludic, but they had Victorian hangovers. They tended to prolong the relationship for the sake of the partner, until the inevitable break was painful. Ovid would not have approved. "Extinguish the fire of love gradually," he admonished, "not all at once . . . it is wicked to hate a girl you used to love."

The legendary ludic lovers, like Don Juan and Alfie, were generally men, and only in recent years—with the pill and penicillin—have women won entry into the game. Ludus is also frequently identified with male homosexual love; the term "gay" may have originated from the assumption that homosexuals adopt a noncommittal, playful approach to sex and love, which is not necessarily so.

There is a variant of this type of love that I call *manic ludus*, in which the lover alternates between a detached, devil-may-care attitude toward the partner, and a worried, lovesick desire for more attention. People in this conflicting state would like to be purely ludic, but they lack the vanity or self-sufficiency to remain aloof from intimacy. They both need and resent love, and they cannot control their emotions long enough to maintain a cool relationship.

STORGE

(Pronounced stor-gay) is, as Proudhon described it, "love without fever, tumult or folly, a peaceful and enchanting affection" such as one might have for a close sibling. It is the kind of love that sneaks up unnoticed; storgic lovers remember no special point when they fell in love. Since storgic lovers consider sex one of the most intimate forms of self-disclosure, sex occurs late in the relationship.

Storge is rarely the stuff of dramatic plays or romantic novels, except perhaps as a backdrop or point of comparison. In *Of Human Bondage*, the hero, Philip, follows a manic love affair with Mildred with a storgic marriage to Sally, whom he has known all along.

Storge superficially resembles ludus in its lack of great passion, but the origins of the two types are quite different. The ludic lover avoids intensity of feeling, consciously aware of its risks. The storgic lover is unaware of intense feeling. It simply doesn't occur to him that a lover should be dewy-eyed and sentimental about a beloved. Such behavior is as out of place in storgic love as it would be for most of us in relating to a close friend. Storgic love "just comes naturally" with the passage of time and the enjoyment of shared activities. You grow accustomed to her face.

In most modern cities people do not live near each other long enough to develop the unself-conscious affection that is typical of storgic love. I found some such cases among people who grew up in rural areas. However, among my urban respondents, who usually had few lasting contacts with their childhood friends, there were some storgic types who based their love on friendship and companionship. This characteristic distinguishes storge from other types of love, in which the partners may not treat each other at all like friends.

When a storgic lover gets involved with another type of lover, serious misunderstandings are likely to occur. The goals of storge, for instance, are marriage, home and children, avoiding all the silly conflicts and entanglements of passion. But to the erotic or ludic lover, storge is a bore. Storge implies a life that is reasonable and predictable; why make it more complicated by engaging in emotionally exhausting types of love? Erotic lovers would never understand that question.

The Strengths of Storge

Storge is a slow-burning love, rarely hectic or urgent, though of course storgic lovers may disagree and fight. But they build up a reservoir of stability that will see them through difficulties that would kill a ludic relationship and greatly strain an erotic one. The physical absence of the beloved, for instance, is much less distressing to them than to other lovers; they can survive long separations (Ulysses and Penelope are a classic example of that ability).

Even if a break-up occurs, storgic lovers are likely to remain good friends. A typical storgic lover would find it inconceivable that two people who had once loved each other could become enemies, simply because they had ceased to be lovers.

In a ludic or erotic relationship, something is happening all the time. In eros, there is always some secret to share, a misunderstanding to mend, a separation to survive with letters and poems. In ludus, inactivity quickly leads to boredom, and a search for new amusement. In storge, there are fewer campaigns to fight and fewer wounds to heal. There is a lack of ecstasy, but also a lack of despair.

Eros, ludus and storge are the three primary types of love, but few love affairs, and few colors, are pure examples of one type. Most reds have a little yellow or blue in them, and most cases of eros have a little storge or ludus.

The color analogy led me to distinguish mixtures from blends (compounds). You can mix two colors and be aware of both components. But it may happen that two primary colors are so evenly blended that an entirely new color emerges, unclassifiable as a hue of either, with unique properties. This is the case with mania, a fourth color of love.

MANIA

The Greeks called it *theia mania*, the madness from the gods. Both Sappho and Plato, along with legions of sufferers, recorded its symptoms: agitation, sleeplessness, fever, loss of appetite, heartache. The manic lover is consumed by thoughts of the beloved. The slightest lack of enthusiasm from the partner brings anxiety and pain; each tiny sign of warmth brings instant relief, but no lasting satisfaction. The manic lover's need for attention and affection from the beloved is insatiable. Cases of mania abound in literature, for its components—furious jealousy, helpless obsession, and tragic endings—are the stuff of human conflict. Goethe made his own unhappy bout with mania the subject of his novel, *The Sorrows of Young Werther*, and Somerset Maugham did the same in *Of Human Bondage*. The manic lover alternates between peaks of ecstasy when he feels loved in return, and depths of despair when the beloved is absent. He knows his possessiveness and jealousy are self-defeating, but he can't help himself.

From God's Curse to Popular Passion

Rational lovers throughout the ages, from Lucretius to Denis de Rougemont, have warned us to avoid mania like the plague. Fashions in love, of course, change. To the ancient Greeks, a person who fell head-over-heels, "madly" in love, had obviously been cursed by the gods. Many parents in the Middle Ages strongly disapproved of love matches, preferring their children to arrange "sensible marriages." But mania has gained popularity in the West since the 13th century; today many young people would consider it wrong to marry unless they loved "romantically."

So popular is mania in literature and love that I originally assumed it would be a primary type. But green, a color that occurs in nature more than any other, is not a primary, but a blend of yellow and blue. Similarly, the data from my interviews refused to reduce mania to one clear type. Instead, manic respondents derive their unique style of love from the primaries of eros and ludus.

These yearning, obsessed, often unhappy manic lovers are typical of frustrated eros. With eros, they share the same intensity of feeling, the same urgency to find the ideal beloved. But erotic lovers are not crushed by disappointment as manic lovers are; they keep their self-respect. Manic lovers, by contrast, are self-effacing, ambivalent, lacking in confidence. They don't have a clear idea of what they are looking for, as erotic lovers do, and they feel helpless, out of control of their emotions. "I know it was crazy, but I couldn't help myself," was a favorite explanation.

Oddly, manic lovers persist in falling in love with people they say they don't even like. "I hate and I love," wailed the Roman poet Catullus. "And if you ask me how, I do not know. I only feel it, and I'm torn in two." Aldous Huxley's hero in *Point Counterpoint* "wanted her against all reason, against all his ideals and principles, madly, against his wishes . . . for he didn't like Lucy, he really hated her."

For these reasons, some psychologists consider mania to be neurotic, unhealthy. Freud was most critical of obsessive love, and Theodor Reik, in *Of*

Love and Lust, explains the obsessiveness of mania as a search for the qualities in a partner that the lover feels lacking in himself. The typical manic lover in my samples seemed to feel, as the song suggests, that he was nobody until somebody loved him.

Pardoxically, manic lovers also behave in ways similar to ludus. They try to hold back to manipulate the lover, to play it cool. But unlike successful ludic types, manic lovers never quite succeed at detachment. Their sense of timing is off. They try to be noncommittal, only to panic and surrender in ignominious defeat.

The Telephone Trauma

Consider this typical caper. The manic realizes that he has been taking the initiative too often in calling his beloved, so he asks her to call the next time. This is a consciously ludic ploy, since no erotic or storgic lover would keep count or care. But it is part of the game in ludus to keep things in balance.

The hour of the expected call arrives, and the phone sits silent. The true ludic lover would not be terribly bothered; he or she would quickly make a few calls and get busy with other lovers. The manic lover falls into a frenzy of anxiety. Either he breaks down and calls the lover, or he is in such a state of emotional upset that he is incapable of ludic detachment when the lover does call: "Where were you? I was so *worried!*"

Manic lovers, in short, attempt to play by the rules of ludus with the passion of eros, and fail at both. They need to be loved so much that they do not let the relationship take its own course. They push things, and thereby tend to lose; mania rarely ends happily. Few lovers go to such extremes as violence or suicide, but most remain troubled by the experience for months, even years. Like malaria, it may return to seize the manic lover with bouts of nostalgia and unrest.

It is theoretically possible for mania to develop into lasting love, but the manic lover must find an unusual partner—one who can ride out the storms of emotion, return the intensity of feeling, and ultimately convince the manic lover that he or she is lovable. A ludic partner will never tolerate the emotional extremes, and a storgic lover will be unable to reciprocate the feelings. A strong-willed erotic partner might manage it.

Ludic Eros

Mania can be reduced by resolving the underlying conditions that create and sustain the lover's lack of self-esteem and his desperate need to be in love. Then the lover may move toward a more confident eros or, perhaps, a more playful ludus. This is the part of the color chart labeled *ludic eros,* the sector between the two primaries.

What enables one lover to mix ludus and eros in a pleasant compromise, while another finds them compounded into mania? Having previous experience in love and many good relationships is one factor. The manic lovers in my sample were discontented with life, but ludic-erotic lovers were basically content and knew what kind of partners they wanted. Ludic-erotic people resemble ludus in their pluralism, their desire for many relationships, but they resemble eros in their preference for clearly-defined types. They do not easily accept substitutes, as ludic types do.

Ludic-erotic love walks an exacting tightrope between intensity and detachment. Most people think this approach is too greedy, and therefore immoral. To the ludic-erotic lover, it is just good sense.

The Art of Passionate Caution

The tight-rope isn't always easy. The lover may spend an evening in the most intense intimacy with his partner, but will always back off in a ludic direction at critical moments. Just when you, the beloved, are about to react to his passion with a murmur of confimation, he leaps from the couch to make a cup of coffee. Or just when he is about to blurt out that he loves you, he bites his lips and says something less committal: "You really turn me on."

The successful combination of ludus and eros is rare, but it exists. The journals of Casanova are a classic example of the bittersweet taste of this type of love. Today many attempts at "open marriages" are in fact advocating a ludic-erotic approach to love: the spouses remain primarily involved with each other, yet may have intense involvements with others so long as these remain temporary.

PRAGMA

Pragma is love with a shopping list, a love that seeks compatibility on practical criteria. In traditional societies, marriages were arranged on similarities of race, social class, income, and so on. In modern society the pragmatic approach to love argues that lovers should choose each other on the basis of compatible personalities, like interests and education, similar backgrounds and religious views, and the like. Computer-match services take a pragmatic view.

The pragmatic lover uses social activities and programs as a means to an end, and will drop them if there is no payoff in partners. By contrast, a storgic lover goes out for the activities he enjoys, and thereby meets someone who shares those interests. The storgic lover never consciously chooses a partner.

Pragma is not a primary type of love but a compound of storge and ludus. The pragmatic lover chooses a partner as if she had grown up with him (storge) and will use conscious manipulation to find one (ludus). Pragma is rather like manufactured storge, a faster means of achieving the time-honored version. If a relationship does not work out, the pragmatic lover will move rationally on, ludic-fashion, to search for another.

The pragmatic approach is not as cold as it seems. Once a sensible choice is made, more intense feelings may develop; but one must begin with a solid match that is practically based. Oriental match-makers noted that in romantic love "the kettle is boiling when the young couple first starts out"—and cools with time, bringing disappointment. An arranged marriage, they say, is like a kettle that starts cold and slowly warms up. Pragmatic love grows over the years.

As pragma is the compound, so storge and ludus may combine as a mixture. The distinguishing features of a *storgic-ludic* affair are convenience and discretion. A typical example is that of a married boss and his secretary, in which the relationship is carefully managed so as to disrupt neither the boss's marriage nor the office routine. Of course, such affairs don't always stay in neat storgic-ludic boxes. In the film, *A Touch of Class*, the affair becomes too intense, threatening to interfere with the man's comfortably companionate marriage.

AGAPE

Agape (pronounced ah-ga-pay) is the classical Christian view of love: altruistic, universalistic love that is always kind and patient, never jealous, never demanding reciprocity. When St. Paul wrote to the Corinthians that love is a duty to care about others, whether the love is deserved or not, and that love must be deeply compassionate and utterly altuistic, he used the Greek word, *agape*. But all the great religions share this concept of love, a generous, unselfish, giving of oneself.

I found no saints in my sample. I have yet to interview an unqualified example of agape, although a few respondents had had brief agapic episodes in relationships that were otherwise tinged with selfishness. For instance, one of my subjects, seeing that his lover was torn between choosing him or another man, resolved to save her pain of deciding; he bowed out gracefully. His action fell short of pure agape, however, because he continued to be interested in how well his beloved was doing, and was purely and selfishly delighted when she dropped the other man and returned to him.

Yet my initial sample of 112 people did contain eight case histories that came quite close to the sexual restraint, dutiful self-sacrifice, universality and altruism that characterize agape. These respondents mixed storge and eros; they had an almost religious attitude toward loving, but they fell short of the hypothetical ideal in loving the partner more than anyone else. They felt intense emotion, as erotic lovers do, along with the enduring patience and abiding affection of storge.

Storgic-erotic respondents felt an initial attraction to their partners, distinguishable from erotic attraction by the absence of physical symptoms of excitement. And unlike eros, these people felt little or no jealousy; they seemed to find enough pleasure in the act of loving another person so that the matter of reciprocity was almost irrelevant.

TESTING ONE'S TYPE OF LOVE

Why construct a typology of love in the first place? Love is a delicate butterfly, runs a certain sentiment, that can be ruined with clumsy dissection. Who cares how many species it comes in; let it fly.

As far as I am concerned, any analysis that helps reduce misunderstandings is worthwhile, and there is no human endeavor more ripe for misunderstandings than love. Consider. A person who has just fallen in love is often tempted to test his sensations to prove it's "really" love. Usually such tests are based on a unidimensional concept of love, and therefore they are usually 180° wrong.

For example, the decision to test love by pstponing sex would be disastrous for an erotic love affair, the equivalent of depriving a baby of food for a week to see if it is strong enough to live. A budding erotic love thrives on sexual intimacy. But delaying sex would be absolutely natural and right for a storgic lover, and it might be a positive incentive to a manic lover.

The advantage of my typology, preliminary as it is, is that it teases apart some very different definitions of love, and suggests which types of love are most compatible. Generally, the farther apart two types are on the color chart, the less likely that the lovers share a common language of love. One of my ludic respondents berated his storgic lover for trying to trap him into a commitment, while she accused him of playing games just to get her body. Different types, different languages. Eros insists on rapid intimacy, storge resents being rushed. Same feelings of "love," but opposite ways to express it.

Obviously, two lovers who represent unlike primaries will have trouble getting along unless they both bend toward a mixture or compromise. But it all depends on what each individual wants out of a relationship. Two storgic lovers have the best chance for a lasting relationship, and two ludic lovers have the worst chance—but they will have fun while it lasts.

The questionnaire at the end of this article will help you identify which of the primary types is most characteristic of you. It is only a general guide, and most useful to see how well matched in attitudes you and your lover arc—which items you agree on, and on which you have serious disagreement. For a more precise way to locate yourself on the color chart, take the test on page 146–47. It lists 35 characteristics and the likelihood of their presence in eight types of love.

Remember to look for overall patterns in your experience. One swallow does not a summer make, and neither does one manic binge confirm you as an obsessive lover. One playful affair in a storgic marriage does not define you as ludus. While some people have enjoyed a variety of love experiences equally, most of us definitely prefer one type. We live with other kinds, as we live with many colors, but we still have our favorites.

The Method of Measuring Love

Literature helped me delimit the scope and varieties of love over the centuries. I began my research by collecting over 4,000 statements about love from hundreds of works of fiction and nonfiction, including Plato and the Bible, Doris Lessing and D. H. Lawrence, romantic Lord Byron and cynical La Rochefoucauld. I recorded each statement on a separate card, and then cross-classified them on topics such as jealousy, altruism, physical beauty.

Some preliminary clusters of ideas about love began to emerge. Some authors, such as St. Paul and Erich Fromm, spoke of love as a universal alturistic quality rather than as an attraction to one person. Others, such as Andreas Capellanus, were sure that true love includes jealousy and possessiveness. Out of the thousands of statements, I discovered six hypothetical types of love to test: love of beauty (eros), obsessive love (mania), playful love (ludus), companionate love (storge), altruistic love (agape), and realistic love (pragma).

A panel of professionals in literature, psychology, sociology and philosophy sorted through an edited number of the cards to select those that would best distinguish these types of love. I gave the resulting questionnaire of 30 statements to a variety of people, and found that they would agree with the most contradictory ideas in love. Almost half of this pretest group, for example, agreed that *Two people can love each other truly, even when they know they have only a short time before they must part, never to meet again*, and also with *The test of time is the only sure way to know if love is real*. Some explained: "It depends on which kind of love."

Since the questionnaire asked only about a respondent's general attitude toward love, I constructed a method that would identify actual experiences in love. This was the love story card sort, in which a lover tells me, in an organized and precoded manner, what happened when he or she was in a relationship defined as love.

The card sort consists of 170 sets of questions, each dealing with steps in the love affair; the questions were the same for men and women except for appropriate pronouns. Each set consists of a green card with a question or incomplete sentence, followed by white cards that represent the range of answers ("other" is included). The respondent simply selects the white card that is his or her answer. For example, one green card asks the resondent for his reaction to the beloved on their first meeting. The answers range from "something seemed to draw us together, like a kind of magnetism" to "I ignored her for a while and we got together casually" to "I rather disliked her."

The questions cover a wide range of events in a person's life and in the love relationship. They begin with recollections of childhood, and move to feelings about work, family, close friends, self-esteem, and life in general at the start of the love affair. The card sort probes what one's expectations of love were like; the ideal lover, if any; how the lovers met; the respondent's thoughts and behavior while away from the lover; sexual intimacy and the nature of the sexual relationship; whether the partners felt jealousy; number and nature of arguments; break-ups and reunions. There is room for variations in love stories: love triangles, homosexuality, serial love affairs, simultaneous ones, and so on.

When I analyzed the individual card selections, three primary approaches to love emerged, which were independent of each other, along with six secondary approaches that were combinations of the primaries. The varied experiences of my respondents broke down to 35 factors that were best able to distinguish the nine types (see chart, page 146–47): for example, memories of childhood, initial frequency of contact, intensity of feeling.

I conducted my pilot study on 112 persons interviewed in four cities: Brighton and London in England, and Toronto and Peterborough in Canada. I simply approached people on the street, told them the purpose of my research, and scheduled an interview with those who agreed. The pilot sample was limited to white heterosexuals under the age of 35, since at the time I did the pilot I wanted only those who had been in love since the World War, an event that significantly changed mores and morals. This was hardly a random sample, but I was more interested in verifying my typology than in determining how many of each type there are. The 112 were approximately matched for age, sex, marital status, and social class.

When I compared the answers to questions according to nationality, sex, social class, and education, few differences emerged. Canadians were slightly more likely than the English to try to "cool off" the beloved's passion. Women were slightly more likely than men to describe their lovers as "holding back" on their emotions, a finding that fits cultural expectations. Younger respondents tended to be slightly more manic than older ones. But the types of love did not vary with education or class. While working-class men reported more sexual difficulties than professional men, they had felt every nuance of passion and imagination that middle-class men did.

Since the pilot study, I have tested the typology on respondents up to age 65, on Americans, and on 60 homosexual males. It remains to study people from other cultures and countries, and non-whites in Western societies. So far, the typology has held up.

Graph Your Own Style of Loving

Consider each characteristic as it applies to a current relationship that you define as love, or to a previous one if that is more applicable. For each, note whether the trait is *almost always* true (AA), *usually true* (U), *rarely true* (R), or *almost never* true (AN).

1 You consider your childhood less happy than the average of peers — R AN U

2 You were discontent with life (work, etc.) at time your encounter began — R AN U R

3 You have never been in love before this relationship — U R AN R

4 You want to be in love or have love as security — R AN AA AN AN U

5 You have a clearly defined ideal image of your desired partner — AA AN AN AN U AN R AA

6 You felt a strong gut attraction to your beloved on the first encounter — AA R AN R AN

7 You are preoccupied with thoughts about the beloved — AA AN AN AA R

8 You believe your partner's interest is at least as great as yours — U R AN R U

9 You are eager to see your beloved almost every day; this was true from the beginning — AA AN R AA R AN R

18 You lose ability to be first to terminate relationship — AN AN AA R U R R

19 You try to force beloved to show more feeling, commitment — AN AN AA AN R

20 You analyze the relationship, weigh it in your mind — AN U R R AA

21 You believe in the sincerity of your partner — AA U R U AA

22 You blame partner for difficulties of your relationship — R U R U R AN

23 You are jealous and possessive but not to the point of angry conflict — U AN R R AN

24 You are jealous to the point of conflict, scenes, threats, etc. — AN AN AN AA R AN AN AN

25 Tactile, sensual contact is very important to you — AA AN AN U AN R

26 Sexual intimacy was achieved early, rapidly in the relationship — AA AN AN U R U

27 You take the quality of sexual rapport as a test of love — AA U AN U AN U R

#		Eros	Ludus	Storge	Mania	Ludic Eros	Storgic Eros	Storgic Ludus	Pragma
28	You are willing to work out sex problems, improve technique	U	R			R	U	R	U
29	You have a continued high rate of sex, tactile contact throughout the relationship	U				R	R	U	R
30	You declare your love first, well ahead of partner				AN	R	AA		AA
31	You consider love life your most important activity, even essential	AA	AN	R	AA		AA	AA	R
32	You are prepared to "give all" for love once under way	U	AN	U		AA		AA	R
33	You are willing to suffer abuse, even ridicule from partner		AN	R	AA			R	AN
34	Your relationship is marked by frequent differences of opinion, anxiety	R	AA	R	AA	R	R		R
35	The relationship ends with lasting bitterness, trauma for you	AN	R	AA	AN	R			R

#		Eros	Ludus	Storge	Mania	Ludic Eros	Storgic Eros	Storgic Ludus	Pragma
10	You soon believed this could become a permanent relationship	AA	AN	R	AN	R	AA	AN	U
11	You see "warning signs" of trouble but ignore them	R	R		AA		AN	R	
12	You deliberately restrain frequency of contact with partner	AN	AA	R	R	R	U		
13	You restrict discussion of your feelings with beloved	R	AA	U	U	R		U	U
14	You restrict display of your feelings with beloved	R	AA	R	U	R		U	U
15	You discuss future plans with beloved	AA	R	R				AN	AA
16	You discuss wide range of topics, experiences with partner	AA	R				U	R	AA
17	You try to control relationship, but feel you've lost control	AN	AN	AN	AA	AN	AN		

To diagnose your style of love, look for patterns across characteristics. If you consider your childhood less happy than that of your friends, were discontent with life when you fell in love, and very much want to be in love, you have "symptoms" that are rarely typical of eros and almost never true of storge, but which do suggest mania. Where a trait did not especially apply to a type of love, the space in that column is blank. Storge, for instance, is not the *presence* of many symptoms of love, but precisely their absence: it is cool, abiding affection rather than *Sturm und Drang*.

THEORIES OF MATE SELECTION*

Bruce K. Eckland

The dissappearance of unilineal kinship systems in Western societies has led to a decline of kinship control over mate selection. The resulting freedom which young people now enjoy has brought about an enormously complex system. No doubt, the selection process actually begins long before the adolescent's first "date." Moreover, under conditions of serial monogamy where it is possible to have many wives but only one at a time, the process for some probably never ends. Determining the "choice" are a myriad of emotional experiences and it is these experiences, along with a variety of subconscious drives and needs, upon which most psychological and other "individualistic" theories are based.

Some of the earliest and perhaps most radical theories of mate selection suggested that what guides a man to choose a woman (it was seldom thought to be the other way around) is instinct. Scholars believed that there must be for each particular man a particular woman who, for reasons involving the survival of the species, corresponded most perfectly with him. A modern rendition of the same idea is Carl Jung's belief that falling in love is being caught by one's "anima." That is, every man inherits an anima which is an "archetypal form" expressing a particular female image he carries within his genes. When the right woman comes along, the one who corresponds to the archetype, he instantly is "seized." However, no one, as far as we know, has actually discovered any pure biologically determined tendencies to assortative mating. . . .

A psychoanalytic view, based on the Oedipus configuration, has been that in terms of temperament and physical appearance one's ideal mate is a parent substitute. The boy, thus, seeks someone like his mother and the girl seeks someone like her father. While it admittedly would seem reasonable to expect parent images to either encourage or discourage a person marrying someone like his parent, no clear evidence has been produced to support the hypothesis. Sometimes striking resemblances between a man's wife and his mother, or a woman's husband and her father, have been noted. Apparently, however, these are only "accidents," occurring hardly more frequently than expected by change. . . .

Another generally unproven assumption, at least with respect to any well-known personality traits, involves the notion that "likes attract." Cattell and Nesselroade recently found significant correlations between husband and wife on a number of personality traits among both stably and unstably married cou-

---

*Eckland, Bruce K. 1968. Theories of Mate Selection. Social Biology 15:71–84.

ples.[1] The correlations, moreover, were substantially higher (and more often in the predicted direction) among the "normal" than among the unstably married couples. As the authors admit, however, it was not possible to determine whether the tendency of these couples to resemble each other was the basis for their initial attraction ("birds of a feather flock together") or whether the correlations were simply an outgrowth of the marital experience. Although the ordering of the variables is not clear, the evidence does tend to suggest that the stability of marriage and, thus the number of progeny of any particular set of parents, may depend to some extent on degrees of likeness. . . .

Probably as old as any other is the notion that "opposites attract"; for example, little men love big women, or a masochistic male desiring punishment seeks out a sadistic female who hungers to give it. Only in the past 20 years has a definitive theory along these lines been formulated and put to empirical test. This is Winch's theory of complementary needs which hypothesizes that each individual seeks that person who will provide him with maximum need gratification. The specific need pattern and personality of each partner will be "complementary."[2] Accordingly, dominant women, for example, would tend to choose submissive men as mates rather than similarly dominant or aggressive ones. The results of a dozen or so investigations, however, are inconclusive, at best. More often than not, researchers have been unable to find a pattern of complementary differences. No less significant than other difficulties inherent in the problem is the discouraging fact that the correlation between what an individual thinks is the personality of his mate and the actual personality of his mate is quite small.[3] Nevertheless, the theory that either mate selection or marital stability involves an exchange of interdependent behaviors resulting from complementary rather than similar needs and personalities is a compelling idea and perhaps deserves more attention.

No firm conclusions can yet be reached about the reasons for similarity (or complementariness) of personality and physical traits in assortative mating. (Even the degree of association or disassociation on most personality characteristics is largely unknown.) To state the "like attracts like" or "opposites attract," we know are oversimplifications. Moreover, few attempts to provide the kinds of explanations we seek have thus far stood up to empirical tests. . . .

In a very general way, social homogamy is a critical point in the integration or continuity of the family and other social institutions. It is a mechanism which serves to maintain the status quo and conserve traditional values and beliefs. And, because marriage itself is such a vital institution, it is not too difficult to understand why so many of the social characteristics which are important variables generally in society, such as race, religion, or class, are also the important variables in mate selection. Thus, most studies in the United States report a very high rate, over 99 percent, for racial endogamy, an overall rate perhaps as high as 90 percent for religious homogamy, and moderately high rates, 50 percent to 80 percent for class homogamy, the exact figures depending on the nature of the index used and the methods employed to calculate the rate.

One possible way of illustrating the conserving or maintenance function of social homogamy in mate selection is to try to visualize momentarily how a contemporary society would operate under conditions of *random* mating. Considering their proportions in the population, Negroes actually would be more likely to marry whites than other Negroes, Catholics more often than not would marry Protestants, and a college graduate would be more apt to marry a high school dropout than to marry another college graduate. In a like manner, about as often as not, dull would marry bright, old would marry young, Democrats would marry Republicans, and teetotalers would marry drinkers. What would be the end result of this kind of social heterogamy? A new melting pot, or chaos?

It seems that, in the absence of "arranged marriages," a variety of controls governs mate selection and, in the process, substantially reduces the availability of certain individuals as potential mates. Many structures in society undoubtedly carry out these functions, sometimes in quite indirect ways, such as the subtle manner in which the promotion of an "organization man" may be based, in part, on how well his mate's characteristics meet the qualifications of a "company wife." Thus, despite the "liberation" of mate selection and the romantic ideals of lovers who are convinced that social differences must not be allowed to stand in their way, probably one of the most important functions of both the elaborate "rating and dating" complex and the ceremonial "engagement" is to allow a society to make apparent who may "marry upward" and under what conditions exogamy is permitted. We are referring here, then, not merely to society's control over the orderly replacement of personnel, but to its integration and the transmission of culture as well.

Rather than reviewing any very well-formulated theories (since there may be none) in the remaining discussion, I have attempted to touch upon a fairly broad range of conditions under which homogamy, as a social fact, relates to other aspects of contemporary societies. . . .

Whether we are speaking about place of residence, school, work, or such abstruse features of human ecology as the bus or streetcar routes along which people travel, propinquity obviously plays a major part in mate selection since, in nearly all cases, it is a precondition for engaging in interaction. (The mail-order bride, for instance, is one of several exceptions.) A person usually "selects" a mate from the group of people he knows. Findings which illustrate the function of distance have been duplicated in dozens of studies. In Columbus, Ohio, it was once found that more than half of the adults who had been married in that city had actually lived within 16 blocks of one another at the time of their first date.[4] Cherished notions about romantic love notwithstanding, the chances are about 50–50 that the "one and only" lives within walking distance.

As many authors have pointed out, people are not distributed through space in a random fashion. In fact, where people live, or work and play, corresponds so closely with one's social class (and race) that it is not quite clear whether propinquity, as a factor in mate selection, is simply a function of class endogamy or, the other way around, class endogamy is a function of propinquity. Ramsey's recent attempt to resolve this issue, I want to note, misses the mark almost completely.[5] Investigating over 5000 couples living in Oslo, Norway, she concludes that propinquity and social homogamy are "totally independent of one another" and, therefore, rejects the long-standing argument that "residential segregation of socioeconomic and cultural groups in cities represents a kind of structural underpinning both to propinquity in mate selection and to homogamy." More specifically, the author shows that "couples who lived very near one another before marriage were no more likely to be of the same occupational status than couples who lived at opposite sides of the city." This is astonishing, but misleading. The author equated the social status of the bride and, implicitly, her social class origin with *her* occupation at the time of marriage. No socioeconomic index other than the bride's occupation unfortunately was known to the investigator and, thus, it was a convenient although poorly considered jump to make. To most sociologists, it should be a great surprise to find in any Western society, including Norway, that the occupations young women hold before marriage give a very clear indication of their social status, relative either to the occupational status of men they marry or to their own places of residence. . . .

An explanation often cited in the literature on mate selection, as well as in that on the more general topic of interpersonal attraction, deals in one form or another with the principle of exchange. A Marxian view, marriage is an exchange involving both the assets and liabilities which each partner brings to the relationship. Thus, a college-educated woman seldom brings any special earning power to the marriage, but rather she typically enters into contract with a male college graduate for whom her diploma is a social asset which may benefit his own career and possibly those of his children. In exchange, he offers her, with a fair degree of confidence, middle-class respectability. Norms of reciprocity might also help to explain the finding that most borderline mentally retarded women successfully marry and even, in some cases marry upward, if they are physically attractive. This particular theory, however, has not been well-developed in regard to mate selection, despite its repeated usage. Also, it may be a more appropriate explanation of deviations from assortative mating or instances of negative mate selection than of positive selection. . . .

In contrast to the inconclusive evidence regarding assortative mating in terms of personality characteristics, numerous studies do indicate that married couples (and engaged couples) show far more consensus on various matters than do randomly matched couples. Even on some rather generalized values, as in the area of aesthetics or economics, social homogamy occurs. Apparently, our perception that other persons share with us the same or similar value orientations and beliefs facilitates considerably our attraction to them.[6]

The importance of norms and values in mate selection, part of the social fabric of every society, also can be illustrated in a more direct way by looking at some of the specific sanctions that we pass along from generation to generation. Without really asking why, children quite routinely are brought up to believe that gentlemen prefer blondes (which may be only a myth perpetuated by the cosmetic industry), that girls should marry someone older rather than younger than themselves (which leaves most of them widows later on), and that a man should be at least a little taller than the woman whom he marries (which places the conspicuously tall girl at an enormous disadvantage). Simply folkways as such beliefs presently are, they nevertheless influence in predictable ways, the "choice" of many individuals....

We have already noted that the field of eligible mates is largely confined to the same social stratum to which an individual's family of orientation belongs. Social-class endogamy not only plays a significant part in the process of mate selection, it may also help to explain other forms of assortative mating. For example, part of the reason why marriage partners or engaged couples share many of the same values and beliefs no doubt is because they come from the same social backgrounds.

There are at least five explanations which can be offered for the persistence of class endogamy, each of which sounds reasonable enough and probably has a hold on some part of the truth.

First, simply to turn the next to last statement around, persons from the same class tend to marry *because* they share the same values (which reflect class differences) and not because they are otherwise aware or especially concerned about each other's background.

Second, during the period of dating and courtship most young people reside at the home of their parents. (Excluded here, of course, are the large minority in residential colleges and those who have left both school and home to take an apartment near their place of work.) The location of parental homes reflects the socioeconomic status of the family and is the general basis for residential segregation. With respect to both within and between communities, the pattern of segregation places potential mates with different backgrounds at greater distances than those with similar backgrounds. Thus, to the extent that the function of distance (or propinquity) limits the field of eligibles, it also encourages class endogamy by restricting class exogamy.

Third, class endogamy in some cases is simply a function of the interlocking nature of class and ethnicity. A middle-class Negro, for example, probably is prevented from an exogamous marriage with a member of the upper-class not so much because class barriers block it but because he (or she) is a Negro. The majority of the eligible mates in the class above are whites and, in this instance, what appears to be class endogamy is really racial endogamy.

Fourth, ascriptive norms of the family exert a great deal of pressure on persons, especially in the higher strata, to marry someone of their "own kind," meaning the same social level. The pressures that parents exert in this regard sometimes are thought to have more than anything else to do with the process and certainly are visible at nearly every point at which young people come into meaningful contact with one another. Norms of kinship regarding the future status of a child may be involved, for example, in the parent's move to the right community, sending a child to a prep school, or seeing that he gets into the proper college.

Fifth, and an increasingly convincing argument, even as the structure of opportunities for social mobility open through direct competition within the educational system, class endogamy persists owing to the education advantages (or disadvantages) accrued from one's family of orientation. Most colleges, whether commuter or residential, are matrimonial agencies. As suggested earlier, despite whatever else a woman may gain from her (or, more often her parents') investment in higher education, the most important thing she can get out of college is the proper husband or at least the credentials that would increase her bargaining power in an exchange later on. Given the fact that men generally confer their status (whether achieved or ascribed) upon women and not the other way around (female proclamations to the contrary notwithstanding), marriage as a product of higher education has far more functional value for women than vocational or other more intrinsic rewards.

To carry this argument a bit further, access to college depends in large measure on the academic aptitude (or intelligence) of the applicants. Moreover, the hierarchical ordering of colleges which is based on this selectivity has led to a system of higher education which, in many ways, replicates the essential elements of the class structure. Differentiating those who go to college from those who do not, as well as where one goes to college, are *both* aptitude and social class. These two variables correspond so closely that despite the most stringent policies at some universities where academic aptitude and performance are the central criteria for admissions and where economic aid is no longer a major factor, students still come predominantly from the higher socioeconomic classes. For whatever the reason, genetic and environmental, this correspondence facilitates the intermarriage of individuals with similar social backgrounds, especially on American campuses where the sex ratio has been declining. It is interesting to note in this context that Warren's recent study of a representative sample of adults showed that roughly half of the similarity in class backgrounds of mates was due to assortative mating by education. . . .[7]

While intermarriage is both a cause and consequence in the assimilation of the descendants of different ethnic origin, various writers claim that the American "melting pot" has failed to materialize. Religious and racial lines in particular are far from being obliterated. In fact, the very low frequency of exogamous marriages across these lines itself underscores the strength of the cleavages. Most authors also agree that nationality is not as binding as either race or religion as a factor in mate selection. Nation-type solidarities are still found among some urban groups (Italians and Poles) and rural groups (Swedes and Finns), but our public school system and open class structure have softened considerably what were once rather rigid boundaries. There is some evidence, too, that religious cleavages have been softening somewhat, and perhaps are continuing to soften as the functions of this institution become increasingly secular and social-problem oriented. On the other hand, racial boundaries, from the view of mate selection, appear to be as binding today as at any previous point in history; at least I have found no evidence to the contrary. The gains that Negroes have made in the schools and at the polls during the past ten years apparently have not softened the color line with respect to intermarrige.

Explanations of racial endogamy in America, some of which would take us back several centuries in time, are too varied to discuss here. It might be well to point out, however, that cultural and even legal prohibitions probably have relatively little to do with the present low rate of interracial marriage. As one author has stated, "the whole structure of social relationships between white and Negroes in the United States has been organized in such a way as to prevent whites and Negroes from meeting, especially under circumstances which would lead to identifying each other as eligible partners. . . . Under these circumstances, the few interracial marriages which do occur are the ones which need explaining.[8]

For the population geneticist, too, it would seem that the deviant cases are the ones which require attention. Elsewhere I have suggested, for example, that genes associated with intelligence may simply drift across the white and Negro populations since it appears that only certain morphological features, like skin color, actually operate to maintain the color line. In other words, if the skin of an individual with Negro ancestry is sufficiently light, he may "pass" (with no strings attached) into the white population. Even just a lighter-than-average complexion "for a Negro" probably enhances his chances of consummating what we socially define as an "interracial" marriage. In neither the first or second case, however, is intelligence necessarily involved.

If intelligence *were* associated in any predictable way with racial exogamy, the drift would not be random and we would then have a number of interesting questions to raise. For instance, do only the lighter *and* brighter pass, and, if so, what effect, if any, would this be likely to have on the character of the Negro gene pool? What, too, is the character of the inflow of genes from the white population? We do know that the great majority of legally consummated interracial marriages involved Negro men and women. Does this information provide any clues? And, what about the illegitimate progeny of white males and Negro prostitutes? How often are they placed for adoption in white households and with what consequences? Before taking any of these questions too seriously, we would want to have many more facts. For obvious reasons, our knowledge is extremely meager. . . .

In conclusion, five brief comments may be made upon the present state of research and theories of mate selection as revealed in the foregoing discussion.

First, there is a great deal of evidence of homogamous or assortative mating but relatively few theories to explain it and no satisfactory way of classifying its many forms.

Second, nearly all facts and theories regarding mate selection deal with engaged or married couples and hardly any attention has been given to illegitimacy (including adultery) and its relationship to assortative mating. It may be, such as in the case of miscegenation, that some of the most important aspects of mate selection occur outside the bonds of matrimony.

Third, our heavy emphasis upon courtship and marriage has obscured the fact that people often separate, divorce, and remarry. Mate selection may be a more or less continuous process for some individuals, affecting the character of the progeny of each new set of partners.

Fouth, the relationships between fertility and assortative mating still must be specified. Are there, for example, any patterns of assortative mating on certain traits, like education, which affect the number of children a couple will have?

Fifth, most of the factors in mate selection appear to covary. We discussed some of the more obvious problems in this regard, such as the relationship between residential segregation (propinquity) and class endogamy. It would appear that much more work of this sort will need to be done.

In regard to the last point, it would also appear that it is precisely here that social scientists, and sociologists in particular, may best serve the needs of population geneticists. Through the application of causal (chair) models and multivariate techniques, it may eventually be possible to sort out the relevant from the irrelevant and to specify in fairly precise terms not only the distribution of assortative mating in the social structure with regard to any particular trait, but also the ordering of variables and processes which restrict the field of eligibles.

References

1. R. Cattell, and J. Nesselroade. " 'Likeness' and 'Completeness' Theories Examined by 16 Personality Factor Measures on Stably and Unstably Married Couples" (Advanced Publication No. 7.) The Laboratory of Personality and Group Analysis, University of Illinois, 1967.
2. R. Winch, *Mate Selection* (New York: Harper and Row, 1958).
3. J. Udry, *The Social Context of Marriage* (Philadephia: J. P. Lippincott, 1966).
4. A. C. Clarke, "An Examination of the Operation of Residential Propinquity as a Factor in Mate Selection" *American Sociological Review*, VXII (1952), 17–22.
5. N. R. Ramsey, "Assortative Mating and the Structure of Cities" *American Sociological Review*, LI (1966), 773–86.
6. E. W. Burgess, and P. Wallin, "Homogamy in Social Characteristics" *American Journal of Sociology*, IL (1943), 109–24.
7. B. L. Warren, "A Multiple Variable Approach to the Assortative Mating Phenomenon" *Eugenics Quarterly*, XIII (1966), 285–90.
8. Udry, *op. cit.*

IS THERE A BEST AGE TO MARRY?:
AN INTERPRETATION*

Marcia E. Lasswell

INTRODUCTION

Since so many thoughtful persons today are asking "Why marry at all?" it may seem insignificant to them to ponder the question of whether there is a best time in life to get married. However, as with so many current challenges to the basic institutions of our lives such as religion and education, a closer look reveals that while many are questioning the necessity for these institutions, most of us still choose to go along with the major tenets, tailoring them to our needs. Our immediate concerns, then, are not whether to go to school or whether or not religion will have any influence in our lives, but instead, how and what the nature of the effects will be. This appears to be true of marriage as well since there is no indication that Americans are marrying any less than they ever have nor does it appear that the future spells the death of marriage.

In spite of what we read about new attitudes toward marriage, and there certainly are new attitudes, most men and women still marry at least once. Marriage is so popular that six out of seven who are divorced remarry. The greater part of those marrying still seem to have high hopes that this marriage, whether it is the first or fourth, will last. Sometimes, it is a shock to very young couples to realize that if they marry at age 22 or 23, and most do, and if they live the average life span to 72 or 73, they are signing up for 50 years. This is a lot of permanence, sometimes based only on very slender threads of romanticism and sexual attraction. It makes George Bernard Shaw's description of the wedding vows have a bitter ring of truth: "When two people are under the influence of the most violent, most insane, most delusive and most transient of passions, they are required to swear solemnly they will remain in that excited, abnormal, and exhausting condition continually until death do them part." It seems like quite an order and yet not many are discouraged.

Ultimately, nearly everyone marries at least once—a figure that comes close to 95 percent of all men and women in the United States who are marriageable. Some are not considered possible marriage partners due to severe mental retardation or incurable mental illness but nearly everyone else is counted in the pool of potential marrieds, even including some with serious disabilities of a physical nature and persons sentenced to prison for life.

*From Marcia E. Lasswell, "Is There a Best Age to Marry?: An Interpretation," *The Family Coordinator* 23, no. 3 (July 1974): 237–242. Copyright by National Council on Family Relations. Reprinted by permission.

MOST POPULAR AGE TO MARRY

One way of investigating the question concerning the best age to marry is to determine what most people actually do. The norm is not necessarily an indication of what is good, but if most people behave in a characteristic way, there may be reasons that are functional behind the behavior.

Recently, the age at first marriage seems to be going up; and in 1971, the largest number of persons under 35 years of age remained single since the turn of the century.[1] The United States had a trend from 1900 to 1960 toward very early marriage both for men and for women. In 1900, for instance, men married for the first time on the average at 25 years and nine months and women were an average age at first marriage of 21 years and nine months. This rate went down very slowly from the turn of the century until 1940 but there was a quick decline in the next ten years to 1950. In fact, the age at first marriage went down as much in those ten years as it did in the previous 40 years.

Speculation has been that the World War I years stimulated those early marriages since many couples hurried to be married before the young man was sent off to battle. It was a time of economic plenty in this country also, enabling young people to support themselves, and this always has been an encouragement to marriage. No such dramatic drop was noticed during World War I, however, so other explanations are needed to account for the rapid decline of the 1940's. It most likely was due, in large part at least, to the length of our involvement in the war endeavor during World War II over World War I and also to the fact that urbanization had taken hold during the 1940's in contrast to the more agricultural nature of the United States from 1910 to 1920. One factor which may have been very influential during the decade of 1910 to 1920 in keeping the age of marriage from dipping was that these were the years of the Suffragettes, and on June 4, 1919, women won the right to vote. Women had new-found freedom, and when the war came along evidently many did not choose to trade that freedom in for marriage.

From 1950 to 1962, the average age at first marriage for women stayed fairly stable at two to three months past the twentieth birthday. For males, it continued to go down until 1959 when it reached an all-time low of 22 years, five months. Since 1960 for men and since 1962 for women, there has been a slow upward trend. In 1972 the average age at first marriage for men was 23 years and three months, the highest since 1948, and for women the average was 20 years and nine months, the highest since 1940. In spite of the trend upward, there are still well over two million women under this age who are married, and nearly as many men under 23 who are. Obviously, most Americans not only marry, but also marry young.

The statistics point to another very interesting fact about the popular age to marry, and that is that there is a very narrow range of years during which most people marry for the first time. It is somewhat broader for men than it is for women. Most men who marry do so between the ages of 20.3 and 26.2 and most of the women are between the ages of 19.0 and 23.4. The years following graduation from high school and college seem to be the favorite years for marrying. The 1970 statistics indicated that by the time men reach the upper limit of this range, nearly 40 million of them are married and nearly as many women are married when they reach the age of 23.4.[2]

In spite of the early marriage picture in the United States generally, there is another interesting trend which needs attention. This trend points to a change in the popular age to marry. Since 1960, the percentage of single men and women under the age of 35 has been increasing. The number has grown by five percent in the past thirteen years for men and the proportion of single women under 35 has increased by seven percent. In 1973, 55 percent of men under 35 were single and 45 percent of the women were single.

What may be even more significant is that the percentage of women marrying between the ages of nineteen and 23.4, when half of those who marry do so, dropped considerably between 1960 and 1972 for each age. For men between 20.3 and 26.2, when half of the men marry, the decline was much less. For instance, for 21-year-old women, marriages declined in the twelve-year period by ten percent, but for 21-year-old men, the drop was only five percent. For 22-year-old women the rate went down by eleven percent compared to seven percent for men. Both 25- and 26-year-old men showed an increase of marriage by one percent during this time period, while women do not show an increase until they are 29.

What these statistics indicate is that currently more young people, particularly women, are delaying first marriage, although just as many as ever will probably marry eventually. Enough are doing this to raise the age at first marriage about one month per year and to account for the six percent average increase in the number of under-35-years-olds who are still single.

There are several factors which are credited with contributing to this situation. They range from attitude changes to social and economic changes. An important factor in the choice to delay marriage is, of course, that many no longer see marriage as the only way to engage in sex. There is no calculating how many young people married in the past in order to make a sexual relationship—whether already in progress or just acutely desired—a legitimate one in the eyes of the partners and society.

Sex before marriage is nothing new historically, although the increased number of women involved and the openness with which it is discussed is new. It used to be that there were two kinds of women—"the ones you had sex with and the ones you married." The data seem to indicate that couples today who have known each other for some time are much more likely to engage in premarital sex than ever before, which accounts in large part for the rise in the number of women involved, while the number of men involved stays relatively the same.[3]

With contraceptive knowledge and increased opportunity for abortion, people no longer have to worry as much about an unwanted pregnancy; "shotgun" weddings are almost a thing of the past. Adding to this, of course, is the increasing number of young women who are keeping the children they bear outside of marriage without feeling that it is necessary for them to marry either for the child's sake or to save their reputation. While it is still not looked upon positively by most of society to have a child out of wedlock, it is certainly not looked upon as negatively as it was even five years ago. In fact, a few celebrities have made a point of having children while unmarried, and no doubt as a result, some young women will begin to believe that this is fashionable.

Other factors involved in delaying marriage, or perhaps causing a decision not to marry at all for some, are the women's liberation movement, which has shown that marriage is not the only socially approved and satisfying life for women; the economic recession, which has made unemployment higher than in recent years; and, to a smaller extent, the Gay Liberation Movement, which is encouraging homosexuals to "come out" openly and, therefore, to resist a heterosexual marriage for the sake of appearances alone.

Another important factor to consider in trying to explain the larger number of singles under 35, particularly single women, is the shift in population which temporarily created an abundance of women of marriageable age following the "baby boom" of the 1950's. This shift created what sociologists have called the "marriage-squeeze." The fertility rates in the United States were understandably low during World War II and then rose to exceedingly high

rates between the years of 1945 and 1957 when they hit a peak. After this they began to go down gradually until 1961 and since then they have continued down at a fast rate until they have leveled off at just over two children per family. The result of the high rates was that those young women who were born in 1945 reached the peak age for marriage of nineteen to 23 in the period of 1964-1968. Because women in this country of this age group typically marry men who are older than they are by an average of two years and four months, this meant that large numbers of young women had no one to marry. They had the choices of marrying men who were younger than they or of waiting until a divorce or a death ended a marriage and so released an eligible man, or of not marrying at all. It seems that they did some of all of these, but for the most part, they delayed marrying.

AGE AT MARRIAGE AS IT RELATES TO SUCCESS

Another way to calculate whether there is a best time to marry is to check the age at first marriage as it relates to the success of the marriage. The two criteria usually employed to measure success are stability and the couple's report of happiness. To be sure, there are serious problems with both of these criteria, but presently the literature affords little research based on any other measures.[4] Based on what is provided by these two measures, it becomes clear that for those who seek a solution to the high divorce rate in this country, the increased age at first marriage is seen as a welcome trend. If there is one unchallenged bit of information we have concerning whether or not a marriage will last, it is that those who are very young when they marry have three strikes against them.

Age itself may not be the critical factor so much as the kinds of problems that go with being young and married in our society—lack of employment opportunities and consequently insufficient financial resources; insufficient experience in coping with problems; disapproval, or at least lack of support, by parents and society; and the fact that so many very young couples have actually been running away from home or from loneliness. In addition, there are still a significant number who marry due to a pregnancy and this obviously can be a major obstacle to marital adjustment.

Getting married in the teen years is unquestionably the worst time to marry, not only in terms of the stability of the marriage, but in terms of the reported satisfaction which the marriage brings to the couple. The divorce rate is correlated with age at marriage and the older the couple is at marriage, the greater likelihood that the marriage will succeed. For men, there is a point of diminishing returns at about age 31 and after age 27 the decline slows down considerably.[5] For women, the divorce rate declines with each year they wait to marry until a gradual leveling off at about age 25. From the standpoint of stability of the marriage, then, men who marry between 27 and 31 and women who marry at about 25 seem to have waited long enough to maximize their chances at a durable relationship. This is more than three years, for both men and women, past the average age at first marriage in the United States currently.

Stability of a marriage relationship may not be the most important factor in a marriage, although it is an easy statistic to keep—either you are married or you are not. However, recent research has made it pretty clear that just staying together for a married lifetime does not necessarily mean that the couple has been happy in the relationship. There have been other studies that have asked married couples how satisfactory their marriage is and their rating has been compared with their age at marriage. The results are not much different from those studying stability. Couples who married in their teen years rate their marriages as significantly less satisfactory than do those who were married later. Women who married at age 28 or even older showed the highest percentage of satisfaction and men who married between 28 and 30 were the most satisfied husbands. Again, it may not be the age itself that is the critical factor but the fact that late marriage is associated with more education, better financial condition, more social and familial approval, and higher social class.

Most of the evidence seems to point to waiting until 25 or 30 to marry for both satisfaction and stability. However, there are some other considerations which merit discussion. An interesting, although perhaps controversial, point which has been made by Allan Fromme in his recent book, *A Woman's Critical Years* is that there is a danger in postponing marriage so long that an adjustment is made to the unmarried state.[5] He feels that a single person's attitude toward the opposite sex is not improved by remaining single. Perhaps there is something to the idea of maturing together as a couple rather than waiting until a style of single life has been solidified beyond being able to adjust to each other in marriage. The statistics seem to be against Fromme's point of view, but it is possible that for some single people giving up a way of life to which they have adjusted is just too much trouble.

One of the problems with seeking a formula for an optimum age to marry is that what may be a good age for one person may be too late or too early for another. There are many varieties of good marriages and the best age to marry is going to depend in large measure upon the style of marriage desired by the couple. Where both desire a career, for instance, there is clear evidence that education is important and a certain amount of freedom is necessary early in the career to move about geographically. Maintaining a home is difficult when both the husband and wife may need to have this freedom. A later marriage which takes place one they are both established may be the only way for such a relationship to work. If they desire to have children also, both need to be well enough established to take time off for child care and to afford household help which is essential in the two-career family.

CONCLUSION

When all of the evidence is in, it appears that women should wait until they are 25 to marry and that they should have their two children at age 28 and age 30. This gives them ample time before they are 35 and it also gives three years after marriage to get the marriage on solid ground emotionally and financially. Men should marry at age 28 and father those two chidren at age 30 and 32. This allows for what still seems to be a popular notion in our society that it is desirable, for whatever reasons this is popular, for the husband to be older. There is much to deny that this works out at the end of the life cycle, however, since women outlive men by several years and consequently the average women is a widow for seven years.

We are a long way from the figures that the evidence supports currently. In 1972, only eleven percent of the men over 29 years old had never been married and eighteen percent of the women. Perhaps not knowing or caring about the optimum time to marry is a part of the reason for the high divorce rate in this country that causes marriages as a whole to last only a little over seven years on the average.

In the United States, the choice of a mate is a relatively free one made by the individual partners and based on their being in love with each other. For many, being in love seems to be enough. There is a romantic notion that if one is in love, everything else will work out. No doubt, this will continue to be important in mate choice and love may not wait for the best time to happen, but if it did, perhaps much of the unhappiness seen a few years later when romanticism has cooled might be avoided.

References

1. United States Department of Commerce, Bureau of the Census, Series P–20, No. 239, September, 1972.
2. *Ibid.*
3. M. Hunt, "Sexual Behavior in the 1970's" *Playboy*, XX (1973), 84–8.
4. M. Hicks, and M. Platt, "Marital Happiness and Stability: A Review of the Research in the Sixties" *Journal of Marriage and the Family*, XXXII (1970), 553–74.
5. United States Department of Commerce, Bureau of the Census, Series P–23, No. 32, July, 1970.
6. A. Fromme, *A Woman's Critical Years* (New York: Grosset and Dunlap, Inc., 1972).

*

4

LEARNINGS

As Section 3 is a time of major decisions, Section 4, "Learnings," is a time for major adjustments and renegotiations. For most it is a rude awakening to move from the romance of courtship to the demands and expectations of life in close physical and emotional intimacy with another person. It is unrealistic to expect to continue life on the intense level of courtship, but there is little in our culture to prepare us for the ordinariness, and at the same time unexpected conflicts, of married life.

That which may have been part of the glamour of courtship may now be dysfunctional for the drama of marriage. Little things loom out of proportion. Love which can survive these tremendous trifles is a different experience than the love which led to marriage. It is tough but resilient, honest but demanding,

165

accepting yet supportive—more than an emotional or physical response to the presence of the beloved. Mature love is being willing to learn what factor of love is needed for what demand of relationship. Those feelings which lead us to the point of commitment may be inappropriate or grossly inadequate for building a life together.

Many couples have not recognized the function of conflict in relationships and often interpret it as indicative of less than the expected perfection in the partner or in the self. For some, conflict may again raise the self-doubts of ego identification and maturity, or lead to similar doubts about the partner. Little preparation has been made for understanding that the fact of conflict is unimportant, that even the why of the conflict may well be irrelevant. Instead, the crucial issue is what to do about inevitable conflict.

The adjustments and renegotiations of the first years of marriage will necessarily cover a wide range of behavior, including the meaning of sexual intercourse. Many a young wife has been both puzzled and affronted by her husband's initiation of sexual play after an evening of conflict. The reverse is the husband's confusion and hurt at his wife's nonresponse. The wife may well see the sex act as a special intimacy that says "I love you because. . ." and therefore it is inappropriate if the conflict is unresolved. For the husband, sex may well be saying "I love you in spite of. . . .," and thus sexual contact can be highly appropriate even when there is no resolution of conflict.

It may be helpful for young marrieds to recognize two levels of existence in their life. One has to do with the conscious adjustments that occur by intention. This level includes establishing a pattern of life together: setting up housekeeping; the purchase of furniture and its arrangement; the evening meal; how often and what activities to share with his friends, her friends, their friends; and the extent and nature of involvement with both sets of in-laws. All of these areas are, in a sense, a surface level of existence, subject to discussion and negotiation. There is a second level of the relationship that may not be recognized or subject to discussion until some near crisis forces its recognition. This is the level of satisfaction and need fulfillment perhaps being inadequately met or even unmet. It then becomes necessary to question the nature of the love itself. Is love the level of commitment that says "I need you because I love you," or is it the more dependent "I love you because I need you"? Indeed, the minimal preparation for marriage we now experience is often limited to the first level issues of conscious intention with little or no attention paid to the deeper level. If deep personal needs are unrecognized and unmet, the level of satisfaction decreases to the point where the expression of that dissatisfaction erupts in all types of tension and conflict—friends, in-laws, money, personal habits, sex. Cultural expectations provide an added dimension to the impact of marriage on men. Women, in a sense, are groomed for marriage and family life from the dolls and miniature housekeeping toys, to the assumption that the daughter will help mother in maintenance of the home. Boys do not prepare to be husbands and fathers but instead prepare for the provider role met by career planning and achievement aspirations.

The one- or two-career family will have different adjustments to make as the couple builds life together. A change of jobs for the one-career family may involve mobility that takes them too far from grandparents. The one-career family in which the woman is employed will have different societal pressure. Negotiations must occur for the two-career family when either has a promotion involving residential mobility. With women becoming increasingly more career oriented, new strains can be placed on the young couple. With men exploring other aspects of job satisfaction besides salary and status, life goals in regard to the level of income and the success syndrome may need to be renegotiated.

One major change in the drama of family life during early marriage has occurred within the last decade. For most, marriage is still a commitment to have children. Widespread usage of the pill has allowed couples greater control over the timing of children, and, in fact, the first child is being delayed to a later age. Only time can tell whether eventual family size will also be smaller. For an increasing number of couples, however, marriage may only be a commitment to each other and exclude having children. Our society is still uneasy about this. Couples opting to have children will find another set of adjustments that must be made: adjustments to the roles as mother and father; life-style changes necessitated by the presence of a baby; financial alterations with increasing costs of children, allocations of time and energy; perceptions by others of themselves as parents.

Reality in the first five years of marriage will include the shock of ordinariness and conflict in the relationship, the impact of tremendous trifles, sexual adjustment, career decisions, parenting choices and adaptation. Married persons who read this book will undoubtedly consider some of these issues irrelevant to their experience. We would suggest that the relative importance of the dramas will differ for couples. However, few couples who have been married five years can deny that the adjustments and renegotiations mentioned here have constituted a fair part of reality for those years.

CONTENTS: SECTION 4

THE HONEYMOON IS OVER*

Frank Cox

A well-known story in American folklore concerns the young couple who find themselves very much in love. He courts her for a year. They are engaged three months. Then they have a storybook wedding and breathlessly look forward to a happy-ever-after marriage. They discuss major problems, such as choice of living area and number of children and resolve most of their differences on these issues before marriage. The first year of marriage goes smoothly but during the second year the couple begins to make certain negative observations about one another. These negative reactions become increasingly serious until they are now causing open conflict between the two. The husband thinks to himself, "She has changed, she is not the girl she was when we first married." The wife silently complains, "But he is so different than he was at first. He used to be so kind and attentive to me. Now he is mad all the time." After one particularly upsetting encounter, one of the partners decides to discuss the problem with an outside third party. Upon meeting this disinterested party, the partner quickly points out what to him is the major problem. Namely, the spouse has changed and is no longer the person he married.

This all too familiar story probably occurs in the majority of American marriages at some time during the early years. Let us call it the "honeymoon is over" period in the modern American marriage.

In order to understand the dynamics of such a relationship it is necessary to know more about typical boy-girl interaction in this country before the marriage. Obviously, there is a great deal of difference between individual dating patterns and the norms. In addition, these patterns evolve and change with time; thus, the reader should be wary of assuming everyone fits the general picture herein described. However, there are certain generalized patterns that emerge upon study, as has been amply demonstrated by such books as *The Natural History of Love*, by Morton Hunt.[1] The couples tending toward an exaggerated "honeymoon is over" period often exhibit certain typical patterns in their pre-marital dating behavior as well as in the first year or two of marriage.

These patterns are chiefly composed of two strong trends. First, these couples tend to be those who lack broad dating experience. They do not "play the field" and limit their dating to a few of the opposite sex, often through the technique of "going steady." When one "goes steady" he essentially dates one person only during the given period of time.

---

*From: Cox, Frank D., *Youth, Marriage and the Seductive Society*, 1974, Dubuque, Iowa, Wm. C. Brown Company Publishers.

169

This tendency to "go steady" combined with a slowly declining average age at marriage* tends to limit drastically the number of meaningful heterosexual relations available to the young person. A study by Schneider indicates that in 75 percent of the cases going steady involves a social commitment to the extent that they report being "in love." Over half have agreed to see each other whenever either of them want to get together. Over 80 percent of the couples have given serious thought to getting married and nearly 40 percent have an informal agreement to marry.[2]

Dating may be thought of as an American social invention and as one of "the most significant new mechanisms of mate selection in many centuries. In place of the church meeting, the formal request to father, and the chaperoned evenings in the family parlor, modern youth meet at parties, make dates on the telephone, and go off in cars to spend their evenings at the movies."[3]

Dating serves numerous purposes. It may be strictly recreation, an end in itself. It also gives one status. Dating aids the socialization process by allowing the sexes to learn about one another. It helps one to learn about one's own personality as well as others. Dating has become the major method of mate-selection in the United States. It enables the young to test out a succession of relationships with persons of the opposite sex. Dating helps one to anticipate marital and adult familial roles.[4]

Limited dating, as in going steady, tends to thwart several of these dating functions, thereby hampering mate selection. Indeed, limited dating experience is one of Burchinal's marital competence and satisfaction predictor variables associated with poor marital risk.[5]

However, going steady yields certain advantages in the eyes of the insecure adolescent. It means that the necessity to compete is reduced, dates for social events are assured, costs may be less, and above all, there is a certain comfortable security about it since one does not risk the possible rejection that might result from interacting with a new individual.

The young adult who engages in "going steady" will, however, also suffer several disadvantages. For one, his field of experience with the opposite sex is reduced. This means that his frame of reference for judging a future spouse may be based on a limited number (perhaps as few as two or three) of meaningful opposite sex relationships.† Secondly, his freedom to grow through having broad experiences with life is now curtailed because of the obligations to his steady. Thus, the period of life that should supply practice in heterosexual relations as well as an invitation to growth through new experience is partly nul-

---

*In 1890 the median age of marriage for men was twenty-six, for women, twenty-two. By 1958, the median ages had dropped to twenty-three for men, and twenty for women. In 1972, the median age of marriage was still about the same as in 1958.

†Even as long ago as 1946, the number of meaningful heterosexual relations was narrow. A survey of Navy men, including those to twenty-five years of age, found that on the average they had dated only seven different girls.

lified by "going steady." Hunt, in his fine book on the history of love supports this view when he states:

> All too soon, they become anxious to "go steady," and tend to do so earlier and more fixedly than used to be the case. Going steady is evidently reassuring in that it signifies they have been accepted by someone; unfortunately it reduces the utility of the dating pattern itself, since it limits the chances for the wider testing of personalities and possible meanings of love.[6]

Even after marriage, the spouse's frame of reference by which to evaluate a marriage partner remains limited and narrow because the American tends to prize and guard his privacy. This conclusion is supported by such general values in the American culture as the private house and yard, strong reaction against living with others after marriage (those interested in communes being the recent exception), dislike of unannounced visits, etc. In a sense, this marriage is analogous to what the psychologist describes as the "loner" individual. This individual operates quite well as long as his narrow frame of reference fits the reality situation. If, however, the reality should change, it is difficult for him to judge the change because of his isolation tendencies. The same holds true for the "loner" marriage. The statistics show that married couples who enjoy many contacts with the society around them; club memberships, church activities, family ties, etc., tend to have more stable marriages. This would im-

ply that the stability of the "loner" marriage is less. When an argument occurs in the "loner" marriage, the spouse tends to react to it in light of his prior limited heterosexual experiences. If these are not appropriate to the new reality, he then has no place to turn to correct this reaction because of the private quality of his marriage (it is no one else's business).

These, then, are the first factors which tend to create the reaction to marital conflict that one's spouse has changed. In short, one has not had enough experience with the opposite sex nor has one a place to turn to understand the reality and judge it in light of the new marriage relationship.

The second trend is the social creation of an over-romanticized and unrealistic image of the marriage relationship. This image stems, in large part, from mass communication media as well as from the failure of the various social institutions, such as school, family, and the church, to present realistically the problems inherent to sexuality and marriage.

Although many new sex education programs have appeared in churches, YMCAs and schools, there is still a great deal of resistance to such programs in many places. Studies have reported that age mates are the major source of sex information for large numbers of American youth.[7] In an informal survey of California city college students taking the marriage and family course, about one-half reported that their major source of sex information up to the time of taking the marriage and family course had been their peers. The following typical excerpt from student reports points up not only the status of sex information received, but the very serious need for adequate sex information.

> Our school had what they called sex education. This was handled by our P.E. teachers. In my case (the respondent is female) the teacher had never been married and had no children of her own. She showed a few films but we were all too uncomfortable to ask questions afterwards. In addition, our library was supposed to have a good collection of sex education books. Unfortunately these were not on open shelves. We had to ask the librarian for them and therefore most of us did not see them. We didn't have the nerve to ask. My parents did give me good information when I asked but often I didn't really know what to ask. I find now that my friends often gave me wrong information but I didn't recognize it at the time.

Obviously, the chances of other adolescents supplying valid information in a clear, understandable manner are small. It is somewhat analogous to the blind leading the blind. Hence, the schools are apparently failing in their efforts to bring sound realistic understanding to the adolescent in the fields of sex and marriage or there would be less necessity for the adolescent to lean so heavily on his peers for this information.

The inability of the parent to communicate this information successfully to his children is so well-known via satirization in cartoons and jokes that it needs no discussion here. The parents and the schools represent two sources that should lead the young adult to realistic attitudes toward sexuality. To the extent that they fail, peers and mass media fill the vacuum.

A cursory examination of mass media's portrayal of modern sex and marriage quickly confirms the unreality of the image projected. Advertising is especially absurd in depicting marital bliss. Basically, the happy marriage, according to advertising, is based on physical charms and material goods. The right deodorant ("don't you wish everyone did?"), correct hair colors ("blonds have more fun," "only her hairdresser knows"), and sex applied from the jar ("the erogenous tones: Faberge introduces nail colors that lead to more than holding hands") appear to epitomize the physical ideal.

Not only do the advertisements subtly undermine reality by exaggeration of the often trivial and superficial, but they directly support the importance of denying truth. For example, the facial cream "Ultra Feminine" advertisement in a popular woman's magazine begins with the following question: "A woman faces so many things. . . . Why should looking her age be one of them?" An example of intellectual distortion can easily be seen in another make-up ad in the same magazine, "A look so nearly nude, it could be nothing at all . . . this is the real you, looking natural as the day you were born." The absurdity of such a statement is obvious. If it were the real you, you would not be covered with makeup and, of course, if you are covered with makeup it is not the real you. One might call the makeup, in reality, a mask hiding the "real you."

The other half of the ideal marriage as depicted by advertising is the material, epitomized by such things as stoves that cook by themselves and play "Tenderly" when the meal is ready; Mr. Clean, which absolves the woman from cleaning chores; the proper car for manly appeal and, of course, the ultimate necessity of the properly colored toilet paper to match the furnishings.*

In addition to advertising, the popular heroine or hero of the serial, novel, movie, or television play bears little resemblance to the statistical norm. He or she is often the stylized, idealized sex symbol, a James Bond, or the bunny of Playboy.

Rose Franzblau makes another interesting and disturbing observation when she writes,

> *Another implication arises when a permitted source of sexual stimulation and excitement on the mass media comes to be a safer form of pleasure and release than personal participation in any sexual activity. Because it is acted out for him by someone else, it*

---

*The general erosive quality of modern advertising on man's values and on his ability to understand reality is made one of the cornerstones of Jules Henry's book *Culture Against Man*.[8]

> *allays his guilt. It is also a form of escape for the individual, within his own home, from the social controls required of him on the outside. . . . This private viewing can become the youngster's total psychosexual life, and keep him from reaching his psychic maturity normally, at the proper age.*[9]

Combining the two trends, a narrow frame of reference and an unrealistic picture of marital bliss, into an individual attitude toward love and marriage, results in a general confusion between the internalized ideal image and external reality. In essence, what the individual with such an attitude does is to marry a projection of his own internalized ideal image. That is, he tends to observe his steady girl, his fiancée or his spouse through a multilens filter system which allows only those rays to pass through which illuminate the imaginary ideal. Erich Fromm, author of the widely read book, *The Art of Loving,*[10] in an interview printed in *McCall's Magazine,* answers the interviewer's question about the meaning of "falling in love" as follows:

> *It is an unfortunate phrase—falling is not standing, and if you take our American phrase "he falls" or "she falls" for someone, what a fantastic phrase this is, to fall for someone. It is the abandonment of judgment, of realism, for an illusion. It is a particular kind of idolatry, where you suddenly build a picture of something wonderful. Only when you come to your senses you see this is not so. Then you start talking to lawyers.*[11]

Such a system works well through courtship and the early months of marriage. But as the months stretch into years, the routine of daily living and the intimate prolonged contact tend to wear out the filter system and more and more realism creeps through. Finally, when the negative can no longer be suppressed, the spouse comes to the belief that his partner has changed. In most cases, nothing could be further from the truth. The fact is that for the first time the couple has really begun to look at one another, not as the stereotyped projections of their own imagination, but as fellow human beings. The partner has not changed. It is the first time that he has been truly observed. The person has married a dream, not a reality, and all dreams come to an end upon awakening. This period marks the end of the "honeymoon." It also demonstrates the working of an age-old human tendency to admit to awareness only that which fits previous wishes or assumptions. What we think we see may tell more about the viewer than about the real situation or person being viewed.

In cases where awakening is too rude or the idealized image is too strongly held, the individual may cling to his first reaction that the spouse has changed. This gives the person a rationalization for leaving the spouse and taking up the search again. It is clear that such a person is doomed to failure since there is a slim change of finding a human who will coincide with his idealized image. John Robert Clark has a pithy description of this occurrence.

> *In learning how to love a plain human being today, as during the romantic movement, what we usually want unconsciously is a fancy human being with no flaws. When the mental picture we have of someone we love is colored by wishes of childhood, we may love the picture rather than the real person behind it. Naturally, we are disappointed in the person we love if he does not conform to our picture. Since this kind of disappointment has no doubt happened to us before, one might suppose we would then tear up the picture and start all over. On the contrary, we keep the picture and tear up the person. Small wonder that divorce courts are full of couples who never gave themselves a chance to know the real persons behind the pictures in their lives.[12]*

On the other hand, the individual who holds a strong idealized image may attempt to change his mate in the direction of his image. Attempting to change one's spouse can lead to trouble. It may arouse hostility on the part of the person being asked to change when they feel they do not want to or that there is no reason to change. It may also arouse feelings when the person does indeed change but fails to meet the idealistic expectations imposed by the partner.

For those who can weather this period of marriage a new potential for true growth, both in marriage and as an individual, is possible. John Sisk in his article, "The Dream Girl as Queen of Utopia" mentions:

> *Lionel Trilling has called attention to a "solution" to the dilemma: the emergence of a low-keyed, open-eyed, realistic kind of "good sexual partnership," the result of a revolution that has "brought the relationship between marriage and passion love to a virtual end." Porphyron and Madeline "learn to see each other without illusion as they are in reality." They "build a life together" in "The mutuality and warmth of their togetherness."[13]*

One's romantic ideal can be a wonderful guideline to give direction to a marriage. But the direction can be maintained and the goals achieved only if there is a firm recognition of the reality from which one may be attempting to move. Realities and idealizations march forward together, not inversely. The ideal realized only when firmly rooted in reality.

References

1. M. Hunt, *The Natural History of Love* (New York: Grove Press, Inc. 1959).
2. C. Broderick, "Going Steady: The Beginning of the End" in *Teenage Marriage and Divorce,* S. Farber and R. Wilson, eds. (Berkeley, Calif.: Diablo Press, 1967).
3. Hunt, *op. cit.*
4. R. Winch, *The Modern Family* (New York: Holt, Rinehard and Winston, 1971).
5. L. Burchinal, "Trends and Prospects for Young Marriages in the United States" *Journal of Marriage and the Family,* XXVII (1965), 243–54.
6. Hunt, *op. cit.*
7. H. Angelino and E. Mech, "Some First Sources of Sex Information as Reported by 67 College Women" *Journal of Psychology,* XXXIX (1955), 321–24.
8. J. Henry, *Culture Against Man* (New York: Random House, 1963).
9. R. Franzblau, "Sex and the Mass Media" in *Sex Education and the Teenager,* S. Farber and R. Wilson, eds. (Berkeley, Calif.: Diablo Press, 1967).
10. E. Fromm, *The Art of Loving* (New York: Harper and Bros. 1956).
11. E. Fromm, "An Interview from Erich Fromm," *McCalls* (October 1965), 215.
12. J. Clark, *The Importance of Being Imperfect* (New York: David McKay Co. Inc., 1961).
13. J. Sisk, "The Dream Girl as Queen of Utopia," in *Sex in America,* Anatole Grunwald, (New York: Bantam Books, 1964).

BUG SPRAY #5*

Wes Seeliger

Our wedding was on October 14, 1966. But our marriage began three weeks later.

We were dressed up and on our way to the swankiest restaurant in town. We had saved all week for the big splurge.

One problem—my bride was wearing the most horrible perfume ever manufactured. Smelled like a mixture of mustard gas, black pepper, and vaporized maple syrup. I still get queasy thinking about it.

We had stopped at a railroad crossing. It was cold outside. The windows were up and the heater was on. My nose and lungs silently begged for mercy. But I didn't want to upset my bride with a comment about her perfume.

I had decided the one perfect marriage in history would be ours. No conflicts . . . no harsh words . . . no hurt feelings . . . no tears . . . nothing negative. My wife had made a similar resolution. For three weeks we had walked on egg shells, protecting each other from the slightest unpleasantness.

Dare I break the spell? Dare I be honest and open? She had soaked in that blasted stuff every day of our marriage. I knew I couldn't hold out forever. So I said, in my sweetest, softest voice, "Honey, that perfume smells like bug spray."

Silence! Like the silence that must have followed President Roosevelt's announcement that the Japanese had bombed Pearl Harbor. I stared straight ahead trying to concentrate on the steady, metallic rhythm of the train cars rolling by.

I glanced at my bride out of the corner of my eye. Her lower lip was quivering slightly. The way it still does when she's fighting a good cry.

We drove on. After an eternity she mumbled softly, "I won't use that brand again."

Any married person can finish the story. We choked down our gourmet dinner. Pouted. Went throught the "it's all my fault, Honey" routine. Shed tears. And were finally reconciled, promising never to be cross with each other again.

The whole episode is now part of our family lore. Our repertory of delightful "young and dumb" stories.

But I still think our marriage began with my observation about the perfume. At that point we began to grow. We discovered marriage is a union stronger than emotions. We began to drop the foolishness about unruffled bliss. We took our first steps toward learning that one all important lesson, a lesson no one ever outgrows—love is a death-resurrection relationship.

As for the perfume . . . I sprayed the rest on roaches. It worked!

---

*Reprinted by permission from *Faith/at/Work* magazine.

THE POLITICS OF HOUSEWORK*

Pat Mainardi

Though women do not complain of the power of husbands, each complains of her own husband, or of the husbands of her friends. It is the same in all other cases of servitude; at least in the commencement of the emancipatory movement. The serfs did not at first complain of the power of their lords, but only of their tyranny.—JOHN STUART MILL, *On the Subjugation of Women*

Liberated women—very different from Women's Liberation! The first signals all kinds of goodies, to warm the hearts (not to mention other parts) of the most radical men. The other signals—*housework*. The first brings sex without marriage, sex before marriage, cozy housekeeping arrangements ("You see, I'm living with this chick") and the self-content of knowing that you're not the kind of man who wants a doormat instead of a woman. That will come later.

On the other hand is Women's Liberation—and housework. What? You say this is all trivial? Wonderful! That's what I thought. It seems perfectly reasonable. We both had careers, both had to work a couple of days a week to earn enough to live on, so why shouldn't we share the housework? So I suggested it to my mate and he agreed—most men are too hip to turn you down flat. You're right, he said. It's only fair.

Then an interesting thing happened. I can only explain it by stating that we women have been brainwashed more than even we can imagine. Probably too many years of seeing media-women coming over their shiny waxed floors or breaking down over their dirty shirt collars. Men have no such conditioning. They recognize the essential fact of housework right from the very beginning. Which is that it stinks.

Here's my list of dirty chores: buying groceries, carting them home and putting them away; cooking meals and washing dishes and pots; doing the laundry; digging out the place when things get out of control; washing floors. The list could go on but the sheer necessities are bad enough. All of us have to do these jobs, or get someone else to do them for us. The longer my husband contemplated these chores, the more repulsed he became, and so proceeded the change from the normally sweet considerate Dr. Jekyll into the crafty Mr. Hyde who would stop at nothing to avoid the horrors of—housework.

*Excerpts reprinted from Pat Mainardi, "The Politics of Housework" *Discrimination Against Women*, Hearings Before the Special Subcommittee on Education of the Committee on Education and Labor, House of Representatives, 91st Congress, second session, Part 1 (Washington: U.S. Government Printing Office, Committee on Education and Labor, 1970), 265–268.

178

So ensued a dialogue that's been going on for several years. Here are some of the high points:

"I don't mind sharing the housework, but I don't do it very well. We should each do the things we're best at.

Meaning: Unfortunately I'm no good at things like washing dishes or cooking. What I do best is a little light carpentry, changing light bulbs, moving furniture. (How often do you move furniture?)

Also meaning: Historically the lower classes (Blacks and women) have had hundreds of years doing menial jobs. It would be a waste of man-power to train someone else to do them now.

Also meaning: I don't like the dull stupid boring jobs, so you should do them.

"I don't mind sharing the work, but you'll have to show me how to do it."

Meaning: I ask a lot of questions and you'll have to show me everything, every time I do it because I don't remember so good. Also, don't try to sit down and read while I'm doing my jobs because I'm going to annoy hell out of you until it's easier to do them yourself.

"I've got nothing against sharing the housework, but you can't make me do it on your schedule."

Meaning: passive resistance. I'll do it when I damn well please, if at all. If my job is doing dishes, it's easier to do them once a week. If taking out laundry, once a month. If washing the floors, once a year. If you don't like it, do it yourself oftener, and then I won't do it at all.

"Women's Liberation isn't really a political movement."

Meaning: The Revolution is coming too close to home.

Also meaning: I am only interested in how I am oppressed, not how I oppress others. Therefore the war, the draft and the university are political. Women's Liberation is not.

POSTSCRIPT

Participatory democracy begins at home. If you are planning to implement your politics there are certain things to remember.

1. He is feeling it more than you. He's losing some leisure and you're gaining it. The measure of your oppression is his resistance.

2. Most men are not accustomed to doing monotonous, repetitive work which never issues in any lasting let alone important achievement. This is why they would rather repair a cabinet than wash dishes. If human endeavors are like a pyramid with man's highest achievements at the top, then keeping oneself alive is at the bottom. Men have always had servants (you) to take care of this bottom stratum of life while he has confined his efforts to the rarefied upper regions. It is thus ironic when they ask of women: "Where are your great painters, statesmen, etc." Mrs. Matisse ran a millinery shop so he could paint. Mrs. Martin Luther King kept his house and raised his babies.

3. It is a traumatizing experience for someone who has always thought of himself as being against any oppression or exploitation of one human being by another to realize that in his daily life he has been accepting and implementing (and benefiting from) this exploitation: that his rationalization is little different from that of the racist who says "Niggers don't feel pain" (women don't mind doing the———work), and that the oldest form of oppression in history has been the oppression of 50 percent of the population by the other 50 percent.

4. Arm yourself with some knowledge of the psychology of oppressed peoples everywhere and a few facts about the animal kingdom. I admit playing top wolf or who runs the gorillas is silly but as a last resort men bring it up all the time. Talk about bees. If you feel really hostile, bring up the sex life of spiders. After sex, she bites off his head.

The psychology of oppressed peoples is not silly. Blacks, women, and immigrants have all employed the same psychological mechanisms to survive. Admiring the oppressor, glorifying the oppressor, wanting to be like the oppressor, wanting the oppressor to like them.

5. In a sense all men everywhere are slightly schizoid—divorced from the reality of maintaining life. This makes it easier for them to play games with it. It is almost a cliche that women feel greater grief at sending a son off to war or losing him to that war because they bore him, suckled him, and raised him. The men who foment those wars did none of those things and have a more superficial estimate of the worth of human life. One hour a day is a low estimate of the amount of time one has to spend 'keeping' oneself. By foisting this off on others, man has seven hours a week—one working day—more to play with his mind and not his human needs. Over the course of generations it is easy to see whence evolved the horrifying abstractions of modern life.

6. With the death of each form of oppression, life changes and new forms evolve. English aristocrats at the turn of the century were horrified at the idea of enfranchising working men, were sure that it signalled the death of civilization and a return to barbarism. Some working men even fell for this line. Similarly with the minimum wage, abolition of slavery, and female suffrage. Life changes but it goes on—don't fall for any crap about the death of everything if men take a turn at the dishes. They will imply that you are holding back the Revolution (their Revolution). But you are advancing it.

7. Keep checking up. Periodically consider who's actually doing the jobs. These things have a way of backsliding so that a year later once again the woman is doing everything. Use timesheets if necessary. Also bear in mind what the worst jobs are, namely the ones that have to be done every day or several times a day. Also the ones that are dirty—it's more pleasant to pick up books, newspapers, et cetera, than to wash dishes. Alternate the bad jobs. It's the daily grind that gets you down. Also make sure that you don't have the responsibility for the housework with occasional help from him. "I'll cook dinner for you tonight" implies that it's really your job and isn't he a nice guy to do some of it for you.

8. Most men had a bachelor life during which they did not starve or become encrusted with crud or buried under the litter. There is a taboo that says that women mustn't strain themselves in the presence of men—we haul around fifty pounds of groceries if we have to but aren't allowed to open a jar if there is someone around to do it for us. The reverse side of the coin is that men aren't supposed to be able to take care of themselves without women. Both are excuses for making women do the housework.

9. Beware of the double whammy. He won't do the little things he always did because you're now a "Liberated Woman, right?" Of course, he won't do anything else either....

I was just finishing this when my husband came in and asked what I was doing. Writing a paper on housework. Housework? He said *Housework?* Oh my god how trivial can you get. A paper on housework.

THE BIG WHEEL: SUCCESS, STATUS, AND THE NEED TO BE LOOKED UP TO*

Deborah S. David and Robert Brannon

One of the most basic routes to manhood in our society is to be a success: to command respect and be looked up to for what one can or has achieved. There are several basic ways to accomplish this, but by definition this kind of status is a limited commodity which not every man can achieve.

WEALTH AND FAME

The most visible and sought-after source of status in our society is what we loosely refer to as "being a success." Success is usually defined in terms of occupational prestige and achievement, wealth, fame, power, and visible positions of leadership. These things usually tend to be correlated; however, *extremely* high standing on any one of them seems to have a very special status quality. The tycoon, the congressman, the movie star, and the sports hero enjoy an automatic kind of status, and will often be viewed as masculine role-models on this basis alone. There's something ineffably masculine about the word "millionaire," or even "the richest man in town." It's also quite helpful to be President of the United States, author of a best-selling novel, or even conductor of a symphony orchestra. Really massive doses of success at almost *anything*, in fact, seem so inherently manly that the "World's Greatest" artist, pianist, chef, hair-dresser, or tiddlywink player is to some extent protected from the taint of unmasculine activity which surrounds less successful members of his profession. Intellectual prominence is also valuable in the right circles, but for most people nothing succeeds quite so well as money. "If Karl, instead of writing a lot about capital, had made a lot of it," said Anna Marx about her famous son, "it would have been much better."[1]

THE SYMBOLS OF SUCCESS

Simply being a doctor, lawyer, or moderately successful businessman is enough to qualify as success in most social circles. A man who has launched a

*David-Brannon (Editors), *The Forty-nine Percent Majority: The Male Sex Role*, 1976, Addison-Wesley, Reading, Mass.

successful career and is earning an impressive salary can usually enjoy the respect of his family, friends, relatives, co-workers, employees—everyone who is *aware* of his accomplishments. Unfortunately though, neighbors, casual visitors, passing motorists, and the waiter at The Ritz may not happen to know who's Vice President For Local Sales at Crump Amalgamated—to them he's just a middle-aged schlepper with thinning hair and a pot belly. The answer is simple: a $300 hand-made suit, glove-leather Gucci shoes, and a hand-made attache case of unborn calf.

These symbols are wasteful of course, but in another more psychological way, they make sense. Quadraphonic stereos playing dusty old Lawrence Welk albums; hosts serving Chivas Regal to business friends who couldn't tell it from Old Overshoe; we may chuckle at what seem to be foolish excesses, but the rewards are not what they seem. What's a little wasted money compared with the precious feeling of Being A Man?

What about men to whom real financial success is out of reach, temporarily or permanently, for reasons of age, social class, or race? Many hunger for it anyway, and seize on its smallest symbols in a parody of material success, for even the fleeting feeling of "being a man" can be precious. Kenneth Clark has described young black men with menial jobs, who carry empty briefcases to and from work. One such youngster wore a white shirt and tie downtown each day to what he said was his "management trainee" job in a large department store; in reality he was a stock-boy.[2]

OTHER ROUTES TO STATUS

Men who haven't "made it" by the standards of the mainstream often find other battlegrounds to fight on, other routes to status before smaller but highly appreciative audiences. A neighborhood bar may have a champion dart thrower, with a standing bet to lick any man in the house. A mailroom may have its fastest sorter, a men's club its stalwart whose record for beer drinking has never been equaled. In truth almost anything pursued seriously can become a source of status. Specialized subgroups often develop their own status ranking systems, sometimes very different from or even opposite to the mainstream male role. Aggressive violence plays a minor part in the general cultural male role, as we'll see later, but in certain juvenile street gangs it serves as the major "currency" on which reputations are based. Miller reports that lower-status gang members committed four to six times as many violent, illegal crimes as the high-status members, who had already "made it." Once the low-status men have acquired reputations for bloodthirsty recklessness, they too can "retire" to the relative ease (and safety) of senior status.[3]

One of the most interesting examples of subgroup status is found in the encounter-group, clinically-oriented "human potential" movement. In the main-

stream male role, showing tender or fearful emotions is distasteful and embarrassing, while being "sensitive" to other people's emotions is fairly irrelevant.
In the clinical counter-culture, sensitivity and being "in touch with one's emotions" have been redefined as extremely good. Naturally, the subgroup leaders
who are most awesomely in touch with every emotion and can "sense" things
in other people that no one else can are . . . men! At such gatherings as Humanistic Psychology and Orthopsychiatry conventions, these super-sensitive Gurus
glide around like whacked-out birds of paradise in beads and Indian gowns,
followed by their retinues of admirers.

BEING "COMPETENT"

"Ask any man a factual question and you'll get an answer," says a single
woman I know. "He may not know a damn thing about it, but he'll make up
something rather than say he doesn't know." Men feel a strong need to seem
knowledgable, on top of things, and generally equal to any situation that arises.
When a husband and wife are driving in a car and get lost, it's almost always
the woman who suggests stopping to ask directions of someone. When a car
won't start, men gather around like flies to peer intently at the mysterious in-
nards. "She's probably flooded," somebody grunts knowledgably.

The act of lovemaking was once considered a natural function, and the
male's prerogative at that. With the widespread discussion of female orgasm,
not to mention multiple orgasm, and the appearance of hundreds of sex
manuals telling men how to bring any woman to the brink of ecstasy in 35 easy
steps, a whole new proving ground for male competence (and status) has appeared. "And I didn't have to consult my sex manual even once!" crowed
Woody Allen after his night of debauchery in *Play It Again Sam.* "My husband
has studied those things so much," said one med student's wife, "I can tell
when he's flipping from page forty-one to forty-two."

THE BREADWINNER ROLE

Most men seek and long for at least part of their lives in which they feel
like a "big wheel." Status of course is a relative thing: A man whose wife looks
up to him can feel like a "real man" in relation to her, but not necessarily to
anyone else. A shopkeeper who is feared and respected by his employees may
feel sublimely masculine at work—but he doesn't look or feel manly when he's
asking for a loan at the bank or being ignored by the maitre d' in a fancy restaurant. The famous "fragile male ego" that marriage manuals warn women to
be so careful of is one symptom of the status vulnerability most average men

must endure. ("Better to let him win a few games of checkers than to put up with a sullen, humiliated man for the rest of the evening," one such guide cautions young women.) For many men the need to feel important is most usually met in role-dictated dominance/submission interactions with women, or with traditional labor divisions in the family.

In the traditional nuclear family the male is the only paid worker, the Breadwinner, the Sole Provider. Even if his job is dull and routine, he leaves the home, labors, and returns with "food for the table"—a computerized paycheck with federal, state, and local withholdings, perhaps—but a direct descendant of Neanderthal's haunch of bison. This bastion of status within the family is traditionally available to virtually every male, a haven in which one basic demand of the male role can be satisfied. When unemployment occurs on a wide scale, such as when the chief industry in a small community fails, the psychological consequences to men are often as severe as the economic.

Despite the importance of having a job, an astounding proportion of men do not especially like what they do for a living, the way they spend approximately two-thirds of their waking hours for the better part of their lives. In a series of interviews I conducted to pretest a questionnaire on masculinity, men's answers about their jobs were notably unenthusiastic. "Well, it's a living," said a restaurant manager. "I guess I like it—I been doing it 15 years," said a window dresser. "Hell, I gotta eat," said a car salesman.

These are all men who are far from the pinnacle of success (as are most of us), so perhaps it's not surprising they don't see their jobs as heaven on earth. But a member of my men's consciousness-raising group had a different problem with his job. He's an executive with one of the largest corporations in America, in his early forties, and was making over $50,000 a year in an assignment he actually enjoyed and was good at. *His* problem was an impending promotion. Having proven his competence at this level of the company hierarchy, he was expected to move on to the next level. It meant more money but a substantially different kind of work, which he was fairly sure he wouldn't like as well, and he'd have to commute a lot further. It made sense to stay where he was . . . but he couldn't. For one thing that would label him as a "quitter" in the company, and his chances of ever being promoted later would evaporate. For another he really couldn't resist the urge to move upward, or live with a reputation as a guy who was headed nowhere. He accepted the promotion, and, as predicted, hated his new assignment.

To the blue-collar worker struggling to make ends meet, such executives are a privileged class of rich mandarins, and obviously, in a way, they are. But based on some close observations I'd say there's another fact that's relevant. They're not very happy.

References

1. A Spiegelman and B. Schneider, *Whole Grains: A Book of Quotations* (New York: Douglas Links, 1974).
2. K. Clark, *Dark Ghetto* (New York: Harper, 1965).
3. W. Miller, "Violent Crimes in City Gangs" in *Politics in the Metropolis*, T. Dye, ed. (Columbus: Charles Merrill, 1967).

TO MY LOVE, AND MOSTLY TO MYSELF*

Martha Whitmore Hickman

I am not a bottle of Jergen's lotion poured out on the
world's pain,
I am not the alter ego of husband, sons, daughters.

I love you and that tells me something important
about both of us.
But it does not tell me who I am.
Before we were together, I was, by myself.
If I were to lose you, I would grieve and feel desola-
tion, but I would prevail.
That I can join with you is an incredible richness to
me.
It is cause for singing and dancing and being glad.

*"To My Love, and Mostly to Myself" on page 72 is reprinted from *Images*, compiled by Janice
Grana and published by the Upper Room, Nashville, Tennessee (© 1976) and is used by permission.

But it is I who sing my song and you who sing yours.
I do not become you. I am myself.
I may dance with you, but I am not you. I am myself.
You can only help me and I, you, if we are apart from
    one another.
Two of us, reciprocal.

SEX IN MARRIAGE*

William J. Lederer and Don D. Jackson

What is the role of sex in marriage?

Like every other element in the marital relationship, sex involves behavior between individuals. The response of each partner varies with his mood, his physical state, and the oscillations of the relationship.

Given adequate physiological and anatomical equipment (which Nature rarely fails to provide) and a modicum of knowledge of sexual techniques, the spouses will enjoy sexual union *when both are in a collaborative mood.* The collaborative exists when each is adding something to the sexual act, not just submitting. When the spouses are not in a loving mood, they still may find in sex release from tension and thus derive another type of pleasure from it, especially if they are in agreement about what they expect, but it is likely to be less fulfilling and often may be frustrating, because one partner has contrary needs which are left unmet.

This sex act—a comparably simple matter—has become the most written about, the most talked of, and the most muddled aspect of marriage. There are several reasons why the role of sex in marriage has become excessively emphasized and distorted.

A cultural fear of sex's losing its effective status in the social structure. This fear is as ancient at least as the Old Testament dictum that "a man ... shall cleave unto his wife." The expectation is that if this pronouncement is violated the species will not fulfill its obligation to procreate in a familial or nurturing setting.

The fear of desertion and abandonment. In our culture, this fear is stronger in women than in men. Women are tied down by the processes of childbearing and childbirth and require assistance physically and emotionally. In response to this fear, and to provide a weapon for fighting it, the belief has developed in our culture that if one is "sexy" enough, one's mate will *not* desert. The result has been an exaggerated consciousness of sexual performance as a ritual to increase personal security in marriage or to induce marriage. Yet if one is "sexy" enough there is the danger of being *too* "sexy" and violating the ancient commandments.

The female's simulation of sexiness. The male requires an erection to enter into the sex act. If he is uninterested in sex, or afraid of it, he will not have an erection. However, a woman does not have any obvious physiological indications of spontaneous readiness. She can fake sexual spontaneity, and the male (at least for a time) may not be aware of the deceit. The female extends

---

this simulation of sexual interest into parasexual areas by means of hair dyes, falsies, girdles, cosmetics, perfumes, and high heels. These parasexual devices scream, "Look, I'm sexy. I'm desirable." This may or may not be true, but it is probable that women resent their need to advertise and would prefer to be accepted as they really are; men resent the necessity for sexual deception even though they foster it.

The economic forces in our culture sustain and stimulate these hypocritical actions. Any attempt to alter the pattern involves resisting the advertising and other merchandising techniques used by multi-billion dollar businesses to peddle false female sexuality. The women who attempt to retain a "natural" appearance, with undoctored hair, no makeup, and so forth, are few in number, and they may (because of cultural conditioning) be regarded by both men and women as deviates. Most of the people who might be inclined to rebel against this type of sexual mores are intimidated by cultural pressures and mass value judgments.

Furthermore, the emphasis upon female sexual paraphernalia is an inherited social custom which long has been associated with the elite. In past ages, makeup, breast accentuators, and the like were worn mainly by the ruling classes, and the tendency to show upward social mobility by imitating the elite still exists. Even today, the wealthier the spouses, the more they exaggerate the difference between the sexes. The wife wears elegant gowns, elaborate hairdos, scintillating jewelry, and expensive furs and perfumes. Her husband may favor dark conservative suits, homburgs, and thick-soled, handmade English shoes.

The erroneous belief that unsatisfactory sexual relations are the major cause of bad marriages. The speciousness here is clear. Unsatisfactory sexual relations are a symptom of marital discord, not the cause of it. It is difficult for the victims to see this because of the mass of propoganda about sex that attacks them day and night, on the street, in the home, in the office. We are such an absurd culture that even mouth-washes and Lysol are related to the sexual aspects of marriage.

John Jones, for example, is dissatisfied with his marriage. On his way to work he may look up and see a billboard with a picture of a nearly nude, beautiful woman, advertising a brand of stockings. John is stimulated sexually and says to himself, "Boy, I'd like to have an affair with something like that." He knows this is wishful thinking, and may even recognize that the beautiful model might be incompatible with him. Next he retreats from the daydream and his thoughts turn toward his wife. But the sexual fantasy he has had about the ad colors his reflections about his marriage relationship, and he thinks, "Golly, Mary's legs might look better in that kind of hosiery." What he means is, "If Mary were a better sexpot we'd both have a happier marriage." He is caught in a double error: the appearance of Mary's legs has nothing to do with the couple's sexual satisfaction, *and* he has forgotten his *own* function in achieving a successful union.

Such a process may be repeated frequently during the day, for John is never permitted to escape advertisements which suggest that sexuality is the key to happiness. Yet there is considerable evidence that an individual's *perception* of the sexual relationship is more related to marital satisfaction than the sexual act itself.

In a survey conducted at an Ohio university, interviews of several hundred couples showed that by and large those who reported their marriages as "satisfactory" gave the frequency of their intercourse as twice a week. Those who reported their marriage as "unsatisfactory" also reported a frequency of twice a week, yet among the unhappy couples the husbands said that twice a week was more than their wives wished but satisfactory from their point of view, and the wives said it was less than their husbands wished but just right for them personally. The "happy" husbands and wives said the frequency of twice a week was satisfying to both themselves *and* their spouses. In other words, the problem was in the couples' communication and not in the actual frequency of their sexual relations.

While sexual problems are often blamed for marital difficulties, one is seldom made aware of the other side of the coin: sexual relations may keep some marriages going, providing virtually the only kind of contact which the spouses have. Psychiatrists and other professionals who treat marital problems are aware that some individuals have been able to establish successful sexual relations with each other although they cannot get together in any other context. Many of these couples have the experience of waking at night to discover themselves involved in sex, with neither partner aware of who took the initiative.

The differences between male and female.   The physical differences between male and female contribute to the novelty and adventure of sex. Heterosexuality is extrafascinating and carries with it the illusion of intrigue. At the same time, the differences make understanding one another more difficult. Also, the excessive emphasis on sex as the major factor in marriage results in a distorted viewpoint. The natural differences between male and female are made to appear crucial for the success of a marriage. Actually, a woman will not improve her marriage by achieving a voluptuous bust, legs like a model, and an aura of exotic perfume. If her marriage is an unhappy one, her husband may develop a preference for small-breasted women who dress plainly and do not wear perfume.

Having reviewed some reasons for mistaken attitudes toward sexual intercourse, let us now take a look at its actual role in marriage. What is special about sexual intercourse, a highly satisfying male-female symbiosis, is that it requires a higher degree of collaborative communication than any other kind of behavior exchanged between the spouses. Sex is consequently precious, but also perilous. It is the only relationship act which must have mutual spontaneity for mutual satisfaction. It can only be a conjoint union, and it represents a common goal which is clear and understood by both.

The reason people keep asking where sex fits into marriage is that they have been hoodwinked, bamboozled, pressured, conned, and persuaded that the sexual act is compulsory in their lives and *must be performed alike by everyone;* the "standards" are established by advertisers, publicity for sexpot motion-picture stars, literature, movies, plays, television, and so on. But these are standards of fantasy. Therefore people ask silly questions. How often should we have sex? What is the best position? How intense should it be? Should we scratch and bite each other? What time of day should it be done? The questions sound like inquiries about the type of gymnastic procedures to be followed for attaining muscles like Mr. America's or a rear end or bust like Miss America's. Perhaps even worse off are the myriads of couples who don't dare ask questions and just assume they *must* be abnormal because their own practice differs from some so-called standard.

The problem is obvious. In sex, trying to keep up with the Joneses is the road to disaster. To decide where sex fits into their particular marriage, a couple must look inward at the marriage, not outward at the deceptive advice and make-believe standards set by others. There are no standards, and most "advice" from friends or family is misleading, for few people can speak honestly about their own sex life. Rather than admit their own sex problems and misgivings, friends often let one assume that their sex experiences are indeed superior; otherwise, the implication is, they wouldn't be giving advice.

Can women and men live without sex and still stay healthy?

Yes, they can. People cast away on isolated islands have gone for years without sex and have not experienced any physiological or psychological breakdowns or deficiencies as a result. Priests, nuns, and many mystics, such as the great Mahatma Gandhi, have eschewed sexual union and not damaged their health or decreased their longevity.

Sex, of course, is necessary for propagation; nature has provided this instinctual drive so that the species will survive. The drive is effective because of the variety of intense pleasures derived from its fulfillment. But no harm will occur to the normal individual to whom sex is denied.

Almost all adult human beings somehow have the feeling that experiencing sex frequently is a requirement for good physical and mental health, even if intellectually they know better. Both men and women who have enjoyed sex at regular intervals become frustrated, sometimes desperate, when it is withheld for (what seems to them) a long time. The sex aggressions of men at war in foreign lands and of sailors who have been at sea for months are well known. Such behavior stems more from a feeling of deprivation than from pure physical necessity. A person who voluntarily renounces or limits sexual intercourse—as priests, nuns, and others do for varied reasons—suffers no ill health or mental anguish as long as the renunciation corresponds to his emotional needs. If, however, a person desires sexual union and has deep, unmet needs for this form of human intimacy, yet is unable for some reason to meet the need, the resulting sense of deprivation and frustration may create emotional problems.

Sometimes unusual sex actions are stimulated by nonsexual deficiencies. For example, male children with a dread of being abandoned by their mother often will masturbate excessively. Men who have repressed homosexual tendencies (frequently the result of having a passive—or dead—father and a dominant mother) often are inclined to act oversexed in order to "prove their manhood."

The *beliefs* (most of them specious) which most individuals have on "what kind" of sex is desirable, and "how much," have several sources:

1. So-called "scientific" information obtained from books, articles, and lectures.

2. Customs, traditions, and advice conveyed by relatives and friends.

3. Customs, traditions, and examples transmitted by literature, radio, television, movies, and advertising.

Tradition molds many beliefs and habits having to do with sex in marriage. For example, consider the barbaric custom of the honeymoon—particularly in past centuries, when the girl's chastity was treasured and important. In those days the bride and groom, who hardly knew each other, departed to a strange geographical area and into sexual intimacy. Usually the bride possessed only hearsay information on sexual matters and the husband's sexual experience had not necessarily prepared him to understand the needs of a virginal bride.

They hurried away from the courtship milieu of jollity, gregariousness, and traditional optimism into a new sexual environment of their own, and were expected to emerge a week or ten days later with all the tenderness, love, and devotion needed to create a successful, happy marriage—whether or not sexual experience had been traumatic for one or both of them.

A modern version of the same ritual occurs today, with an additional cultural expectation introduced: the newlyweds are expected to achieve *mutual* sexual satisfaction during the honeymoon. The young couple usually is launched with a lavish wedding and a tremendous amount of effort and expense on the part of both their families. The newlyweds are under pressure to "have fun" on their honeymoon and to return looking radiant and serene. Frequently the opposite happens. We estimate that most honeymoons are periods of frustrating sexual disappointment. The honeymoon may be an exciting novelty, but usually it results in confusion even when there has been premarital sexual experience. The situation of the bride who cried all through her honeymoon is a common one. Sex, like anything else, has to be learned; and even if the two have had relations before marriage, the marriage state places them in a new psychological milieu to which they must adjust. Now they are "legitimate," and they believe that their sexual experience will therefore be better. Now they are legally tied; they cannot walk away from each other. They feel the sex act *must* be a success every time; otherwise, the marriage is disintegrating.

This situation is aggravated by the pronouncements of most sex consultants, books, and articles on marriage. They usually indicate that sex is the keystone of marital success. We disagree. Sex is significant; and good sex is satisfying and emotionally nourishing. Sex is highly desirable, but it is not the only vital force in marriage, either during the honeymoon or later.

The situation is muddied further by the conflicting views of "experts" who give "scientific" information on sex. It is important that all "expert" opinions on sex be taken with a grain of skepticism.

Most "scientific" information on sex comes from two sources: psychiatrists and other physicians writing about data obtained from the experiences of their patients, and social scientists generalizing from data obtained in surveys conducted by means of some type of questionnaire.

In point of fact, conclusions based upon the medical data obtained from patients are not necessarily applicable to most people. Patients go to doctors for the treatment of one or more problems. If they have come for psychiatric therapy, they expect to spend many hours discussing sex and exploring the negative aspects of themselves, their spouses, their friends, and so on. Few (if any) will pay twenty-five or thirty dollars an hour and then spend time discussing pleasant and satisfactory experiences. The gynecologist or the family physician who writes a sex book is scientific only in regard to anatomy. The nonanatomical aspects of the text are based upon his own personal sex experiences plus whatever his ailing patients have told him.

Some of the most popular tracts on sex and marriage are written by gynecologists whose practices consist to a great extent of women who *spontaneously and voluntarily* talk freely to the physician in their efforts to describe their personal discords. The fact that a person talks and answers questions in a doctor's office (instead of in a public bar or a living room) does not prove that the individual is accurate or objective, and certainly does not indicate that his conclusions are generally applicable. Almost all patients' views on sex are subjective and weighted, especially since those who feel the need to discuss their sex lives usually have special problems.

The same difficulty causes the flaws in the Kinsey reports (and in most other studies whose data comes from question-and-answer procedures). Although Kinsey made an important study, one that required courage to initiate, we cannot overlook one important fact: he depended primarily on *volunteers* to answer his questions. Can we be sure that the people who volunteer to answer sex questions are representative? Some of the Kinsey interviews talked two or three hours about their experiences—evidently revealing intimacies was fun for some.

Also, there were considerable differences in experience and ability among Kinsey's interviewers. Only recently, the work of the Department of Psychiatry at Harvard has demonstrated that the nature of an interviewing context (including the interviewer's attitude) has a tremendous influence on the interviewee's response. An interviewer who strongly believes that, say, many wives have intercourse with other men when their husbands are on trips, will come up with much more evidence to support this view than will an interviewer who holds the opposite opinion at the start of the investigation.

Nevertheless, the Kinsey material provides the most complete and reliable data we have on the sexual practices of middle- and upper-class Americans. It reveals that increasingly in our culture, sexual intercourse is not confined to married people; and it is certainly not limited to sexual congress between men and women.

The bulk of the Kinsey material and of other surveys (which primarily relate to college students) concerns homosexuality, masturbation, premarital intercourse, perversion, post-divorce sexual activities, the activities of spinsters and bachelors, and adultery. To our knowledge, *no one has studied a sample of normogenic (average) married couples in significant numbers* and scientifically determined what married people think and do in relation to sex. Little is known about socioeconomic class differences, let alone ethnic idiosyncrasies.

Where does sex fit into marriage? It is almost impossible to estimate (except with respect to a specific married couple, after many hours of interviews) because so few studies have been made on the subject, and those which do exist are limited in scope and objectivity.

The answer to this question also depends upon time and circumstances, for sexual needs are fundamentally psychological. Middle-income spouses who have been married for a year and have no children, but want some, may have different sexual needs from the husband and wife without jobs, so poor they

can't pay the rent, who therefore are afraid to have children. A couple married for thirty years, with four children in college, may have different sexual needs from a couple married for five years, with only one child. Such differences are not merely due to age. Boredom plays a more significant role in decreasing the frequency of intercourse than do withering sex glands. Also, a couple whose sex experience is beautiful and satisfying may engage in sex less frequently than an unhappy pair frantically experimenting for a solution to their discord.

There is no accurate sex information which gives exact answers for everyone, since there are so many variables. Yet in the United States, the sex ethic has become all important. As we have already stressed, the fallacious concept that sex determines our lives is spread far and wide by those promoting the tremendous sales of products supposed to enhance sexual attractiveness. Also, "authorities" on sex lecture, write, and give sexual advice *for a fee*. Naturally, they exaggerate the importance of sex in marriage. Offering complicated sex techniques is a profitable profession, and the more difficult the techniques, the longer the expensive counseling will last. The most popular sex manual has been through countless revisions and has outsold all other books except the Bible.

The myth that perfect and heavenly sex must be experienced by an individual before he can consider himself normal has become the foundation for a national mania. Sex success is the theme of social instruction and of almost all advertising, even for products not in any way associated with the sex act.

Spouses who are disappointed in sex are profoundly concerned about their difficulty. This is a reasonable reaction, if the disappointment is well founded. Men often wonder about their manhood or suspect that their wives are frigid or malicious. Wives wonder about their frigidity and suspect that perhaps their husbands are having affairs or that they are effeminate or at least inconsiderate or ignorant of satisfying sexual techniques.

Spouses will try anything to bring about a happier union, *one closer to the sex-success image* which is our national demi-god. Many a man and wife have spent a small fortune to go to a posh luxury lodge where they hoped they would miraculously achieve a sexual congress they couldn't bring about in their own bedroom. If the weather is nice and the view is good, something may come of the weekend, but it is not apt to result in unusual sexual satisfaction. People frequently buy new houses, hire interior decorators—with the hope that a fresh environment will improve sexual relations.

If the various manifestations of sex were accepted as natural, and if people could abandon the view that there is a single absolute standard to be reached by all who are normal, the unhappiness of many couples would decrease—*and their performance would automatically improve.*

Our concern in this chapter has been with the problem: Is great, *great,* GREAT SEX necessary for a satisfactory marriage, for a workable marriage? If sex is not up to culturally created expectations, is the marriage a failure?

It need not be a failure. It can be a good marriage even if the partners don't find heaven in bed.

Next, is a less-than-heavenly sex performance "normal"?

No one knows the answer, neither clergymen nor doctors. No one knows what normogenic sex performances are in marriage. Scientists have studied pathological marriages, but not normal ones. Small-sample research (such as that by Epstein and Westley at McGill University) supports our contention that sex is not essential; it has been found that some apparently well-adjusted spouses have "given up" sex after a few years of marriage.

In summary, the important thing to remember is that there is no absolute standard against which the success of married sex can be measured as one would clock a hundred-yard dash. Occasionally, there are medical abnormalities (such as disfigured or diseased genitals, impotence, a pathological fear of sex), but assuming that these are not present, there is only one important question: Is sex a source of pleasure—in the spouses' own judgment?

What is a satisfying sex experience for two people may well be undesirable for two others, and vice versa. For example, it is estimated by most physicians that more than half of all women married an average of ten years and having three children have never experienced an orgasm. In a sampling made of such cases most of the women were not aware that they had not had a full sex act. They derived varying degrees of pleasure from the physical intimacy with their husbands. Equally interesting is the fact that the husbands frequently did not know that their wives voluntarily made the same noises and motions which they *had heard or read* were performed by passionate women; the husbands had accepted these as spontaneous and derived satisfaction from them as evidence of the wives' pleasure.

Spouses should not permit their satisfactions to be influenced by authority figures (such as actors and actresses), advertising, art, literature, and social customs and traditions. Personal sex values concern the two people involved. For example, we know a couple in their seventies. Every evening they bathe and dress elegantly for dinner. They treat each other with the dignity and courtesy of blossoming courtship. At night when they go to bed they hold each other throughout the night, even though they have not exercised their genitalia for years. The elderly gentleman has described their experience as "having a ten-hour orgasm every night." For these two, it is a complete and wonderful sex act, and a very satisfying and nourishing one. Who is to differ with them?

Is sex important in married life? Yes, it is. It is *one* of the cements which hold the bricks of married life together. But the when, the how, the how often, and the quality can only be determined by the people involved.

LOUIE*

Shirley Holzer Jeffrey

Louie: Tall, slender, sixteen. He had lived in at least seven different homes, and had no one but an elderly grandmother, who cared enough about him to stand by him and help him to grow into the person he had the potential to be. And the old grandmother was becoming senile, and lived in a nursing home. The seven homes where he had lived had each decided, for one reason or another, that the nurturing of a young boy into manhood was more than they cared to undertake.

That was when he entered our lives. He had been living at the YMCA while attending school at our local high school. He came to live with us—a shy, sensitive boy, afraid to trust people, and struggling hard to know who he was. He was a pleasant boy who tried hard to convince himself that there were positive things in his experience. He emphasized what he had learned about people by living in many homes. He protected himself from the anger of so many rejections by building walls of rationalization which allowed him to cope with his experience. But buried deep inside there had to be much anger and hurt. People could not be trusted because they had let him down too many times.

As Louie sought the answer to the question, "Who am I?", he was unable to point to a family of flesh and blood. He treasured the pictures and articles about the family from which he came. His parents were both dead by the time he was five. The mementos were little help to a teenage boy seeking his identity. He chose to find identity with his peers in the only way he knew. He became the best dressed boy in the school. In clothes he found recognition. He wanted to be judged to be "college", which was the expression of the day used to describe someone noticed and admired by his peers. He bought a sports car and with it gained mobility and recognition. He sensed dimly that security did not really rest in these things. But his experience had taught him well that it did not rest in relationships with people either. In late night talks we often were able to penetrate the wall a little and witness our own deep concern for his being.

Louie chose to go on to college, and in that choice he opened a door to many new struggles. The vacation conversations revealed the depth of the struggle that was his. He dated a warm and outgoing girl who attracted him because she obviously cared about him and she reminded him of the one adult woman in his background whom he admired. She was attracted to him partly because of his background. He was different. She wanted to make up for what he had missed. After college they married, but she was not prepared for the

*"Louie" by Shirley Holzer Jeffrey, copyright 1975. Reprinted by permission of author.

199

walls of protection that he had maintained. In marriage those walls that had protected him so long were being threatened and he had to agonize over the desire to be close and yet the great fear that risking trust produced. "If I trust her she may let me down too. How can I be sure I won't be hurt again? Do I dare to trust?"

That struggle was great enough for one life. But then he became ill. He went to the Mayo Clinic, where after a number of tests the doctor came into his room and announced: "Well, we know what is wrong now: you have Hodgkin's Disease." With that the doctor turned on his heels and left Louie and his wife, Diane, in the wake of shock. Horror swept over them. There were a thousand thoughts, and many many questions that beat upon their beings. The questions needed answers: What was involved in Hodgkin's? What does the future hold? What are the chances for survival? How long? What will be done? What kind of treatment is there? Is there any hope? These questions a doctor could face with them. Instead the two young people sat in that hospital room away from home and friends, and faced a vast and dark unknown in utter agony. And there was no one there who would take time to listen to their hurt, to their questions, to their anguish. There was no one.

The chaplain stopped in. He might have provided a listening ear to hear the feelings that were being encountered. Instead he engaged in inane chatter and superficial talk about their home town. When he walked through that door to the hospital room he had an opportunity to minister. By the time he had set the tone for informal chatter, the two young people wanted only to get rid of him. His hollow words rang as clashing cymbals in the closed and tight room of their agony.

Louie and Diane came home from the clinic with the knowledge that Louie's disease had already progressed far. Hope was at best very thin. What does the future hold? What is going to happen? Why do others grow old while life for him will be short at best? Hodgkin's Disease!!! What is it going to mean? The greatest fears burn through the body like electric shocks. "I'm going to die. I'll lose my good looks. My hair will fall out. I'll get puffy. I'll become unattractive. How will Diane take it? She married me because I was strong and she wanted a normal life with home and children. I won't be able to give her that. It makes me feel guilty and angry and helpless. She married a good looking, healthy young man, with dreams of home and family, and she is stuck with an ugly, sick creature, who will get sicker and who can give her nothing. Every time I see an old person I hate them just because they are alive." Such feelings gave rise to much hostility, and anger, and self rejection, and self indulgence. Coupled with the loss of his image as a strong man came the loss of hope to be a success. "I'm not going to live long enough to prove to all those who didn't believe in me, that I can be a success." Despair, frustration, anger, fear, and terror became daily companions.

Notes of concern began to come. Louie discovered that people did care about him, and hurt because he was hurting. There were those who said, "It's so hard to understand why God lets such a thing happen." They made Louie feel guilty and intensified the natural question, "Why me?" Someone said, "God does not will for you to be sick, but he does will for you to grow in the experience that is yours." Others told of people they knew and tragedies with which they were familiar in hope that another person's misfortune would ease Louie's hurt. Such stories only made Louie feel that the person did not want to identify with his hurt and feel with him. One person wrote, "Thinking of you in faith, hope and love." That note was much appreciated. It communicated that someone cared and hurt and hoped. That is what Louie needed to know. No one could erase his situation, but people could offer him the support of their caring. Someone sent him the words of the Twenty-second Psalm. That psalmist captured utterly much of the feeling that Louie and Diane were experiencing.

The Christmas season came and Louie was worse. He had to be hospitalized. He was frightened and felt so alone and vulnerable. The cards began to come; flowers arrived; and then someone from work brought a hundred dollars collected from fellow workers to help with expenses. Louie was amazed and moved to tears. He couldn't believe that people could care so much about him. He had built his life on the foundation that people did not care. After the hospitalization he said one day, "One good thing about Hodgkin's, if there can be a good thing, I've found out that people really do care about me. It's hard for me to handle, but I am glad."

In the first months he struggled with a question that he would have to deal with over and over. "If I'm not going to live long, why shouldn't I do anything at all that I want to do?" It hooked itself into specifics at different times: "Why should I work?", "Why shouldn't I eat steak every night?" "Why shouldn't I buy anything I want?" "Why shouldn't I stay high on drugs if I want?" Louie had to discover for himself that neither escape nor indulgence give life meaning.

Louie did become puffy as he had feared, but he did not lose his hair. The daily agony of living with the knowledge of the disease made him fantasize that he would meet a girl who had Hodgkin's and they would go off to an island somewhere together. This fantasy described the deep longing for someone who would really understand his feelings, and that person would know them only if she had actually experienced them.

A year passed. Another Christmas came. And Louie found himself in the hospital again. This time he learned that the disease had progressed, and that the drug that they had been using no longer worked. His lungs were bad and his backbone was near breaking. They would have to give large doses of cobalt to strengthen the weak spot. A new drug would be used and it would not be as comprehensive as the other, but neither would it produce the terrible nausea. The news brought about a new wave of terror. After two weeks he completed the cobalt treatment and went home only to return within seventy-two hours nearly dead. His condition was critical. He responded to no one. And we had to deal with the prospect of losing him. At four in the afternoon he opened his eyes and said the first words of the day. We were relieved. He would make it this time. Platelets poured into his bloodstream had brought Louie back with great rapidity. One day he was nearly dead, and the next he was up shaving. He was confronted with how rapidly he could change—both directions.

We talked. He said he was glad to be in the hospital because then people realized how sick he is, and that his condition is serious. "I don't have to pretend to be strong when I am in the hospital. People come to see me and they know that I am really sick." There was another side of him, though, that feared being weak. "I can't accept being weak. I'm so angry. And I don't know what to do. I cry over every little thing. I can't control my emotions." He was so frustrated and frightened. He later said, "The thought of what is going on inside my body is terrifying. I can get so much worse and not even know it. Before I checked my nodes every morning. Now I'll have to check the bones too????" The unknown is an awful monster to encounter.

In the weeks following this last hospitalization Louie felt that death was around the corner and he became terrified. The only way he knew how to cope was to take sleeping pills and other drugs in such quantity as to knock himself out. He nearly succeeded in knocking himself out permanently and thus had to return to the hospital.

The terror itself frightened him. He hated it. "Why can't I be like the man who didn't tell anyone that he had cancer? Wasn't he a much more noble person than I am?" I told him, "Perhaps the man was even more terrified. If no one knew, then he could pretend he wasn't sick and didn't have to admit it even to himself." A look of relief ran across Louie's face. He went on, "When I went down for a liver scan there was a man crying out, ''Why can't you stop all this and let me die?'' I said, ''You are worrying about what it will be like.'' He told me how scared he was. And finally he told of reading of the football player with Hodgkin's who was going to the Mardi Gras, but died before he got there. The future is so unknown. When will death come? Will there be warning? Will it be gradual or fast? Can it be avoided? The fears came tumbling out.

I went home and wrote to Louie:

> I do not know
> If you feel it
> As I feel it.
> Maybe not
> But for me
> There is a dimension
> Of love
> That I have for you
> That is absolutely
> Unique!!
> I know for sure
> That with each passing
> Month you become
> More precious to me.
> And one of the reasons
> This is so,
> Is because you do not
> Hide behind a mask,
> But share
> Your hurts and sorrows,
> Worries and dreams,
> Fantasies and pleasures,
> Anger and insights.
> Your struggles shared
> Have brought a dimension
> To my being
> That was not there before.
> And I thank you for sharing with me.
> I hurt with you just a tiny bit of your hurt.
> And even that tiny bit
> Is sometimes hard for me to handle.
>
> There is no doubt that I feel weak
> As do you.

And I say ''Praise God for weakness felt.''
For somehow or other
In weakness feelings shared
There is a meaning never experienced
By the so called strong,
Who need to deny their weakness feelings.

Louie framed the tribute and hung it on his bedroom wall. Its assurance had meaning for him. Too often feelings do not get verbalized. The permanence of the written word is often treasured by the recipient.

Louie has died. His fears of a lingering death were unnecessary. His agony was but a week. But in that week there was so much physical pain and so much frustration. What he had feared for two years had come to pass. There was the agony to be endured. Perhaps it is as necessary for growth of the spirit as is heat for the tempering of steel. The agony was followed by the great affirmation three hours before he died. For one entire half hour he communicated with all the tones of the conquering spirit. There were no words, just a continuous and intense, ''Ummmmmm Hummmmmm, um hum, ummmmm hummmmmm!!!!!!'' What did it mean? Surely it involved gratitude; gratitude for what had been, but also for what was to be. As his spirit remained with us it seemed to take on a bit of the eternal. There was such strong and intense tone. It was hard to believe that enough strength could be summoned for such a witness. UMMMMMMM HUMMMMMM!!!!!!! ummm hummm! HUMMMMMMM HUMMMMMMMM!!!!!!!!!!

Death, it is no longer just a word I wish to avoid. It is an experience the near side of which I felt as I sat by and hurt and agonized as Louie was engaged in the act of dying. Early in the week I felt the pain, the frustration, the fear and the anxiety. He said he would wait to talk about it until Friday. Later in the week I felt the courage, the confrontation, the agony and the frustration. I was afraid. I wanted to escape. I wanted to be free.

On Friday I felt the conquest, the conquering, and finally the anticipation. I felt my soul bared as it had never been before. Surely those were by far the most emotion filled moments of my entire life. His eyes were wide, he held Diane's hand with great strength and uttered his song of affirmation: Ummmm Hummmm! Ummmmmm hummmmmm!! Ummmmmmm Hummmmmm!!!!!!! An before my very eyes I saw that dying is a birth. It is terribly, terribly hard. It may be the hardest thing a person ever does. But one does emerge from the dark into the light.

Louie's conquering spirt bore witness to a new chapter about which we have only been given a hint.

I shall be richer all my life for this sorrow! New insights about life have been born. Life is to be lived by striking a line through every minus and turning it into a plus. If agony must be experienced, there are those who are ready to bear some of the burden. Where there is suffering the gift of courage is given. Courage comes from without as well as from within. The important moments in life are those shared with others, whatever the cost may be. When hurts are shared, closeness is born. The gift of love is a most precious gift, and it is possible to express it most fully at the end of earthly life. I shall be richer all my life for this sorrow. New insights about death have emerged. Death is another beginning, not an end. Death is but a new birth into a new state. Death is not to be feared, any more than is birth. When the body ceases to be, the spirit emerges, free and unencumbered. I shall be richer all my life for this sorrow!

> Sorrow:
> It hurts deep down inside.
> One feels diminished,
> Less than he has been.
> Empty,
> Bereft—
> Forlorn and incomplete.
> Sorrow is a painful word
> But if someone is there
> To share the feeling
> It becomes endurable
> And in the scheme of things
> A time of being
> That includes great emotion
> And thus a time of closeness,
> Growing and becoming someone more
> Than we have been before.

> *IN MEMORIAM*
>
> We sprinkle the ashes—
> All that tangibly remains
> Of Louis Peter Knudsen.
> But thank God for the intangibles—
> The impact of his life on ours.
> We remember:
> —the smile
> —the frown
> —the quizzical look
> —the love

—the courage
—the hurt
—the sorrow
—the significant moments
—the fun times
—the searching times
—the moments of risk
—the great time of affirmation
As long as we live
We will bear the imprint
Of that influence.
He opened many doors for us—
Doors to whole new sets of meanings.
We will forever be sensitized
As to the importance of life.
Because of Louie we will live differently.

LOVE—GRATITUDE

The agony is so great . . .
And yet I will stand it.
Had I not loved so very much
I would not hurt so much.
But goodness knows I would not
Want to diminish that precious love
By one fraction of an ounce.
I will hurt,
And I will be grateful to the hurt
For it bears witness to
The depth of our meanings,
And for that I will be
Eternally grateful.

AN ATTEMPT AT REFORM*

August Strindberg

She had noticed with disgust the way in which girls were brought up to be housekeepers to their future husbands. She had therefore learnt a trade, by which she would be able to support herself under all possible circumstances: she could make artificial flowers.

He had noticed with pain that girls sat about waiting to be kept by their future husbands. He wanted to marry a free, independent woman, who could support herself. Then he would be able to regard her as his equal, and have a comrade for life, not a housekeeper.

Fate willed that they should meet. He was a painter, an artist, and she, as I said, made flowers, and it was in Paris that they had picked up those new ideas.

Theirs was a marriage in good taste. They had rented three rooms in Passy. Their studio was in the middle, his room was on one side of it, and hers on the other. They were not going to share a bed, a beastly idea, that had not the remotest counterpart in nature, and which only gave rise to excesses and disorderliness. And fancy having to undress in the same room! Ugh! No indeed! A room each and a neutral room in common: the studio. No servants, for they would do the cooking together, just an old woman who would come in morning and evening.

It was all carefully calculated and rightly conceived.

"But what if you have children?" enquired the doubters.

"We're not going to have any children."

Bon! They were not going to have any children.

It was delightful. He went down to the market in the morning and did the shopping. After that he made the coffee. She swept, and made the beds, and tidied up. Then they sat down to work.

When they tired of this they chatted for a while, gave each other a bit of advice, laughed and enjoyed themselves. As dinner-time drew near he lit the stove, and she cleaned the vegetables. He saw to the *pot-au-feu*, while she ran down to the grocer's. Then she laid the table while he dished up.

But they did not live as brother and sister. They said good night in the evening and they each went to their own room. Then would come a knock at her door, and she would say: come in. But the bed was narrow, and there was never any nonsense. They each woke up in the morning in their own bed. And then there'd be a knocking on the walls.

"Good morning, my pet! How are you today?"

"Very well, thank you, but how are you?"

Their meeting in the morning was always new, and it never grew stale.

Sometimes they went out together in the evenings and met their fellow-countrymen at Syrach's. Tobacco smoke did not embarrass her, and she never embarrassed anyone.

People thought it was an ideal marriage; they had never seen such a happy couple.

But the girl had parents who lived a long way off. In their letters they constantly asked if Lisen wasn't expecting yet, for they were longing so much to have a grandchild. Lisen must remember that marriage was created for the sake of the children, not for the parents. Lisen told them that their ideas were old-fashioned. Whereupon her mother asked if they intended to exterminate the human race with their newfangled notions. Lisen had not thought of this, but it did not worry her. She was happy, and so was her husband, and now the world had at last seen a happy marriage, and consequently it was jealous.

What fun they had. Neither was the other's master, and they went shares on expenses. Sometimes he earned more, sometimes she did, so things evened up in the end.

Then there were birthdays. She would wake up to find their madame entering with a bouquet of flowers and a little sheet of notepaper with flowers painted on it, on which was written: "Mrs. Rosebud's dauber wishes her Many Happy Returns, and invites her to a tip-top breakfast in his room—ready now." Then they'd do a bit of knocking on the wall, after which she'd put on her dressing-gown, and there'd be more knocking, this time on his door. Come in! And they'd have breakfast in bed, his bed, and their madame would stay there for the whole morning. It was delightful.

And it never grew stale. For it lasted for two years. All the prophets were proved wrong, and that's what marriage should be like.

Then something happened. The young wife became ill. She thought it was the wall-paper, but he suggested bacteria. Yes, of course, it must be bacteria.

But something else was wrong too. Things were definitely not as they should be. It must be a chill. But she was getting so fat! Could it be that she had one of those growths you hear so much about? Yes, it must be a growth. She went to a doctor, and when she got home she wept. It really was a little growth, but one which would emerge into the daylight in due course, and turn into a flower, and set seeds, it too!

Her husband did not weep. He thought it was stunning. And would you believe it, the wretch went and boasted about it at Syrach's. But his wife wept again. What would happen now to their relationship? She wouldn't be able to earn anything now. She'd have to live on him. They'd have to have a maid too. Ugh! those maids!

All their planning, all their prudence, all their foresight had gone aground on the inescapable.

But mother-in-law wrote enthusiastic letters of congratulation, and repeated time after time that God had created marriage for the sake of the children, and that the parent's pleasure was only a side issue.

Hugo swore that he would never give a thought to the fact that she didn't earn anything. Wouldn't she contribute quite enough to their home by the work she did for his child, and wasn't that also worth money? What was money but work? That meant she'd be paying her share. All the same the thought that she'd be living on him nagged for a long time, but when the child arrived she forgot about it. She was his wife and his comrade, just as she had been, but she was also the mother of his child, and to him that was best of all.

ARE YOU READY FOR A BABY?*

Lynn Forman

Back in the days when I had my children, people married young, and the patter of bootied feet followed closely, if discreetly, on the heels of the bridal procession. A proper wedding to a husband who could afford diaper service was considered adequate preparation for parenthood.

Now with improved methods of family planning, and the easing of societal pressures, there is increased freedom of choice—whether to opt for parenthood or to pass, and when. But with increased freedom comes increased complexity.

"Readiness" for parenthood can be glibly defined in terms of chronology, biology, psychology or even ecology. But attempts to determine it by a single factor are bound to be frustrating: one important consideration invariably conflicts with another. If, for example, one postpones parenthood in order to launch a career, one may have to pay a price in increased chances of birth complications. Conversely, if one bears children at physical "prime time," one may later regret the premature sacrifices of personal freedom.

What seems apparent in talking to women who became mothers at ages ranging from eighteen to forty-two is that no one age is "right" for everybody. One woman may need years of relative freedom before settling down happily to parenthood. Another may prefer to have children early and have her freedom, as one woman put it, "when you're young enough to enjoy it but mature enough to appreciate it."

Some very young parents raise children easily enough while getting through college and into careers; others flounder and feel helplessly trapped. Some older parents feel resentment at the upsetting of already established routines or are overwhelmed by the demands; others, like Adele Ribolow, are flexible and take it all in stride.

Director of a New York employment agency and mother of two young daughters, Ms. Ribolow was married for ten years before having her first child at thirty-four. Although she feels that, in her case, the advantages of waiting till she was "really ready" outweighed the disadvantages, she stressed that readiness "is a state of mind, not a fact of chonology."

"If you don't feel trapped by motherhood, I think you can have a child at *any* age," says Ms. Ribolow. "A lot depends on how tied down you *want* to feel. I took my infants everywhere and never felt trapped, while other women feel incarcerated and very bitter." Another woman, the thirty-eight-year-old mother of two preschoolers, takes the latter view: "After doing exactly as I pleased for so many years, I resent the curtailment of my activities much more than I would if I hadn't gotten used to having such freedom.

Ms. Ribolow is one of many whose experience disputes the popular notion that the physical side of motherhood is rougher as a woman gets older. She delivered both children by prepared childbirth and had eventless pregnancies. "I worked till Thursday," she says, "and had my daughter Friday morning. I really think a lot of it depends on your attitude. I'm actually more energetic and more physically active at the age of forty-three than I was at twenty."

While some young parents feel they missed out on something by having children very early, others were "blissfully unaware" of what they were missing. One woman who had her first child at nineteen, less than a year after she was married, is glad—now that her kids are grown—that she did. "When I had them, I had no idea of who I was or what I wanted. I might just as well have been washing diapers as pounding a typewriter. By the time I started to think about doing something, the kids were in school and I had a second chance. I'd rather be free at thirty-nine (and now that I've reached it, it doesn't seem as 'over the hill' as it once did) than at twenty, when I was too young to know what I wanted, let alone how to go about getting it. In a way though, I think I missed a lot of my kids' childhoods. I was so into my own youthful preoccupations and so impatient to get the children off to school. In retrospect I'm glad I had them early, but I wouldn't want my daughters to do it that way. I'd like them to explore and experience a bit first and get a sense of their own identity."

Many women feel that it is important to attain a personal identity before becoming a parent, not only to avoid limiting one's world to diapers and playgrounds, but also because having a child can be a significant test of who you really are. One woman, who was twenty-two when her son was born, puts it this way: "Your child is constantly throwing your own values and ideas back at you. Unless you have a strong sense of yourself, that constant confrontation can be very threatening."

To some women, a sense of identity is strongly connected with a career, and some advocate postponing a family until a woman has developed confidence in her abilities and gotten a career off the ground.

Gail Tavares, a thirty-one-year-old art director, switched to free-lance work until her three-year-old son recently entered nursery school. Temporarily adjusting her schedule didn't upset her since, as she says, "I had already proven myself and I knew that as long as I kept my hand in, there would always be a place for me in my field." Having recently returned to a full-time job, she is surprised to discover that employers take her more seriously now. "They know I'm not just marking time. Since I already have a child, they're not afraid I'll quit to have one."

Some women, however, resent putting an active career aside even for a while, or diluting it with family responsibilities. And many feel the strain of "being pulled into two directions."

Sharon Bermon, president of New York City's Counseling Women, was married at twenty, but waited until she was twenty-nine to have her daughter, Jenny. "A lot of women wait until they've established a career befor having a child," she says, "but then when they do, they don't have time for a child. I feel guilty about the fact that I resent the time that Jenny takes now when I'm finally hitting my stride. A couple of years ago I was more patient with her because I had fewer demands on my time." She admits to being a little envious of women who had children young and are free now, "while I'm in my mid-thirties and my child is still in pre-school. If I could do things differently," she muses, "I'd probably have had a child sooner, at twenty-three or twenty-five or maybe even in college. But I don't think people usually know what they should do until about ten years after the fact."

Although some women with young children feel guilty about working, they concede that being at home doesn't automatically make a good mother. "If you really have a strong urge for a career but stay home resenting your kids, you might as well go out and work," says Ms. Bermon. "You may feel the increased pressure of two pulls, but at least you're satisfying an important need."

In addition to the emotional factors connected with parenthood at various stages of a woman's life, there are also serious physical considerations.

According to Dr. Louise B. Tyrer, Vice-President for Medical Affairs of Planned Parenthood World Population, the risk of all pregnancy and birth complications (to both mother and child) is highest when a mother is under eighteen or over thirty-five.

Women at the older end of the reproductive age span have the highest incidence of hemorrhage, toxemia of pregnancy, prolonged labor, delivery complications, abnormal fetal presentation, elevated diastolic blood pressure, Caesarean section, fetal death, stillbirth, early spontaneous abortion (often of a genetically defective fetus) and incidence of congenitally malformed offspring (although mongolism, which used to be the biggest concern to mothers over forty, may now be detected during pregnancy by sampling the fluid around the baby, and if possible, the fetus may be aborted). The maternal mortality rate also rises sharply with increasing age. From a low of 10.3 maternal deaths per one hundred thousand live births at age 20–24 and 15.6 at 25–29, it climbs to 27.6 at 30–34, 67.7 at 35–39 and 97.7 at 40–44.

Teenage mothers, on the other hand, run a higher than average risk of anemia infant mortality, and premature and low birth-weight babies. Statistics for the under 20 age group, however, can sometimes be misleading, since they tend to lump ages from 15 to 19 together in one category. While the *early* teens are dangerous years for motherhood because of biological immaturity, many experts feel that by the age of 18 or 19 a woman has reached her prime physical condition for reproduction. Even though the maternal mortality rate—which is slightly higher for mothers under 20 (18.5 deaths per 100,000 live births) than for women in their 20's—makes no distinctions between 15 and 19 year olds, the rate for younger mothers is still considerably lower than that for women over 30.

It is important to bear in mind when considering such statistics that, while the *relative risk* of complication is far greater in much older or much younger age groups, factors such as poor general health and inadequate medical care contribute substantially to *actual incidence* of complications. Improved medical knowledge continues to reduce the risks in *all* age groups (the U.S. maternal mortality rate, for example, has declined over 94% since 1940), and chronological age alone should not cause a woman to rule out having children if other conditions are favorable.

Clearly, the "ideal" physiological age to have a child is in the 20's, when all physical risks are minimal and the chances of having an uncomplicated pregnancy, a normal delivery and a healthy child are best. But to be truly "ideal" in our culture Dr. Tyrer feels the range should be narrowed even more: "When you add the psychological factors, I think it would suit a woman better to have pregnancies between 25 and 30 when her life and her marital situation are usually more stable."

The stability of one's marriage not only affects one's decision to have children but is frequently affected by that decision as well. When parents are very young, it is often for the worse.

Several women who became mothers at a very early age felt they became "old and settled" before their time; they say that struggling with family responsibilities while still in their teens or early twenties put tremendous strains on their marriage. Many of them are now divorced. An added strain occurs when young parents extend their own adolescence by becoming increasingly dependent on their own parents.

Regardless of a couple's age, experts feel it is best to wait several years after marriage before having a child—long enough to get to know themselves and to allow sufficient time for their marriage to stabilize, but not so long that the couple becomes too settled in a childless lifestyle. Since a child may be seen as more and more of an intrusion as time goes by, a couple who continually postpones having children for "one more year" and then another may not get around to having them at all.

An "ideal" age for parenthood becomes even more difficult to pinpoint when one considers the child's point of view. As Dr. Sirgay Sanger, a Manhattan child psychiatrist, points out, different age children benefit from different age parents. "A forty-year-old mother may do beautifully with a baby," he says "but when that child gets to be ten or eleven and the mother is in her fifties, she may find it difficult to keep up physically. Children themselves prefer younger parents, but the teenager who's great when it comes to getting down on the floor to play games with three- to ten-year olds may not be nearly so great when she's confined to the house with the responsibilities of an infant."

In general, children of teenage parents and of those over thirty-five tend to have more problems than those of parents in other age groups. But, since individuals vary even at the same age, one parent may be "old" at 25, and another may be youthful in spirit, if not in years, at fifty or even older.

The experts feel that parent-child difficulties are apt to occur when older parents have forgotten how it feels to be an adolescent and are unable to empathize with their children's problems and to the turmoil involved in growing up.

According to Dr. Sanger, "Older parents sometimes have such clear ideas of what they want their children to be that the child doesn't have a chance. Their standards and expectations are so rigidly set that it's more difficult for the child to live up to them, to make mistakes, to just be different." This problem is especially acute for an only child of such parents.

Since one person's asset is often another's liability, a decision that's right for your best friend may be all wrong for you. But whatever your choice, it is important to realize that, while a situation may be good, nothing is perfect. If you have unrealistic expectations—if you insist on holding out for circumstances that are nothing less than idyllic, on waiting until the world situation has improved, you can "easily" afford to feed extra mouths and you have no second thoughts whatsoever—the "right" time for parenthood may very well never come at all. As one woman put it, "Nobody's ever *really* ready to have children."

ARE YOU READY TO BECOME A PARENT? ASK YOURSELF THESE QUESTIONS BEFORE YOU DECIDE:

1. *Identity:* a) Do you have a pretty clear idea of who you are and what

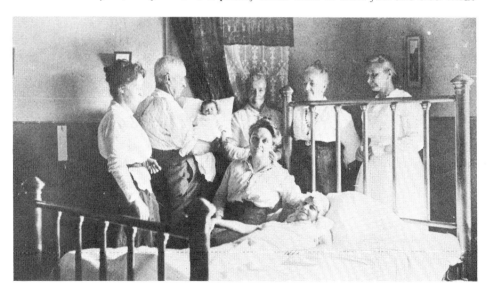

you want, or are you clutching at parenthood to provide you with it? b) Have you had sufficient time and freedom to explore, experiment and do the things you wanted to do?

2. *Motivation:* Do you really *want* a child, feel you're ready and believe you can contribute substantially to that child in terms of love, time and attention, *or* would you like a child in order to feel grown up, to have security in your old age, to avoid making decisions or facing problems, to save your marriage, to define your identity or because your friends, family or the calendar say you should?

3. *Attitude:* Are you flexible in your attitudes and your lifestyle, or do you have rigid standards, firm ideas and precise expectations of what your child "should" be like and exactly how he or she will fit into your life?

4. *Marital situation:* a) Have you been married long enough to adjust to marriage, to know your husband and to feel that your relationship is strong enough to sustain added responsibilities? b) Is your husband supportive, does he want a child as much as you do, and do you honestly believe he'll be a good father? c) Have you discussed your views on parenthood, including your idea about child-raising and your feelings about sharing chores? And have you freely aired any reservations either of you may have about becoming parents? d) Regardless of the stability of your marriage, would you be willing and able to raise your child alone if it turned out that you had to? (If that sounds negative, remember that even "stable" marriages sometimes end, and it's a lot harder to face the reality when you hadn't even considered the possibility.)

5. *Financial situation:* Are you independent enough financially (as well as emotionally) so that you won't have to lean on your parents for help in handling increased expenses? And if you can't afford occasional paid sitters, are you resourceful enough to consider alternatives (like cooperative swap-sitting with neighborhood mothers) so you won't have to stay home and feel trapped or rely on your parents as constant unpaid baby-tenders?

6. *Career:* If you plan to continue working, have you given serious thought to how you'll arrange your schedule and started to check out possible child-care arrangements? Are you willing, if necessary, to adjust your timetable for the first two or three years or put your career on hold for a while? Or will you resent the intrusion on your established routine?

7. *Physical health:* Are you reasonably healthy, with a fair degree of stamina? While you don't have to have a letter in sports, parenthood does require a certain amount of energy.

8. *Are you on the pill?* If you are, it is best not to plan to conceive as soon as you go off it. During the first few months after stopping the pill, there is a lower likelihood of conception, as well as an increased occurrence of congenital deformities that result in spontaneous abortions. It's a good idea to use another birth control method for a few months before trying to conceive.

9. *Do you have some idea of what parenthood is really like?* While it's impossible to know until you've been there exactly what the experience is all

about, you're in for a rude awakening if *all* your images begin with a closetful of cute maternity clothes and fade out romantically on a madonna and cooing child. It might be worth your while to talk candidly with mothers. And, if you feel you need it, pre-family counseling offered by some counseling centers can help you get more in touch with what you can expect from parenthood and from yourself as a parent. A helpful book is *The Mother Person* by Virginia Barber and Merrill Maguire Skaggs.

10. *Where do you want to be a quarter of a century from now?* At the age of 20 or 25, it may be fairly easy to think about having a baby "in the future" when you're 35. But don't stop there; project even further ahead. When you're 50 (and you will be someday), would you rather be free, with an occasional visit from grandchildren . . . or still on active duty? Will the freedom now be worth the responsibilities later? And if a large family sounds appealing, have you figured out how old you'll be when the youngest one is grown? While you can't know until you get there what your life will be like at a given future time, a little planning in the present can prevent a lot of regretting later on.

*

5

AND THEY LIVED HAPPILY EVER AFTER

Admittedly, the family during child rearing years continues to deal with major issues. Some of these may develop into problems severe enough to result in divorce. Still, there is the tendency to consider the marriage relationship as a type of clock that is to be wound and set in motion, needing little further attention. After all, the major decisions on career, residence, number and spacing of children have been made, and the initial adjustments to the "stranger" across the table and in bed are in the past. In Section 5, "And They Lived Happily Ever After," we examine some of the crucial issues that prompt the question, "What else is to be done to ensure a lasting and fulfilling relationship?"

The question itself holds a key to the problem. Many, in fact, feel they have done all that is necessary and that they can now relax, be comfortable, and enjoy the stability of a dependable relationship. Both persons, however, continue to change in response to each other, to jobs, aging, children's growth, and to external factors. If they do not make a creative response, they may find disruptive problems with which they cannot cope.

Family roles and role expectations change over time. The full-time homemaker/wife may want to reenter the job market or continue education when children are in school, or the part-time employed wife may opt for the 40-hour week. Such change necessitates a renegotiation of homemaking responsibilities. Even if the homemaker does not decide to work outside the home, her responsibilities and the demands on her time change when children are all in school. Expectations of the male role also change as children grow, needing and wanting the companionship of shared activities that are more time-consuming than when the children were younger. Camping, fishing, sports activities, joint projects, help with homework—all take more time and effort than changing diapers, reading the comics or building a tower of blocks for a preschooler.

By the time men reach 35, they can begin to see their career more clearly. Only a few will make it big in the business world; most must face the reality of settling for a place well down the ladder. Women entering the job market and developing careers also will face the issue of how high they are going. For both men and women, the future may be couched in the question, "Is this all there is?" The stimulation of the early years of marriage can fade, the comfortable life long anticipated can become a rut.

The relationship between a husband and wife also changes. Where wives/mothers with small children may have needed support from their husbands, now they may need encouragement for greater independence in activities or careers of their own. As the needs change, responses vary. They can include disenchantment or disengagement, divorce or rebuilding on the basis of new needs. If the family drama of this period is to have the "happy ending" desired by the couple and by society, family members must be active participants and change the script as the drama develops. Unfortunately, many prefer not to change or may be unable to do so. Life for them will likely continue with less satisfaction than it might have. However they choose, the issues presented in this section will be a part of the drama of this stage.

CONTENTS: SECTION 5

FEMALES IN THE WORLD OF WORK*

Janet S. Chafetz

... Most females in our society marry at some time in their lives. Most also work at some point. Indeed, 31 million adult females are employed, comprising 40 percent of the total work force.[1] The effects on their job opportunities of the fact that women marry and work cannot be overstated. One of the most important is the problem of role conflict. The term "role conflict" refers to two phenomena: a conflict of expectations arising from two or more roles that an individual holds simultaneously, and a conflict of expectations built into a single role. Employed females, especially but not solely if they are married and have children, are subject to both.

It has been noted that the mere fact that males have wives is important in helping to advance career aspirations. More than two thirds of all American wives are employed outside the home at some time in their married life, and nearly 40 percent of all married women in 1968 were working wives.[2] Such women are trying to fulfill two separate roles, each of which makes strong (and often conflicting) demands on time, energy, and attention. Wives and mothers who work outside their homes (and even about one in three mothers of young children are employed) are not excused by society, nor do they excuse themselves from the many time-consuming activities involved in these family roles.[3] When daughter Jane has the flu, Mother is somehow expected to arrange her work day to get daughter to the doctor. The ironing and vacuuming get done at night or on Saturday, but they are expected to be done by the wife (few employed wives can afford the services of even part-time household help). An "understanding" husband-father may, out of "the goodness of his heart" "help" his wife by drying the dishes; he may even "babysit" while his wife attends an important evening or Saturday meeting (but have you ever heard of a mother "babysitting" for her own children while father is out?). However, he is always a "helpmate," and the responsibility remains hers.

The working wife ends up working at two full-time jobs, and the time and energy commitments of these must necessarily conflict, as well as exhaust her. Since the husband and father roles specify so little by way of actual, expected tasks at home, few such conflicts are apt to arise for the male. In short, most work roles are currently structured for people whose main, indeed sole, important task is that of "provider" and who have little else to divert their attention. Wives and mothers are simply not by social and personal definition in that situation.

---

*Reproduced by permission of the publisher, F. E. Peacock Publishers, Inc., Itasca, Illinois. From Janet Saltzman Chafetz, *Masculine/Feminine or Human? An overview of the Sociology of Sex Roles.* 1974 copyright, pp. 119–132.

The work role, then, is structured by our economy for males (which is perhaps the real meaning of "sexism"). It is hardly likely that a research scientist, a lawyer, an artist, an administrator, or anyone else can compete for excellence in their chosen field, and the promotions and raises that result, if they are diverted constantly by worries about what to defrost for dinner, running noses, dry cleaning, the plumbing, and so forth. This is especially the case if the competitors are freed from such concerns. In addition, many women lose valuable years of work and experience on the dubious assumption, reinforced by media and "scientific" experts such as Dr. Benjamin Spock, that newborns need the constant presence and attention of their mothers. This, too, puts them at a competitive disadvantage. Indeed, a number of organizations which have routinely granted leaves to males for the discharge of military obligations, guaranteeing their jobs on return, have no parallel policy for pregnancy leave. This virtually forces females to quit work when pregnant, only to have to begin again from the bottom when they return to the labor market.

The problems faced by women who are both wives and employees exemplify one kind of role conflict, namely, interrole conflict. This second type of conflict exists for female workers regardless of marital status and may even be somewhat worse for the unmarried. The modern work environment in postindustrial societies is heavily bureaucratic and administrative. A premium is placed on brains rather than brawn, since few jobs today require a degree of physical strength greater than that probably possessed by all healthy adults. Thus females today should be in an infinitely better position to compete in the economy than previously, when physical strength was a more important component of most work. The fact that this is not the case results from the values instilled in females by the kind of upbringing documented in the preceding chapter and strongly reinforced by male-dominated media, science, and religion.

Females are trained to be sensitive, emotional, intuitive, passive, unaggressive, and so forth, but the modern work environment increasingly requires rational, logical, aggressive, ambitious, competitive, and mechanical traits. It has, in fact, a "masculine" orientation. On the one hand "feminine" females lose out in the job market because they lack the requisite mental habits to function in any but the most menial jobs. On the other, females who enter the world of work at higher levels, unlike males, are forced to behave in one way on the job and another with dates and families. Moreover, if they exhibit too strongly those "masculine" traits that enable success, they are labeled "bitches" or "castrating females" and shunned by male colleagues, to both their personal and professional detriment.[4] Females in more responsible positions are thus faced with a "catch 22." They must maneuver on a narrow balance beam between the contradictory traits that on the one side would win them admiration as females and on the other would enable them to function professionally. The psychic costs and waste of valuable energy are immeasurable, and the result again is a strong competitive disadvantage with males.

Several other considerations make matters worse for women in the world of work. Faced with psychologically distressing and physically exhausting role conflicts, females who compete for good jobs find their male "peers" expect little of them—after all, they're "only" females. If she performs as well as a mediocre male a woman will often find herself loudly praised, and when she does poorly it's dismissed with a "Well, what did you expect of a woman?" These kinds of responses come to constitute self-fulfilling prophecies and hardly comprise the kind of spur that promotes excellence.[5]

When a woman finds herself discouraged at work, as everyone, regardless of gender, does from time to time, she will know that she can quit without suffering social criticism. Indeed, she will generally be praised for leaving career behind and devoting herself full time to home and family. She must, therefore, constantly recommit herself to work. By comparison, males are rarely free to leave the world of work and are thus, ironically, freed from the psychological stress entailed in worrying about whether or not to remain employed. From youth she has been encouraged by schools, parents, and peers to view work in terms of "contingency plans" in case she "has to work," and she has been told to leave enough options open to avoid conflict with the career needs of whatever male she eventually marries.[6] As a result, many females find themselves in fields they dislike but have chosen because they can practice them anywhere their husbands might go. They only too eagerly give them up when possible, or at least they approach their jobs with something less than enthusiasm.

Finally, "victimized" people, whether black or female, tend to suffer from a lack of self-confidence, or an inferiority complex. The feminine stereotype explicitly encourages such a self-concept in regard to males, and males are taught from an early age that they are indeed "superior" to females. These attitudes will hardly benefit a female in pressing for the acceptance of her ideas or in any aspect of job competition with males. Indeed, most employed females have had the experience of finding themselves virtually "invisible" to their male colleagues—their ideas ignored or stolen—and incapable of asserting themselves in response.

JOB DISCRIMINATION AGAINST WOMEN

These competitive disadvantages rooted in the feminine sex role are strengthened by overt, as well as more subtle, forms of discrimination on the part of employers, who are overwhelmingly male. Rationalizing on the basis of a series of myths, employers still blatantly disregard the law, refusing to hire females for a large number of high-status and well-paid positions, failing to promote them, and paying them less than males engaged in the same work. As of the 1964 Civil Rights Act and a number of subsequent executive orders, discrimination on the basis of gender is illegal. It is noteworthy that this stipulation was added by Senator Harry Byrd as a "joke," in an effort to block passage of a law designed chiefly to end racial discrimination.

Let us consider first some of the more subtle forms of discrimination. To a large extent, policy is formed, "deals" are closed, contacts are made, and information is exchanged in male-only clubs, bars, and such lofty sites as men's rooms and locker rooms. When feminists picket men's grills or such an establishment as the all-male Detroit Economic Club they are not engaged in a trivial exercise. Among other things, they are asking that the key sites for important business dealings be made accessible to females—how else can they hope to achieve anything in the business world, even if they manage to reach positions with grandiose titles? The "protégé" or apprentice system, especially in academia and other professions, constitutes another subtle form of discrimination.[7] Top positions in many fields are filled by an informal process in which the potential employer calls around to his (male) friends and asks whom they recommend. They recommend their protégés, who, given the sponsors' own prejudices, are rarely female. Only open advertising of all openings can avoid this type of discrimination, a major demand of many professional women's groups. There is, finally, what Cynthia Epstein refers to as "status-set typing."[8] This "occurs when a class of persons shares statuses (that is, certain statuses tend to cluster) *and when it is considered appropriate that they do so*". For instance, most top-level administrators of large corporations also share other statuses in common, namely, they are white, Protestant, and male. Although these other statuses are theoretically irrelevant to their functioning as corporate administrators, people who do not share the cluster make the others "uncomfortable"; something doesn't seem to "fit." The irrelevant statuses then become the most salient ones to the individual as well as to colleagues, in the process obscuring the chief status, which in this case is that of corporate administrator. Under these circumstances the individual will find it difficult to function effectively. Virtually all economic positions of much prestige have as part of their status-set the attribute of maleness.

Discrimination scarcely ends with these subtle forms. On the basis of a series of myths and half-truths, employers often outspokenly defend their "right" to grant males preferential treatment in job considerations.

Myth 1: Females are only working for "pin money."   The idea behind this myth is that since their husbands are supporting them, females do not need as much income as males. One thing is certain, females do not *receive* as much pay as males, even those in the same positions. In 1972 full-time employed females earned 60 percent of the males' average income; the median female income was $5,323, compared to $8,966 for males.[9] Where in 1969 13 percent of all employed males earned in excess of $10,000, the corresponding percentage for females was 1.4. The median wages of white females are considerably below those of black males, and the doubly discriminated-against black females are at the very bottom of the salary scale.[10] [11] Moreover, college-educated women earn about the equivalent of a male with an eighth-grade education.[12] [13] Females in sales positions earn only 42 percent of the salary of males in sales; those in the census category "professional, technical and kindred," about 68 percent; craftsmen and foremen, 58 percent; clerical personnel, 68 percent, and so on.[14] Finally, females have an unemployment rate that is double that of males.[15]

The "result" of this myth is obvious; the only problem is that the "cause," namely, the lesser need for income, is simply not true. Five and a half million American families are headed by females—single, widowed, divorced, or separated—and in 1969 their median income amounted to a mere $4,000. It should therefore come as no shock to learn that 2.4 million of those families live below the poverty line, accounting for 4.5 million dependent children.[16] The divorce rate has been rising so sharply that no female can assume any longer that she will be supported for the rest of her life. Those husbands who are supposed by many to be supporting their estranged wives in luxury averaged a mere $12 per week in support payments a few years ago.[17]

But what about working wives with husbands present and employed? The simple truth is that the bulk of employed wives are married to men who do not earn very much, and it is often their wages that maintain the family above the poverty line.[18] In short, women who work are generally either the sole support of self, and frequently family, or they provide much-needed income to maintain life above the poverty line. Salaries are scarcely "pin money" to these millions. Salary discrepancies are also not irrelevant to businesses. A recent newspaper report *(Houston Chronicle)* estimated that if females were paid at the

same rate as males, the annual national payroll would have to be increased by $59 billion! Exploitation is only too profitable.

Myth 2: The wealth of our nation is mainly in the hands of females. Females comprise only one third of the top wealthholders in this country and about half of the adult, individual stockholders. Moreover, they acquire their wealth at a much later age than males, primarily through widowhood. Of the younger women in this group, much of their wealth is largely a matter of assets assigned them in name only by husbands and fathers for tax purposes. In any case, *de facto* control of wealth usually remains in male hands, be it father, husband, or trustee in the form of a lawyer, banker, or broker.[19] Kristen Amundsen concludes that "The implications of these findings are quite clear: Women wealth-holders are not likely to have the expertise, the experience, or the opportunity for putting their resources to use in an attempt to influence the trend and shape of the economy".[20]

Myth 3: Women aren't worth hiring where any training or investment is involved, since they just get married or pregnant and quit. Females do indeed quit jobs more often than males, and frequently they give family-related reasons. However, when occupational level and income are held constant, males and females do not differ significantly in turnover rates.[21] What does this mean? Females are more frequently hired for menial, routinized, duller jobs than males. Moreover, they are often "overeducated" for them. The college-educated female working as a receptionist or clerk-typist (while supposedly "proving" she is worthy of more serious consideration) is no rarity. Among all such jobs turnover rates are very high; the overwhelmingly male, but dull, routinized auto-assembly industry is plagued with the highest job turnover rate of any. Where females and males in the *same* job and income categories are compared, little difference is found.

It is only because of their differential distribution within the occupational structure that females have a higher turnover rate. Thus, for instance, 14 percent of all male workers but only 4 percent of females are in proprietary or managerial positions; the corresponding figures for craftsmen are 20 and 1. These are relatively interesting and well-paid jobs. Looking at the more routinized, poorly paid occupations, 42 percent of the employed females are clerks or sales workers (mainly retailing the less expensive items for poor wages), compared to 13 percent of the males (mainly wholesaling industrial products or retailing expensive items on commission); 6 percent of the females and less than 1 percent of the males are household workers (servants); and the corresponding percentages for service workers are 16 and 7.

Myth 4: Women are weak and frequently sick, thus missing too many days of work. This is seen as a justification for not giving them much responsibility. The facts are that females miss more days due to acute health conditions than males, but males miss more for chronic conditions. In total, females average 5.3 and males 5.4 sick days in the course of a year.[22]

Myth 5: No one wants a woman boss. This is really not a myth; most employees of both genders seem to resent the idea of a female superior. Given our notions of "masculinity" and femininity," it would be surprising if this were not the case. But most whites resent a black boss, and that is no longer considered a legitimate reason for not having them. When faced with the reality of a superior who is black or female, most employees manage to adjust quite readily.

Myth 6: Women don't want the responsibility entailed in many high status jobs. Given the upbringing of most females, again it might be a shock to find any who do want the responsibility, but there are in fact many. And again, to assume that a particular Jane does not want responsibility because most females do not want it is nothing less than discrimination. At any rate, it is clear that females are not to be found in substantial numbers in decision-making positions. For instance, in the federal Civil Service, where discrimination is supposedly nonexistent, only 4 percent of the top-level bureaucrats are female. In the predominantly female field of social work, where almost all workers have about the same educational accomplishments, 58 percent of the males but only 43 percent of the females function in any kind of administrative capacity. Moreover, the very top positions in social work agencies and departments are almost all filled by males.[23] A similar phenomenon is evident in two other "female" fields: nursing and public school teaching. In 1966 46 percent of all male nurses but only 32 percent of the females were functioning in an administrative capacity.[24] It is also clear that males are disproportionately promoted to principalships and school district administrative positions. Thus, where 90 percent of the elementary school teachers are female, only 50 percent of the principals

of elementary schools are, and this proportion is declining.[25]

As virtually all semiprofessional and professional fields have become more bureaucratic and "scientific" in recent years, the few "havens" for ambitious women that existed in such traditionally female occupations as library science, social work, nursing, and public school teaching are being taken over at the top levels by males (the converse has not happened to traditionally male fields). The female professions in the past represented something of an extension of traditional female duties within the home. It was considered "legitimate" and "feminine" to be employed teaching children, nursing the sick, and caring for the needy—all activities females normally do for free as housewives. Because it was "only" females who were engaged in such activities, salaries and prestige were uniformly low in the "feminine professions."[26] As they changed somewhat in character, males entered them and salaries gradually increased (although which came first is unclear). The result is that the female social worker or teacher who might readily have worked her way into an administrative role years ago has less chance today, since the newly entering males are preferred for such jobs.

Myth 7: Females lack the physical strength for many highly skilled and well-paid manual jobs, especially in the crafts. Unions are often guilty of perpetuating this myth. Given current machinery, most such jobs rarely entail more physical exertion than that involved in carrying a 60-pound child or transporting a desk typewriter from one office to another—both tasks done frequently by a large number of the "weaker sex." In any event, . . . it is clear that some males are physically weaker than most females, while some females are stronger than most males.

Myth 8: Well, anyway, a woman who is really ambitious and qualified can get ahead and acquire an interesting, responsible job. True. If she has somehow managed to avoid the tremendous pressure to conform to stereotypical "femininity"; and if she has put up with many years of drudgery, poor pay, and discouragement from everyone; and if she still has energy, creativity, and ambition left, *then*, when she reaches middle age, she may be in a position commensurate with that of a male 15 years her junior who has less experience, ability, and frequently less by way of formal credentials. Personal "horror stories" abound among working women to document this. Typically, Jane was graduated from college and headed for the "big city." There, at office after office, she was administered a typing test while classmate Dick took an aptitude test. Finally, she settled for a secretarial job at under $100 a week on the promise that "if things work out" she would be promoted to research, editing, copywriting, administration, or whatever. Meanwhile, Dick was hired at $8,000 as a management trainee. She worked overtime and Saturdays (without extra pay) and gradually took over many of the duties assigned to her $20,000-per-year boss. If she was lucky, five or so years later her boss was promoted or quit, and she moved up to his job (which she had been doing all along)—for less than half his pay and a new, less official-sounding title. The bigger the company, the more apt this scenario is to be played. Even with all this, her advancement opportunities were not infrequently tied to sexual favors granted to various levels of bosses, or at least the willingness to play flattering "alter ego."

Myth 9: "I don't know what American women today are complaining about; they are much better off than ever before." (You know, "you've come a long way, baby.") Those who espouse this myth also maintain that American women are much better off than their sisters in other nations and that it takes time to change things, but "we're getting there." Nothing could be more incorrect than these assertions. In a now-classic article written in 1969, Dean Knudsen documented the declining status of females in American society from 1940 to 1966. He concluded that:

> . . . *women have experienced a gradual but persistent decline in status as measured by occupation, income, and education. The sources of the lowered status include diminished efforts by women and institutionalized discrimination, both of which derive from a normative definition of sex roles based upon functionalist assumptions and presuppositions about the nature of society and reality. Thus, given the conviction that women should not pursue occupations in competition with men, women and employers together develop a self-fulfilling prophecy.*[27]

Taking a closer look at some of these trends, where in 1940 41.6 percent of those in professional and technical jobs were female, in 1966 this figure had declined to 37.9 percent; among those in routine jobs like clerical positions the proportion of females rose sharply from 53.9 to 71.3 percent; even the proportion of private household workers who were female increased from 94.4 to 98.0 percent, and service workers jumped from 38.4 to 55.0 percent.[28] More specifically, and with reference to professional occupations, the proportion of females in college teaching and administration dropped from 32 percent in 1930 to 19 percent in 1960; dentistry from 3.2 percent in 1920 to 2.1 percent in 1960; science, from 11.4 percent in 1950 to 9.9 percent in 1960; mathematics, from 38.0 percent in 1950 to 26.4 percent in 1960, and so on.[29] In short, even as women began increasing their numbers as a proportion of the job market from the fifties to the present, their proportion in high-status fields declined; they were and are entering the labor market at the lowest levels and remaining there. The income gap, too, has widened in many cases. In 1939 female managers and proprietors earned 57.3 percent of the income of similarly employed males, in 1966, only 54.0 percent. Between 1939 and 1966, clerical females went from 78.5 percent of the income of their male counterparts to 66.5 percent; in sales, from 51.3 to 41.0 percent; craftsmen and foremen, from 63.7 to 60.4 percent; and service workers, from 59.6 to 55.4 percent. In virtually no case was the gap decreased.[30] As with blacks, females' salaries have increased, but nowhere near as rapidly as those of white males. This places females in a position that is *relatively* worse as years pass.

Females in our society are no better off than many other places in the world and are in a worse relative position than women in some nations. Females in the United States comprise 6 percent of the medical doctors, where in Sweden they represent 13 percent; India and Japan, 9 percent; France, 22 percent; Great Britain, 25 percent; and the U.S.S.R., 76 percent.[31, 32] In 1960 over 40 percent of the medical students in China were female. Of all U.S. lawyers, 3½ percent are female, a figure considerably below that for France, Denmark, Sweden, Germany, Poland, and the Soviet Union, where females comprise 38 percent of the lawyers.[34, 35] Comparative figures reveal similar findings with reference to engineering, science, university-level education, judgeships, and so forth. Clearly, many European societies are somewhat ahead of the United States in opening the professions to women, and the Soviet Union is very far ahead. It is true that some of these professions are less prestigeful and less well paid abroad than here, especially medicine (which in the U.S.S.R. is considered a "woman's occupation," as grammar school teaching or social work is here), but the fact remains that interesting, responsible positions are more open to women in many nations than in America.

When relative income is considered, females in this country seem to fare about the same as their counterparts abroad. Women in France earn about 70 percent of males' income, somewhat better than in this country, but in Great Britain the figure is about 50 percent, or somewhat below ours. In no case does it seem to approach real equality.[36] However, in a number of nations, including Austria, Denmark, France, Germany, Italy, Spain, Sweden, and Yugoslavia, postnatal maternity leave varying from four to ten weeks is a right granted by law, and in many instances such leave is either with partial pay or accompanied by governmental allowances.[37]

In addition to these common myths, two other factors have a strong bearing on the job prospects of females—age and "looks." Quite bluntly, male employers often look at female employees as sex objects and "good looks" are for women an important consideration in acquiring many jobs; the unattractive female, regardless of qualifications, is seriously handicapped. This is compounded by the fact that our society generally has as its model of feminine pulchritude the looks of an attractive 20 year old. In contrast, good looks are far less important for males in the labor market. The model of an attractive male is also taken to be the successful, middle-aged man, graying slightly at the temples, and having "character" in his face (those "unsightly lines" in females). A quick check of advertising in television or magazines will verify this difference. A female is thus considered "old" about the time a male is considered to be in his "prime."[38, 39]

The implications of this emphasis on looks and age are very important for women. Females are most frequently in the labor market at two times in their life cycle: for a few years before marriage and childbearing, and for a much greater number of years after age 35. Today most females have had their last child by about age 30, and this child is in school full time by the time the mother is in her mid or late thirties. Since females now have a life expectancy of about 75 years, increasing numbers are looking to the job market to provide a functional role for the many years after the main child-rearing tasks have been completed. However, by that age they are already considered "old" and "unattractive," and therefore unsuitable for many jobs. Thus, for instance, in 1965 between 40 and 50 percent of the women in the labor force aged 45 and over were officially unemployed.[40] In a study of want ads Inge Bell found that 97 percent of all advertisements for females asked for a "girl" or a "gal," compared to a mere 2 out of 2,272 male listings requesting a "boy."[41] When asked what these terms meant, employment agencies explained that employers were seeking females generally under 30, or 35 at the outside. When females over 35 were sought, the term "mature" was employed. In addition, ads for females, but almost never for males, frequently employed descriptive adjectives such as "attractive."

References

1. K. Amundsen, *The Silenced Majority* (Englewood Cliffs, N.J.: Prentice-Hall, 1971).
2. *Ibid.*
3. M. Paloma and N. Garland, "The Married Professional Woman: A Study in the Tolerance of Domestication" *Journal of Marriage and The Family,* XXXIII (1971), 531–40.
4. A. Rossi, "Job Discrimination and What Women Can Do About It" *Atlantic Monthly,* CCXXV (1970), 99–103.
5. C. Epstein, *Woman's Place* (Berkeley, Calif.: University of California Press, 1970).
6. S. Husbands, "Woman's Place in Higher Education" *School Review,* LXXX (1972), 261–74.
7. Epstein, *op. cit.*
8. *Ibid.*
9. *Time* Magazine, March 20, 1972.
10. C. Bird, *Born Female* (New York: David McKay Co., 1968).
11. Amundsen, *op. cit.*
12. Bird, *op. cit.*
13. Amundsen, *op. cit.*
14. P. Sexton, *The Feminized Male* (New York: Vintage Books, 1969).
15. Amundsen, *op. cit.*
16. *Ibid.*
17. *Ibid.*
18. M. Suelzle, "Women in Labor" *Trans-Action,* VIII (1970), 50–8.
19. Amundsen, *op. cit.*

20. *Ibid.*
21. M. Mead and F. Kaplan, eds. *American Women: The Report of the President's Commission on the Status of Women* (New York: Charles Scribner's Sons, 1965).
22. M. Suelzle, *op. cit.*
23. A. Stamm, "NASW Membership: Characteristics, Deployment, and Salaries" *Personnel Information, NASW,* XII (1969), 34–45.
24. J. Grimm and R. Stern, "Sex Roles and Professional Labor Markets: Intra-Occupational Structuring" Paper delivered at the annual meeting of the Southwestern Social Science Association, San Antonio, 1972.
25. E. Lewis, *Developing Woman's Potential* (Ames, Iowa: Iowa State University Press, 1968).
26. J. Chafetz, "Women in Social Work" *Social Work,* XVII (1972), 12–18.
27. D. Knudsen, "The Declining Status of Women: Popular Myths and The Failure of Functional Thought" *Social Forces,* IIL (1969), 183–93.
28. *Ibid.*
29. Epstein, *op. cit.*
30. Knudsen, *op. cit.*
31. Epstein, *op. cit.*
32. E. Sullerot, *Women, Society and Change* Translated by M. Archer (New York: McGraw-Hill, 1971).
33. C. Cohen, "Women in China" in *Sisterhood is Powerful,* R. Morgan, ed. (New York: Vintage Books, 1970).
34. Epstein, *op. cit.*
35. Sullerot, *op. cit.*
36. *Ibid.*
37. *Ibid.*
38. I. Bell, "The Double Standard" *Trans-Action,* VIII (1970), 75–80.
39. Z. Moss, It Hurts to be Alive and Obsolete: The Aging Woman" in *Sisterhood Is Powerful,* R. Morgan, ed. (New York: Vintage Books, 1970).
40. Bell, *op. cit.*
41. *Ibid.*

THE FATHERING INSTINCT*

John Leonard

Andrew is eleven. Amy is seven. Her mother took Amy this Saturday afternoon to the ballet. His father took Andrew to the park to ride his bike. Andrew and I are bored by the ballet. If we have to see people running around in their underwear in public, we would prefer a basketball game. I doubt whether this preference says anything significant about either the Y chromosome or the way I discharge my responsibilities as a male role model. If Andrew were modeling himself consistently on his father, he would be a lousy chess player instead of the school champion; he would loathe double acrostics; he would not read books on rabbits and military history; his eight cacti, two philodendrons, coleus, ailanthus, hibiscus, and jade plant would all wither in their pots instead of thriving. (I have merely to walk into a room and the vegetable kingdom perishes.)

For that matter, if Amy were modeling herself consistently on her mother, Tiana—a scientist who has gone off to work almost every day of her adult life—she would listen to Mozart instead of "Jesus Christ, Superstar"; she would never have asked for a Suzy Homemaker Oven for her birthday; she would not have announced an ambition to become a nurse; and she would have refrained from prancing around in a tutu while her mother was trying to write a report on sex bias in the university.

In the park, while Andrew is riding his bike, I could be reading the galleys of a novel translated from the Hungarian or I could start to write this article in my head. Actually, I sit with a brain full of the usual New York paranoid fantasies: maybe they are mugging Andrew near the reservoir; maybe his bike will be ripped off; maybe Kohoutek will land on him. Also: doesn't everybody suppose that fathers alone with their children in the park on weekends are divorced—refugees from emotional wars that have been lost—exercising visitation rights? The park is a demilitarized zone. How does one manage to look happily married?

When Amy was born, I quit my job in Boston to stay home and take care of her. This was not really very liberated. I disliked my job; I wanted to write a book; Tiana was nearing her doctorate at the Massachusetts Institute of Technology. Once before, I had dragged her out of graduate school, across the country, and into the woods where I would finish a novel and she would read Freud, while Andrew learned to walk and there were mice in the wainscoting. Now she had a career and I had mixed reviews, and a certain amount of reciprocity seemed appropriate. If her grant could get us through to her Ph.D., then, and

---

*By permission of John Leonard. First appeared in *Ms. Magazine*.

234

only then, would we seek our mutual fortunes elsewhere. So Andrew went off each morning in a Volkswagen bus to nursery school, Tiana went off on an ordinary bus to the Institute, Amy went off in disposable diapers to her crib, and I went off with a cigarette in each ear to my typewriter.

Our neighbors, strangers, disapproved. The idea of a grown man staying home during the day to care for a baby was subversive. The houses on our block were mostly rented. On Saturdays, the men washed their new cars; on Sundays, their families piled into those cars and cruised the suburbs. It didn't help my image in their eyes that my car was a thirdhand Edsel, a huge yellow boat almost Wagerian in its vulgarity. To see me in the middle of the afternoon pushing my daughter up the hill in a stroller, or carrying her strapped to my back like kitchen utensils for an Alpine ascent, was offensive enough. To see my Edsel, my glowering submarine, leaking oil on their street, was to stare at downward mobility.

Finally, I had to explain to the mailman that I was a writer. The packages he was forever lugging up the steps and pitching in the porthole were manuscripts. He relayed this information to the neighborhood. It was exculpatory. Writers, properly, are presumed strange, but not dangerous. Thereafter, I was tolerated, and Amy was regarded with profound sympathy. Children came after school to play with her, as though she were a doll with a key in her back. "Can we push Amy around and see if she gurgles?"

That is, they played with her when she bothered to get out of bed. From the beginning, she seemed incredibly lazy. Breast-fed in the morning and evening, she had no use for the blue plastic bottle of Similac I tried to plug into her at lunchtime. Strained spinach, puree of apricot, and reconstituted chicken fat understandably disgusted her. Three days out of five, she took simply to sleeping until her mother came home, or until I started washing the dishes, which was the same thing because I never washed the dishes until the last second. Nor was she a night owl. Having been fed, bathed, packaged, and poked at, she was ready for another 12 hours of oblivion.

Nobody had ever told me how *humorless* it is, staying home with an infant. Whether or not the baby sleeps, there are no jokes.

But Amy's perfect consideration, her *tact*, meant that I got a lot of work done. I attributed her naps to the soothing effect of my electric typewriter, like a giant hummingbird on the other side of the wall; or perhaps to an innate regard for literature. Tiana thought maybe there was something wrong with her. Andrew, after all, fought sleep as though it were a cannibal, had almost to be nailed to his bed. We know now that Amy was hoarding herself until the world became more accessible. She held in check her greed, her intensity, building up reserves, until she could explode on a situation and send pieces of it flying about the room.

I think children are their own thermostats, self-regulating their emotions and their abilities. I don't want to tamper with the mechanism—as long as I smoke, I won't stop Andrew from salting his bread or Amy from watching reruns of "I Dream of Jeannie"—unless the clockwork seems likely to do harm to itself or to others. When they decide to, children even become interesting.

Two years ago Amy became interesting, a friend instead of a responsibility. I took her with me on a business trip to California, on an overstuffed jumbo jet. Antlered with earphones, she was watching the movie, listening to music, consulting a Babar book, picking at her food, asking questions about Kansas. How could such a complicated intelligence have slept so serenely next door while I typed her mother's doctoral dissertation on "Prefrontal Cortex in the Rat"? We talked.

This was in the spring. That summer I took her for swimming lessons. She wanted to swim because her brother could. At age five, she was the youngest and smallest in her class, and one of the few females. It is chilly in New Hampshire at 10 o'clock in the morning, and water is shock therapy. Blue-gilled in bath towels at the edge of the pool, nobody wanted to jump in. The instructor always asked Amy to begin. Amy always dropped her towel, plunged, foamed the water like a motorboat, climbed out, retrieved her towel, and huddled there, skin so transparent you could just see the fist of brain inside the skull, clenched around a single idea, a hammer of willfulness. The instructor was a tactician in shame. Immediately, the parents of the other children, most of them mothers, began to keen and vituperate behind the wire fence. That little girl did it, they screamed at their sons; go on, you coward! Deplorable, but I enjoyed it. After so many generations, at last an athlete in the family. Perhaps even a President.

She wears her nerves like a leotard. Everything bruises her, and she rages, because she is going to get on with it anyway, and the bruises are unfair. She shouts, she cries, she slams doors, and 10 minutes later I will find her in the living room, like a child dropped from the moon, using the stereo as a crib, so absorbed in rock music that it seems her whole body is an ear. Hair in her eyes, a psychic crater, a well of feeling, playing with her emotions as though they were blind puppies, having at age seven eaten suffering for breakfast, plucking on gut-strings of permanent loss before she's even learned long division—I sometimes find this a little difficult to take seriously, but it is a privacy I won't invade without invitation. Reciprocity, again: when in *my* privacy I type, she will not invade, at least not often, and then only to present me a drawing or a story she knows will scour the brainpan and fry six eggs of astonishment.

Sometimes you are invited. A couple of years ago we watched in silence a TV special called "The Littlest Angel," about a shepherd boy who died and went to heaven shortly before the birth of Christ. When I took her to bed after the program, she burst into tears. That was an invitation to ask why. She finally explained that when the shepherd boy returned to earth to pick up his box of "favorite things," his parents couldn't see him. That's death, when your parents can't see or hear you. Back downstairs, my son had hidden my cigarettes, matches, and ashtray, and refused to tell me where.

When Andrew was born, in Oakland, California, I worked for a radio sta-

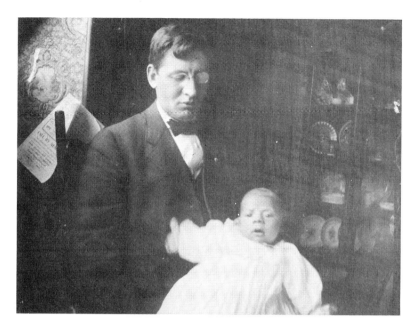

tion. I described him to KPFA as looking like a peeled orange. Forceps marks. I was pleased, confirmed in a secret and disreputable pride, at the fact of a son. But the day of his birth was also the day I received in the mail a contract for my first novel. I was pregnant, too, and about to become a mother. This good news had to be concealed for a while from Tiana. You don't try to upstage the mother of your child.

And you are terrified. His neck seemed as snappable as a stalk of celery. The sections of skull on top of his head hadn't grown together yet. Heat waves came out of his brain. Tiana, breast-feeding him, once spilled a martini full into his face, and it was as if we had personally insulted the San Andreas Fault. The earth heaved, and the roof came down. Clumsiness was criminal. I wanted him to learn to lock his knees, to stand. He hauled himself up on the edge of a coffee table. He swept everything onto the floor: magazines, newspapers, books, ballpoint pens. His hauteur was Churchillian. See how I unhinge myself from objects! He grinned.

He went to a baby-sitter during the day, and came home with every epidemic in the neighborhood. He paid no attention to his bruises, but the gods were always dealing him a karate chop—the incapacitating earache, pneumonia, skull concussion, bad eyes, broken teeth. While I wasn't noticing—books to write, work to do—these wounds mended into character. Slow to talk, slow to read, now he never stops doing both. Awkward, stoic about it, generous, intensely loyal, maker of mazes, diary-keeper, collector of smaller children who are devoted to him because he takes them seriously. . . . I think the world is not good enough for him. His sister will bend the world, break its arm;

Andrew innocently expects its approval. His sort of saintly intelligence fills me with qualm. What am I doing, bringing up such a person in a city like New York?

If breakfast weren't prepared for him, he would starve while reading *The Chronicles of Narnia*. Objects—pencils, coins, stamps, mittens—disappear into him as if into a void. Gone. He doesn't know where. His awareness is buried in *National Geographic* or the Nimzo-Indian defense. Instead of the public school around the corner, he belongs in the mountains of California or in the apple orchards of New Hampshire, where his grandparents share him each summer. But our children are told that their parents have their own lives, and for the time being they must share ours, even if this means that one of the two gerbils brought home to run loose as pets will climb into the oven for warmth and be accidentally baked to death; if the typewriter late at night seems more like a giant mosquito than a great hummingbird; if we are never home in the afternoons when they return from school.

At least we are always there in the evenings. We go out just once a week. We are allowed to nurse a drink before Andrew launches into his day, retailing its complications as though they were yard goods. As they are: psychic yard goods. The pattern, the figure, is amazing. He will dissect a hamster—both our children peer unflinchingly into the microscope; they regard with equanimity a jar of hamster testicles; their mother's work is real in a way that mine is not; things *happen*; there are consequences—and lose a spelling bee. He will dance on one leg, food forgotten. Chairs will topple, glasses spill. His own glasses need cleaning; his hair needs brushing; his shoes need laces. He is talking about medieval courts, Willie Mays, qualities of sandpaper, puns, Nixon, hobbits, and semisweet chocolate. This is the young man who last Thanksgiving defeated a grown man who prides himself on his chess game in a two-hour match, complained that his head hurt because his brain was tired, and went upstairs to read for relaxation.

Increasingly, we take our children wherever we go, and we tend to take longer to get there. By train, for instance, to Chicago for a wedding—because they should see the horseshoe curve outside of Pittsburgh, because we see more when they are around, and because they oblige us, by their presence, to be somewhat better people than we might otherwise settle for being. My role in these adventures seems to be that of someone explaining that once upon a time, I also was excited or disappointed, neglected this, ignored that, felt as bad, was pleasantly surprised, forgiven, encouraged, equal. Before my eyes, my children are acquiring dignity; they would be nice people to know. This is not something I ever really expected. My fathering had always taken the form of a friendly cloud that floated across the lives of the children, and paused occasionally to cast a shadow. That they would turn out to have their own weather, and that I would profit by the climate, was an immense satisfaction.

It may be, unfortunately, that it is easier for a father than for a mother to be a friend of the children. A father's attentions are so casual. He may have paid for a housekeeper, say, or bought the house, or even purchased the lamb chops. But, I was recently reminded, who *conceived* of the lamb chops as a problem? Who had to think about them beforehand? I may take Amy to California; who worries about the appropriate clothes, the gum, the Babar, the special blanket, the allowance? Mothers, mostly, who, by their attention to the details, liberate fathers to become friends with their daughters, and then find that when daughters have grown up and don't need the details to be taken care of, they suddenly want their mothers to be friends. That may come too late. If motherhood is a storm of details, a million conceptions of lamb chops and gum and mittens and thank-you notes, the habit hardens even if the object has escaped the necessity. And if fathering is usually evoked as a principle of authority, judicial, rectitudinous among the disorders of emotion and behavior, the leading player in a counterinsurgency scenario, he is merely a bumpkin with a gun. We will not have enjoyed our children, and we will not respect their adulthood. We will have punished, and then quibbled.

In our house, where like everybody else, I have accidently become an adult, they are trying to teach me that money nd authority are not substitutes for details of feeling. My children, by being more interesting than most other people I know, may make me earn the credit I intend to appropriate for their excellence.

MAKING IT TOGETHER: GROWTH FROM WITHIN*

John F. Crosby

The difference between a "rut" and a "groove" seems to be the difference between losing variety and making constructive use of routine. A rut is negative in that variety and spontaneity have been choked to death; a groove is positive as long as the routine and the ordinary are continually used as springboards into experiences involving variety and spontaneity. People who wish to deny the need of "routine" and the "ordinary" may find fulfillment in one of the emerging marital patterns, but they probably will not find it within traditional monogamy. Two people cannot live together over a long period of time without coming to terms with the routine and the ordinary. The only option (but a most important one) available to couples who commit themselves to a monogamous, sexually exclusive union is the option between the rut and the groove.

TO KILL A MARRIAGE

If someone were to appoint a presidential commission on "how to destroy marriage" we could offer some cogent suggestions on strategy. The first maneuver should be to use the mass media to condition people to believe that change and variety are wrong—and to be resisted at all costs. Such a step would allow cultural traditions and patterns, myths, and taboos to be absorbed into a rigidity of form and function within marriage. Isn't it true that we often oblige the commission by commiting "maricide" and "familicide" the very instant we say "I do"? Oh, not intentionally, but in a rather subtle, sneaky way don't we conclude that since he or she is now mine there is no need to continue to score points—no need to be creative, imaginative, spontaneous, or interesting? Many promising relationships begin to die when the relationship becomes legalized—not because a legal bond works some sort of deadly witchcraft but because legalization becomes an open invitation to take the partner *too much* for granted. Our second suggestion on how to kill a marriage is therefore, Take each other for granted—always!

There is no doubt that marriage should provide a couple with a haven in

*From *Illusion and Disillusion: The Self in Love and Marriage* by John F. Crosby. © 1973 by Wadsworth Publishing Company, Inc., Belmont, California 94002. Reprinted by permission of the publisher.

which they can bask in the luxury of not having to put on facades or false pretenses for anyone. This freedom to be oneself provides the joy of being taken for granted, of being loved (agape) "in spite of" one's faults, idiosyncrasies, and hang-ups. Yet there is something in us that doesn't like to be taken for granted, even though we may persist in defending our right to take the other for granted. To be taken for granted is both a relief and a threat; it is both a security and an insecurity; it is both a joy and a peril. Thus, a delicate balance must be maintained in a marital relationship; agape must never be too much out of balance with philos and eros. (In-spite-of love must be balanced with friendship love and physical, passion-filled love.) Whenever equilibrium is upset, it is probably because one or both partners are demanding the right to take the other for granted while claiming that it is not the other's prerogative to take him for granted. . . .

The rut . . . brings us to the third suggestion we will make to the presidential commission: create a cultural milieu in which no one is rewarded for creativity and imagination. Once we convince people that deviation from the traditional role assumptions and marital expections is wrong, risky, and unnecessary, we can then quickly proceed to the marriage funeral. The rut will become unbearable. I suspect that such a commission would suggest that "imagination" be checked permanently at the door of the (church) (courthouse) (J.P.) (Synagogue)—check one!

Answers to the following questions would indicate that the presidential commission had been highly successful. Answers implying "seldom," "a long time ago," or "we never would" indicate a rigidity in marital roles and a successful campaign to destroy marriage.

When was the last time the couple was separated for at least several days? When was the last time the husband stayed home with the children while the wife went away? When was the last time the couple went away together, leaving the children with a sitter, alone if older, or with friends? Where did the

couple go? A nearby motel for overnight? Away with another couple?

How often are the traditional roles of male and female reversed? When did "he" last cook dinner? Does he even know how? Or clean house? Or go to his child's teacher's evaluation conference instead of his wife? When was the last time sexual intercourse was engaged in other than in the bed the couple ordinarily sleeps in? Outside? In the living room? On the floor? Indeed, the sexual technologists have a good point when they lash out at our sexual rigidities and suggest positions in intercourse, changes in technique, and exploration of intimacies beyond coitus.

When has the couple varied the time of sexual intimacy? Must it always be evening, or morning, or on certain night of the week? When has the couple last reversed the so-called traditional sex-role which assumes that the male is always active and the female passive? A passive male and an active female may be a welcome relief and change for both.

How many couples have ever seriously attempted to learn transactional analysis? How many married couples and/or families use transactional analysis as a means of learning to cope with the conflicts, changing moods, and everyday situations that are common fare in family life?

All of the foregoing questions and statements presuppose a motivation to change, to grow, to explore, and to enrich and enliven. Once a couple agrees to give up, however slowly and gradually, the defense mechanisms and safety devices that they have used to avoid intimacy there is no limit to what can change, with or without outside help. People may protest that centers for development of human potential are out of the question for ordinary people with limited means. Perhaps, although even a growth workshop can be given priority over more traditional vacations or a new car.

Church groups have been increasingly concerned about marital and familial interaction and some have become involved in sensitivity training. It is becoming more and more common for clergy in the more liberal religious traditions to receive training in group marital enrichment. Thus, couples who complain of a lack of understanding friends who might share such group training might not need to look further than their own church, or the YMCA, YWCA, or community educational program.

Many larger cities have pastoral counseling centers where clergymen with specialized training are available for individual counseling, for group therapy, and for marital enrichment groups. Many county and city mental health clinics and Community Chest family agencies also have special groups and classes pertaining to marital growth and family interaction.

But a couple can also work together, separate from an organized counseling group, to improve their marriage. Indeed, transactional analysis is emphasized . . . because anybody can learn it, as has been shown with children, older people, and the mentally retarded.

Two married people can also learn role taking in a matter of minutes—that is, he plays the wife and she plays the husband. Using this for-mat, many conflicts can be dealt with and many feelings explored, for when any one person tries to think and feel himself into the role of another he is bound to have an increase in understanding and empathy. Further, when another assumes my role (plays me) I am bound to get insight and find myself reacting in interesting ways. Others who know us deeply and intimately can give us a glimpse of how we come across to others—can give us feedback. Feedback in human relations can be either divergent or convergent. Divergent feedback is a communication (whether verbal, written, or symbolic) we usually don't want to hear; convergent feedback is welcome because it agrees with or confirms our self-image. Role taking can drastically reduce the divergent feedback and increase the convergent feedback because it can help one "feel into" the other person and learn to change one's attitude and behavior. More positive feelings (positive feedback) are bound to result from such new insight. Role taking can also help us cut through idealized images of the self and the other by forcing us to see ourselves the way we come across to others. Since idealization militates against a realistic acceptance of oneself and of others, role playing may serve as a tremendous aid in learning authentic self-acceptance and acceptance of others.

Role playing can also help a husband and wife uncover some of their traditional expectations. Thus, a fourth suggestion that the presidential commission should implement is to mount an attack on those who would test traditional male-female and husband-wife roles. The commission should demand role rigidity and a strict sex division of labor, duty, and responsibility to guard against honest self-examination of role expectation, which can often change a conflict-ridden, rut-oriented marriage into a growth relationship. A husband may relate to his wife for ten years on the mistaken assumption that because his mother starched his shirts and cheerfully made a career of housekeeping and mothering, his wife should also be contented to stay at home as sole housekeeper. Similarly, a wife may expect her husband to be domineering and sole bread-winner like her father was, even though she may consciously dislike her father or bear animosity or resentment toward him. Such role expectations, which are deeply embedded in cultural and religious traditions, often provide fertile ground for manipulation of the mate.

A government thrust to "freeze" traditional husband-wife, male-female, father-mother, and parent-offspring roles would go a long way toward killing the potential of monogamous unions. Whenever either partner fails to measure up to the sacred institutionalized expectations of the other, feelings of hurt, anger, resentment, and hostility are likely to run rampant. Thus, a fifth suggestion might be, "Create a national climate that encourages perfection and harmony." A careful manipulation of the mass media could be used to create the illusion that happy successful marriages are those in which there is no conflict, and everybody is improving day by day in their quest for perfect relationships.

Analysis of so-called happy, vital marriages often reveals a total absence of perfectionism and a total acceptance of each other despite character defects, personality flaws, and hang-ups. *Perfection* and *lack of conflict* may yet prove to be the most reliable predictors of *unsatisfactory* marriage—perfection because it is blatantly nonhuman and stupid; lack of conflict because it signals a fundamental dishonesty through denial of feelings.

A final suggestion for our commission (the reader can carry on from here) is to create a marriage ritual law which prescribes phrases of the wedding ceremony that define the marriage contract once and forever as nonnegotiable and nonamendable. Such a nuptial requirement would prevent the constructive orientation that Sidney Jourard describes as "serial polygamy with the same spouse." By serial polygamy Jourard means the reinvention of marriage by the same husband and the same wife. Impasse is struggled with; the old union dies, and a new union is born—between the same two people. The fallacy in traditional marital relationships has been the assumption that people do not really change. While a case may be made for a person's "core" personality as relatively consistent over time, it is also true that we are always changing, growing, reverting, regressing, progressing, or discovering. Hence, it is totally unrealistic to think that two adults should be confined to the (implicit) contract they both agreed upon at the time of marriage. What Jourard calls reinventing marriage is perhaps better described as "redefining," "recreating," or "revitalizing" the present relationship. Redefinition (by that name or by any other name) needs to take place if the marriage is to be a self-actualizing contract for both spouses. Redefinition is an ongoing occurrence; the two partners are committed to the fulfillment of each other and to the fulfillment of their relationship.

Perhaps redefinition springs from a certain set of values. If the highest values held by a couple are aliveness, creativity, authenticity, vitality, health, lovingness, intimacy (sexual and spiritual), and productivity, then redefinition will come as naturally as day and night. On the other hand, if the most basic values are loyalty to past traditions, conformity to societal expectations, ancestral beliefs and mores, and the authoritarian triad of obedience, respect, and duty to one's parents, then redefinition will be difficult at best.

THE RESIDUAL

What remains after we have torn down our defenses in a marital relationship? What is left upon which to build? The residual remains after the tearing-down process has taken from us our defense mechanisms and our safety devices. The residual is the foundation beneath the taboos and myths in which we took refuge; it is the sperm and ovum which united to conceive the marriage in the first place. Many marriages have far more going for them than the partners permit themselves to see. People seem to celebrate failure and divorce by pointing out the things that went wrong—the incompatibilities, the impasses, the drudgery, the disillusionment. Yet at the conception of each union there are legitimate hopes, dreams, and possibilities; there are trust and love, commitment and spontaneity.

What is love's legacy? What is the residual we seek to uncover and re-create? What is it to which we seek to give vitality and fulfillment? The question may be approached in several ways but the underlying assumptions are much the same. Monogamy as it has evolved in our society has tended to work against the development of individual potential; it has tended to create rigidity, joylessness, frustration, monotony, boredom, hostility, anger, and pleasureless sexuality.

Perhaps the initial step in the direction of change is to opt for a continuing revision and updating of the marital contract. Herbert Otto has spoken of the "New Marriage," which is a framework for developing personal potential. In another article Otto asks, "Has Monogamy Failed?" Both articles are variations on the theme of monogamous marital enrichment:

> *Has monogamy failed? My answer is "no." Monogamy is no longer a rigid institution, but instead an evolving one. There is a multiplicity of models and dimensions that we have not even begun to explore. It takes a certain amount of openness to become aware on not only an intellectual level but a feeling level that these possibilities face us with a choice. Then it takes courage to recognize that this choice in a measure represents our faith in monogamy. Finally, there is the fact that every marriage has a potential for greater commitment, enjoyment, and communication, for more love, understanding and warmth. Actualizing this potential can offer new dimensions in living and new opportunities for personal growth, and can add new strength and affirmation to a marriage.*

Virginia Satir has also spoken to the issue of "marriage as a Human-Actualizing Contract." Another way of presenting this view would be to advocate the ongoing process of defining the relationship. There are times when marriages peak; there are times when these same marriages are void of vitality and joy. We have noted that the actual wedding ceremony can be an open invitation to decay and stagnation, simply because the two people now legally possess and are possessed by each other. Duty, responsibility, and obligation, however important and necessary, have a repressive intonation and may be cited as the reason for loss of spontaneity in marriage.

Growth centers and organizations for actualizing human potential have sprung up all over the United States. The basic purpose of these centers is to help individuals and couples break out of the binds which constrict the full expression of oneself. In order to do this there must be a willingness to experience some discomfort as one permits the breaking down of barriers and defenses against intimacy. Reawakening of the senses, openness to others, spontaneity in self-expression and honesty in interpersonal relationships are encouraged, usually in a group context.

The history and background of such centers is a story within itself. Our concern here, however, is to suggest that traditional monogamy is still the overwhelming marital pattern within our society and that much can be attempted to revitalize and to actualize the marital relationship.

Yet in defining marriage as a "human actualizing contract" it is all too easy to fall back into the same trap as before—the trap of excessive and unrealistic expectations. Just as romantic and societal expectations often lead one to post-honeymoon disillusionment, so also expectations regarding marriage as the heart-bed of psychic intimacy may lead a couple to discontent and disillusionment. Is it possible for a couple to have peak intimacy experiences day-in/day-out? If the answer to this question is "no," why do we conclude that something is wrong with the marriage? Richard Farson has pointed out that discontent in "good" marriages arises from several sources, including heightened expectations about sexual and psychic intimacy, comparison with other marriages, and comparison of the marriage with itself in its better moments. Farson says: ". . . probably the most important source of discontent is the comparison of the marriage with its own good moments in the present. . . . These peaks, however, are inevitably followed by valleys. Couples lucky enough to have these moments find themselves unable to sustain them and, at the same time, unable to settle for ordinary moments. They want life to be a constantly satisfying state. But to be a constant state, to avoid the valleys, it is necessary to eliminate the peaks. . . . Good marriages are not like that, but the price they exact in depression and pain is high."

If the residual, the core of the marriage, is to be secured and cultivated it must be tempered with realistic expectations, "realistic" meaning what is considered real in line with what we know about human life through experiences and the testimony of others, including historical and literary confirmation. For example, when Farson speaks of "peaks" and "valleys," he is giving witness to a basic human experience. An idealistic person might say, "Why? Why can't life be filled with peaks?" A pessimistic person may claim in the name of "realism" that Farson is wrong because "life is basically valley after valley with no peaks."

We cannot secure our residual, let alone cultivate it, until we are able to see through the self-destructive tendencies born of unrealistic expectations. As illustration consider the rather common occurrence of a meeting between two strangers on a bus or plane. In a matter of an hour or two, such relationships often yield deep-felt emotions and problems from one or both of the travelers. A common reaction to such an experience is the wish that one could attain and remain in such an intimate level with one's own spouse. But is this a realistic expectation? Can a married couple live day-in and day-out in such an emotionally charged manner? In the majority of bus-airplane instances, the two people involved will never see each other again . . . and they know it! And if, perchance, they do meet again, the odds are that any effort to recreate a semblance of the intimate moment of the past will end in frustration and disappointment.

Thus, the residual has great potential only if it is intellectually and emotionally placed in a context of balance and perspective. If, as we discussed earlier, variety is a desirable quality in human experience, then it follows that we would do well to welcome variety in the range and type of marital relationships as well as in any particular relationship. A couple may achieve a great deal of variety in their sexual relationship, but even this desirable quality will not fill the need for variety in meeting other basic needs.

The residual is, in short, more than enough to sustain the great majority of monogamous and sexually exclusive marriages providing the residual is placed within a congruency of life values and goals which form a configuration. Once the romantic expectations stemming from the media and the conditioning process of socialization are seen through and placed in perspective, there follows the challenge of seeing through the double-bind created by unrealistically expecting our mate to fill all our basic human needs. Let us hope for meaningful peak experiences between husband and wife, yet without either feeling guilty or apologetic about the transitoriness of such experiences. In a very real sense they are meaningful *because* they are transitory.

There are those who will claim that the residual can survive only if the marriage includes the standard of sexual permissiveness. The argument is advanced that if we embrace the value of psychic intimacy with people other than the spouse, we therefore should also embrace sexual intimacy with people other than the spouse. OK for those who so define it. I do not think it is either necessary or logical. What is often desired in sex is an affirmation of the self by the other. It is no more logical to conclude that psychic intimacy must culminate in sexual intimacy than it is to conclude that sexual intimacy must culminate in psychic intimacy. A fair statement about the relationship of psychic and sexual intimacy seems to be this: sometimes and in some situations psychic intimacy progresses into sexual intimacy and in other situations psychic intimacy is destroyed by sexual intimacy. Sexual intimacy often creates only an illusory facsimile of psychic intimacy; that is, when one fails to experience psychic intimacy he deludes himself into believing that sexual intimacy will be an effective substitute. Significantly, a common manner of seduction depends on the manipulation of desires for psychic intimacy as a means of achieving sexual intimacy.

WHAT PRICE FULFILLMENT?

The quest for fulfillment comes at a price, both for the individual and the marital relationship. The price is paid in the form of pain and discomfort, the slow process of learning new patterns, the break with security mechanisms, or the parting with games and strategies calculated to manipulate or dominate the other.

The growth toward maturity, toward self-acceptance, toward learning to deal with conflict and unlearning standards of perfection are four specific areas of growth which exact a toll upon those who would build on the residual in their quest for marital fulfillment within a monogamous relationship.

The maturity required to make it together reveals itself most forcefully in the ability to see through the illusions of romantic, societal, and parental expectations of marriage. Further, maturity is manifested in the ability of a person to make viable assessments of the expectations posited for a "human actualizing contract." The more we thirst for the peak experiences the greater will be our discontent with the "down" experiences. This discontent is predictable and inescapable to the extent that we fail to see through the dynamics that we allow to play through us.

Marital fulfillment requires, probably above all other qualities, the grace of self-acceptance. The self-accepting person is the one who is best able to recognize his own foibles and hang-ups without becoming defensive or unnecessarily compulsive in compensating for them. Consequently, he is most free to analyze societal and cultural data and to consciously decide his own level of content and/or discontent. There is little doubt, either experimentally or clinically, that the self-accepting person is best qualified to accept others, most especially his mate. . . . Suffice it to reiterate that acceptance and confrontation of conflict are essential requirements for human growth and development. Once we accept conflict as an amoral fact of life, we are in a position to be done with old patterns and voices that told us we would not be loved if we expressed our deepest and innermost feelings. In dispelling one myth, we run the risk of falling prey to another myth—the myth that all conflict is resolvable. It is not! To believe otherwise is to add to one's own level of discontent.

Perhaps the greatest price to be paid in building on the residual is the death of perfection. I can hear murmurs and protests to the effect that this villain had been put to death years ago (or at least several pages . . . back). Maybe so. Likely not! The perfectionist tendency has been reinforced by one's family, competition with siblings, the educational establishment (nursery through postdoctoral), the mass media, and the ecclesiastical establishment. Perfectionism may have been conquered in one or several areas of one's life without having been recognized in one's marital expectations. The purists will maintain that to settle for anything less than perfection is a cop-out or a compromise, yet perfection and the perfectionist fallacy have, in my opinion, been among the greatest curses with which mankind has been historically enslaved. The fallacy of perfectionism is its tacit promise that we will one day be satisfied, when at last we reach the coveted goal. Even if the perfectionist claims he is realistic and that he knows the goal is unattainable but that the meaning is in the striving, he deceives himself precisely because he is unable to live in the present. How can he? He doesn't accept the present without superimposing his own qualifications and improvements. He is then thrust into the future—where all perfectionists dwell—and hence, happiness itself becomes part and parcel of the future illusion.

NEW HORIZONS*

Jean Spencer

You're a woman now, my daughter,
I can see it in your eyes
Feel it in your enthusiasm.
Your world is no longer
bounded by ours.
It stretches out
to new horizons
with pathways
of your choosing.
Go quickly now
else I'm too tempted
to call you back
to continue the interweaving
of twenty beautiful years.
But
when you're free
come back—
come back as my friend
so that
our worlds can meet
at the intersection
of love
and respect.

*"New Horizons" on page 68 is reprinted from *Images*, compiled by Janice Grana and published by The Upper Room, Nashville Tennessee © 1976 and is used by permission.

MARRIAGE AND MIDDLE AGE*

Richard K. Kerckhoff

The problems created by being in the middle generation are numerous. Sartre has noted that when the generations struggle with each other, "children and old people often join forces." Sandwiched between the demands of youth and the needs of the aged, the middle-aged person often reports feeling caught, pressed, squeezed. Economists and political scientists have described the financial pressures put upon the middle age, middle income categories of society by the young and the old: old people and young people cost a lot of money—money which to a large extent is being earned by middle-aged people. Clark Vincent has described the more psychological behavioral aspects of this uncomfortable position of what he calls the "caught generation":

> "If you are between 35 and 55 years old, you may belong to the caught generation—caught in between the demands of youth and expectations of the elderly. The respect you were taught to give your parents may have been denied you by your children. . . The threat of 'love withdrawal,' used by your parents to keep you in line as a child, may now be used by your children to keep you in line as a parent. As a child, you were to be seen and not heard, now as a parent you may feel you are to be neither seen nor heard."[1]

The middle-aged person may feel caught, too, between the job and the family. The world of work and the world of family have different, and competing, expectations, and it often seems impossible to meet the demands of both realms. Early middle age, when there are children in the home, may sometimes be accurately schematized as a triangle. At one point of our lives is our job. Another point represents our marriage. And the third point is our child-rearing, our parenthood. The wife's triangle interfaces with the husband's. Triangles are used, symbolically, to represent stressful human relations. A *double* triangle may appear to be positively explosive!

Later in the middle years, the world of work may provide us with a different kind of problem or disappointment. Our work—at least in some occupational classes—may not be as demanding (as competitive with our family life,

*From Richard K. Kerckhoff, "Marriage and Middle Age," *The Family Coordinator* 25, no. 1 (January 1976): 5–10. Copyright 1976 by National Council on Family Relations. Reprinted by permission.

that is), but it may also not be as rewarding. Middle class workers, reared on the reward system which involved promotions and salary raises, may find that they are suffering from a "plateau phenomenon." Salaries do *not* keep going up, and the promotions may be going to people ten years their junior. Those economists who claim that we are going through the "liquidation of the middle class," are describing, particularly, the plight of middle-aged workers whose incomes are not keeping up with rising consumer prices. In the managerial occupations, according to surveys made by the American Management Associations, "career discontent" reaches alarming proportions under these conditions, influencing about half of managers to change or consider changing occupations. Mostly, it would seem, the middle-aged, middle-level executive suffers from fears of his ability to compete, and from doubts as to the value of competing; the doubts are epitomized by the title of a recent book, *The Failure of Success.*

On an even more traumatic note, the middle-aged person often becomes aware, as did Freddy Landon in Richard B. Wright's novel *In the Middle of Life,* that the people who are dying from cancer and heart disease are no longer some old people his parents knew—they are his own friends and acquaintances.[2] Illness and death tend to become more personal. Writing about the special health problems of middle-aged men, Berland says that these fellows are prime targets for cardiovascular disease, cancer and other ills "ranging from baldness to prostate trouble." More than his wife, the middle-aged man is apt to have an ulcer, poor hearing, bad eyes and diseased gums!

A common phenomenon of middle age is the shock experienced by the recognition of the distance between ourselves and youth. Two subjects in Neugarten's research told her:

> *"I used to think that all of us in the office were contemporaries for we all had similar career interests. But one day we were talking about old movies, and we realized that the younger ones had never seen a Shirley Temple film or an Our Gang comedy . . . Then it struck me with a blow that I was older than they. I had never been so conscious of it before . . ."*

> *"When I see a pretty girl on the stage or in the movies—we used to say 'a cute chick'—and when I realize, 'My God, she's about the age of my son', it's a real shock. It makes me realize that I'm middle-aged."*[3]

McMorrow has observed that the shock of recognition of the distance from our own youth often occurs to male characters in creative literature as they gaze into the bathroom mirror.[4] A Nelson Algren character looks into the mirror and sees his father. Harry Haller, "Steppenwolf," looks into the mirror and wonders about using the razor to cut his own throat.

Having said that the pressures and disappointments of middle age are among the aspects of this period which make for interest and which should stimulate research, educational and therapeutic programs for middle-aged people, we should hasten to add that this has been a purposely lopsided characterization of mid-life. Middle-aged people are not to be accurately characterized as *just* squeezed, pressured, disappointed, exploited and exhausted. They are often that, but they are also, according to our studies, comparatively well-off, and they know it. Being as Barbara Fried said, "wiser than the young and stronger than the old," the middle-aged person has a lot going for him. The middle years can be a time of recognition of our value, not just a time of doubt about our worth. They can be for many a time of reassessment, of withdrawal from energy-consuming activities to which we were never really committed, and of focus on those things in life which we now feel sure are worthwhile. There is some room for contemplation and for feelings of satisfaction in the lives of many middle-aged people—time for learning from past experiences, for taking stock and for finding perspective. Middle-aged people, studies indicate, may feel squeezed by being in the middle, but they may, in addition, feel their own importance. They often know that they are the nation's decision-makers; they set the tone for life in this society. Society depends on middle-aged people's leadership and productivity.

Deutscher noted a decade ago that the mixed reports that we receive on the quality of life in the post-parental years—anything from the terrible despair to the wonderful freedom that is supposed to characterize this age—make excellent hypotheses just waiting to be tested.[5]

Deutscher's own Kansas City investigation, reported in the Neugarten book, found the middle-agers to be a pretty contented group of people, as have the studies of other scholars from Axelson to Gingles.

Neugarten's sample of influential middle-aged men and women certainly saw advantages to their position in life. Being in the middle put pressures on them, but it also allowed them to serve as a bridge between generations. Being more mature, they recognized their special competencies:

> "I know now exactly what I can do best, and how to make the best use of my time . . . I know how to delegate authority, but also what decisions to make myself . . . I know how to buffer myself from troublesome people . . . All this is what makes the difference between me and a young man, and it's all this that gives me the advantage . . ."[6]

Neugarten concludes one report by claiming that, "The successful middle-aged person often describes himself as no longer 'driven,' but as now the 'driver'—in short, 'in command'."

Creative literature also points to the many advantages of being middle-aged. Poet Carolyn Wells compares this period favorably with those which precede and follow it:

> "Youth is a silly, vapid state;
> Old age with fears and ills is rife;
> This simple boon I beg of Fate—
> A thousand years of Middle Life!

Novelist Hervey Allen's character says, "Grow up as soon as you can. It pays. The only time you really live fully is from thirty to sixty . . . The young are slaves to dreams; the old servants of regrets. Only the middle-aged have all their five senses in the keeping of their wits." *(Anthony Adverse)*

The major theme of Eda LeShan's book on middle age is that the "crisis" of these years offers a wonderful chance for growth: "And this is the wonder of the crisis of middle age: *its challenges are the greatest opportunity one has*

ever had to become most truly alive and oneself."[7] She takes her theme from Carl Jung who, she says, saw middle age as a time for turning away from our concern with what other people think of us, and turning toward our own good opinion of ourselves. "If ever," says LeShan, "there is to be a moment that belongs to us, it is now, in our middle years."

When we focus on *marriage* in middle life, we find a similar mixed report. Older studies emphasized the general down-hill path of marital satisfaction between the time of the honeymoon and the time of the death of one spouse. More recent studies point to an upsurge of satisfaction with the marriage during the empty nest stage. Cuber and Harroff have described the middle years as a time of unhappy decisions for many couples: They know now that their marriage will not ever be what once they simply assumed it would become.[8] Decision: Should they separate and try to find Shangrila with new partners? Or should they stay together and settle for second best—a second best which is often epitomized by the phrase, "at our age, that's just how marriage is"?

Other writers, as will be noted below, emphasize the special opportunities middle age offers for marriage enrichment and for couples helping each other fulfill themselves and grow their personalities. In essence, this opportunity occurs because the double triangle that I suggested earlier may become less complicated. The pressures exerted by our children and our jobs *may* decrease, allowing us more time, energy and wisdom to apply to our marriages. David Mace of ACME, the Association for Couples for Marriage Enrichment, has reported that these opportunities are real and middle-aged couples are taking advantage of them.

Most impressive have been the reports of middle-aged couples themselves. Various studies fairly ooze with the contentment these couples find in their marriages.

> *"My wife and I always did get along well together, but it seems that there was a better understanding, even better as we got older . . . It's extremely pleasant, gets more pleasant as the years go by."*[9]

> *"It (sex) hasn't changed. There's never any problem . . . I think we have the best relationship right now that we've ever had."*[10]

Merely ridding the house of the children does not always bring the magic back into a marriage, however. LeShan sees this event as a challenge to the marriage:

> *"When the children leave, marriage faces a moment of truth; is there strength enough to sustain it without the excuse of parenthood?"*[11]

In his fine play, "Double Solitaire," Robert Anderson, who has been called "the playwright of middle-aged loneliness," has a character named George who relates: "I have friends who wrangled along in the city, always with the illusion that if they get away from the clutter of their lives and be alone in the country, things would be better for them . . . When their kids left home, they took to the woods, and looked at each other across the uncluttered space and promptly got a divorce." Recognizing the seductive quality of this romantic notion, George adds: "I try to confront my illusions as rarely as possible."[12]

In fact, the reduced pressures on life in middle age—if they occur—may lead not to marital bliss, but to the marital blahs. Middle age has been characterized in creative literature as a period of self-satisfied smugness. James Russell Lowell preferred old age to the "pompous mediocrity of middle life," and Clive Staples Lewis wrote of "the long, dull, monotonous years of middle-age prosperity or middle-aged adversity." Middle-aged men, especially, have been portrayed in literature as feeling drowned in the dullness of life. Hermann Hesse's Steppenwolf seethes with "a wild longing for strong emotions and sensations . . . a rage against this toneless, flat, normal and sterile life."[13] Charley Potter in "Double Solitaire" senses that he is slipping into an abyss of nothingness:

> *"Christ George . . . do you know there's nothing I'd die for. It's an overblown way of putting it. But these few days have made me wonder, 'Jesus, what do I feel strongly about?' . . . My life seems to be spent in discussing the day's news and the latest movies . . . Entirely superficial . . . Suddenly I'm examining everything I do and feel, and so much of it seems so damned pointless. I mean, yesterday I'm up there making out the monthly checks, and I found myself stopping and asking, 'Which of these damned things I'm paying for do I really care about?' . . . I sense something about myself, that I could be the damnedest most detached person, and I could freeze to death somewhere out there in the cool world, without this connection with life through my feelings for someone . . . That's why this blandness terrifies me. I feel my spirtual temperature dropping, and I get scared, and I reach out desperately for some saving intensity and intimacy . . ."[14]*

Middle-aged marriages may be considered "good" then when they are to a great extent unpainful and unexamined rather than when they are stimulating and challenging. They may be comfortable when they are easy to endure and easy to ignore.

Marriage counselors have long noted that when trouble arises in middle-aged marriages, it is often related to boredom of the union, not to its traumatic qualities. Infidelity, alcoholism, hypochondria and divorce and suicide must, in middle age, be as much related to the deadliness of the marital union as to any pain it can produce.

As Cuber and Harroff have noted, this deadliness may pervade even those unions which we are tending to categorize—with the contented compliance of the husband and wife—as happy marriages.[15] And Troll viewing the self-reported good marriages of some of our studies, concludes that in Cuber-Harroff terms, they are indeed nice, comfortable "devitalized" and "passive congenial" unions.[16]

Middle age and marriage in middle age, then, can be characterized as suffering from success. The comfort and security that have been achieved by many individuals in many marital relations may incorporate seeds of destruction—destruction, Charley Potter would say, by freezing, not by burning.

What I am hypothesizing, then, is an ideal type developmental marriage characterized during the early years of middle age by terrible pressures and competing demands, and during the later years of middle age by smug complacency and comfortable rot. If this is an accurate description of a common phenomenon of the middle years of life, our salvation may be in another characteristic of the age as a noted by numerous observers. Middle age is often compared in the literature with adolescence because both periods provide developmental encouragement for facing the great questions of human existence: Who am I? Where am I going? What is life all about? Writers who compare middle age with adolescence and who discover an identity crisis in both periods, differ, naturally, in their enthusiasm for these phenomena. McMorrow, who spells middlescence with an "o" (midolescence) so as to emphasize its similarity to adolescence, sees middle age as characterized by a reverting to the bizarre, irrational, sexually confused status of adolescence.[17] The crisis that he notes, then, is to be avoided if at all possible. A decade ago, Brayshaw came from Britain to tell us that the resemblances of middle age and adolescence might be frustrating, but could be growth-producing: "There are significant parallels between adolescence and middle age. The task of the adolescent is to integrate into life not only his sexuality but the powerful resurgence of idealism . . . Now in middle life there is a sudden breaking through of this suppressed and neglected . . . element in life . . . We come then to the central question. What is the second half of life for? Man has always asked himself 'What are we here for?' ' What is the purpose of life?' 'What is our prime duty?' But in practice, ordinary people find that the cares of bringing up a family obliterate these philosophical questions. We are too busy earning our livings and running our homes and caring for our children. We have no doubt that this is our duty and purpose in life. It is when the children go that these ancient questions become acutely personal for the second half of life."[18]

The most optimistic observer of middle age—the writer who refers to the "wonderful crisis" of that age—LeShan, urges us to grasp the opportunity that this crisis offers us: " 'Middlescence' is the opportunity for going on with the identity crisis of the first adolescence. It is our second chance to find out what it really means to 'do your own thing,' to sing your own song, to be deeply and truly yourself. It is a time for finding *one's own* truths at last, and thereby to become free to discover one's real identity."[19]

LeShan is not a *foolish* optimist, however, and her book clearly describes the pain and the danger middle-aged people will experience in reexamining their identities. She compares the process with a lobster's periodic shedding of its shell; it makes the lobster vulnerable, but it allows him to grow.

It is no wonder, then, as Brayshaw implied, many middle-aged people choose to use their marriage as *an escape from* facing the existential challenge of that age.[20] They do not ask the important questions because they assume their marriage is answer enough. Who am I? I am Mrs. John Jones. What is life all about? I am a faithful wife and good housekeeper. Where am I going? We hope to take a trip to Cape Cod next summer. My marriage is my answer.

But to those couples who dare, the crisis of middle age can offer a chance to grow, and the marriage of middle age can become a vehicle for that growth. Marriage enrichment for the middle-aged couple, as I see it, is not to be focused on the improvement of the marriage so much as on the improvement of the human beings in it. It is an antidote for middle-age character deterioration. LeShan says: "One of the most valuable attributes of marriage is that one's partner can truly be one's best friend, and friendship was never more important. If one defines a friend as someone who loves you in spite of knowing your faults and weaknesses, and has even better dreams for your fulfillment than you have for yourself, it can surely be the foundation for what each of us needs most in middle age—permission to continue to quest for one's own identity."[21]

As is so often the case, it is an irritatingly simple and excruciatingly difficult conclusion we recognize after this journey through fields of conflicting data. It is not so much what happens to us in middle age as it is what we do with what happens to us; that's what counts. We all experience some kind of crisis in this as in other ages; but how do we use the crisis? Education, therapy and research will surely be of more help to us in the utilization of middle-aged crisis as they more and more treat this fascinating time period with the respect it deserves instead of viewing it as a kind of big-people's latency period.

References

1. C. Vincent, "An Open Letter to the 'Caught Generation' " *The Family Coordinator*, XXI (1972), 143–50.
2. R. Wright, *In the Middle of Life* (New York: Farrar, Straus and Giroux, 1973).
3. B. Neugarten, ed., *Middle Age and Aging* (Chicago: University of Chicago Press, 1968).

4. F. McMorrow, *Midolescence: The Dangerous Years* (New York: Strawberry Hill Publishing Company, Inc., 1974).
5. Neugarten, *op. cit.*
6. *Ibid.*
7. E. LeShan, *The Wonderful Crisis of Middle Age* (New York: David McKay Company, Inc., 1973).
8. J. Cuber and P. Harroff, *The Significant Americans* (New York: Appleton-Century, 1965).
9. H. Mass and J. Kuypers, *From Thirty to Seventy* (San Francisco: Jossey-Bass, Inc., 1974).
10. *Ibid.*
11. LeShan, *op. cit.*
12. R. Anderson, *Solitaire and Double Solitaire* (New York: Random House, 1972).
13. H. Hesse, *Steppenwolf* (New York: Holt, Rinehard and Winston, Inc., 1957).
14. Anderson, *op. cit.*
15. Cuber and Harroff, *op. cit.*
16. L. Troll, "The Family of Later Life: A Decade Review" *Journal of Marriage and the Family*, XXXIII (1971), 263–90.
17. McMorrow, *op. cit.*
18. A. Brayshaw, "Middle-aged Marriage: Idealism, Realism and the Search for Meaning" *Marriage and Family Living*, XXIV (1962), 358–64.
19. LeShan, *op. cit.*
20. Brayshaw, *op. cit.*
21. LeShan, *op. cit.*

HOLY DEADLOCK: A STUDY
OF UNSUCCESSFUL MARRIAGES*

E. E. LeMasters

Not all cases of marital maladjustment arise from major crises and not all end in divorce. This article traces the history of thirty-six couples, caught in a chain of conflict situations that had extended over at least ten years' time. The study covers such items as degree of personal disorganization, effect on children, and reasons that held the couple together.

INTRODUCTION

Some years ago Waller demonstrated that divorced persons in our society suffer personal disorganization as the price of marital failure.[1] More recently, in a careful study of divorced women, Goode has shown again that divorce is no bed of roses, sociologically speaking.[2]

In the present study a somewhat different problem has been posed: what happens to married couples whose marriages have failed but who *don't* separate or divorce? More specifically, the study attempts to answer the following questions: (1) Do the couples who don't separate or divorce escape personal disorganization, as measured by such indices as alcoholism, mental illness, etc.? (2) Do couples with a long history of marital conflict (ten years miminum in this study) ever "solve" their marital problems? (3) What are the effects of such marriages on the children?

In an attempt to discover some tentative answers to these questions, 36 marriages characterized by chronic husband-wife conflict were anlyzed. To be included in the sample, the cases had to meet three requirements: (1) both spouses had to regard the marriage as unsuccessful; (2) this condition must have persisted for at least ten years; and (3) the marriage had to be intact—that is, they were still living together. No case which met these requirements was excluded.

The couples were located through friends, attorneys, physicians, ministers, and marriage counselors. An average of three hours was spent interviewing each couple. With four exceptions, both spouses were seen.

The sample is basically white, urban, Protestant, and middle-class, with

*E. E. LeMasters is Professor of Social Work and Lecturer in Sociology, University of Wisconsin-Madison. Reprinted by permission of the Sociological Quarterly, vol. XXI, no. 2 (The Midwest Sociologist), July 1959.

scattered cases falling into diverse socio-economic categories. No claim is made for the representativeness of the sample. In view of the limited nature of the study, the findings are presented as being suggestive rather than conclusive.

THE FINDINGS

Data bearing on the three questions posed for the study will be presented first. Other material which might be of interest to research persons and practitioners in this field will be discussed later.

1. Do the couples who don't separate or divorce escape personal disorganization? The evidence from these cases is that they don't. Of the 36 married couples, objective evidence of personal disorganization could be demonstrated for one or both spouses in 27 cases (75%).[3] The most frequent types of disorganization were alcoholism, chronic psychosomatic illness, neurotic or psychotic behavior, occupational disorganization, extramarital affairs, and a syndrome of patterns best described by Schulberg's term, "disenchantment."[4] The table on 36 unsuccessful marriages summarizes the distribution of these types of personal disorganization.

Types of Personal Disorganization in 36 Unsuccessful Marriages

Type	Husbands	Wives
Alcoholism	14	6
Psychosomatic illness	5	12
Neurotic-psychotic behavior	8	10
Occupational disorganization	17	0
Extramarital affairs	12	6
Disenchantment	18	22

It is not known, of course, what these persons would have been like had they married someone else (or not married at all). Nor is it possible to know what their adjustment would have been had they separated or divorced. Keeping these limitations in mind, it still seems well established that these couples did not escape the destructive impact of marital failure by avoiding separation or divorce.

2. Do couples with a long history of marital conflict ever "solve" their marital problems? A recent follow-up of these couples revealed that of the 29

still living together, not one couple had been able to work out what seemed to them to be a satisfactory marriage. the implications of this finding will be presented later.

3. What are the effects of such marriages on the children?   One would assume a high incidence of disorganization in the children of these couples. The data, however, do not seem to support such an assumption. Of the 76 children in these marriages, only 7 have ever been referred to a child guidance clinic or school psychologist for diagnosis or therapy for emotional or behavioral problems. And only 3 children in the sample have ever been booked for a juvenile offense. Furthermore, of the male children who have served in the armed forces (17), none has been rejected or discharged for psychiatric reasons or behavioral problems.

It is recognized that the above "tests" are very crude and that a psychiatric screening might prove these children to have been damaged emotionally in various ways. Most certainly they have not had an optimum opportunity to develop their capacities as human beings. But using such crude measuring devices as school and community adjustment, plus performance in the armed forces, these children appear to be a relatively "normal" group.

This finding does not agree with that of Despert,[5] who concludes that chronic marital conflict is often more damaging to children than separation or divorce. It is also not entirely in line with the findings of Goode, whose divorced women felt their children to be better adjusted after the divorce.[6]

If other studies should support our findings in this point, how could one explain the ability of these children to be well organized in spite of their negative home environment? The writer suggests several possible interpretations: (1) the conclusion of Orlansky that children are tougher emotionally than has generally been thought;[7] (2) the possibility that children are not as aware of parental conflict as child psychiatrists have supposed—for example, the findings of Burchinal and his co-workers that the relationship between parental acceptance of children and the adjustment of the children was negligible;[8] (3) that modern society permits the child enough contacts with other human beings that the parents are custodians of personality rather than its shapers;[9] (4) that genetic factors are crucial in personality disorganization and that these operate independently of parental conflict—for example, the findings of Kallmann on schizophrenia.[10] The work of Sewell in which infant care techniques did not correlate significantly with later school adjustment might also be fitted into this analysis.[11]

Regardless of the interpretation of this finding, it could be maintained with some logic that the results of this study support the argument that parents should continue their marriage "for the benefit of the children."

OTHER OBSERVATIONS ON THE CASES

Differential Reaction Patterns of Husbands and Wives

The husbands and wives in this sample utilized quite different substitute satisfaction patterns to soften the blow of marital failure. The men tended to turn to (a) their job, (b) liquor, (c) other women. With the wives, however, the major substitute satisfactions were (a) their children, (b) a job, (c) religion, and (d) community service.

As Kinsey would have predicted, extramarital affairs were reported for twice as many husbands as wives.[12] It is interesting to note that the extramarital affairs tended to follow rather than precede the marital failure, thus raising the question whether this so-called "cause" of marital difficulty may be an effect instead.

Of the two sets of substitute satisfactions, it appears that those of the husbands are potentially more destructive. The writer has the distinct impression from these cases that husbands are more likely to be severely damaged by chronic marital failure than are wives. This is contrary to the old saying that "the woman pays," but it may be true nevertheless. Unfortunately, the best study available on divorced persons, that cited by Goode, did not cover the post-divorce adjustment of the husbands, hence gives us no comparable data.

If it is true that men do suffer more damage than women from marital failure, the interpretation would seem to be that the substitute satisfactions of the women are more in line with the basic values of the society—increased interest in their children, greater participation in church affairs, etc.

The Process of Disenchantment

Given the romantic approach to marriage in American society, it would seem logical to expect some degree of trauma in these couples. Of the 72 husbands and wives in the sample, 40 (56 percent) exhibited what we have chosen to call "disenchantment." These persons have lost their faith in romance and are cynical (if not bitter). In the most severe cases they refer to love as "a joke"; some perceive themselves as "suckers." They also use the expression "kid stuff" in referring to the romantic complex.

Careful study of these 40 persons reveals a process of disenchantment; (a) the feeling of concern that the marriage has not gone as they had expected; (b) a stage of determined effort to be brave and to solve their problems; (c) this is followed by a stage of hostility toward the partner for not "cooperating" in the effort to save the marriage; (d) and then resignation and perhaps bitterness.

It is worthwhile to note that these couples do not exhibit a stage (e) described by Waller and Goode—namely, the therapeutic excitement of a new love affair and the possibility of another marriage. If it is true that the best treatment for a broken love affair is a new one, as the above studies seem to indicate, then one of the prices paid by these couples for not terminating their marriage is their inability to form new meaningful love relationships. With a very few exceptions, the extramarital affairs reported by the couples failed to be deep enough to heal the wounds from the marital failure.

Counseling Efforts with These Couples

Marriage counselors, ministers, and psychotherapists consulted by this sample (14 had consulted at least one of the above) seem in general to have been committed to keeping these couples together. In view of the fact that not one of the couples eventually succeeded in building what they regarded as an adequate marriage, one wonders why more effort was not directed at helping the couples dissolve what was for most of them essentially a destructive relationship. It would seem that professional practitioners working with such couples may be reflecting a cultural bias in their counseling efforts—that the function of the counselor is to keep the marriage intact no matter what the cost.

It is undoubtedly true that the counselor who suggests separation or divorce is open to the charge of "undermining" marriage and of not being able to "save marriages." It is also true, however, that the counselor who fails to consider separation or divorce for marriages such as these must face the fact that some of these couples will deteriorate seriously if the relationship is continued for any length of time. Actually, not even the Catholic moral code demands that destructive marriages be continued. And as Gold says, divorce (with or without remarriage) can be therapeutic for some persons.[13]

How Did Some of the Couples Escape Disorganization?

It will be remembered that of the 36 couples, disorganization could not be demonstrated for nine (25 percent) of the couples. If marriage is so crucial in our society in meeting basic needs, how is one to explain the fact that one-fourth of these husbands and wives apparently succeeded in living constructive lives in spite of what might have been a disastrous marital relationship?

It is suggested that the following interpretations may be helpful in understanding these cases: (1) Differential ability to tolerate frustration. It is well recognized in psychiatry that humans vary widely in their ability to absorb physical or psychic punishment. World War II supplied ample evidence of this for the men in the armed forces. Sociologists who specialize in crime, alcoholism, and the entire field of deviation are well aware of the fact that what drives one man to murder (or drink) will scarcely upset another man (or woman). (2) Displacement of hostility and other forms of negative emotion. Some persons express their hostility directly onto the marriage partner, others turn the emotion back on themselves, whereas still others displace the feeling onto the outside world—employees working under them, employers, minority groups, the economic system, etc. Whatever the device, the emotion which might damage the married partners is not released within the primary group, thus minimizing the destructive effects within the family itself. It could be maintained that these nine marriages did produce damage but that it was to persons outside the intimate circle. As one wife said of her husband: "He doesn't get ulcers—he gives them to *other* people." (3) The development of separate worlds for the husband and wife. Difficult as it may be to believe, it is possible in modern society to live as man and wife and hardly interact with each other. One man, for example, seeing that his marriage was unsuccessful, arranged to be assigned a wide territory which kept him away from home six weeks at a time. Another case was more ingenious: the man would arise about five A.M., prepare his own breakfast and leave for work. He lunched downtown (although he could easily have come home for lunch), had an early dinner in the evening and went to bed about seven. His wife, on the other hand, always stayed in bed until her husband had gone to work, and she usually stayed up until two or so in the morning. As this pattern developed, it became possible for them to live together while spending only about two hours together in the evening (from 5 to 7). They each slept with one of the children, so that part of the day or night did not involve interaction either. In a very pragmatic way, this couple worked out a style of life which held to the barest minimum their opportunity to express hostility.

A more common pattern involving separate worlds finds the husband becoming increasingly absorbed in his career, while the wife immerses herself in the children, community service, the church, etc. This sort of behavior represents what has been called "sublimation" in the redirection of sexual drives—the energy which might normally go into husband-wife interaction is expressed through other channels which meet with society's approval. Thus these couples minimize the potential destructiveness of the marriage and are actually industrial and community leaders in many cases. Sloan Wilson describes such a marriage in *Man in the Gray Flannel Suit.*[14] Oddly enough, society and the community often do benefit from such marriages—in these cases there was one children's hospital and one low cost housing project which owe their existence to a poor marriage.

In view of the above, it appears that there are various ultimate reactions to an unsuccessful marriage, some of which are more socially desirable than others.

Why Did They Stay Together?

In a few cases only psychiatric theory would appear to explain why some of these couples continued living together. In perhaps the "worst" case, the man and wife seemed to hate each other, yet were unable to separate. They had no children, nor did their religious beliefs prevent separation. Yet they lived on together for over twenty years. One might say that they were locked together in a deadly struggle to see which one would break first. The man finally became an invalid, at which point the wife seemed to feel that she had "won." In such cases there seems to be a desire to "get even" with the partner. The reasoning (if such it can be called) seems to be like this: you have ruined my live by marrying me, and the only way I can pay you back is by living with you and ruining your life too. Separation, it seems, is too good for the partner: he or she must be made to pay. Oddly enough, such marriages are recorded statistically in our society as being "successful," since no separation, desertion, or divorce is ever recorded. It should be said that only a small number of cases (three) exhibited such psychopathic characteristics.

A more typical reason for continuing the relationship was the desire to give the children a normal home life. And in these cases, there seems to have been some reality content in this desire. This reason for living together was mentioned by 24 of the couples (66%).

There was also the hope, at least in the early years of discord, that matters would improve. Then by the time it became clear that the problems were not being solved, there were children to think of, community position to consider, financial complications, etc.

How Did They Choose Each Other?

Although it is beyond the scope of this paper to attempt to answer this question, two observations can be made: (1) lengthy dating and courtship in themselves do not necessarily prevent unsuccessful marriages in our society—14 of these couples (39%) had gone together for over three years before marrying. This supports Goode's finding that the divorces in his sample could not be explained by this variable. It appears that we need some way to measure the depth and intensity of courtship rather than just its duration in time. (2) Winch's theory of the unconscious nature of psychodynamic attraction between future marital partners merits further attention.[15] Some of the most incompatible couples in this sample seemed to be pulled toward each other by forces of which they had no real understanding.

CONCLUSION

The sample and the research design in this study are not adequate to support any definitive generalizations. But as suggestions for further research two findings seem of special interest: (1) that marital failure not terminated by separation or divorce has a differential impact on the two sexes, with the male suffering the more severe damage. (It is unfortunate that the best study we have of divorce, that by Goode, focused on wives exclusively, thus providing no comparable data on this finding.) (2) That the adjustment of the children in these marriages did not seem to reflect that of the parents. Although the indices of adjustment used in this study are admittedly very crude, their direction is so impressive that the matter merits systematic study. Furthermore, they are not entirely unsupported by more carefully designed research published in recent years.[16]

It is hoped that these two findings in particular will be subjected to further analysis by other sociologists.

References

1. W. Waller, *The Old Love and the New* (New York: Liveright, 1930).
2. W. Goode, *After Divorce* (Glencoe: The Free Press, 1956).
3. For a discussion of the concept of personal disorganization, see M. B. Clinard, *Sociology of Deviant Behavior* (New York: Rinehart and Company, 1957).
4. B. Schulberg, *The Disenchanted* (New York: Random House, 1950).
5. J. Despert, *Children of Divorce* (New York: Doubleday, 1953).
6. Goode, *op. cit.*
7. H. Orlansky, "Infant Care and Personality" *Psychological Bulletin*, XLVI (1949), 1–48.
8. L. Burchinal, G. Hawkes, and B. Gardner, "The Relationship Between Parental Acceptance and Adjustment of Children" *Child Development*, XXVIII (1957), 65–77.
9. This is partly implied in Cohen's analysis of the impact of the peer group on gang behavior. See A. K. Cohen, *Delinquent Boys, The Culture of the Gang* (Glencoe: The Free Press, 1955).
10. F. Kallmann, "The Genetic Theory of Schizophrenia" in *Personality in Nature, Society, and Culture*, C. Kluckhohn and H. Murray, eds. (New York: Alfred A. Knopf, 1949).

11. W. Sewell, "Infant Training and the Personality of the Child" *American Journal of Sociology,* LVIII (1952), 150–59.

12. A. Kinsey *et al., Sexual Behavior in the Human Male* (Philadelphia: W. B. Saunders, 1948).

13. H. Gold, "Divorce as a Moral Act" *The Atlantic Monthly,* CC (1957).

14. S. Wilson, *Man in the Gray Flannel Suit* (New York: Simon and Schuster, 1955).

15. R. Winch, *Mate-Selection* (New York: Harper and Brothers, 1958).

16. See references 7, 8, 9, 10 and 11.

*

6

STARTING AGAIN

Section 6, "Starting Again," raises the issues involved when we begin new relationships. We, of course, start over for a variety of reasons—the children leave home, the need to rebuild a relationship gone stale, divorce, or the death of one of the couple. Although parents do not end their parenting, it is now definitely of less importance. An important issue at this stage thus becomes the quality of the dyadic relationship.

The diminished parent role may be a factor in the joy often associated with the onset of grandparenting for women. Mothering in the United States is not just to have a child, but to have a child who will have a child. Status is often accorded the grandmother because of her expertise. Grandfathers also excel, as they are more free to indulge grandchildren without the responsibility of discipline which accompanied fathering. With changes in American life-styles, however, there are changes in the traditional grandparenting roles. Residential mobility may remove or constrain the opportunities for grandparenting, women with careers may have neither the time for nor the interest in grandparenting patterns of a previous generation, and men who take early retirement to create a second career may be reluctant to fulfill the grandfather role.

However grandparenting is experienced, physiological aging is an inescapable issue of this stage of family life. Although aging is a reality from the day of birth, "aging" has the connotation of changes from the middle years through retirement and then death. Many cultures honor the aged; ours does not. That we all age is a reality of life. The way we accept, reject or fight the reality is a crucial issue for these years.

There is another form of "starting again" which results from the disruptions of death or divorce. Starting again for most persons means remarriage, especially after divorce. With remarriage there are again the crucial issues of the earlier years, but now with added concerns. Now children may be his, hers or theirs. There are also those who might want to remarry but do not have the opportunity to do so. Persons who are single again find a couple-oriented society and have difficulty making a place within that group arrangement. We do not have any easy reentry patterns to facilitate starting again as a single. Those who choose not to remarry also begin a new life full of adjustments to single status, complicated by the continuing parental role. Whether the person chooses remarriage or remains single, problems will include issues of income and status changes, career adjustments, residential decisions and changes in friendship networks.

Starting again may be disturbing, but it also offers opportunity for growth. New roles demand change, whether as a grandparent, as one among the "aging" or following remarriage or death.

CONTENTS: SECTION 6

REINVENTING MARRIAGE*

Sidney M. Jourard

One man, one woman and no, or some, children, all living together in a household separate from others—this is the pattern, or better, the cliche, of marriage and family life that has evolved in the Western, industrialized world.

If this design evolved as an economic necessity, as the most efficient way for people to live in order to keep the economy going, and the social structure with its power elite unchanged, the design has been successful. In fact, throughout history people at the top have seldom lived the same pattern of marriage and family life as have the larger, working majority. The rich and aristocratic have invented ways to live that have scandalized the majority as much as they have evoked envy. The conventional marriage, while preserving the *status quo*, has failed to serve such important functions as facilitating personal growth and self-actualization in the married couple and their children. In fact, I see compulsive adherence to conventional definitions of husband-and-wife roles or son-and-daughter roles as a factor in disease.[1] Entrapment in forms of interaction that merely preserve a system imposes stress on those who are trapped, saps them of zest and morale, and contributes to illness.

As a psychotherapist, I have often been called upon to do "marriage counseling," and I have been struck by the incredible lack of artistry and creativity in marriage partners. Either person may be imaginative in making money or decorating a house, but when it comes to altering the design for their relationship, it is as if both imaginations had burnt out. For years, spouses go to sleep night after night, with their relstionship patterned one way, a way that perhaps satisfies neither—too close, too distant, boring or suffocating—and on awakening the next morning, they reinvent their relationship *in the same way*. There is nothing sacred to the wife about the last way she decorated her house; as soon as it begins to pall, she shuffles things around until the new decor pleases her. But the way she and her husband interact will persist for years unchallenged and unchanged, long after it has ceased to engender delight, zest or growth.

I have similarly been impressed with the same lack of creativity in inventing and reinventing oneself. A man can retire and, if one sees him asleep, his facial expression changes, the chronic neuromuscular patterns which define his "character" all dissolve, and he is unconscious for a few hours.[2] On

*Sidney M. Jourard, "Reinventing Marriage: The Perspective of a Psychologist" from *The Family in Search of a Future: Alternate Models for Moderns*, Herbert A. Otto, editor, © 1970, pp. 43–49. Reprinted by permission of Prentice-Hall, Inc., Englewood Cliffs, New Jersey.

274

awakening, it is as if a button has been pushed; his facial musculature reproduces the mask that defines his physiognomy, he holds his body as he did yesterday, and he behaves toward everyone he encounters as he did yesterday. Yet, in principle, he has the possibility of recreating himself at every moment of his waking life. It is difficult but possible to reinvent one's identity, because man is human, the embodiment of freedom; his body and his situation are raw material out of which a way to *be* can be created, just as a sculptor creates forms out of clay or steel. The medium imposes limitations, but the sculptor has many degrees of freedom to create forms, limited only by the extent of his imagination, his courage, and his mastery of technique. The sculptor confronts a heap of clay, imagines a possible form that will be pleasing and meaningful to him, then sets about transmuting this image into a structure that can be *perceived.*[3] He may create and then destroy dozens of approximations of his image, until finally he hits upon the form that "works." But that same sculptor, confronted by the "clay" of his being and the being of his wife, can neither imagine nor make new ways for him and her to interact that please, that fulfill needs and values other than the visible *form* of their relationship.

It is both possible and difficult to reinvent a relationship. The difficulty has to do with barriers to change that exist in persons and in the environment. If I begin to change my ways of being myself, I feel strange: I feel I am not myself. The different ways of being may make me anxious or guilty. And so I may revert back to familiar, but stultifying, ways of being myself. If I persist in my efforts to reinvent myself, and begin to behave before others in new ways, they may become angered or affrighted. They don't recognize me. And they may punish me in any way at their disposal for changing a part of *their* world—namely myself—without first "clearing it" with them. Much invaluable growth and change in persons has been invalidated and destroyed by the untoward reactions of well-intentioned others. Perhaps it is because if I change a part of their world, the part that I embody, there is an invitation or demand presented to them to change *their* ways of being. They may not be ready or willing to change their ways. If I lack "ontological security,"[4] I may withdraw my changed being from their gaze, wipe out the new version of myself and, in a moment of cowardice, reproduce the being I used to be. I then become an impersonation of past identity.

When one is involved in a relationship like marriage, the difficulty in reinventing the relationship is compounded because there are two persons, two imaginations, and two sets of needs to be considered; two sets of change-possibilities are involved. But it is still possible for two people of good will to discuss images of possibility, reconcile differences that arise, and then set about trying to actualize themselves. It is possible to play games with a relationship, to experiment with new forms, until a viable way is evolved. What seems to thwart this kind of interpersonal creativity is failure in imagination on the part of either partner, dread of external criticism and sanctions, and dread of change in oneself.

One barrier to change in any institutional form is economic. People have to make a living, and they must find a way to interact with others which facilitates, or at least will not interfere with, the necessities of producing goods and maintaining the social, political and economic *status quo*. Societies that are under external threat and societies that have an insecure economic base are "one-dimensional" societies.[5] Their techniques for socializing the young and for social control of adults are powerful, and incontestable. Deviation from the norm is severely censured, by necessity, because the security of the whole society is endangered.

But in America, the most affluent nation that ever existed, objective reasons for enforcing conformity are diminishing. At last, we have the power and the wealth (despite protestations from conservative alarmists to the contrary) to ground *a fantastically pluralistic society*. Indeed, *not* to capitalize on our increased release from economic necessity, *not* to "play" creatively with such existential forms as marriage, family life, schooling, leisure pursuits, etc., is a kind of madness, a dread of, and escape from, freedom and the terror it engenders. Forms of family life that were relevant in rural frontier days, or in earlier urban life, that mediated compulsive productivity and produced a mighty industrial complex and immense wealth, are obsolete today. I think that our divorce rate and the refusal of many hippies, artists, and intellectuals to live the middle-class model for marriage and family life attests to this obsolescence. There exists, in fact, in this nation a great diversity of man-woman, parent-child relationships; only the middle-class design is legitimized. The other pat-

CAMPING AT WALNUT GROVE.

terns, serial polygamy or communal living where the nuclear family is less strong, are viewed with alarm and scorn by the vast, conforming majority. These patterns exist as a kind of underground. But both the myriad ways for living married that are secretly being explored by consenting adults in this society, and the designs that have existed since time immemorial in foreign and "primitive" societies, represent a storehouse of tested possibilities available to those who would experiment with marriage. Polygyny, polyandry, homosexual marriages, permanent and temporary associations, anything that has been tried in any time and place represents a possible mode for existential exploration by men and women who dare to try some new design when the conventional pattern has died for them. *Not to legitimize such experimentation and exploration is to make life in our society unlivable for an increasing proportion of the population.*

If it is sane and appropriate for people to explore viable ways for men and women and children to live together so that life is maximally potentiated, then we must ask why it is not being done with more vigor, more openness, and more public interest. We must wonder why divorce laws are so strict, why alimony regulations are so punitive, and why people experience the end of one way of being married as so catastrophic that they may commit suicide or murder rather than invent new forms or patterns of life.

I suppose it is the task of sociologists to answer this question. But from both a clinical and existential point of view, something can be done.

I have encouraged couples who find themselves in a dead marriage but still find it meaningful to live together, to begin a series of experiments in their ways of relating. The image or metaphor that underlies this experimentation is the view of *serial polygamy to the same person.* I conjure up the image of two people who marry when they are young, who live a way of relating that gratifies needs and fulfills meaning up to the point of an impasse. One partner or the other finds continuation in that way intolerable. The marriage, in its legal form, is usually dissolved at this point. But it is also possible that the couple may struggle with the impasse, and evolve a new marriage with each other, one that includes change, yet preserves some of the old pattern that remains viable. This is their second marriage to each other.

The end of the first can be likened to a divorce, without benefit of the courts. The new marriage, whatever form it takes, will also reach its end. It may last as a viable form for five days or five years, but if both parties are growing people, it must reach its end. There is then a period of estrangement, a period of experimentation, and a remarriage in a new way—and so on for as long as continued association with that same spouse *remains meaningful for both partners.* Any one of these marriages may look peculiar to an outsider. For example, one marriage of perhaps seven months may take the form of separate domiciles, or weekend visits, or communication through the mails or by telephone. But the idea is that, for growing people, each marriage is, as it were, to a new partner anyway. So long as both partners are growing, they have had a polygamous relationship. The "new" spouse is simply the old spouse grown in some new dimensions.

This model of serial polygamy with the "same" spouse must be viewed as only one of the myriad possibilities for persons who desire marriages to try. The cultural storehouse can also be drawn upon for other models. We could even envision a new profession, that of "marriage-inventor," who would develop and catalogue new ways for men and women to cohabit and raise children, so that no one would be at a loss for new forms to try when the old forms have deadened and become deadly. It is curious to me that college courses and textbooks on marriage all turn out to be propaganda for the prevailing cliché of marriage for the middle class.

I could invent a course that might be called "Experimental Marriage," complete with laboratory. The laboratory would consist of households where every conceivable way for men, women, and children to live together would be studied and tested for its viability, its consequences for physical and mental health of the participants, its economic basis, etc. If the prevailing ways of marriage are outmoded, if men find it necessary to live with women or with somebody, on an intimate basis, and if children need parents, then experimentation is called for to make more forms of cohabitation available, on an acceptable basis, for everybody. The present design is clearly not for everyone.

There is an implication here for those counselors and therapists who engage in marriage- and divorce-counseling. Elsewhere I have discussed the politics of psychotherapy:[6] Is the therapist committed to the social *status quo*, or to a more pluralistic society? *If to the former, he then functions as an agent of socialization, a trainer of persons so they might better "adjust" to the* status quo. *If to the latter, he is more akin to a guru, or existential guide.* If he follows the latter model, then he will indeed function as a marriage counselor in ways different from his more conventional colleagues. He will encourage people who find themselves in marital impasses to explore new ways; he will be able to help his client invent a new way of being married to someone, rather than persuade him to perpetuate the conventional marriage form with his present partner in despair, or with a new partner in unfounded hope.

The inventive counselor of spouses or entire families, as I say, does not aim toward fitting human beings to a marital design that was invented by no one for no particular human beings. Rather, he is more akin to a consultant to artists whose creativity has dried up as they pursue tasks of vital concern to them. If Picasso, or Gilbert and Sullivan, ran out of ideas, or the courage to produce them in action, we might hope that they would have available to them a consultant who would help them turn their imaginations on again, and inspire them with the courage to produce what they imagined

Since each man, woman, and child is a potentially creative artist in the invention of family roles, the marriage and family counselor should certainly be no less than a family-invention consultant. It happens that everyone is the artist-of-himself, whether he is reflectively aware of this or not. He is responsible for what he creates out of what he has already become. But the banality of self-creation that we see everywhere attests to alienation of each from his self-creative powers. The stereotype of family relationships in a society with an economic base that enables and requires creative diversity further attests to this alienation. A good therapist brings his patient back into contact with his powers. A good family counselor awakens his clients to the experience of their freedom or powers, and to their responsibility to reinvent their situation.

Concretely, this way of being a counselor requires that the counselor himself be more enlightened than his clients regarding barriers to inventing or changing patterns of life. It helps if he is himself continuously engaged in inventing and reinventing his own interpersonal life, so that he is, and exemplifies, a vital and growing person. His imagination and knowledge can then draw upon a repository of family life possibilities larger than that possessed by his clients. The criterion of a successful solution to marital- and family-relationship problems is not the *appearance* of the relationship, but rather *the experience of freedom, confirmation, and growth* on the part of the participants. Thus, "seeking" spouses can be encouraged to try such things as: living apart from time to time; lending their children to foster parents for a while; trying to be radically honest with one another, etc. So long as the counselor is not himself existentially or professionally committed to one image of family life, he can encourage spouses to explore any and all possibilities, the criterion of their success being, not "saving the marriage" in its present form, but rather a richer, fuller experience of growing existence and honest relationship.

The group structure most effective for fighting an enemy is an army with its platoons and regiments. The group structure most effective for providing care and training to infants, as well as companionship, love, and sex for the adults, is the now-outmoded family structure. The family structure for the emerging age of affluence and leisure cannot be prescribed or described in advance—only invented.

References

1. See my book, *The Transparent Self* (Princeton, New Jersey: Van Nostrand, 1964) especially Chapters 6, 9, 15, for the sick-making potentialities of various family and occupational roles.
2. Wilhelm Reich has discussed "Character" in terms of neuromuscular patterning: significantly enough, he speaks of both character *and* muscular armor. See W. Reich, *Character Analysis* (New York: Orgone Institute Press, 1948).
3. My existentialist bias is showing here, as rightly it should. See S. Jourard, *Disclosing Man to Himself* (Princeton, New Jersey: Van Nostrand, 1968) especially chapter 14 for a discussion of creativity that applies as much to the creation of self and of

relationships as it does to such productions as a painting, a symphony, a dance or a sculpture.

4. R. Laing, *The Divided Self* (London: Tavistock, 1960).
5. H. Marcuse, *One-Dimensional Man* (London: Routledge and Kegan Paul, 1964).
6. Jourard, *Disclosing Man to Himself, op. cit.*

THAT'S NO LADY...
THAT'S MY SECOND WIFE*

Art Buchwald

My wife and I had this problem. We had been married for 20 years and neither one of us knew what to do about it. It just isn't natural in America to be married to the same person for that long, at least in our generation, and as time went on, we kept feeling more and more isolated.

I guess I'd better start at the beginning. We met in Paris when our hearts were young and gay and we lived in sin for two years before she threatened that she would go back to the States if I didn't do something legal about it.

Well, I figured I might as well humor her. After the wedding, when the novelty of marriage wore off, she could run off with Gene Kelly and I'd move in with Leslie Caron.

SAID IT WOULDN'T LAST

Our friends all thought it was very funny and had a great time at our wedding, although they predicted the marriage wouldn't last either. After all, we came from such different backgrounds. She was from Western Pennsylvania and I was from Eastern New York.

We went through the motions of moving into an apartment and furnishing it and calling each other endearing terms. But both of us were waiting for the other shoe to drop.

Then something happened—or maybe nothing happened. Everyone we knew was breaking up. We kept getting Christmas cards from Paul and Virginia and Sarah and Eddie. This used to confuse us because the only Paul we knew was married to Edith and we were almost certain we had been to Sarah and Lyle's wedding.

School chums used to write and tell us how anxious they were to have us meet their new spouses. Divorcees would stop by with ski instructors they had just met.

As time went on, it seemed like we were the only ones in our group who were still married to each other.

I remember discussing it with my wife on our seventh wedding anniversary.

"What do you think we're doing wrong?"

"I don't know," she said sadly "The statistics say we should have been split two years ago."

"Maybe we're just slow starters?"

"We seem to do everything other couples do," my wife said. "We fight over petty things; we don't agree on how to raise the children; you flirt with other women; I flirt with other men; and yet here we are seven years later still together. We must have goofed somewhere along the line."

"Why don't we drift for a while and see what happens. The thing can't last much longer."

Before we knew it, we were facing up to our 10th anniversary. Several of our friends were already on to their third and fourth husbands and wives. It had gotten so bad we decided not to give wedding presents any more. We could also detect a change in the people we knew.

They were becoming downright hostile.

My wife's friends kept asking her if she wasn't worried that I was horsing around with some French mistress.

She said she didn't think so, but since she wasn't sure, she'd ask me. The night of our 10th anniversary she said to me, "Are you horsing around with anyone?"

"No," I replied. "Should I be?"

"My girl friends seem to think so. You see, if I caught you *en flagrante* with a woman, then we could call it quits. I'd be civilized about it, but I couldn't have you sleeping in the house after that. We could see our lawyers and work out a decent settlement, and you could see the children when you wanted to. I would never show my hurt."

"Gosh," I said "that would solve all our problems. The only thing is I don't know how to get involved with a French gal. Why don't you get involved with a French guy and I'll be the hurt party."

"I hate Frenchmen," my wife said.

"I guess that takes care of that. It looks like we're still in this marriage thing together."

"Ten years," my wife said, looking into her wineglass. "How can two people live together for 10 years?"

"It beats me," I said. "We must be more screwed up than each of us wants to admit."

We ignored the 11th, 12th, 13th and 14th years of marriage after we moved to Washington. But as we approached the 15th anniversary, I said to my wife, "Should we do something about it?"

"Like what?" she asked.

"Have a party or something?"

"And let everybody know we've been married that long? Have you no feelings at all?"

"Don't you think people suspect we've been married a long time, just by the way we act?"

"I don't care what they suspect as long as we don't make it official. One of the reasons I left Paris is that I couldn't take it any more. People talking behind our backs, whispering that we were still together. You don't know what it's like to go to a bridge party and have no first husband to talk about."

QUESTION OF ALIMONY

"Oh yeah." I said defensively. "Well it isn't that easy for me, either. The first question a guy asks me is how much alimony I'm paying."

"I don't know what to say. If I say I'm not paying any alimony, he gets sore. You should hear the way those guys talk about their first wives. I sit there like a dumdum living in deathly fear they're going to ask me about mine."

"Don't yell at me," she said. "It isn't my fault we've been married 15 years. I've given you plenty of opportunities to get out of it."

"Like when?" I retorted. "Just tell me one time you gave me an opportunity to get out of our marriage."

"The week I went to visit my mother in Warren, Pennsylvania."

"Yeah, and then you told every friend in town you were going to be away and for them to look after me. That was some opportunity."

"Why are we quarreling? We're going to be stuck together for a long time," she said resignedly.

"You mustn't get discouraged," I said, holding her hand. "Something will happen. Look at the Larsens. Seventeen years of heavenly bliss and then, boom! One day he moves out, just like that. You'll see, we'll figure something out. Don't forget, marriage isn't forever."

"People are so sick of us," my wife said. "Do you know our children are the only ones in our circle who don't get to visit their father on weekends?"

"Why should they visit me?" I said. "I'm home."

"Exactly," she said. "The children feel so out of it."

"Tough," I said. "Why do you always blame me because we're still married? You had dozens of chances to walk out of it. Why didn't you?"

"Because," she screamed at me, "I had the car pool."

"Oh," I said "I forgot about that. So what you're saying, in effect, is no party for our 15th anniversary?"

"No way," she said, "I couldn't stand the contempt in everyone's eyes."

Okay, so forget about the 16th, 17th, 18th, and 19th anniversaries. It's the 20th one that changed our lives.

We went up to this party in New York City with a lot of the radical-chic and jet-set people in attendance. I must say my wife looked beautiful in a black pants suit with this flimsy lace hanging over her shoulders, and I was very proud of her.

I was standing around with a glass in my hand and this guy, I guess he was a broker or something, said to me pointing across the room, "She yours?"

"Yeah," I said.

"How many times around for you?"

"Times around?"

"Is that your second wife, your third or your fourth?"

I don't know what possessed me, but I blurted out, "My second. She's been around three times, though."

"Pretty sexy," he said. "You're lucky."

"By this time," I replied, "we both know what we want."

My wife came up to us. "Darling," I said, staring right at her, "I've just been telling Jeff here . . ."

"Gerry," he said.

". . . Gerry here about my first wife."

"Your first wife?" She looked at me as if I'd spit on the floor.

"You know, that crazy blonde I met in Paris years ago that drove me up the wall."

Gerry said, "I don't know what he had before, but I would have given up my first wife for you."

My wife said, slightly perplexed, "You would?"

"You bet your sweet life. I hear you made a couple of mistakes before you met him," Gerry continued.

"You know, Darling—your other two husbands," I said quickly.

"My other two husbands?"

"I know you don't like to talk about them," I said, "but Gerry and I were doing some comparison shopping."

My wife said, "Of course. My motto's always been, 'Love 'em and leave 'em.' "

Gerry laughed. "Well, when you're ready to leave him, call me at Merrill Lynch, Pierce, Fenner and Smith. Remember, we're the ones who are bullish on America."

We all laughed at that one.

I knew I was in for it when we got back to the hotel. She hadn't said a word in the taxi.

As soon as I got to the room, I said, "How could I tell the guy we've been married for 20 years? They would have laughed us out of the party."

She pursed her lips. "I just want to know one thing. Why did you tell him I had been married twice before and you had only been married *once?*"

"Well, the way you looked tonight, you just seemed like a woman who would be married three times. It was a compliment. Nobody would believe I was more than a one-time loser."

"You put yourself down."

"But there was nothing wrong with it," I protested. "Once you got over the shock, you seemed to enjoy the idea of having had three husbands."

"I guess I did," she said thoughtfully. "It certainly was more fun than talking about being married for 20 years. Let me ask you, as long as we're on the subject, what was your first wife *really* like?"

"Terrible," I said. "All she ever talked about was the car pool."

"My first husband didn't even know how to have an affair."

"What about your second husband?"

"I though we promised never to talk about him."

"I forgot," I said, taking the black veil off her shoulders.

Well, all I can tell you, it's been great ever since. We don't talk about anniversaries any more. But we do talk a lot about people we used to be married to and we are both in total agreement that we made the best deal the day we got rid of them.

It's nice to be part of the human race again.

THE QUALITY OF POSTPARENTAL LIFE: DEFINITIONS OF THE SITUATION*

Irwin Deutscher

The life cycle of the family may be thought of as the sequence of realignments of family structure and relationships ranging from the time of marriage through the death of one or both partners. In a stable society, such a sequence remains relatively fixed. A body of cultural norms related to appropriate family organization and intra-family relationships develops. Obligations, responsibilities, and privileges appropriate to each phase of the family cycle become established, and anticipatory socialization for each phase takes place during the preceding period. When, however, the society itself is in a state of general transition rather than stability, the phasing of the family cycle may change, and discontinuities in socialization from phase to phase may occur. Thus, for example, rapid advances in medical and related areas of knowledge during the preceding half-century have been followed by sharp increases in life expectancy, resulting in an increased population of aged couples, many of whom remain healthy and active. This phenomenon, in effect a new stage of the family cycle, has received (and continues to receive) considerable attention from both medical and social science. Although certainly striking, this is not the only, and perhaps not the most radical, modification of the family cycle to occur during recent generations.

This paper is concerned with an emergent phase of the family cycle referred to by Cavan as the postparental: "The postparental couple are the husband and wife, usually . . . in their forties and fifties. . . . The most obvious change is the withdrawal of . . . children from the family, leaving husband and wife as the family unit. . . ."[1] This new phase of the family cycle is, in large part, a consequence of the increasing longevity mentioned above, coupled with a decline in the average number of children as compared with earlier generations.[2]

Paul C. Glick has observed that the typical couple of two generations ago had a life expectancy which enabled them to survive together for 31 years after marriage, two years short of the time when their *fifth* child was expected to marry.

But, "the decline in size of family and the improved survival prospects of the population since 1890 not

---

*From Irwin Deutscher, "The Quality of Postparental Life: Definitions of the Situation," *Journal of Marriage and the Family* 26, no. 1 (February 1964): 52–59. Copyright 1965 by National Council on Family Relations. Reprinted by permission.

*only have assured the average parents of our day
that they will live to see their children married but
also have made it probable that they will have one-
fourth of their married life still to come when their
last child leaves the parental home."*[3]

If median ages of death of husband and marriage of last child are taken as
the criterion, the postparental phase of the family cycle did not begin to appear
until about 1900. In 1890 the average woman was a widow before her last child
was launched; by 1950 she could expect her marriage to endure for some 14
years beyond the marriage of her last child. Looking at Census data from another perspective, Nelson Foote[4] remarks that of the 42 million married couples
in the United States, little more than half have children at home. Of these childless couples, more than two-thirds, that is, as many as 15 million couples, are in
the post-parental category. "It is about time," Foote suggests, "that our
writers consider the vast audience that is waiting for relevant knowledge
about marital relations during the years from 45 onward."[5]

It is this new period of marriage with which this paper is concerned—
when husband and wife must, for the second time during their marriage, anticipate a childless household.

THE CURRENT STATE OF KNOWLEDGE

The natural history of such a phenomenon is that generally there is a lag
between the time of its appearance and the advent of more widespread occurrence, and an additional lag before its problematic aspects become apparent.
The appearance of a social problem (family or otherwise) then becomes the
subject of considerable discussion among those clinicians or practitioners who
find themselves most directly confronted with it. Customarily, debate among
such professionals, grounded largely upon their personal experiences, results
in the polarization of conflicting explanatory and therapeutic theories. Finally,
more detached and objective research efforts are brought to play upon the
problem.

Research focusing directly upon the postparental phase of the family cycle
was practically nonexistent prior to the mid-1950's. Since that time there have
been a few efforts made to determine some of the characteristics and processes of this stage. The work of Sussman is highly relevant although he
focuses almost exclusively upon the parent-child relationship during the
middle years.[6] Gravatt had made a preliminary effort to determine the relationship between the departure of children and marital adjustment.[7] Others, such
as Rose and Gass, have provided the beginnings of descriptions of some of the
variables related to favorable and unfavorable evaluations of life during the

postparental years.[8] What is perhaps the most intensive study of the middle years, The Kansas City Study of Adult Life, remains partially unreported at this writing.[9] A study dealing directly with adaptations to postparental life was conducted almost simultaneously, but in complete independence from the one reported in this paper, by Axelson.[10] The demographic-baseline analysis provided by Glick has been referred to above.

In contrast to this dearth of research on the postparental period, clinical observations, speculations, and inferences from other kinds of situations are plentiful. Commentaries based on such sources tend to be polarized. On the one hand there are those who warn that this is a period which places a severe strain on both the individual adult and the husband-wife relationship; at the other extreme is the school of thought which suggests that this is the time when life reaches its fullest bloom and the husband-wife relationship is reinforced with renewed vigor.

The arguments for the first position point to a complex of almost simultaneous changes which confront the parents at this time. It is the age of the climacteric, of physiological changes in both male and female with concurrent psychological and social manifestations. It is also the time when many American men, conditioned to the drive to "get ahead," find success a disillusioning word. The forties and fifties are the periods of diminishing sex appeal. "The critical middle years are those in which men are most likely to 'jump over the traces,' when a man must prove his virility to himself by 'making passes' at more youthful partners."[11] In addition to all this, there is the disruption of established interpersonal relationships caused by the departure of the children from the home to get married, to get jobs, to go to college, or to seek their fortunes.[12]

At the opposite pole are writers who point out that this is a period of lessened responsibility and increased leisure, freedom, and privileges. For the American woman it is an era when "Her husband is earning more now than when he was younger, and her children have flown. . . . In one sense she has everything."[13] It is observed that, "With child-rearing completed, time and strength remain for an active share of civic affairs, etc. . . . For some time the totality of cerebral function increases and the opportunity for its use is at hand."[14] Stieglitz claims that the menopause has long served as a "diagnostic catch-all, glibly presented to explain almost any symptoms which may arise between forty and fifty years."[15] He concludes that, "More frequently than not, the menopause is cause for relief and increasing pleasure for maturing women."[16]

AN OBJECTIVE DESCRIPTION

There is, then, a substantial amount of disagreement regarding the quality of life during this newly evolving and as yet largely unexplored phase of the family cycle. In addition, the opinions held by the experts are based to a considerable extent on experiences with clients or patients—a selectively disturbed segment of the population. The present paper reports the results of an attempt to locate and describe the quality of postparental life within one stratum of the urban population and among a more representative sample of that population.

The method is reported in detail elsewhere.* Briefly, the investigator conducted a door-to-door survey in two socio-economic areas of Kansas City, Missouri. One of these areas can be described as upper-middle class and the other as lower-middle class.† Approximately 540 households were contacted in these areas. A brief questioning at the door with anyone who answered was sufficient to determine whether or not the household met the operational criteria of postparental, i.e., husband and wife both alive and living together, both between the ages of 40 and 65, and having had from one to four children, all of whom had been launched.

The survey technique resulted in the identification of 33 postparental households. Efforts to obtain intensive interviews were successful in 31 of these households, with 49 of the spouses being interviewed. Most of these open-ended interviews, which lasted from one to three hours, were tape recorded. This paper examines the way in which these urban, middle-class couples orient themselves to a new phase in the family cycle: to what extent do they define the postparental situation favorably and unfavorably?

DEFINITIONS OF THE SITUATION

The clearest clues to the manner in which postparental spouses evaluate their present situation lie in the place they reserve for it in their discussion of the total life line. This place was revealed by respondents in their discussion of such questions as, "If you could divide your life into parts, which part would you say was the best time?" and "which part was the worst time?" "How is your life different now from what it was when the children were home?" "Now that the children have left, do you notice any difference in your husband (or wife)?" "How did you feel when the last of the children left home?" "How is your life different now than it was ten years ago?"

As Table 1 indicates, clear evaluations of the postparental period as being "better" than life during earlier stages of the family cycle appear in 22 of the

---

*This study is reported in full in the author's unpublished doctoral dissertation.[17]

†The areas were identified with the help of a social area map of the city, developed by R. Coleman. The investigator allowed himself the freedom of shifting respondents between the upper- and lower-middle-class brackets when, in his opinion, either occupation or house type suggested the appropriateness of such a change.

49 interviews. Equally clear negative evaluations occur in only *three* instances.* This sample provides little support for those observers who suggest that postparental life is a time of great difficulty.†

What kinds of comments provide the basis for the classification which appears in Table 1, and what lies behind the frequencies; i.e., what are the criteria by which people judge their lives as "better" or "worse"? Let us examine first the majority, for whom postparental life, far from being a time of crisis, is the "good" time—or, at least, better than the periods immediately preceding it.

For such people, it is a time of freedom—freedom from financial responsibilities, freedom to be mobile (geographically), freedom from housework and other chores, and finally, freedom to be one's self for the first time since the children came along; no longer do the parents need to lead the self-consciously restricted existence of models for their children. They can let their hair down: "We just take life easy now that the children are grown. We even serve dinner right from the stove when we're alone. It's hotter that way, but you just couldn't let down like that when your children are still at home."

Table 1. Evaluation of the Postparental Phase of the Family Cycle by 49 Spouses According to Sex

Evaluation	Total	Husbands	Wives
(+) Postparental is "better" than preceding phases	22	8	14
Postparental is as "good" as preceding phases	15	7	8
(0) Value orientation or changes not clear	7	5	2
Postparental is as "bad" as preceding phases	2	1	1
(−) Postparental is "worse" than preceding phases	3	0	3
Total	49	21	28

*In contrast, a study of persons aged 60–88 revealed a great majority expressing dissatisfaction with their present stage of the life cycle: "Only 2 per cent of the group looked upon the age beyond sixty years as the happiest period of life."[18]

†It should be pointed out, however, that couples whose difficulties during this period were reflected in extreme husband-wife friction—so extreme that the couple no longer lived together—were selected out of this sample by definition.

These new-found "freedoms" are expressed in many ways by respondents. A newly postparental wife provides the following typical summary statement in response to the inquiry concerning how life is different now that the children are gone:

> *There's not as much physical labor. There's not as much cooking and there's not as much mending and, well, I remarked not long ago that for the first time since I can remember my evenings are free. And we had to be very economical to get the three children through college. We're over the hurdle now; we've completed it. Last fall was the first time in 27 years that I haven't gotten a child ready to go to school. That was very relaxing.*

In this group, typical male comments are "It took a load off me when the boys left. I didn't have to support 'em anymore. I wouldn't mind having a dozen if I could support 'em right." Or, as one businessman expresses it: "I think the happiest time was when our children came into the world, but I'm looking forward to our life together now; we're getting our dividends." In a manner of speaking, these become the years of the payoff.

The wives, on the other hand, respond typically in this manner:

"We're not tied down with children anymore, because they're old enough to take care of themselves now."

"I don't have as many meals to prepare anymore, and my health is better now, and we have had more to live on in the past few years; our income is better now."

"We have given all for the children and that was the most important thing. We lived for the children, and after they were raised we looked for comfort for ourselves. Now when I make up my mind to get something important, I get it in time."

But even more important than these "freedoms" is the re-definition of self and the marital partnership which appears to result from them. It may be this new form of interpersonal relationship and self conception that is the real dividend for these particular families. They speak of "better" relationships with each other, of a sense of accomplishment—a job well done—and refer to postparental life as a time of "contentment" or "satisfaction." As mentioned above, the "freedoms" culminate in the freedom to be oneself. Such a freedom could, of course, lead to either a strengthening or a weakening of the husband-wife relationship. For the moment only the former cases are considered:

> *My husband was a very nervous, jumpy man when the children were younger. If he wanted to do something, he would do it. We would have an argument if I tried to stop him. Now he is altogether a different*

> man. *(Q.: What do you think brought about this*
> *change in him?) Well, I think that when the girls*
> *grew up and he saw how well I was trying to raise*
> *them that he was really proud of them. Of course, as*
> *a man grows older he doesn't want to go out so much.*
> *He gets to more of a homebody.*

Nor is this a one-way picture. This woman's husband also finds her more amiable now that the children are gone:

> *We get along better—we always got along very well*
> *but we get along so much better since we're by our-*
> *selves. I know I appreciate and enjoyed her company*
> *more in the last year or two than I did before. The*
> *main change is like with myself; she's not as nervous*
> *since the children left home.*

For some of the older postparental couples, retirement has accompanied the departure of the children, but the result is the same:

> *The happiest time of my life? To tell you the truth, I*
> *believe it's right now. We're happier than we've ever*
> *been because we're together constantly, you know.*
> *He's home and I don't have to worry about him going*
> *out and going on the road, and I believe we're just*
> *the happiest now that we've ever been. Of course,*
> *we were happy when we had the children.*

"Of course," they were happy; however, her husband, who commented that raising four children was a "hard row to hoe" agrees: "I think it's more like home since I retired. As I told you before, I'm really enjoying my life now." It is a long, hard row to hoe, not only economically, but emotionally as well. The prelaunching years are a time of uncertainty and of anticipation—will the children turn out all right? "You put part of the tension on the children in younger lives"—

> *Just about now we have a comfortable home, two*
> *children, a grandchild, and I feel relaxed. That is a*
> *rather comfortable feeling—to be our age—to live*
> *for each other.*

Things have not always been so good for this couple: "About ten years ago, my boy came home from the service, and I had a lot of worry and responsibility. Then, I had a teen-age daughter, and there was the uncertainty of their life." As one husband puts it, "Life didn't start settling down until the kids got grown up." He feels that now is the best time in life: "I'm more content, and there is more satisfaction."

Unfavorable evaluations made by postparents, although they rarely occur, bear examination in order to determine their quality. The difficulties appear to center around three areas: (1) the advent of menopause and other disabilities associated with the aging process; (2) the final recognition and definition in retrospect of oneself as a "failure," either in terms of the work career or the child-raising process; and (3) the inability to fill the gap—the empty place in the family which results from the departure of the children.

All of the respondents are familiar with the advent of menopause. To some it had no meaning or impact on their existence; to others it was a difficult time which had to be hurdled with a conscious effort; to a few it was a disrupting force which left a permanent impression on their lives and family relationships. Survival of the menopause is described by one respondent in terms of keeping "a healthy attitude:"

> *I've had a little trouble with menopause. (Q.: Is menopause very bad?) Yes, it is sometimes. You just get so terribly depressed. You have all kinds of silly feelings. You hate your best friend, and you are irritable and critical and cross. You just feel crazy sometimes. But I make a joke out of it. You got to keep a healthy attitude.*

This woman confessed to the interviewer that no mother ever really wants her daughter to get married, picked the best years as those when the children were in school, and described the postparental period as "a difficult time." Nor are husbands unaware of difficulties which may be attributable to menopause:

> *(Q.: Do you find your wife easier or harder to get along with during these last few years?) Well, I don't know, maybe—in some ways a little harder. I don't know just how to explain it to you. Of course, uh, my wife, uh, is in a period of life now that's a little difficult. (Q.: Through menopause?) That's right, so I feel that maybe that has something to do with it. I, uh, I'm a little more economical-minded than she is, and maybe we, uh, differ there a little bit. I find bills on my desk in there every day. First one problem and then another.*

This is a man whose wife describes him as being a penny-pincher and who apparently has patiently tolerated his miserliness for many years. With the advent of menopause, both her patience and her tolerance seem to have dissipated, and family arguments occur with increasing frequency.

Even more telling, however, is the final assessment—the summing up—which some respondents make of their own lives. Now, in late middle age, they gain some perspective on their own histories, and to a few, the story is a tragedy of unattained goals—of "failure." One kind of failure involves the shattering of hopes and ambitions for children:

> *It seems like life spaces itself. You look forward to finishing up one space, but then something else—another space—always pops up. Things hurt you a little deeper when you get older. (Q.: What kinds of things?) Oh, if you have real trouble, it hurts you worse. If your children have traits—you never can tell about traits because they don't show up sometimes for three or four generations, and by that time grandpa is dead and gone and everyone has forgotten that he had those traits—so it is a surprise when they show up in your children. (Q.: What do you mean by traits?) Maybe you've been religious and gone to church and sent the kids to Sunday School regularly and, you know, put yourself out. Well, sometimes it ends up that the kids won't go near a church. They just say, "I had all the church I need." And education—well, you can't help but feel that they are foolish there. You have to know their personality. You can't make them over; you have to find out the hard way . . . (pause) . . . . He had a voice like Nelson Eddy. Just beautiful. I tried to encourage him, but it didn't do any good. He would never do anything with it.*

Another kind of failure which "hurts," and which becomes apparent at this time of the life cycle, concerns the work career. Mistakes have been made; things have been left undone, and now it is too late for anything but regrets:

> *In my case, I've always had to take a job and stay with it, because I've always had so much responsibility that—that's what I feel about this job I'm with. I feel that I'd have been better off if I'd have stayed with the paint company. I know now; I can see my mistake there. However, financially I'm making more money now than I was over there. I don't feel that I should get out and look for another job. My age is against me. I've got so much responsibility here. I wouldn't take a chance on falling down on my job. We've never let our family down. We've always put*

> *the kids first. So here I am. A man my age, of course,*
> *if I had gone in the operating end of it when I was*
> *younger, why, I could have been an engineer—could*
> *have had a little seniority. They used to paint us a big*
> *picture down there when we were young—tell us*
> *we'd be vice-presidents you know, or something like*
> *that. I've always noticed that the vice-presidents*
> *came in from outside. (Q.: What is the worst thing*
> *that ever happened to you?) Well, I feel maybe, uh,*
> *the worst thing that ever happened to me was to*
> *work for a company 17 years and quit. I feel maybe*
> *that was a mistake.*

The third general area of postparental difficulties lies in the vacuum perceived by some parents after the departure of their children. There are both men and women who describe the best time of life as that period when the children were teen-agers or even younger. For them, life no longer holds much interest; it is, as one ex-mother puts it, "monotonous."

> *(Q.: What would you say is the biggest difference*
> *now from what your life was like when the children*
> *were at home?) Well, don't you think that anybody*
> *will strive to do things and enjoy it if you know you*
> *have something you can do with your family? That's*
> *the way it was with us. I got my children ready every*
> *Sunday and went to Sunday School with them. I think*
> *you enjoy it because you have something to plan for.*
> *(Q.: And now you don't feel that you have that?) No,*
> *not like we did, because it just gets monotonous and*
> *you need a change—something to look forward to.*

There are couples who have clung to marriage "for the sake of the children" or some other such rationale for as long as 25 years. But it is now, with the children gone, that it is possible for "the worm to turn:"

> *(Q.: Have you ever seriously considered divorce?)*
> *Sure, anybody that says no is a darn fool. Seriously,*
> *yes, several times. (Q.: More often when you were*
> *younger or when you were older?) Ha!—more often*
> *since I have gotten older. I've threatened it plenty of*
> *times when I was younger, but I didn't do anything*
> *about it. (Q.: What things made you threaten di-*
> *vorce?) His bad disposition. And it is terrible—a ter-*
> *rible temper. (Q.: And this isn't calming down with*
> *age?) No. I think it gets worse with age. He used to*

> *scare me but he don't anymore. I let him have it right*
> *back now. I think he is afraid of me now—the worm*
> *has turned.*

There is one respondent who illustrates in extreme form the kinds of limits which can be approached during this period; here is postparental life at its worst!

> *(Q.: Both of your daughters are married?) Yes, both*
> *are married and have children. Yes, here I am fifty-*
> *five—fifty-five, but I don't feel old. I feel disgusted*
> *but not old. (Q.: What are you disgusted with?) Just*
> *life in general; I can't see much reason for it. You live*
> *and worry, but where does it get anyone? I believe in*
> *a hereafter, and that's the only thing that keeps me*
> *going. I can't see anything from now on but getting*
> *old and ugly. I would lay down and die if I wasn't a*
> *coward. I was kinda depressed when my first girl*
> *married. I thought that was the end. I just died. I*
> *don't even care very much how I look. Look, I'm*
> *thirty pounds overweight. My daughters were both*
> *nineteen when they married. I didn't want them not*
> *to marry, but I missed them so much. I felt alone. I*
> *couldn't play golf. I couldn't even play bridge. I don't*
> *have a profession, and I couldn't take just any job. I*
> *just didn't have a chance to learn anything. My*
> *father used to say, "Every tub sits on its own bot-*
> *tom." I didn't know what he meant then, but I do*
> *now. Old age is lonesome, especially without a*
> *family. This is not the way I wanted life to be. It's not*
> *good; it's bad and disappointing. Why have a bunch*
> *of kids and worry about them and then have them*
> *worry? You have dress-up days—gay days. If you*
> *could stay 18 or 25 forever, it would be a grand*
> *world. I wanted my girls to wait until they were 30*
> *before they got married.*

CONCLUSIONS

These, then, are the evaluative outlooks on postparental life, from its best face to its worst. If the sample employed for this analysis should prove to be typical of urban middle-class postparental couples, it can be concluded that the overwhelming majority of them define the situation favorably, although serious problems present themselves for a small minority. When this gross overview is examined for sex, age, and class differences, some variations appear. A larger percentage of wives evaluate the postparental period *both* more favorably and more unfavorably than do husbands. It would appear that this is a crucial time of life for the woman and that it is being clearly resolved one way or the other as far as she is concerned. It may be that the men have not yet been forced into self-evaluation or reconciliation to any major revisions in life. They are, for the most part, still employed in their occupations as they have been for many years, and the interviews reveal that in an overwhelming majority of cases, the children were closer to the mother and her primary responsibility. Her hand has been forced; her husband's showdown may lie in the near future when retirement comes.

Any explanation of the general blandness of the husband's interviews must be qualified in terms of some of the more universalistic sex-role characteristics in our society. Whereas a woman may be expected to be volatile, emotional, expressive, and sentimental, such qualities are hardly considered masculine. The interviews with husbands were characterized by a lack of emotional quality—of expressiveness. They were not nearly as communicative as their wives. This does not mean that their tendency toward neutral responses was an artifact of the methodology; the impression of the writer (and interviewer) is that it is more likely an artifact of the culture.

Insofar as the evidence obtained in this study is concerned, there seems to be no difference between older and younger postparental spouses regarding their evaluation of that time of life. In terms of class, however, a different picture presents itself. Table 2 shows that the upper-middle-class spouses have an appreciably more favorable outlook on postparental life than do their lower-middle counterparts.* On the other hand, there is no noteworthy difference between the two terms of unfavorable evaluations; the explanation lies, as it did with the sex difference, in the neutral category.

Although the sample employed in the study is small, it does not suffer from representing only those people who seek help, and it does reveal some extreme differences. In addition, what little nonclinical research is available appears to agree with the present findings. Basing her conclusions on a study of 85 upper-middle-class women between the ages of 25 and 50, Gass found that they obtained little satisfaction from childrearing and that they were glad to be freed of the confining element of homemaking: "For these women, then, the fact that they were in their middle years increased, rather than decreased, their contentment."[19] Axelson studied postparental couples in two "medium sized communities" in Idaho and Washington at about the same time the field

---

*The percentages in Table 2 are derived from the frequencies in Table 1. The five categories described in that table have been combined into three for Table 2. The five categories left frequencies far too small to be converted into the percentages which are needed to facilitate visual comparisons. Even with this reduction, the percentages are based on small frequencies—too small for statistical manipulation and small enough to be misleading if the reader is not aware of them.

work for the present study was undertaken. His mailed questionnaire returns from over 800 parents of wedding-license applicants lead him to conclude that "this period of life seems as satisfying as earlier periods."[20]

These data seem to indicate that the postparental phase of the family cycle is not generally defined unfavorably by those involved in it. This finding evidently holds true despite the relative newness of this phase of the family cycle and the assumption which might be made that little opportunity for role-taking or anticipatory socialization has existed.*

Table 2. Percentage of Spouses Evaluating the Postparental Period Favorably, Neutrally, and Unfavorably, According to Class

Evaluation	Lower-Middle (N=28)	Upper-Middle (N=21)	Total (N=49)
Favorable	68	86	76
Neutral or indeterminate	21	5	14
Unfavorable	11	9	10
Total	100	100	100

References

1. R. Cavan, *The American Family* (New York: Crowell, 1963). For a restatement of Cavan's position on the family cycle as well as selected readings related to the cycle, see Cavan *Marriage and Family in the Modern World* (New York: Crowell, 1960), Chapter 2.
2. Although it may appear superficially that this decline has reversed itself, there is reliable evidence that the reversal is more apparent than real. See R. Freedman, P. Whelpton, and A. Campbell, *Family Planning, Sterility, and Population Growth* (New York: McGraw-Hill, 1959).
3. P. Glick, "The Family Cycle" *American Sociological Review*, XII (1947), 161–69. For a more recent demographic analysis of the family cycle see P. Glick, "The Life Cycle of the Family" *Marriage and Family Living*, XVII (1955), 3–9. Glick's data are derived from the decennial *United State Population Census*.
4. N. Foote, "New Roles for Men and Women" *Marriage and Family Living*, XXIII (1961).
5. *Ibid.*

*Although most of these people were not provided with role models whom they might emulate, there were a variety of ways by which they learned to anticipate the postparental role. For a discussion of the ways in which spouses are prepared to make the transition to postparental life.[21]

6. M. Sussman, "Family Continuity: A Study of Factors Which Affect Relationships between Families at Generational Levels" unpublished Ph.D dissertation, Department of Sociology, Yale University, 1951. Some relevant papers published by Sussman on this subject are: "The Help Pattern in the Middle-Class Family" *The American Sociological Review*, XVIII (1953), 22–8; "Parental Participation in Mate Selection and its Effect Upon Family Continuity" *Social Forces*, XXXII (1953), 76–81; "Family Continuity: Selective Factors Which Affect Relationships between Families at Generational Levels" *Marriage and Family Living*, XVI (1954), 112–20.

7. A. Gravatt, "An Exploratory Study of Marital Adjustment in Middle-Age," published Master's thesis, Department of Sociology, University of Oregon, 1951. A report based on this thesis appears in A. Gravatt, "Family Relations in Middle and Old Age: A Review" *Journal of Gerontology*, VIII (1953), 197–201. Gravatt's efforts, in the opinion of this writer, were premature insofar as he attempted a rigorous operational testing of relationships based on variables of which the importance had not yet been determined.

8. A. Rose, "Factors Associated With the Life Satisfaction of Middle-Class, Middle-Aged Persons" *Marriage and Family Living*, XVII (1955), 15–19; G. Gass, "Counseling Implications of Woman's Changing Role" *Personnel and Guidance Journal*, XXXVII (1959), 428–87. These studies do not isolate the effects of being postparental in contrast to being a middle-aged person located in some other stage of the family circle.

9. E. Cumming and W. Henry, *The Process of Growing Old* (New York: Basic Books, 1961).

10. L. Axelson, "Personal Adjustment in the Postparent Period" *Marriage and Family Living*, XXII (1960), 66–70.

11. W. Waller and R. Hill, *The Family: A Dynamic Interpretation* (New York: Dryden, 1951).

12. These arguments and variations of them may be found in H. Christensen, *Marriage Analysis* (New York: Ronald Press, 1950); E. Duvall and R. Hill, *The Dynamics of Family Interaction*, (National Conference on Family Life, Inc., 1948, Section 6, 3; mimeographed), cited by Waller and Hill, *op. cit.*; C. Tibbitts, "National Aspects of an Aging Population in *Growing in the Older Years*, C. Tibbitts and W. Donahue, eds. (Ann Arbor: University of Michigan Press, 1951); E. Burgess and H. Locke, *The Family, From Institution to Companionship* (New York: American Book Company, 1945); L. Lowrey, "Adjustment Over the Life Span in *New Goals for Old Age*, G. Lawton, ed. (New York: Columbia University Press, 1943); O. Pollak, *Social Adjustment in Old Age* (New York: Social Science Research Council, Bulletin 59, 1948); A. Kinsey *et al., Sexual Life of the American Female* (Philadelphia: Saunders, 1953).

13. R. Benedict, "The Family: Genus Americanum" *The Family: Its Functions and Destiny*, R. M. Anshen, ed. (New York: Harper and Bros., 1949).

14. C. Weller, "Biological Aspects of the Aging Process" in *Living Through the Older Years*, C. Tibbitts, ed. (Ann Arbor: University of Michigan Press, 1949).

15. E. Stieglitz, *The Second Forty Years* (New York: Lippincott, 1946). For further discussion of the climacteric and its relationship to postparental life see M. Ross, "A Psychosomatic Approach to the Climacteric" *California Medicine*, LXXIV (1951), 240–42; O. English. "Climacteric Neuroses and Their Management" *Geriatrics*, IX

(1954), 35–45; L. Biskind, "Modern Concepts of the Menopause" *Modern Medicine,* XXIII (1955), 145.

16.   *Ibid.* In addition to Benedict, Weller and Steiglitz, this second point of view is reflected in M. Frohlich, "Mental Hygiene of Old Age" in Tibbitts, *op. cit.;* T. Benedek, "The Emotional Structure of the Family" in Anshen, *op. cit.;* and N. Foote, *op. cit.*

17.   I. Duetscher, "Married Life in the Middle Years: A Study of the Middle-Class Urban Postparental Couple" (Department of Sociology, University of Missouri, 1959).

18.   T. Tuckman and I. Lorge, "Old People's Appraisal of Adjustment Over the Life Span" *Journal of Personality,* XXII (1954), 417–22.

19.   G. Gass, *op. cit.*

20.   L. Axelson, *op. cit.*

21.   I. Deutscher, "Socialization for Postparental Life" in *Human Behavior and Social Process,* A. M. Rose, ed. (Boston: Houghton-Mifflin, 1962).

SOME THOUGHTS ON DIVORCE REFORM (EXCERPT)*

Paul Bohannan

WHAT A DIVORCE ENDS AND HOW

Spouses do not simply cease to be associated at divorce; they become ex-husbands and ex-wives. Your wife cannot become your non-wife (as all the girls you never married might be considered); rather she becomes your ex-wife. Although it may not involve seeing her or doing anything to maintain a relationship, nevertheless the basis for a relationship and the history of a relationship are still there. It was DiMaggio who made the funeral arrangements for Marilyn Monroe. Your ex-wife or ex-husband may cease to be your responsibility in a legal sense—but in some attenuated sense or other, no matter how completely you have accomplished the psychic divorce, you choose autonomously to take a new kind of responsibility.

Divorce also shatters the household. This may be devastating if there are young children involved. It is the isolation of American and European households from stable and long-term association with the kinsmen of the spouses that leads to many of the sharpest problems at the time of divorce. Americans have a word for this shattered household—they need it. It is a "broken home." The single-parent household is understaffed, and hence the division of labor is altered. Our do-it-yourself world assumes both an adult male and an adult female in the household. When one or the other is not there, but children are, a harrowing lack of services results.

There is also a lack of role models for everyone in the household. The absence of father at home (no matter how present father is in every other sense) leads to a different structuring of a child's world. A good and workable relationship can be built, but it is not the same relationship. In many societies of the world, the married couple moves in with the husband's parents—and that, of course, may include all his brothers and their wives and his grandfather and his wife or wives. In these extended households, a divorce makes less difference. If the child goes with his mother at her divorce, he enters another large household—either her father's household, or that of her new husband. If he stays with his father, there are many adult females in the compound who are "mothering" their children, including him. He is not uniquely dependent on his very own father or mother in order to have a good idea of what fathers or mothers do.

Divorce, therefore, shatters the alliance between husband and wife—which can be rebuilt into a thinner compact between ex-husband and ex-wife. It breaks the household and so thrusts the family members into a condition in which the economic system of our society does not provide adequate services. It also disrupts the larger community in which the divorce occurs, but does not "break" it in the same way it does the household. There is, in the community of friends nothing analogous to the kinship system which must be repaired and maintained at the time of divorce. Americans join and leave groups and communities—and divorce is just another time for regrouping, no matter how painful an experience it may be when one is undergoing the process.

WHAT A DIVORCE DOES NOT END

Divorce never sunders a kinship relationship. And once a child is born, his parents are kinsmen to one another. Westerners have for centuries thought of kinship in terms of "blood." This idea, under the pressure of modern science, has given way to the more correct expression in terms of genes, but has not changed in essence. Many other peoples of the world, however, trace kinship through descendants as well as through ancestors. Thus, through the mixture of their genes in a child, a man and woman become kinsmen—and all of their kinsmen become kinsmen of one another.

The most important thing that a divorce cannot cancel is the kinship. Moreover, if a ritual was performed at the time of marriage, no civil divorce can set it aside (although a church may choose to honor the divorce as tantamount to breaking the ritual, others do not).

Divorce does not break clean. There is always a residue to be dealt with.

WHAT A DIVORCE BEGINS

Just as a wedding institutes a marriage, a decree institutes a divorce. The things about a marriage that a divorce decree does not end provide the basic content of the institution of divorce. Divorce is a social institution as much as marriage is. And it has a purpose, residual though it may be: the divorce must achieve the unfinished tasks of the broken family. Children must still be loved and educated; household tasks must still be done.

Divorce may be, for the participants, just as difficult an institution as the family it replaces. Although there is less pressure on divorcees today, and although divorced women are not unusual or unfairly treated (at least because of their divorces) in the labor market, there is still no public image of the way a divorce ought to be run. The divorce (like the marriage) devolves on the stability and organizing sense of the people concerned—everyone else is likely to stand back. After the searing experience of legal divorce, this new relationship will not be easy.

There is, moreover, no built-in sanction except the courts for ex-husbands and ex-wives to apply to one another. The parent-child relationships, backed by court orders when necessary, keep it together. Courts take a vast amount of time trying to make ex-husbands pay alimony and divorced fathers carry out obligations of support.

Thus, one of the areas in which we are weakest and in which a lot of social ingenuity must be put is into the contractual aspects of divorce. Our present system occupies judges, social workers, lawyers to an end for which a simpler solution would be cheaper and more comfortable. I do not know what that solution is, but we must search for one.

Divorce also begins a housing problem. The living arrangements that divorced persons must make all tend to be considered inadequate by them, unless they are single individuals with no dependents. Here are some of the solutions—most of them considered haphazard by the people who life in them.

The Bachelor Household

Bachelor apartments, for men or women, are part of the American scene and do not provide much difficulty. Therefore, the ex-spouse without the children passes into this category: "single householders." American culture provides adequate services to single householders.

The Mother-Centered Household

Just as a bachelor household can be called "individual centered" and the ordinary "normal" home can be called "couple centered," so the household of a divorced woman or widow is a mother-centered home. (Widows, however, do not run into the full range of complications.) We have seen that American tradition and economy are geared either to the individual-centered or the couple-centered households. The mother-centered household, on the other hand, has difficulty in carrying out the routine tasks of living, especially when children are young, because services are not provided except at the most exorbitant prices. Who does the man's job is always a problem; for children, there is a single source of both authority and affection—what we might call a direct current instead of an alternating current.

Obviously, there is a tendency in mother-centered households to search for a second adult. Several interesting forms have resulted.

The Bar-Bell Household

One not unusual form of household results from the compound of the mother-centered household with the bachelor household of the divorced husband/father. The bar-bell is composed of a house on one end, the apartment on the other, joined by an automobile. I know several instances in which reduction

of interaction between spouses more or less cured their problems, so that they have been able to live for some years in these compound households. The ex-husband (and this form of household may of course occur without divorce) comes back to do some of the chores around the house—I have found no instance in which the ex-wife ever does any chores in the bachelor-household unit, but we have already seen that such services are available.

The bar-bell household offers maximum opportunity for a rapprochement between ex-spouses. I know instances in which the ex-husband sometimes eats with the mother-centered family and may ultimately come to spend two or three nights a week there, sleeping with his ex-wife.

This kind of household results when spouses are not ready to give up their associations with one another, but have never learned to live within the confines of a single house. Theirs is a tenuous solution, and this kind of arrangement is brittle, but it seems to occur with some regularity.

The Odd-Couple Household

Two men, one or both of them divorced, may try to move into a single apartment in order to save money. As Neil Simon's play, *The Odd Couple*, reported vividly, they react to one another just as they reacted to their spouses. This play is about roles, more or less independent of sex—some households (and therefore some marriages) fall apart because the close interconnection between people in a household is unbearable. Anyone who is not capable of close intimacy has trouble in an American household—it doesn't matter who the other people are.

The Inverse Odd-Couple Household

Sometimes two divorced women, both with custody, form a household. One takes care of the children of both, while the other works. Sometimes both women work, trying to dovetail their hours so that one of them is always home. They thus form a sort of dark image of the normal household. Sanctions are difficult—those based on love and kinship are seldom there, and hence one must fall back again on the weaker links of respect and good will: and the threat that if this household should break up, there is no ready substitute that provides any services at all. Not surprisingly, such households are full of tensions; they seem to be short-lived.

Sibling Households

Sometimes brother and sister, one or both with children from a broken marriage, live together in what they consider to be imitation of a normal household. Such households are usually full of tension, and there may be a great deal of guilt if there is unconscious sexual attraction between the siblings (and I venture that there often is). I have found no households made up of two sisters or of two brothers, but do not see why they should not exist. I have found one uncle-niece household that tried to imitate normal household patterns.

Grandfamily Households

Many divorced women take their children back to their own parents to form a three-generation household. I have known many who tried, few who were happy with the arrangement. The greatest difficulty is to be found in conflict for the woman between her daughter role and her mother role. Public opinion is also hostile: Her return may be interpreted (perhaps correctly) as her being "tied to the apron strings." American values may say very specifically that "you can't go home again."

Occasionally men are offered a place by their parents, and a few accept. My information on this type is limited—perhaps because such men do not join organizations, but I believe this is because of the rarity of the arrangement.

All these types of household have one thing in common: They show individual adaptation to an overall social situation that is poorly defined and morally unsolved. Every person in such a group feels that he has to make compromises in order to get along.

It makes little difference whether the mother-centered family is isolated in a mother-centered household or whether it is grafted onto some other form of household, the division of labor is at odds with that of the majority group. Husbands return to mow the lawn; children learn to iron shirts at a "tender" age; women become more or less adequate plumbers. And perhaps most important of all, they all resent it.*

THE KINSHIP ASPECTS OF DIVORCE

Although divorce does not alter the relations in the kinship system, it necessarily has a great effect on the way they are carried out. The relationship between one parent and the children ceases to be any business of the other parent. If you are a man, it is now none of your business what their mother—your ex-wife—does with the children so long as she does not expose them to situations that the court (not you, the court) would consider physically or morally dangerous, and as long as you get your visitation rights. That is true even when the parents have joint legal custody.

Similarly, a divorced woman cannot control what her ex-husband does with the children when they go for vacations or visitations with their father. She cannot make issues about where they will or will not go, what he will or will not teach them to do, what influences he will or will not expose them to. Unless the court decides that what he does has a morally disruptive influence on the children, there is nothing she can do about it. It is "officially" none of her business. After divorce, being wife and mother no longer "go together," because a man is no longer husband to the mother of his children.

Both parents have, of course, some say in the education of their children, and in some of their life decisions, but unless the ex-wife communicates about it with the ex-husband, and unless he is willing to discuss matters with her, such rights are difficult or impossible to enforce.

The difficulty shows up in many ways: the children either no longer want to stay with the mother, or they do not want ever to go with father at all, even for an afternoon. They may be grouchy and cranky, and perhaps physically ill. After such a visitation, their mother may try to stop all visitations. The father sees this as an infringement of his rights (which it is, unless she has done it with the consent of the court), and therefore uses the only weapon he has in the divorce institution—he stops child-support payments. The mother then has to go through legal channels to make him pay. It is difficult not to use the children as means of communication in all this—especially if direct communication leads to bitterness and recriminations.

---

*Editors' note: Increasingly fathers are awarded custody of children; an alternative overlooked by Bohannon.

The ideal of the mother image does not change on divorce. But the activities and practices of the mother must change. The responsibilities which the cultural tradition puts on a father do not change—but the means of meeting or compromising these responsibilities certainly do. The relationship among brothers and sisters may be altered—it may become more or less intense, either for good or ill.

The kinship aspects of divorce are even further complicated when remarriages ensue. Remarriage does not change divorce structurally, but only complicates it further. If marriage is not easy, divorce may be no easier. And divorce and remarriage may become almost impossibly complicated. Unless, of course, we laugh and turn it into farce—*Divorce, American Style.*

THE NATURAL HISTORY OF DIVORCE

. . . During courtship, the couple participate in what I have elsewhere called an adventure in intimacy,[1] as a part of which they work out an agreement to seek a major proportion of their companionship in one another, and to intertwine their lives in an emotional interdependency—what might better be called "interautonomy." Although both spouses can be independent if they like or if they are pushed to the point that they have to do so, they prefer to depend upon one another materially and emotionally. They therefore make a pact, in part presumed by the culture, in other part overtly stated. Although companionship and emotional interautonomy are subject to tremendous change and to ebb and flow during the course of a normal marriage, the foundations are usually in place before the wedding.

At the time of the wedding, a legal relationship between the spouses is cemented. This means, among other things, that in the eyes of the state and of its various communities, these two people have entered into the civil status of married people. They lose the legal right to marry again until the extant marriage is canceled, either by death or by divorce: They acquire some specific legal rights in each other.

The wedding establishes rights to form a financial unit composed of husband and wife. Many states in the United States create of this unit a property-owning corporation; all states regard financial co-operation as a requirement on the parties. In the ideal case, the husband is expected to support the wife, and the wife is expected to spend her portion of the husband's income (as well as any income of her own) wisely and judiciously.

Still at the wedding, the basis for a domestic union is recognized. The husband and wife now have claims on each other that a household will be established, and that together they will form a team to provide for the needs of one another and of their children. A choice must also be made by the spouses as to where the new household will be located. Most of the American states have laws stating that the husband has the ultimate right and duty to decide where

	Accreted during Courtship	Assumed at Wedding	Accreted during Marriage	Eroded during Marriage	Canceled or Solved at Decree	Institution of Divorce	Inadequately Institutionalized for Divorce
CONTRACT							
Companionship and Emotional Interautonomy					1		6 *
Legal Relationship						2	|
Financial Cooperation						3	|*
KINSHIP and HOUSEHOLD							
Sex Rights							|
Coparents						4	|*
"Coupleness"							|
Child Support							|*
Domestic Rights							|*
Community Choice						5	↓*

Legend:
1. The Emotional Divorce
2. The Legal Divorce
3. The Financial Divorce
4. The Coparental Divorce
5. The Community Divorce
6. The Psychic Divorce

*Areas of interaction between ex-spouses which are inadequately resolved by divorce. These are areas in which divorce reform is needed.

the couple, and eventual family, shall live. The wedding also indicates community approval of sexual cohabitation.

In the course of the marriage, new characteristics are added. One of these characteristics can be called "coupleness." Coupleness is different from the emotional interautonomy that continues to grow throughout a successful marriage. Whereas emotional interautonomy is related to the psychic welfare of the two individuals and to their personal and private relationship with one another, "coupleness" is the way in which they function together as a unit, vis-à-vis third parties and the outside world. Many of us know of couples who function socially as a unit long after emotional interautonomy has been abandoned. These are the people who have experienced emotional divorce but have not proceeded through the rest of the stations.

With the birth of children, of course, the husband and wife take on obligations to one another. Child support—both financial and emotional—is taken as a matter of course to be the responsibility of both parents.

Only two of these many aspects of marriage are unequivocally dissolved at the time of divorce. The legal relationship of spouses ends, and both are remarriageable. The law also says quite unequivocally that their legitimate sexual rights in one another are canceled. By indirection, the domestic rights are also canceled.

Though domestic rights may be "canceled" by a decree, domestic problems are not solved by it. The decree accomplishes only what we have called the legal divorce.

The institution of divorce is left with those problems the decree failed to solve. The institution of divorce involves a new form of financial co-operation between the ex-partners. Financial co-operation may be settled once and for all at the time of the decree, but if there are children, this financial co-operation is subject to reconsideration by the court. Child support remains the responsibility of both parents, but now their responsibilities are spelled out in somewhat greater detail—and therefore there are more loopholes. The normative sort of child support known in the course of the marriage is no longer enough to ensure the support of the children. The activities and expectations of coparents are greatly different in divorce from what they were during marriage.

Most divorcees change communities at the time of the decree, as they changed communities at the time of the wedding. Choice of community is now open to each, although the court may circumscribe the right of the parents to remove children from a specific state.

We are left with the residue—those aspects and factors of the marriage that have not been solved either by the decree or by the institution of divorce. The spiritual task of developing autonomy again; working out satisfactory emotional and training relationships with the children; creation of adequate domestic groups so that physical and emotional security of adults and children is assured; the community into which divorced people move.

WIDOWHOOD STATUS IN THE UNITED STATES: PERSPECTIVE ON A NEGLECTED ASPECT OF THE FAMILY LIFE-CYCLE*

Felix M. Berardo

Widowhood is rapidly becoming a major phenomenon of American society. National census data indicate that there are close to 11 million widowed persons among our population today, the large majority of whom are women.† Over the past several decades the widowed female has, in fact, been outdistancing her male counterpart by a continually widening margin. Whereas the number of widowers has remained relatively constant from 1930 to the present, female survivors have shown a substantial rise during this period. Thus, in 1940 there were twice as many widows as there were widowers. During the following decade widows increased by more than 22 percent while the number of widowers rose by only 7 percent. By 1960 the ratio of widows to widowers had risen to more than 3½ to 1, and throughout the decade has continued to climb to a present ratio of more than 4 to 1. Currently, there are well over eight and three-quarter million widows in the nation, and their total is expected to continue expanding.†† Widowhood then is emerging as an important area for sociological inquiry because of the growing and extensive population involved. (Unless specified otherwise, the term widowhood as used in this paper will have reference to female survivors and their families only.)

For a variety of reasons, however, widowhood as a topic of study has not engaged the specific interests of *sociological* investigators to any appreciable extent, although there has been occasional recognition of the need for empirical data regarding their patterns of accommodation. Over a decade ago, for example, Kutner and his associates pointed out that "the effects and sequelae

---

*From Felix M. Berardo, "Widowhood Status in the United States," *Family Coordinator* (July 1968), pp. 191–202. Copyright 1968 by National Council on Family Relations. Reprinted by permission.

†The national data, of course, reflect the marital status of individuals at the time of the census enumeration only. It should be noted that people in the status of widowhood today may not be in this status tomorrow. Moreover, many currently married persons were once in the widowhood status.[1]

††Three *major* factors are generally cited to account for the growing excess of widows in the United States, namely: (a) mortality among women is lower than among men and, therefore, larger numbers of women survive to advanced years; (b) wives are typically younger than their husbands and, consequently, even without the sex differences in mortality have a greater probability of outliving their husbands; (c) among the widowed, remarriage rates are considerably lower for women than men. Other major factors which also have an impact on widowhood status are the effects of war casualties, depressions, and disease pandemics.

of widowhood have received little attention in empirical research. Widows are coming to represent a sizeable group in American life and there is a growing need for information regarding their pattern of adjustment."[2] In the more recent *Handbook of Social Gerontology* one reviewer particularly notes the lack of references to widowhood in the various publications of that specialized field and related areas, remarking: "It is striking that this inevitable and universal phase of life would be so patently neglected as an area of serious study"[3]. In 1965, a sociologist employed with the federal government made a similar observation, stating: "While much is made of the shock of retirement in gerontological literature, little is made of the shock of bereavement. Both are the common expectation of mankind and each should be studied. But in our society there is a strange silence about death and fear of death that is present with older people."[4] Finally, an informal survey of textbooks currently utilized in marriage and family courses reveals that in many instances the topic of widowhood is given only cursory attention and in still others the subject is not even raised. Such apparent disregard and lack of research concerning this special phase of the family life-cycle appears somewhat anomalous, indeed, in light of the fact that three out of every four wives in the United States survive their husbands.

This paper seeks to call specific attention to this neglected aspect of the family life-cycle. It will attempt to accomplish this goal primarily in two ways: (a) by highlighting the acute and problematic aspects of widowhood status through a concentration on significant socio-demographic indicators which characterize the contemporary condition of the widow and her family, and (b) by critically assessing the interdisciplinary scientific efforts concerning the study of widowhood, with particular emphasis on the sociological research orientation. In the latter connection, this paper represents an argument for a more extensive and systematic development of sociological knowledge concerning the phenomenon of widowhood in the United States and by emphasizing some needed areas of research on the social correlates of widowhood status.

SOCIO-DEMOGRAPHIC PROFILE ON AMERICAN WIDOWHOOD

Widowhood has long been known to entail a variety of social problems at the local level, being related to adult and child dependency, poverty, unemployment, illness, and the more significant facts of family disorganization and of women's insecure industrial status.[5] In order to more fully portray the magnitude of the problem in contemporary society it is necessary to present a concise but somewhat abbreviated demographic profile on American widowhood. In addition to serving as a point of information regarding certain baseline data, the picture to be presented hopefully will also provide proper amplification of the current social conditions surrounding female survivors and will set the stage for exploring the sociological dimensions of their status for both the family and society.

It should be noted at the outset that from a statistical standpoint widowhood is largely a problem of the aged woman. As a result of the impact of advances in medical technology, pervasive health programs, etc., on decreasing mortality prior to midlife, widowhood for the most part has been postponed to the latter stages of the family life-cycle. Around the turn of the twentieth century about 1 in 25 persons was 65 years old or older, as compared to 1 in 11 in the present decade. Since the gains in longevity have been more rapid for females than for males, the growing proportion of elderly women in our population is accentuating the problem of widowhood. Thus, currently more than three-fifths of the widows in the United States are 65 years of age or over (almost another fourth are between 55–64) and "unless the trends in male and female mortality are sharply reversed, the excess of women over men at the upper ages will increase, and our older population will contain a larger proportion of widows."[b]

Widowhood and Income

Because the majority of widows are aged, their economic circumstances are usually below average. A special survey of widows 55 years of age or older, for example, revealed that almost two-thirds of the husbands left a sum total of assets (including cash, savings, life insurance, property value of the home, and other assets) of less than $10,000 to their families; 44 percent left assets of less than $5,000. Equally significant, the median income of the wives in the year preceding the survey was less than $2,000.[7] These figures are comparable to some extent with census data on the aged which shows the median income of the widowed as a group to be less than $1,200 per year, in comparison to almost $3,000 for the aged married. The census data also indicate that widows have substantially lower assets than non-widows in all age groups.[8]

One thing is clear—the available evidence on income levels lends little support to the occasional stereotype of "the wealthy widow," as a statistically prevalent type among our aged population. In this connection, it is frequently stated that women, as a consequence of outliving their husbands, control a great deal of the inherited wealth in the United States. It is said, for example, that they are beneficiaries of 80 percent of all life insurance policies.[9] It is true that as beneficiaries, women in the United States received more than two-thirds of the nearly $5 billion paid in 1965 following the death of a policyholder. Such gross figures, however, can be misleading. In the study cited earlier, for example, almost three-fourths of the husbands owned *less* than $5,000 in life-insurance at the time of their death, and an additional 20 percent owned less than $10,000. Moreover, many of these women have to use what small amounts of insurance their husbands did carry to pay for funeral expenses, medical bills, taxes, mortgages, and so on, leaving them with only small savings on which to survive.

There is no doubt that life insurance has become a principal defense against the insecurity and risk of widowhood in our urban, industrial society with its attendant nuclear family system. It is a concrete form of security which in some instances may help the bereaved family to avoid an embarrassing and reluctant dependence on relatives and or the state in the case of untimely death. Nevertheless, it has been the experience of investment bankers and the like that few female survivors are capable of handling the economic responsibilities brought about by the husband's death, inasmuch as they know very little about matters of real estate, titles, mortgage, contracts, stocks, bonds, and matters of property.*[10]

---

*Actually, the economic dilemma in which widows often find themselves is frequently brought about as a direct result of the failure of husbands to plan their estates and advise their wives. "The truth is that most men leave their affairs in a jumble. This is not because their lives are unduly complicated, but simply because they can't seem to get around to the task of setting up a program for their families that would automatically go into operation upon their death. Death is un-

(footnote continued on page 314)

Widowhood and Employment

Because they frequently encounter serious economic problems soon after their husbands have passed away, many wives find it necessary to seek employment. This is particularly the case where dependent children are involved; approximately 900,000 female survivors carried this responsibility in 1960. Moreover, at that time over half of all widows under age 35 were either employed or else seeking work. At ages 35–54, this proportion rises to nearly two thirds.[11]

While women entering widowhood at the older ages are not as likely to have dependent children in the home, they are nevertheless often faced with a similar problem of self-support, since Social Security benefits provide for the minimum necessities only. Moreover, the obstacles to securing employment at this stage of the life-cycle are often rather difficult to overcome. Typically, these women have been absent from the labor market for several years and are, therefore, at a disadvantage with respect to the educational and occupational demands of current employment. In addition, they are frequently confronted with a subtle but pervasive discrimination on the part of the employers who are not in favor of hiring older persons, let alone older women. Since the majority of all widows, but in particular the aged widows, are unemployed, they are unable to support themselves and consequently are partly or wholly dependent on the assistance of children or relatives, and on public or private funds. While the 1965 amendments to Social Security Act broadened and substantially increased benefits available to widows and their dependent children, their economic circumstances still remain far from satisfactory.[12]

Female survivors who have obtained employment are heavily concentrated in the low-paying jobs. Over one-third are private household or other service workers; one-fifth are clerical and kindred workers, and one-seventh are operatives and kindred workers. Less than one-tenth of all widows are engaged in professional or technical occupations. In any event, research indicates that playing a role in the productive economy is predictive of favorable adaptation to widowhood. Kutner, *et al.*, for example, found that an employed widow in later life tends to be better adjusted, that is, to have higher morale, than both a housewife who has never worked or a retired widow.[14] The acts of preparing for work, carrying out one's tasks, and returning home are viewed as being intimately connected to feelings of personal worth, self-esteem, and significance in life. This has led to the suggestion that "for widowed women, there is a need for a service that will provide occasional jobs, such as baby-sitting, service as companions for bedridden persons, and occasional light

---

(continued from page 313)

pleasant to think about and always seems remote. The tendency is to put the problem off and plan 'to get to it one of these days'."[13] Moreover, many husbands themselves are incapable of making sensible financial decisions and preparations.

housekeeping tasks. Many widows have never been in the labor force and have never acquired skills in any other line. These kinds of jobs frequently coincide with their experience as homemakers."*[15]

Widowhood Mortality and Mental Health

That widowhood presents serious problems of personal adjustment and mental health is rather well established. Empirical research has consistently demonstrated that the widowed typically have higher death rates, a greater incidence of mental disorders, and a higher suicide rate than their married counterparts. More specifically:

The Widowed Die Sooner.   Analyses of National Vital Statistics and Census data for the United States reveal that the widowed have a significantly higher mortality rate than married persons of the same age, and that among young widowed people there is a particularly high excess of mortality.[16] Additional investigations in this country and abroad have supported these findings. Moreover, recent research by Rees and Lutkins has provided rather dramatic statistical confirmation of the long-standing hypothesis that a death in the family produces an increased post-bereavement mortality rate among close relatives, with the greatest increase in mortality risk occurring among surviving spouses.[17] At present, little is known of the primary causative agents underlying this association between bereavement and mortality. Homogamy, common affection, joint unfavorable environment, and loss of care have all been suggested as possible influences. Moreover, "Personality factors, social isolation, age (old people withstand bereavement better than young), and the nature and magnitude of the loss itself all seem to be important factors. When the bereaved person is supported by a united and affectionate family, when there is something left to live for, when the person has been adequately prepared for the loss, and when it can be fitted into a secure religious or philosophical attitude to life and death there will seldom be much need for professional help. When, however, the bereaved person is left alone in a world which is seen as hostile and insecure, when the future is black and the loss has not been prepared for, help may be needed."[18]

Widowhood and Suicide.   Durkheim is generally recognized as the first well known sociologist to stress the connection between widowhood and suicide. "The suicides, occurring at the crisis of widowhood . . . are really due to

---

*A federally sponsored program which dovetails rather nicely with the employment needs of older widows who lack specialized technical skills is the recently initiated Foster Grandparent Project developed by the Office of Economic Opportunity. Under this project, the federal government awards grants of money to the states to be used to employ older people as "foster grandparents" to work with and serve as companions for the mentally retarded, physically handicapped, delinquent, emotionally disturbed, and dependent and neglected children in institutions, day care centers, and homes.

domestic anomie resulting from the death of husband or wife. A family catastrophe occurs which affects the survivor. He is not adapted to the new situation in which he find himself and accordingly offers less resistance to suicide."[19] Numerous investigations have since demonstrated that within a given age group, the suicide rates of the widowed are consistently higher than the married. A review of these studies indicates that suicide—whether attempted or actual—frequently tends to be preceded by the disruption of significant social interaction and reciprocal role relationships through the loss of a mate.[20] Moreover, these studies further reveal that the death of one or both parents in childhood is common among attempted and actual suicide victims; that the incidence of suicide among such persons when they attain adulthood is much greater than that for comparable groups in the general population.

Widowhood, Social Isolation, and Mental Health.   That a high correlation exists between marital status and mental illness has been repeatedly noted in the scientific literature. While considerable professional controversy prevails over identification of the exact sequence of the antecedent-consequent conditions which predispose individuals toward various forms of organic and psychogenic disorders, there is little disagreement with the general hypothesis that "the emotional security and social stability afforded by married life makes for low incidence of mental illness."[21] Again, the evidence is quite consistent that the widowed experience a substantially higher rate of mental disorders than the still married, particularly among the older populations.

The association between marital status and mental disorders has been shown to be a function of several intervening factors, including age, socio-economic status, physical condition, and the degree as well as duration of social isolation.[22] [23] [24] Problems of social isolation, often accompanied by distressing loneliness, are especially germane to the personal adjustment of aged female survivors, a very high proportion of whom are residing alone as occupants of one-person households. Fried and Stern, for example, found that almost two-thirds of the widowed in their study were dissatisfied with the single state and were lonesome even after 10 years of widowhood.[25] The loss of a husband not only creates many practical problems of living alone, but also produces a social vacuum in the life of the aged widow which is difficult to fill. She may find herself "marooned" in an environment which generally requires paired relationships as a prerequisite to social participation.* Consequently, various researchers have found that, compared to married women, widows are more apt to feel economically insecure, unhappy, to suffer from fears of being alone and from loss of self-esteem as women, to exhibit undue anxiety and emotional tensions, and to lack self-confidence. In the case of widows who are still mothers: "There are the objective problems of limited income and the need to find the time and energy for a job to augment it and still be the kind of mother children

---

*Blau has demonstrated that the degree of social isolation among older widows is partially conditioned by the prevalence of similar age-sex peer groupings in the social structure.[27]

need in the circumstances—a mother who can maintain a home, discipline and educate young people, and insure their positive emotional growth. Then there are the countless problems of guilt, fear, frustration and loneliness, ever-present and always the threatening."[26]

To summarize at this point, it can be seen that a rather dismal picture of widowhood status emerges from the brief sociodemographic profile presented in the preceding pages. Clearly, the majority of women survivors generally have had to face a multiplicity of personal and familial adjustment problems while at the same time attempting to establish a satisfactory adaptation to a new and relatively undefined social role. Their economic position is likely to be insecure; more often than not they will need to seek employment, especially if young children are still in the home, and we only have touched on the various difficulties associated with these conditions. Moreover, in comparison to the still married, the widow faces the possibility of an early mortality, and there is a more than average probability that she will develop some mental disorder or even commit suicide.

References

1. U.S. Bureau of the Census, *Statistical Abstract of the United States: 1967* (88th Edition) (Washington, D.C., 1967, p. 33, Table 32, Marital Status of the Population, by Sex: 1890–1966).
2. B. Kutner, D. Fanshel, A. Togo and T. Langner, *Five-Hundred over Sixty* (New York: Russell Sage Foundation, 1956).
3. R. Williams, "Changing Status, Roles and Relationships" in *Handbook of Social Gerontology*, C. Tibbitts, ed. (Chicago: University of Chicago Press, 1961).
4. D. Kent, *Aging-Fact and Fancy* (U.S. Department of Health, Education, and Welfare Welfare Administration, Office of Aging, OA No. 224 Washington, D.C.: U.S. Government Printing Office, 1965).
5. H. Phelps, *Contemporary Social Problems* (New York: Prentice-Hall, 1938).
6. H. Sheldon, *The Older Population of the United States* (New York: John Wiley and Sons, 1958).
7. Institute for Life Insurance, *Some Data on Life Insurance Ownership and Related Characteristics of the Older Population*, 1964 (mimeographed).
8. L. Epstein and J. Murray, *The Aged Population of the United States* (U.S. Department of Health, Education, and Welfare, Social Security Administration, Office of Research and Statistics, Research Report No. 19, U.S. Government Printing Office, Washington, D.C. 1967).
9. National Consumer Finance Association, *Finance Facts* (Educational Service Division, Washington, D.C., January, 1964).
10. A. Schwabacher, Jr., "The Repository of Wealth," in *The Potential of Women*, S. M. Farber and R. H. L. Wilson, eds. (New York: McGraw-Hill, 1963).
11. Metropolitan Life Insurance Company, "Widows and Widowhood" *Statistical Bulletin*, XLVII (1966), 3–6.
12. E. Palmore, G. Stanley, and R. Cormier, *Widows with Children under Social Secur-*

ity (The 1963 National Survey of Widows with Children under OASDHI. U.S. Department of Health, Education and Welfare, Social Security Administration, Office of Research and Statistics, Research Report No. 16 Washington, D.C.: U.S. Government Printing Office, 1966).

13. *Changing Times*, "How to Help Your Widow" (1961), 9–14.
14. Kutner, Fanshel, Togo and Langner, *op. cit.*
15. *Ibid.*
16. A. Kraus and A. Lilienfeld, "The Widowed Die Sooner" *Journal of Chronic Diseases*, X (1959), 207.
17. W. Rees and S. Lutkins, "Mortality of Bereavement" *British Medical Journal*, IV (1967), 13–16.
18. *Ibid.*
19. E. Durkheim, *Suicide: A Study in Sociology* (Glencoe: The Free Press, 1951).
20. W. Rushing, "Individual Behavior and Suicide" in *Suicide*, Jack P. Gibbs, ed. (New York: Harper and Row, 1968).
21. L. Adler, "The Relationship of Marital Status to Incidence and Recovery from Mental Illness" *Social Forces*, XXXII (1953), 185–94.
22. S. Bellin and R. Hardt, "Marital Status and Mental Disorders among the Aged" *American Sociological Review*, XXIII (1958), 155–62.
23. M. Lowenthal, "Social Isolation and Mental Illness in Old Age" *American Sociological Review*, XXIX (1964, 54–70.
24. M. Lowenthal, "Antecedents of Isolation and Mental Illness in Old Age" *Archives of General Psychiatry*, XII (1965), 245–54.
25. E. Fried and K. Stern, "The Situation of the Aged within the Family" *American Journal of Orthopsychiatry*, XVIII (1948), 31–54.
26. M. Ilgenfritz, "Mothers on Their Own—Widows and Divorcees" *Marriage and Family Living*, XXIII (1961), 38–41.
27. Z. Blau, "Structural Constraints on Friendships in Old Age" *American Sociological Review*, XXVI (1961), 429–39.

MINNIE REMEMBERS*

Donna Swanson

God.
My hands are old.
I've never said that out loud before
but they are.
I was so proud of them once.
They were soft
like the velvet smoothness of a firm, ripe
peach.
Now the softness is more like wornout sheets
or withered leaves.
When did these slender, graceful hands
become gnarled, shrunken claws?
When, God?
They lie here in my lap,
naked reminders of this worn-out
body that has served me too well!

How long has it been since someone touched me
Twenty years?
Twenty years I've been a widow.
Respected.
Smiled at.
But never touched.
Never held so close that loneliness
was blotted out.

I remember how my mother used to hold me,
God.
When I was hurt in spirit or flesh,
she would gather me close,
stroke my silky hair
and caress my back with her warm hands.
O God, I'm so lonely!

---

*"Minnie Remembers" on pages 118–119 is reprinted from *Images*, compiled by Janice Grana and published by The Upper Room, Tennessee © 1976 and is used by permission.

I remember the first boy who ever kissed me.
We were both so new at that!
The taste of young lips and popcorn,
the feeling inside of mysteries to come.

I remember Hank and the babies.
How else can I remember them but together?
Out of the fumbling, awkward attempts of new
lovers came the babies.
And as they grew, so did our love.
And, God, Hank didn't seem to mind
if my body thickened and faded a little.
He still loved it. And touched it.
And we didn't mind if we were no longer beautiful.
And the children hugged me a lot.
O God, I'm lonely!

God, why didn't we raise the kids to be silly
and affectionate as well as
dignified and proper?
You see, they do their duty.
They drive up in their fine cars;
they come to my room to pay their respects.
They chatter brightly, and reminisce.
But they don't touch me.
They call me "Mom" or "Mother"
or "Grandma."

Never Minnie.
My mother called me Minnie.
So did my friends.
Hank called me Minnie, too.
But they're gone.
And so is Minnie.
Only Grandma is here.
And God! She's lonely!

FACTS AND FORECASTS ABOUT
THE FAMILY AND OLD AGE*

Gordon F. Streib

There has been an increasing interest among scholars, scientists, and journalists in what life will be like in the year 2000.[1] It is surprising how little attention is given in this growing literature to family structures and relations, especially those of the latter part of the life cycle.

Why has the older family been ignored? First because the study of old age is not as popular and interesting as predictions of technological advances. It is concerned with decline, deceleration, and death, and thus tends to be avoided or ignored. In our youth-oriented culture, old age is not considered a captivating topic to study.

Some of the older utopian societies, such as the Shakers or the Oneida community, were concerned with the roles of older people.[2][3] However, in the descriptions of new forms of family relationships which one reads so often these days in the popular press, the entire emphasis is placed on the family relationships of young people. There is no mention of the problem of "Grandma in the commune."

Finally, the family is regarded as a dependent social form which is influenced by technological and economic factors; thus it can respond to change but cannot stimulate or influence it.†

The major information base which will be drawn upon for our discussion and analysis will be the United States. We assume, however, that many if not most of our observations, particularly the facts and the forecasts which we make, would apply to other Western industrialized countries. The primary reason for assuming the basic similarity of family structures and relations in Western industrialized societies is the fact that the detailed, careful, cross-national study of Denmark, Great Britain, and the United States by Shanas et al. has shown strikingly similar findings for these three societies.[4]

*"Old Age and the Family: Facts and Forecasts," by Gordon F. Streib is reprinted from *American Behavioral Scientist* Vol. 14, No. 1 (Sept/Oct. 1970) pp. 25–39 by permission of the Publisher, Sage Publications, Inc.

†William J. Goode is one sociologist who has stressed that the family may be an independent factor influencing the process of industrialization.[6] William F. Ogburn in his early work stressed the impact of technology upon other institutions. In Ogburn's later work, his approach was much more intricate for he analyzed technology linked in complex ways to other causes of changes in the family.[7] The statement of Fred Cottrell would probably be accepted by many as a summary of the issue: "There is probably nothing on which social scientists agree more completely than upon the thesis that, to a very great extent, social change is tied up with technological change."[8]

It should be stressed that the forecasting of family structures and relations for a generation ahead is not a scientifically well-grounded operation.[5] The fragmentary body of knowledge which we possess is based upon limited samples of information gathered with the use of crude instruments. Moreover, the theories of social change pertaining to the family—as well as to other social institutions—are rudimentary, and this is particularly true about the future of industrialized societies.*

FORECASTS FOR THE FAMILY IN OLD AGE

In this section we will outline some of the major facts and trends concerning the family and old age, and on the basis of this knowledge, we will forecast the characteristics of family life and family structures pertaining to later maturity in the year 2000. For the sake of clarity we have assigned these trends to three broad categories: (1) Biosocial, (2) Sociocultural, and (3) Social-Psychological. There is obviously some degree of overlap in these categories, but they can be regarded as constituting three distinct analytical levels.

Biosocial

These characteristics are rooted primarily in biological phenomena. Social and Cultural factors impinge upon them, and social scientists consider them usually as demographic factors or variables.

1. The life expectation for white males is approximately 68 years and for white females about 75 years.[9] We forecast that the length of life will not be greatly extended for most persons.[10] Major scientific discoveries may well be made in the biological and medical sciences which will alter this possibility. However, some investigators seem to be rather conservative in their expectations about major scientific breakthroughs regarding major causes of death for older persons such as heart disease, cancer, and stroke. Medical gimmickry, involving such things as heart transplants, may contribute to our knowledge of human anatomy and physiology, but major organ transplants will not be widely practiced and, therefore, will not affect the longevity of very many older persons.

2. Women live longer than men. The life expectancy of men and women has increased over a long period of years, but since the turn of this century, the differential in the expectation of life between the sexes has steadily increased.[11] The universal fact that throughout the animal kingdom, the female of the species is longer-lived appears to be a persistent biosocial trend. The con-

---

*Goode has offered an excellent analysis of both the major theoretical questions concerning social change and the family and also the kinds of data required to obtain some tentative answers.[12]

tinuation of this trend implies that the present tendency for many more women than men to become widowed should be a stubborn fact of family life for at least a generation and probably longer.

Sociocultural

These facts and trends are more closely linked to social and cultural components of society than those listed under Biosocial. They are more closely related to the norms, attitudes, and values shared and transmitted by most members of the society.

1. About nine out of ten persons eventually marry. The trend for more adults to marry at least once will continue to be a major cultural pattern.

2. Men marry women who are on the average three or more years younger than themselves. The tendency of men in most cultures, and specifically in the United States, to choose younger women for marital partners will not change. This culturally influenced pattern will continue to accentuate the larger proportion of widows than widowers in the older population.

3. We anticipate that the increasing concern with environmental problems—many of which are highly correlated with population pressures—will result in smaller families. More families will have one, two, or no children than in the present older generation. The smaller family will result in fewer grandchildren.

Social-Psychological

These trends can be conveniently classified under three kinds of family role relationships: husband-wife, parent-child, and sibling.

Husband-Wife Relations.   1. The basic family unit in old age is the marital dyad, for among persons 65 and older, 53% are married couples.[13] A broad picture of all persons over age 65 in the United States shows that 71% live in families with other persons to whom they are related and 22% live alone.[14] Only about 12% of older married couples live with their children.[15] "Intimacy at a distance" will continue to be preferred by both old and young as the living arrangement for older persons. Unless there is a radical decline in the standard of living—which might necessitate some doubling up in housing—married older couples will prefer to live separately from their children.

2. American society has more permissive sexual norms than a generation ago. The forecast for the next generation is that there will be an increased understanding of the fact that sexual activity is normal in older persons. The fuller understanding of man's sexuality and the greater permissiveness in which the present generation has been reared will result in more tolerance of older persons having platonic and sexual liaisons than is common at the present time.

3. Mid-life divorce is on the increase in American society. This trend will

continue into the next century. Marriages may be continued for the sake of children, but when children reach maturity, there will be a greater proneness to terminate a marriage. Greater numbers of divorces among the old will probably be associated with more remarriage. There will also be more remarriage of widowed persons.[16] The remarriage of older persons will have repercussions for parent-child relations because of the problems related to the transfer and disposition of property, visiting patterns, and family assistance patterns.[17]

Parent-Child Relationships.   1. Contrary to some of the stereotypes about the rejected old person, there is considerable contact between old parents and their adult children. Even though the residential family may consist of only one person, the modified extended family remains an important part of the older person's life.

In the study of three industrialized societies it was reported that most older parents (over three-fifths) had seen at least one child the same day of the interview or the previous day, and another fifth had seen a child within the previous week.[18] The percentage of older persons who had not seen a married child in the previous year was very small (three percent). This existence of an extended kin network in which parents and children are in regular and frequent contact with one another will continue and may increase in the decades ahead. The assertion by some theorists that the isolated nuclear family is the modal pattern in American society is not supported by a variety of studies in the contemporary situation, and isolation will not characterize modal family patterns in the future.

2. Reciprocity patterns are evidenced; adult children and their parents maintain a viable kind network involving mutual patterns of assistance. Small services are rendered reciprocally by each generation. In the United States more than half the older persons reported they helped their children.[19] Moreover, the aged are independent of regular monetary aid from their children. In the United States, only four percent report receiving regular financial aid.

The reciprocity of help—shopping, housework, baby-sitting, home repairs, and so on—as a form of kin assistance will continue as a family pattern into the next century. The overwhelming percentage of the old now report receiving no regular financial aid from children. This pattern will persist, unless there is a major economic depression, a catastrophe, or a major social restructuring.

3. The postparental period is not a traumatic and negative experience for most families, in spite of gloomy reports of the "empty nest" syndrome.[20][21] A number of cultural trends will tend to perpetuate this pattern in American older families. The fact that more women will be employed outside the home suggests that their lives will have other foci than child rearing. Furthermore, the increasing emphasis on the dangers of overpopulation and the desirability of small families, coupled with the pronouncements from women's liberation groups that women have a destiny other than as breeding machines, will encourage women to have broader interests. Opportunities for travel and other leisure pursuits also suggest that parents will be able to find substitute interests for family-centered activities. With the problems of the "generation gap"

and the increasing cost of higher education for children, many families will find the "empty nest" period a time of contentment and fulfillment.

Sibling Relationships.   Living with siblings will not be an important form of living arrangement except for the single—never married—person. Even the widowed or divorced do not live with siblings. This pattern will continue into the generation ahead.

SOCIETAL TRENDS

The following trends are more remote from the family itself, but they will have profound effects upon family structures and relations. These trends are an integral part of the larger trends in post-industrial American society.

1. Most older persons will live in their own homes, but there will be more specialized communities and residences which will be age segregated.[22]

2. The average age for retirement of men is about 65. There are an increasing number of retirement plans which permit an early retirement option. The retirement age will decline in the years ahead as a result, in part, of economic benefits received by a person when he elects to retire early. The probable consequences of more persons retiring early will be that a larger proportion of older persons will change their residence for climatic reasons, kinship consideration, (to be near children or other kinsmen) or to have a smaller and more comfortable home. However, the large majority of retirees will continue to live in their long-term place of residence.

3. There will be improved health and medical care provisions which will release the immediate family from some of the health care costs which it assumed in the past.

4. Assuming no major restructuring of the economic and political systems, there will be improved pension and social security benefits. More persons will be able to retire earlier on special early retirement plans. Despite these gains and also assuming some moderate growth in the economy, the aged in general will continue to be an economically underprivileged segment of the society.

QUALIFICATIONS AND VARIATIONS FROM THE MAJOR PATTERNS

These generalizations must, of course, be qualified for subgroups and subcategories of the population. The importance of major variables which have been found to influence social relations and human behavior in the past may be changed to some degree in the next generation. But it seems probable on an intuitive basis, projecting past trends into the future, that ethnic, religious, racial, residential, occupational, and educational factors and variables will be significant in qualifying, modifying, or accentuating most of the above generalizations. We believe that the struggle for racial, religious, and social justice will continue and will probably accelerate in the decades ahead. Moreover, there will be definite positive changes in the social, economic, and political situation of the underprivileged and those groups and categories of the population which suffer discrimination.

The major ethnic and racial minorities—Blacks, Mexican-Americans, and the American Indians—will receive more opportunities than in the past, yet a pragmatic forecast suggests that substantial numbers of these minorities will continue to be underprivileged compared to the majority of white Americans. The most difficult and unresolved internal social problem will be the situation of Black Americans. The matri-focal family continues to be a significant pattern among lower-class Blacks, and it is forecast that increased social insurance benefits will alleviate somewhat the stringent economic situation of the lower-income Black family in their gerontological phase.[23][24]

Among lower-income and less-educated white Americans, one can also expect that socioeconomic differences will continue to be observed concerning the latter period of life. For example, Kerckhoff found that professional and managerial couples welcome retirement and have a more favorable experience in retirement while lower occupational levels tend to be more passive in advance of retirement and they report their retirement experience more negatively.[25]

RADICAL RESTRUCTURING OF THE SOCIETY AND THE FAMILY

Social scientists do not have a very high batting average in predicting the broad course of human affairs, and it is probably risky to make prognostications about these matters. However, with all of the hazards that such activity entails, we propose the following possibilities.

We believe that there is a low probability of radical restructuring of American society. The general institutional structures will continue to be organized in about the same way—government, the economy, education, and so on. There will be modifications, of course, but it is unlikely that in the next decade or two the capitalistic economic system with government intervention in some sectors will be changed in its major contours.

How will this affect the family? Even if there should be a major restructuring of the society—for example, governmental ownership and control of major industries, banks, utilities, and the like—the family as an institution and as an interacting group will tend to operate basically in the ways which are familiar to contemporary Americans, with emotional and mutual help patterns of prime importance. We note that in other countries having undergone drastic change—Communist China and the Soviet Union—family structures, because of their resiliency and tenacity, are not quickly altered. There may be some adaptations to meet the exigencies of possible inefficiences which might result from the drastic alteration of the political and economic systems, but the family members will continue to interact as a primary group.

If a radical restructuring of the society does occur in the next generation, the likelihood of the present middle-age cohort faring better under the restructured society is not great. First, the radical restructuring is more likely to be initiated and carried out by young people and if successful, younger persons would tend to be the power wielders in the new system, such as has occurred in Cuba. Second, assuming even the most orderly radicalization and smoothest transition, there are likely to be periods of strain and areas of neglect. Even if the reorganization should be carried out with a minimum amount of force and violence, the old are likely at best to find themselves in a state of "benign neglect" unless the new regime can maintain a high level of productivity equal to that of the old order. The care and treatment of the old is rather highly correlated with the general level of economic development and social security of the society as a whole. Hence, it is unlikely that the aged will receive any special consideration.

In this connection, it is interesting to observe the situation of the aged in Russia since the time of the complete restructuring of that society with the goal of more humane treatment of all Soviet citizens. One of America's leading students of the Soviet family reported in 1968 that a half century after the Bolshevik revolution, only about half of the Soviet population is covered by social security.[26] Coverage is provided only to those who have worked for an extended period. Geiger also reported that only 38% of the women over the legal retirement age of 55 were receiving pensions in 1959. The Soviet family has adapted to the lack of adequate pensions for the aged and the shortage of homes for the aged by the use of a three-generation extended family form. Geiger summarized the situation in these words: In the marketplace of mutually desired services it has been a good bargain; in exchange for a home, the aged have taken over, according to capacity, the functions left undone by the working wife and mother. In past years this arrangement has been such a standard practice that it was defined as desirable. In the words of a worker: "It is good when both spouses work and have someone to do the laundry and cooking, etc." All benefit from this arrangement, including the Soviet regime itself, which saved itself the expense for many years of becoming a true welfare state.[27]

NEW FAMILY STRUCTURES ON A MICRO-SCALE

We have asserted that there is a low probability there will be a major alteration of the political and economic structure of the United States in the next generation. Further, if a major restructuring should occur, its immediate chief effect upon many older families will be a decline in the standard of living.

There is another way in which *some* American families might be changed in their basic structure and relationships and that is by the creation of collectivities, enclaves, cultural islands, and settlements which would foster or develop family forms which would differ from the modal pattern found in the larger society. The number of persons who might live in collectivities would probably be relatively small in proportion to the total population, but their influence might be greater than their sheer numbers might suggest.

Historically, the United States has been the haven for the settlement of peoples from abroad who desired to pursue a way of life which might be variant from that of their neighbors. The United States has also spawned a variety of indigenous groupings with norms and values which differ from those of the larger society. Some of these ethnic, religious, or cultural enclaves survive, while others have been short-lived. Among those from abroad which have maintained their cultural identity for a long period have been pietistic groups like the Amish who have lived in the United States for over two centuries.[28]

Broadly speaking, these American communities can be dichotomized into those which were (or are) organized on the basis of private property or those in which property is collectively held—communal societies. The study of these communities indicates that those in which property is held privately by individuals or by blood relatives are longer-lived than those which have the communal ownership of property.

In this connection, it is pertinent to study the communes of Israel. The kibbutzim have had to confront and cope with the problem of an aging and aged population. To my knowledge, the communes now being organized in this country have given no attention to gerontological issues. This is, of course, quite understandable because their major concerns are ideological, membership recruitment, internal tensions, and sheer survival in many cases. However, if any remain viable long enough, at the turn of the century, they will face similar problems to those which the kibbutzim of Israel have encountered. One of the interesting facts found in the perceptive report by Talmon is that Israeli communes have a form of benign disengagement in which persons disengage gradually, and probably with less strain than may be true of older persons in the larger Israeli and American society.[29] However, what is more significant from the standpoint of the family in old age is that parents of the members who move into the kibbutzim in later life are happier and more contented than the aging members who have lived in the commune for long periods, for the latter are often very critical. Moreover, the parents of the members, as new residents, do not have the ideological commitment to youth, work, and productivity, and are not pressured by group norms and behavior as are the older members. They are grateful to be there and do not suffer the decline in status and power which the older members must face. The aging member who has had an integral position in the settlement and adheres to its values must face more pressure and strains.

There is a marked increase in retirement communities in the United States, and it is instructive to compare them in terms of structure and ideology with the communal settlements of Israel and of this country.[30] This comparison offers valuable clues about some family and community issues in the decades ahead. The retirement village or retirement home usually requires the payment of a substantial fee for the purchase of an apartment or house, or for lifetime lodging. The terms, conditions, and housing may vary considerably but our concerns here are not real estate and economics but family structures and relations. The person who moves into a retirement community buys his house or apartment as an individual private investment and pays for it and the community facilities which are involved. It is primarily an individual economic decision and occurs because the person or his family can pay the cost involved. There are few, if any political or ideological aspects involved. On the contrary, young people who join communes (this was and is true of the Israeli kibbutzim) have strong and deep ideological reasons in almost all cases. Idealism is high and the economic considerations are rather low in the priorities. It must be pointed out that while ideological motives can be very powerful, they have a certain fragility and instability and are subject to alteration due to shifts in beliefs and also because of the economic and social pressures which arise internally and in the larger society. Hence, in the long run the ideologically organized commune faces a different set of problems from those of the retirement community which is established primarily for economic reasons.

It is predicted that retirement villages, based on economic considerations combined with community interest, will continue to flourish in the United States. However, they will remain a middle-class phenomenon and will not involve any real sharing of resources, but will continue as contractual arrangements based on the ability of the person or his family to buy this style of life.

CONCLUSIONS

In the future old families will find that they are increasingly in competition with other groups in the society, such as militant youthful, racial, or ethnic minorities who will be seeking a larger share of the community's funds. There will continue to be a struggle for federal and local funds and resources. Unless the old become more militant, which is doubtful, they will never get as much concern and attention in American society as they would like. Furthermore, there are three inescapable problems over which they have little or no control: inflation, declining health, and for the women, widowhood.

Yet there are many optimistic aspects to the forecast of life ahead for the family in old age. With increasing social security benefits, improved medical insurance, and more widespread pension plans, more older families can look forward to declining years of comfort and fulfillment. If they are adaptive, they will be able to maintain their own residences, as they overwhelmingly prefer, and still remain in close emotional contact with their kin networks.

References

1. H. Winthrop, "The Sociologist and the Study of the Future" *American Sociologist,* III (1968), 136–145.
2. C. Nordhoff, *The Communist Societies of the United States* (New York: Schocken Books, 1875).
3. M. L. Carden, *Oneida: Utopian Community to Modern Corporation* (Baltimore: Johns Hopkins University Press, 1969).
4. E. Shanas, *et al., Old People in Three Industrial Societies* (London: Routledge & Kegan Paul, 1968).
5. W. J. Goode, "The Theory and Measurement of Family Change" in *Indicators of Social Change,* E. B. Sheldon and W. E. Moore, eds. (New York: Russell Sage Foundation, 1968).
6. W. J. Goode, *World Revolution and Family Patterns* (New York: Free Press, 1963).
7. W. F. Ogburn and M. F. Nimkoff, *Technology and the Changing Family* (Boston: Houghton-Mifflin, 1955).
8. W. F. Cottrell, "Technological and Societal Basis of Aging" in *Handbook of Gerontology,* C. Tibbitts, ed. (Chicago: University of Chicago Press, 1960).
9. M. W. Riley, *et al., Aging and Society* (New York: Russell Sage Foundation, 1968).
10. H. Kahn and A. J. Weiner, *The Year 2000* (New York: Macmillan, 1967).
11. Riley, *et al., op. cit.*

12.   Goode, 1968, *op. cit.*
13.   Riley, *et. al., op. cit.*
14.   *Ibid.*
15.   *Ibid.*
16.   W. C. McKain, *Retirement Marriage* (Storrs, Conn.: Storrs Agricultural Experiment Station, 1969).
17.   *Ibid.*
18.   Shanas, *et al., op. cit.*
19.   *Ibid.*
20.   I. Deutscher, "The Quality of Post Parental Life: Definitions of the Situation" *Journal of Marriage and the Family,* XXVI (1964), 52–59.
21.   G. Gurin, *et. al., Americans View Their Mental Health* (New York: Basic Books, 1960).
22.   R. P. Walkley, *et al., Retirement Housing in California* (Berkeley: Diablo Press, 1966).
23.   E. F. Frazier, *The Negro Family in the United States* (Chicago: University of Chicago Press, 1939).
24.   A. Billingsley, *Black Families in White America* (Englewood Cliffs, N.J.: Prentice-Hall, 1968).
25.   A. C. Kerckhoff, "Husband-Wife Expectations and Reactions to Retirement" *Journal of Gerontology,* XIX (1964), 510–16.
26.   H. K. Geiger, *The Family in Soviet Russia* (Cambridge: Harvard University Press, 1968).
27.   *Ibid.*
28.   J. A. Hostetler, *Amish Society* (Baltimore: Johns Hopkins Univ. Press, 1968).
29.   Y. Talmon, "Aging in Israel, a planned society" *American Journal of Sociology,* LXVII (1961), 284–95.
30.   Walkley, *et al., op. cit.*

section

7

OTHERWISE

In the first six sections of this book, we looked at the crucial issues of family life as reflected in the traditional patterns for American families. This perspective assumed that there are children in the family, that they make reasonable progress in school, eventually marry and have children of their own. The American family pattern tolerates minor alterations but essentially reflects middle-class values of the desirability of family, work and achievement. The final section "Otherwise," recognizes that there is a large number of persons who have made major alterations from this traditional pattern. These variant forms are still within the mainstream of middle-class life in most values and behaviors, although they differ in one or more important elements.

In every generation and in most families there have always been those who did not marry. This is not new today. What is new is the increasing acceptance of the adult single without apology or explanation. Previously, such persons were the "spinster" aunts or "bachelor" uncles. The point of reference and first fact of identification was their nonmarried state. Those who choose singleness today are not as likely to feel deprived but see singleness as acceptable within the mainstream of family life. Some have parented their own child without marriage or have adopted, wanting the family experience without the commitment of marriage. Some have chosen a career in which marriage would represent conformity without value. Still others prefer a life unencumbered with responsibility for others. Whichever form of singleness, it is a choice that will still include many of the crucial issues discussed previously. Family ties will be maintained with parents, siblings, and other relatives. There will be career decisions, and he/she will age. These experiences are realities independent of the married state.

Another variant form is the swinging subculture. Most participating couples are traditional, except in sexual expression. Swinging may involve a threesome, foursome, or unrestricted sexual access to a selected group. Some devise a regularized though nonlegal "menage à trois." There will be crucial issues unique to this subculture while sharing issues in common with other stages of the drama.

A third form consists of those couples who choose not to have children. In our culture, the nuclear family includes a wife, a husband and at least one child. Otherwise, the literature refers to the solo-parent family, the childless family or other hyphenated form to represent some deviation from the norm. We suggest this norm may be changing to include as families those who choose not to have children.

Except for couples who choose to be childless, the alternative family forms mentioned above vary primarily because of sexual expression. There are other alternatives, one of which involves role reversals: the husband a househusband and the wife the provider. These might be either for a contracted short-term arrangement, perhaps to allow the husband to paint, sculpt or write, or might be because the wife wants to develop a career.

One final variation is just living together, which can occur without commitment or intention to marry. This alternative has been around a long time, as evidenced by legal interpretations of common-law marriages, but is probably more openly practiced now than before.

To the mainstream of American life, these variations undoubtedly support fears that the "family" is deteriorating as a viable institution. We believe that families that fit the idealized pattern are relatively few, and that all generations have had alternate forms, although less openly practiced or widely publicized in the past. And yet, contemporary alternatives are just that: alternatives. Most still choose traditional life-styles consonant with parental values accorded marriage, family life with children, careers and achievement. Within that basic pattern, there is a wide range of behavior considered "normal" in all areas of family life, from child nurturance, parenting roles, homemaking responsibilities, employment and sexual behavior, to grandparenting, retirement and aging.

Even as we have dealt with these alternate styles, we know that we may justifiably be charged with ignoring other models of family life. The audience for this book consists almost entirely of young people in college who have had enough control and options in their lives to choose college. It is from this perspective, then, that we have chosen to deal with family reality. We have not considered the unique realities that face the jet set or minority and ethnic families that may differ significantly from the middle class. We further recognize that within the middle class there is a wide variation. It is impossible for a single book of readings to deal with all variations. We believe the readings we have selected represent crucial issues to a large majority of our audience and are the realities of family life to be faced by that audience.

One further point: the institution of the family is being challenged as having outlived its usefulness. Cultural expectations have placed heavy demands upon the family. Some of the readings in this book explore these issues, both as reality and unreality. That there is change is obvious. All institutions and all persons change. While in the midst of change, however, it is difficult to assess how radical that change may be. The alternate forms of family life examined in this book may be atypical, temporary variations, perhaps reflecting a pendulum that has swung too far and will return to more customary patterns. Or they may, indeed, be the forefront of dramatic long-range change in family lifestyles. The point is that it is impossible to know from the middle of change. One is reminded of the political activity on college campuses in the late 60s and early 70s and the expressed fears of the growing radicalism. By the mid-1970s, student concerns centered around employment, social activities and athletics; the environmental concern is essentially quiescent; the extreme radicalism of the early women's movement has not sustained enough momentum for passage of the Equal Rights Amendment. Where are the revolutions and the revolutionaries?

Two quotations accentuate our perspective on change as fad or future. Except for certain quaintness of expression, many grandparents (and parents) of today would echo the sentiments expressed in the following:

> *The children now love luxury; they show disrespect for elders and love chatter in place of exercise. Children are tyrants, not the servants of their households. They no longer rise when their elders enter the room. They contradict their parents, chatter before company, gobble up dainties at the table, cross their legs, and tyrannize their teachers.*

The quotation is not contemporary; it is attributed to Socrates.

John F. Furbay, in speaking to a large audience in Chicago, read from a morning newspaper. The article said:

> *It's a gloomy moment in history. Not in the lifetime of any person who reads this paper has there been so much grave and deep apprehension. Never has the future seemed so dark and formidable. Our country is beset by racial strife, industrial and commercial chaos, and where we are drifting with the politicians in charge, nobody knows. Of our troubles no one can see the end.*

In the aftermath of Watergate and Vietnam, and in the midst of inflation and recession, Dr. Furbay says it well. But the article was written in 1847.

As our society becomes increasingly complex, it is difficult to know whether change is fad or future. To the extent that the future family resembles our present form, the commonness of issues presented here will continue to be reality for the family drama.

CONTENTS: SECTION 7

THE KITCHEN SINK PAPERS*

Mike McGrady

I had it made.

At the age of forty I had been married for sixteen years to a woman of intelligence and beauty. The three children seemed to be growing up straight. My job—writing a newspaper column—brought prestige and a measure of artistic satisfaction. I had a home in a quiet suburb, a new swimming pool, two cars and the rest of it.

I was a happy man who had been rewarded by life, one of those rare individuals who feels good driving toward work in the morning, good again driving toward home in the evening.

Then one day, late in 1973, with all my affairs in order, I quit my job and became a housewife. I don't know the exact moment when I decided to quit —but one reason was certainly that I had done the job long enough. Time was a key issue. After a dozen years I had done it as well and as poorly as I was apt to do it in the future. And it seems that I had an offer, an intriguing job offer from my wife.

Actually the offer was not new, but it had remained general in nature. Never once did we sit down and work out the specifics; at no time did we consider all the ramifications that a trade of roles would involve. The agreement was simplicity itself. I would do what she had been doing. She would do what I had been doing.

Like many women who came of age in the 1950s and 1960s, my wife, Corinne, had been charting a course toward liberation ever since our third child was out of diapers. . . . . Sensing that her freedom was connected somehow to her ability to produce, she had tried a number of projects on her own and finally had begun designing plastic furnishings—plastic because it was readily available and because it could be bent into any of a thousand shapes with equipment no more elaborate than a simple hot wire. Gradually the business, which had started in the basement of our home, grew. When she rented an office above a candy store on the main street of town to house Corinne McGrady Designs, it was no small thing. As another woman once explained to me: "Corinne is an inspiration to us all; she's the first woman to move up from the basement to an office—it's our goal."

The year that I decided to become a housewife, Corinne's income finally had risen to $10,000. From time to time in the past she had suggested it—why didn't I stay home and take care of the children? I would threaten to accept;

she would threaten to accept my acceptance; I would warn her that I just might accept her acceptance of my acceptance.

There were aspects of her life that provoked unqualified envy on my part. All that free time. I would say: "But if I became a housewife, you'd have to devote full time to your business. You'd have to go to the office every day and work eight hours . . . and of course I'd need an allowance. I'd have to buy all the food. . . ." At last she said, "How does a hundred a week strike you?"

"I wish we could talk seriously about this," I said.

"Who's not being serious?" she said.

And so it happened. . . . .

"A deal's a deal," she says.

The check is for a hundred dollars. It is an unpracticed exchange, accomplished awkwardly. I don't know which of us has more difficulty, which of us is more embarrassed. I guess Corinne handles her side of the exchange more smoothly than I do.

It is the easiest hundred dollars I've ever made. But the reversal feels strange. In a marriage of any duration the two people become tied together by hundreds of threads—habits, understandings, obligations—and a single strand would not seem to matter all that much. But the money thread does. This ritual, the giving of an allowance by one human being to another, bespeaks whole planets of meaning; it has to do with independence, gratification, reward, punishment, resentment. The feelings are so intertwined that I doubt whether they can be understood until the situation is reversed. Believe me, when the child starts to give the parent an allowance, whole worlds shatter.

My own reaction on receiving money—this first day and every week since then—has not been what I anticipated. It is not a pleasurable experience, not in the least. In fact there is on my part inevitably an effort to minimize the transaction, to snatch up the check and stuff it into my wallet as rapidly as possible, to pretend that the transaction doesn't really matter. I can see, in Corinne, opposite tendencies, an effort to ceremonialize the offering, to announce it in advance—"Ah, today is the day you get your allowance"—to make a production number out of locating the checkbook and the pen, to sign it with a flourish, to hand it over with a kiss.

I know her feeling all too well. I'm sure there is at least a small sensation of triumph in turning the tables after all these years. And surely there is a strong element of pride—after all, she is pulling not only her weight but *our* weight. And maybe, just maybe, there is a trace element of resentment—as in, "Why should I have to take care of everyone else?" I know how hard it can be to make a hundred dollars, how much work it can represent, but if Corinne has ever felt those feelings, she has not allowed them to surface. . . . .

Corinne is in a bad mood. The mood seems possibly linked in some fashion to the vacuum-cleaner hose she is holding in her hand. Of course. She had been vacuuming the living room, just as she had done before the great role switch.

"I don't want you doing that kind of work," I said to her. "Part of our deal was that you don't do any work around the house anymore."

"But I can't stand it any longer. Mike, I don't want to say anything . . ."

"You're already saying it."

"Well, I don't want to complain," she said, "I really don't. I know you're just starting out. But I can't go on living this way indefinitely."

"I was going to get to the cleaning myself." I said. "Today as a matter of fact."

"But you've had two weeks, and you haven't gotten to it," she said. "As long as I've got to live here, I don't want to live in a pigpen."

Harsh words. I looked around the living room, and it seemed no worse than usual—better in fact. But of couse it had just been vacuumed, and I couldn't take credit for that. My vision of myself as a successful homemaker started to dissolve, in the heat of Corinne's criticism.

"Maybe you're beginning to think that this whole experiment is a mistake," I said. "Maybe you're starting to feel I should be back in the office."

This conversation, with variations, was replayed several times during the first weeks of the experiment, and it had to be an indication of our doubts. But it always stopped there, the dare offered but not picked up.

What I did this time, by way of apology, was get the window-cleaning fluid and start polishing the panes in the living room. If Corinne noticed, she didn't find it was worth mentioning. But then she still wasn't finding much worth mentioning. . . . .

I've since learned that cleaning a house is very much like ironing clothes—the first experience is dreadful and the second one worse. These tasks require a numbness that, if lacking at the outset, one soon tends to acquire. At times even the simple mechanics of the job seemed beyond me. I've watched Corinne as she wades through a room, all motion and efficiency, and in my attempts to imitate her, I come out as kind of a slow-motion version, taking twice the time to accomplish half the work.

As I write these words I have tried most of the housewifely chores, and my Achilles' heel, my downfall, is clearly the ancient task of housecleaning. I am, I can only conclude, an incurable slob, and this is a fact that has, during my year as a housewife, caused not a little anguish. . . . .

As the year progressed, my attitude toward money began going through some changes. This could be attributed to the fact that for me money had stopped coming in. I had decided to stay within the hundred-dollar allowance, but it was not working out. The money always seemed to disappear by Wednesday, and that was the eve of my big weekly food-shopping trip. I could have asked for a raise, but I kept thinking back to all those years when Corinne had come to me. Forty-five dollars a week was not enough, she said. Seventy-five was not enough. Ninety was not enough. I could remember being very patient with her, even fatherly, and going over the receipts and adding everything up and showing her that she should have—oh, at least four and a half dollars left over for her own amusements every week.

Undoubtedly this was the reason she decided early in the marriage to make money on her own. Not until this year did I realize what I had put her through for the weekly pittance. This past history with Corinne made it next to impossible to bring up the subject myself. Early in January I started trying to cut corners—having two meatless nights a week, making do with meat loaves for dinner and sandwiches. My own pleasures were modest, but even they started to seem expensive. A visit to the pool hall ate up five dollars. A quick stop at the Pier Three, a few rounds with the boys, ate up another five or ten.

Corinne's business was flourishing, and she was paying the bills without a murmur of complaint. There was no reason she couldn't give me a cost-of-living raise, but there was no way I could come out and ask for it. I began leaving my grocery bills where she might notice them. On Saturday, April 13, I hit a new high—a $63.45 tab from the A & P. . . .

Four months into the year, Corinne added twenty-five dollars to my weekly allowance check. I put up some resistance that didn't fool anyone. At least it prevented me from turning into a miser.

Throughout my year as a housewife I didn't meet one woman who understood why I was doing it. They looked at me the way a lifer might look at an innocent person trying to break into prison. They knew something I didn't know. And as the year crept along, I was able more and more to understand their point. . . . .

It strikes me that in writing of my year as a housewife I've often presented too bleak a portrait of the housewifely existence. There have been compensations, rewards, moments I wouldn't have traded with anyone.

For example, the trip to Washington. This year, when the upperclassmen of the Norwood Avenue elementary school made their annual trip to the nation's capital, Liam went along. He was the third and final McGrady youngster to go. In a sense it was more than a visit to Washington; it was also three days away from home and family, a passage into apprentice adulthood.

The only unpleasant aspect of it was the time of departure. Four o'clock in the morning. And, as so often during the year, I was a solitary male figure in a female world. It is important that the breadwinner face the new day with a full night's sleep, and so the chauffeurs in the early morning were the mothers and myself.

"You going to eat all your food down there?" I asked Liam.

"Sure," he said.

"What if you don't like it?"

"Well, I made five sandwiches just in case," he said. "Peanut butter. I've got them in the suitcase."

"Peanut butter? Inside the suitcase?"

"Don't worry," he said. "I wrapped them up in the shirts."

"Liam . . ."

"Just kidding, Dad."

My eleven-year-old son got out of the car then and joined the procession toward the chartered bus. There he was, neighborhood tough guy, wearing new trousers, blue blazer and a necktie we had chopped down from one of my old models that very morning. Liam McGrady, carrying camera and overnight bag and maybe some peanut-butter sandwiches, openly enthusiastic about his debut in the outside world.

As I watched him climb up onto that airport bus with his fellow sixth-graders, there was a lump in my throat that couldn't be swallowed. I had missed this moment with the other two children. Through the years I had missed quite a bit by being no more than a father. . . .

The year before I would have slept through Liam's departure, would have been the one running out of the house with a coffee cup in my hand. This year I was part of everyone else's life. True, I was the servant, the deliveryman, the cook and the chauffeur—but at least I was part of their lives. Let them put the knock on my Russian dressing; let them order me around; at least they were using me. At the end of the year they had all accepted me in the role and that was not a bad feeling. So don't let me neglect to mention some of the joys of motherhood, even this belated and male motherhood of mine.

"Did you have a hard day at the office, dear?" I would ask Corinne in the evening.

"Don't ask," she would say.

The fact was, being a business person was taking a toll on Corinne and it could be measured in visible ways. Her appearance seemed increasingly run-down, her face seemed paler and there was a tightness that reflected the new tensions she was feeling.

One of the motivating factors behind the experiment had been to permit Corinne to spend more time on her business. I must say she took advantage of it, working longer and longer hours as the year wore on. And although her business prospered, the pressure on her was mounting at a similar rate.

The pressures were felt by all of us. On a Tuesday night in October, for instance, Corinne was late as usual. I was trying to decide whether to feed the kids or make them wait. Meanwhile the food was losing its moisture, its freshness, its coloration. It was a good thing I am not a suspicious sort; Corinne had been late so often lately that she could have been conducting three or four affairs simultaneously. Finally I called the kids to the dinner table, and as they were sitting down, we heard the sound of the car driving up to the house.

"I wonder what she's going to say tonight," Siobhan said.

"She's going to say, 'I'm sorry I'm late,' " Sean guessed. "That's what she always says."

"No," Siobhan said, "it's not late enough for that. She's going to see us sitting at the table and she's going to come in and she's going to say 'Oh, what time is it?' "

"You're both wrong," I said. "She's going to come in and she's going to say, 'Oh, am I late?' "

The sound of a car door. The sound of footsteps up the walk. The front door slamming. The quick footsteps as she came from the hallway into the kitchen.

"Oh, am I late?" she said, and seemed slightly surprised when her question was greeted by applause and laughter.

One reason Corinne was late was Vinnie. Vinnie, a truck owner, was one of her new associates. Vinnie was six-foot-three and constructed exclusively of muscle, muscle that seemed to extend from his feet all the way to his scalp. Corinne stayed late night after night while Vinnie loaded cartons onto his truck. One night she was explaining to him that the larger cartons contained the larger items in her line and that, furthermore, it was impossible for one of the small cartons to contain an object larger than itself. Suddenly she was aware that Vinnie was edging closer to her, and she was simultaneously aware that they were the last two people left in the building. . . . .

"Hey," Vinnie said, "would you wanna give your truckman a little kiss?"

"Whaaaaaat?"

"Wanna give your truckman a little kiss?"

"Vinnie, my husband wouldn't like that one little bit." How quickly even the most liberated woman resorts to ancient tactics. "And he's a very big man. Much bigger than you are."

"Ah, I just meant on the cheek," he said.

"Vinnie, let's cut the nonsense and get these boxes moved."

The conversation ended there but not in Corinne's mind. When she came home that night, she was furious.

"It makes me so damn mad when men behave like that."

"What do you want?" I asked. "Do you want me to go beat up Vinnie?"

"Of course not."

"Well, it's a good thing."

"What makes me angriest is the way I reacted," she said. "I still don't know what I should have told him."

"Tell him that you're going to tell his wife," I suggested. "That always slows me down."

"Not funny."

The next few days were not easy ones for Corinne. Her upset over the incident seemed to grow—not so much because of the proposition but because of her reaction to it. My feeling was that Vinnie did not even realize he had said anything out of line, that in his world a woman would accept the invitation as a frank compliment. And, in fact, the next time Vinnie saw Corinne, he repeated the compliment.

"Oh," he said, "I'll bet you've decided to give your truckman a little kiss."

This time, however, Corinne was ready for him.

"Vinnie, you are sadly mistaken. You may think you're being flattering, but it is the most insulting thing I can imagine. I've been doing a lot of business with you. And if you expect me to go on paying good money for your services, you better stop treating me like someone you picked up on a street corner. Is that clear?"

"Yes," he said.

"And besides, if you try anything funny, I'm going to tell your wife." . . . .

At last it was November, and the trade had been for a year, only a year. In point of fact, the year had gone by quickly, and by the end of it I was just becoming accustomed to some aspects of the housewife's life. In many ways it had not been a true test for me. Any woman saddled with infants will know just how easy I had it. When babies are still in diapers, there is no simple escape, no way to slip off to the pool hall or the tavern for a break in routine. If I had had the problem of a baby in addition to the problems I faced, I might not have endured.

Then, too, money was never the problem it might have been. Had we tried the same trade a few years earlier, before Corinne's business was well launched, it would have been much more challenging. The main challenge would be to remain alive without food or money; by my calculations our money would have run out about midway through the third week of August.

Another key factor, one that I always kept in mind, was the temporary nature of the switch. No one tells a new bride that she is only going to be a housewife for a year. The difference between a year in prison and a life sentence is considerable.

Not only had Corinne been an excellent wife; she was a better husband than I'll ever be. There were no all-night poker games, no carousing with the boys until all hours, no hiding out weekends on the golf course. Moreover, I can't say enough about her as a provider. She paid the bills without a whimper, raised my allowance before I had to ask for it. I'm telling you, if more women could find husbands like Corinne, there would be fewer divorces.

I'm writing these words on the last day of the year, New Year's Eve. Starting tomorrow, I'll be paying the bills again. How will it go? The economy continues to look bleak; unemployment rises; I have no assurance that there will be room in that jungle for me. It has been months since I've seen any payment for my work—what right do I have to go out and try to be a provider again? What right do I have to ask Corinne to come home again, particularly since there is no guarantee that I can contribute as she has?

I'm not the first housewife to face these questions. I could hold back and be a housewife for another few months, at least until everything seems more settled economically, but the longer I stay away, the harder that return trip is going to seem. I'm not the first housewife who has to take a gamble to go back to work; nor will I be the last.

The closer we've come to understanding the nature of the roles in a marriage, the more important money seems. The freedom of a housewife can be purchased. Once she is in a position to assume some of the financial responsibilities, she can argue most effectively for the sharing of other responsibilities. Unsurprisingly there is an enormous conspiracy to prevent her from doing just that. The jungle awaiting her is a tangle of lower salaries and slower promotions, a solid wall of obstacles and attitudes all seemingly aimed at keeping the servant in the home. The trip is taken one step at a time. A small amount of money purchases a small amount of time; the time can be used for earning more money, for buying more freedom, and so on.

It isn't easy, and it doesn't happen overnight. Husbands are not notoriously keen about coming home to frozen dinners and unmade beds. Untended kids can complain as much as neglected husbands. And what is required in these instances is not a soft and loving heart so much as some tough-minded self-interest. It's all a matter of priorities. What is more important, a clean house or a person's future? A hot dinner or a human being free to function? It is entirely possible to have both, but there are times, particularly when the escape is being initiated, when hard choices have to be made.

I'm not for a minute advocating role reversal; replacing one unpaid servant with another doesn't change the system. The sole benefit of an experiment such as the one we have been going through is that each person will begin to understand the problems of the other; the heart of much real progress rests in one person's ability to put himself in another's shoes.

What we are after is an equal distribution of rights and responsibilities, a classless family.

The old marriage contract, sometimes seen as a trade of male protection for female servitude, never seemed to apply to us. More than sixteen years ago, when Corinne and I drove down to Virginia to elope, Corinne had a sudden change of heart. Why should we bother getting married? What did the vows really mean? I argued that it had been a long drive and that we had forked out for the license and gone through the blood test and—well, why not?

She finally agreed—but only reluctantly, and only if we would sit down first and write out our own private marriage contract. We wrote it on a napkin in a roadside diner. All in all, there were two dozen clauses covering such things as the guaranteed care and feeding of her old alley cat. One other stipulation provided that we wouldn't let a day pass by without making love......

In time the alley cat died and I would have too, if we had followed the contract to the letter. That first contract may not have withstood the test of time, but at least it was an attempt to live up to our own expectations, not society's. I think now we're ready for another contract, one that will someday undoubtedly seem as out-of-date as our first try.

The idea is hardly unique, and I have no idea whether our contract would work for any other family. Our family is in a somewhat enviable position; beginning tomorrow, it will have two breadwinners and two housewives—a sum total of two people, each with the capability of being a husband and each with the experience of being a wife.

The new year is fast approaching, and this may be a little rough. But I would like to have it completed by the time I make my last dinner as a full-time housewife. Lobster thermidor. I wish you could be here. Over the champagne the family will consider the following agreement:

THE MARRIAGE CONTRACT

General

The goal is to gain as much freedom as possible—freedom for everyone in the family to grow, to realize potential, to enjoy life to the full. The hope is to have a family that is supportive, each member promoting the well-being of the others. The base is to be one of sharing, an equal division of all responsibilities.

The Exchequer

It is understood, at the outset, that the money earned by either Corinne or Mike belongs to all members of the family. Our intention is to distribute the financial burden as equitably as possible, thus freeing us all for other pursuits. Although there will be an equal sharing at the beginning, if either of us suffers an economic setback, the other will simply make up the difference. On the other hand, should either of us enjoy a surprising increase in fortune, we will contribute a proportionately larger share to the family exchequer without expectation of compensatory privileges.

Household Expenses: All regular household expenses—heat, electricity, gas, mortgage, medical, charity, education, telephone and so forth—are to be paid from a special joint checking account set up for just this purpose. Corinne and Mike will handle the bookkeeping on alternate months.

The Household Account: This will be set up on the first of the year by depositing two one-thousand dollar checks. The account will be maintained by adding additional deposits whenever the total on reserve falls below two hundred dollars.

Major Purchases: All agreed-upon major purchases for the family—such as furnishings or appliances—are to be paid for in equal shares.

Personal Expenses: Individual expenses will be paid from individual accounts. These would include such items as creditcard expenses, personal clothing, car repairs and, generally, any expenses involving the individual but not the family.

Adult Responsibilities

All the responsibilities of keeping the home and the family are to be divided as fairly and as equitably as possible. To this end we here initiate the wife-for-a-week program. . . . .

The weeks of the year are to be divided equally between Corinne and Mike. On alternate weeks each is to act as wife and assume the wifely duties for that week. Since this is a nonbinding agreement—in fact, the intention is not to bind anyone—we understand there will be exceptions to the pattern, emergencies and times when days or weeks must be traded.

Food: The wife-for-a-week is to be responsible for shopping and preparing food in that week. The wife-for-a-week will also assume full responsibility for preparing breakfast and lunch for the three children; also for fixing coffee for the husband-for-a-week. Exception: Company meals are to be prepared by both Corinne and Mike.

Wife's Night Out: One night each week, the wife-for-a-week is given an evening away from all wifely duties. This is intended to offer some respite, also to allow each person to follow individual interests without concern to what the rest of the family is doing on that night.

Cleaning: The wife-for-a-week is to see that the house is cleaned thoroughly at least once during the week, either with or without the aid of hired help. The house should be turned over on Monday morning to the new wife-for-a-week in fairly good shape.

Hell Week: Four weeks a year—the first week in January, April, July and October—will be set aside for doing those jobs that no one wants to do. At the end of Hell Week—and full participation is mandatory—the basement will be clean, the yard will be neat, the trash will be gone, the clothes will be purchased, the sewing will be done and all other agreed-upon tasks will be accomplished. The responsibilities of Hell Week will be equally shared.

Children's Responsibilities

Servant-for-a-day Program: The wife-for-a-week will be assisted by the servant-for-a-day. Each of the three children will assume this role in turn. The primary responsibility for the servant-for-the-day is the kitchen's sanitation-maintenance program. The servant will be responsible for: 1) setting and clearing the table; 2) doing the dishes; 3) cleaning the kitchen; 4) taking out the garbage; 5) feeding the pets.

Shared Responsibilities

Cleaning of Bedrooms: Individuals will be responsible for seeing that bedrooms do not become pigpens.

Laundry: Each individual is responsible for taking care of personal laundry. The entire laundry cycle—washing and drying—is to be done at one time. Clothes never to be left in the laundry room.

Towels: Each individual has one color of towel and is responsible for all towels of that color. Liam—green; Sean—blue; Siobhan—yellow; Corinne —brown; Mike—red.

Violence: No hitting anyone ever.

Yelling and Swearing: No yelling or swearing; especially no yelling or swearing in voices loud enough to be heard by the neighbors.

General Philosophy: 1) Never do anything that bothers, hurts or inter-feres with another member of the family. 2) It's a home, not a house, and it should be treated accordingly. 3) Do unto others as you would have them do unto you.

WE'RE NOT HAVING CHILDREN*

Joan Rattner Heilman

Around this time of year, while other young women wheel their babies in the bright spring sunshine and sit in the park comparing their children's weight gains, toilet training and school grades, Rosemary Vaccaro is bumping along in her green pickup truck loaded with flower arrangements or maybe a set of dining-room chairs. When the sun dips down in the Georgia sky and the others are changing diapers, wiping junior dinners off the kitchen floor, and imploring their children not to jump on Daddy because he's just come home from work and he's tired, Rosemary and Jere Vaccaro sit peacefully in their cozy kitchen sipping drinks and talking over their day.

The Vaccaros have been married 11½ years and aren't planning to have a baby—ever. And people haven't stopped asking them, "When's the baby?"

"We don't *need* a baby," Rosemary says. "We enjoy each other so much that we've never felt there needed to be any addition, someone else in our family—which is the two of us. It's nice just the way it is."

Jere concurs. "There are other things in life besides having children. We do a lot more interesting things than anybody I know—we just can't find enough hours in the day."

Rosemary and Jere are now 33 and 39, two handsome people, with warmth and charm enough for six. Both of them grew up in Atlanta, Georgia, where they now live, met when Rosie and Jere's kid sister, Valerie, were best friends in the seventh grade. Their ways parted and Rosie and Jere met again when they were both involved with Theater Atlanta. Rosie, a tall, lanky, striking brunette who has a fine arts major and now works part-time as a free-lance interior decorator, drives around in her pickup truck in jeans and shirt. Jere, with dark hair, straight white teeth, broad muscular shoulders, is vice-president for U.S. marketing and operations of a German optical medical equipment company.

"We both adore children," Rosie says. "We think they're neat. Some of the kids around here come over all the time and ask if Jere can come out and play.

"Jere's sister's children are here a lot and we really enjoy them. But then they go home again! It's different having children 24 hours a day. You can't have a trial child—once you've got one, you've got one. You can't be sorry you did it; you can't give them back and start all over again.

"I think most people give less thought to having children than buying a

---

new washing machine. I think women are programmed into recreating themselves. It's pushed on them. They're supposed to get married and go off to a vine-covered cottage, and after a year or so, have a baby. Most of the time they don't even wonder why they're doing it or if they really want to.

"We don't have kids, because we decided not to. We didn't really talk much about it before we were married and then, after we were married, we knew we didn't want a baby right away. We wanted to learn how to live with each other, enjoy each other, go places, have fun. Jere was with the airlines then; he was manager of an airlines reservation office, and we had a chance to travel."

"It wasn't," Jere interjects, "that we made a firm resolution never to have children. We just didn't want them *then*. After three or four years, we realized we didn't want to change the way we were living or our relationship. Everybody we knew around our age had children or was about to have them, and, to tell the truth, we didn't like what was happening to their life-style. Something changed between the two people; there was this wedge between them. It didn't bring them together; it pushed them apart."

"There was a year or so when I thought I wanted a baby," Rosie says. "We were living in Virginia then, in 1966 and 1967, and I was unhappy and I felt isolated. I was away from my family for the first time and we had no friends around. I had a job I didn't like and I thought maybe I'd have a baby. I was bored and I thought, 'If I have a baby, I won't have to go to work any more, I'll have something to do, I'll have an identity, I'll be a mother.' I think a lot of women have babies because they can't think of anything else to do.

"Then I realized that wasn't what I wanted. When Jere and I discussed it, we decided we didn't feel we were missing anything by not having children, at least not yet. You don't miss what you've never had. I don't miss a yacht, because I never had one. All I'd be missing would be two o'clock feedings and diaper rash and orthodontists. I love playing with other people's babies but I have no urge to have one any more."

The Vaccaros live in an Atlanta suburb now, in a two-floor town house condominium set in a patch of woods near a stream. Children play in the short U-shaped street and in the small but pleasant front yards. Hilda, the Vaccaros' elderly 160-pound St. Bernard, rises to her four arthritic feet and wags her tail. "That old dog," says Rosie, "is almost as much resonsibility as a child. She takes thyroid pills and tonics and we have to give her a tranquilizer when we go out for a while. You know, you can get babysitters, but it's pretty hard to ask someone to come over and sit with your dog!"

Their house is warm and inviting, with a comfortable mixture of antique and contemporary furnishings, tastefully put together. Rosie has accidentally become an interior decorator since they have returned to Atlanta. When Robert Griggs, who is the city's top party decorator, found out the Vaccaros were back in town, he asked Rosie, whom he'd known in art school, if she'd help him occasionally. She agreed with alacrity, and has assisted him on many projects, notably the Piedmont Ball, "the biggest social event in Atlanta." Then a friend asked her to decorate his office, another wanted her house done over, and she was in business on her own as well. "It isn't full time," she says. "I fit the stuff into my day. And I'm planning to go back to art school and get my degree, too."

Jere, who got into the medical field 10 years ago and has been with his current firm three years, headquarters in the house, travels at least two or three days a week on business. When I interviewed them, there was talk of a possible move to Los Angeles where Jere would work out of the head office, promotion included.

Their day is packed. Both of them jog for two miles every morning at the local high-school track. ("I alternate two miles with two-and-a-quarter miles," says Rosie. "That way every other day I can say, 'Boy, I only have to go two miles today'.") Jere works out for at least an hour a day at a nearby gym and neither of them carries around an unnecessary ounce of fat.

The two spend much of their free time in the combined kitchen-dining-sitting room where there's a fireplace, a long old table and space to sit around. "I love to cook and I love to talk. This way I can do both at the same time," Rosie states. "And we both like to eat!"

I asked Rosie if people had ever accused them of being selfish because they didn't want children.

"Sure they have. Sometimes I think they're jealous of the way we live. Some people have the attitude: We have kids and we have problems; you should have them too. Women have griped to me about their kids and how they're stuck in the house and how they wouldn't have another one for a million dollars. Or I see mothers in the supermarket yelling and knocking their kids around, and then they turn around and push the mother instinct. I don't get the message. People say you're selfish because you're free to come and go, but I honestly feel it's much more selfish to have children for any other reason than just because you want them and will take care of them and love them. Some people use their children to give themselves meaning, to live through them or to have someone to take care of them when they get old. These are little human beings and shouldn't be used that way."

"Very few people consider the awesome responsibility when they have children," Jere adds. "They owe those children their complete attention. People say, 'Well, we're not going to let our children interfere with our lives.' That's wrong. If you have children, you *must* care for them, devote your time to them. Because those kids did not ask to be born. They *should* interfere. They should be the most important part of your existence. And if they're not, you shouldn't have had them, it's been a big mistake."

"Yes," says Rosie. "Somehow there's no stigma put on a mother who belts her kids around, because she did the natural thing and had children. But there's a great deal of stigma if you choose not to have any. Then 'there's something wrong with you.'

"I don't think I'd mistreat my kids, but I've seen such horrible things

people have done to children. I've got a lot of talents, and I think I have sympathy and empathy and the ability to love, but one thing I don't have is a lot of patience. I'm impatient, and I think it's wrong to be impatient with children. I don't know if I could cope. I don't know if I'm the motherly type, and I don't think it's right to have a baby just to find out. Anybody can get pregnant. Just because you get pregnant doesn't mean you're qualified to be a mother.

"Of course, this isn't for everybody and I don't think people who choose to have children are crazy or stupid—it would be awful if everyone said no to children. People who want them should have them. But they should respect our right *not* to have them. I don't want to offend anybody with children and I don't want to be offended because I don't have them.

"Now, I always tell people, when they ask if we have kids, 'No, by choice, we don't.' If you just say 'No,' they're sorry for you. Something's 'wrong.' It's a funny thing, people feel free to ask about it. People who wouldn't think of asking how you vote think nothing of asking whether or not you're fertile, or if your husband's 'the one.' Of course, once you tell them you chose not to have children, then they feel free to criticize."

The Vaccaros aren't the only couple in the U.S. who've made a conscious decision not to have children. There's a small but rapidly growing number of couples who have chosen the same route. According to the U.S. census figures, the number of American married couples who *expect* to have no children has quadrupled in the last six years. In 1967, one of every 100 wives between 18 and 24 planned to have no children; in 1973, one of every 25 wives in that age group expected to have none. Of all married women, 18 to 39, 4.2 percent expect no offspring.

In addition, studies made on California campuses in 1965 found that 10 percent of the students wanted no children after marriage. By 1970, the number had risen to 24 percent.

Margaret Mead, the 72-year-old anthropologist, said recently: "We are going to see fewer parental families, and those we do see will be better families, because the people who are doing it are wanting it."

"Parenthood is so important," says Dr. Lee Salk, a well-known child psychologist, "that people shouldn't take on that role unless they're willing to take on the responsibility. They should consider the alternatives. I don't think all people should be parents."

Until very recently, the "child-free by choice" were quite definitely a silent and often repressed minority, unaware of others who felt the same, taking their lumps from unsympathetic families and neighbors who couldn't imagine anyone rejecting the age-old tradition of having babies. But now some of them have banded together in chapters all over the country, in their own club, the National Organization for Non-Parents, whose object is to give them the strength of their convictions, let them communicate with other non-parents, help them deal with the outside pressures.

"NON is not against parenthood," asserts Audrey Bertolet, its executive director. "I have two children myself. But we feel it is a matter to be thought over. It will be a better world when parenthood is truly a choice and not a requirement, an automatic thing. Parenthood is permanent—there's no trial period. So we suggest people should postpone it until age 22 at the earliest, plan an interval of at least three years between marriage and the first child. This way, the people who have children will know they want them."

"There is definite prejudice against non-parents," says Ellen Peck, author of *The Baby Trap*, who with her husband founded NON, which now has 27 chapters and 10 more in the works. "People without an aptitude to be good parents, or those who are concerned about population control, or who simply want a child-free life should be allowed to have that option. It should be socially acceptable."

DEVASTATING PRESSURE

Rosie and Jere Vaccaro haven't joined NON—"I'm not a joiner," Rosie says. "But we certainly agree with them. People like us need bolstering because the pressure can be pretty devastating. We need to know we're not alone or crazy or un-American. We aren't hurting anyone; if anything, we're helping them by keeping the world less crowded. We don't hate people with children—anybody who truly wants kids should certainly have them—but they shouldn't hassle us either.''

I asked the Vaccaros all the questions posed most often to child-free couples. Like, if something happened to her or Jere, wouldn't the one who's left behind want a family, children?

"Now that really is a selfish reason to have children. To keep you company. Jere and I have enough resources, we have our own identities. We're both very capable of love. I'm sure there will always be somebody to love."

And in their later years? Who will take care of them? "Look at all the old people whose children don't want anything to do with them, shunted off into old folks' homes, ignored except for their birthdays or Christmas. Anyway, that's no reason to have children, to take care of you in your old age. What could be more selfish than that?"

Wouldn't a baby make you closer? If you were having problems in your marriage, wouldn't it bring you together?

"I don't know how we could be any closer," Jere answered. "We enjoy each other so much, how could a baby make us enjoy each other more? Certainly we know people with children and a beautiful marriage, so it's perfectly possible to have both. But we don't need children, basically we relate to each other; and our relationship has gotten stronger the longer we've been married. We're *growing* together. And if a couple has problems, how could children solve their difficulties? That's a way to cover things up and could drive people further apart, I think. And what if they then decide to break up? What about the kids then?

"My parents were divorced when I was twenty-one," Jere relates. "Rosie's parents separated when she was a teenager and her little sister was eight."

Rosie says, "I've seen it happen to so many people. But that didn't have anything to do with our choice; or maybe it did a little bit. But we've grown to know each other so well and we feel we have a better marriage than anyone else I know."

Hasn't Rosemary ever felt the need to be "fulfilled as a woman," to do what nature intended her to do, to prove she could do it? Doesn't she ever feel "unfeminine"?

"I think that could be a problem and I've thought about it, If I said I didn't, I'd be lying to you. But motherhood is really not the ultimate in femininity. I'm a woman. I'm a female. I know that, even though the idea did disturb me for a while. But I don't have to go through nine months of pregnancy and give birth just to prove it. Jere has never made me feel less of a woman because I didn't. I'm always *the* woman to him, you know, so what more of a woman could I be?"

And Jere, to prove he's "a real man"?

"A man who feels he has to have children to show his masculinity has a hangup," he says. "I've never felt the need."

Do the Vaccaros think they may ever change their minds about children?

"I don't think so," Rosie answers, "but you never know. You can't say how you're going to feel next year. But probably, if we felt we needed an addition, we'd adopt a child."

Don't they want to give their parents grandchildren? Haven't their parents put the pressure on?

"Well," says Rosie, "we've had pressure, certainly, but not too bad. Things like: 'Val (Jere's sister) is *pregnant*! Do *you* have any news for us?' The worst pressure came from friends and neighbors. Our parents have grandchildren on both sides, and they've accepted our position, though I guess they don't understand it. Jere's mother was pretty upset for a while, and I was told once by a member of our family that if we didn't have children, we wouldn't be left any money. That's comical, you know."

NOT THE ULTIMATE

While I was talking with the Vaccaros, Rosie's mother and father came by separately to visit. I asked them what they thought of the situation. Her mother told me: "Some people are child-oriented and others are not. Rose would make a wonderful mother, but I don't think children are necessary for a happy marriage. Having children isn't the ultimate, at least not anymore."

Her father's attitude was also accepting, although he was sorry about it. "It's their own prerogative and certainly they can do just as they please without my butting in. I love them the way they are. But I will say that I wouldn't take anything in the world for the three children I've got. I'm real thankful for them. I just think Rose and Jere will be sorry in later years that they didn't have a child."

"We don't know what the world will be like in a few years," Jere points out. "Little kids are going to grow up and have to get jobs and have to eat. They'll have to breathe. They'll need a decent place to live. And this isn't the greatest world today. People who have children need to think about this and what is going to happen to them when they grow up. What's the world going to be like in 50 years?"

"Whatever our reasons are," Rosie adds, "the real point is that having babies should be something people think about, not just *do*. If they really want to be parents, they'll do a much better job of it; they'll really love those kids. That's what kids need. If people know they have a choice, that it's not just pushed on them, then they'll have to be more loving."

"The truth is," says Jere, "we don't need children to be happy. I'm not saying this is for everybody, but it's right for us. It's not necessary for us to have a family—the two of *us* are a family."

CHANGING GROUND RULES AND EMERGENT LIFE-STYLES*

Robert N. Whitehurst

The measurement and evaluation of social changes affecting male-female relationships continues to be a popular sport for futurists. This may in part be a reflection of the power of the media and its concern for saleable messages, but it most likely is as well a reflection of some real changes occurring in the lives of a great number of people. It is suggested in this paper that real social change affecting men and women is occurring and that the changes are as of this time poorly understood by our usual sociological conceptions. The standard works on the sociology of the family simply fail to depict underlying currents of change within male-female relationships—partly because of the framework and traditionalist mold in which they are cast, partly because some of the change is taking place underground. Usually, family sociologists ask their questions in terms of a closed-system functionalist model which implies stability. Our concern will be to develop some ideas about what relationships will be like in the future based on the observation of some more general indicators of social change then survey data. The paper is thus speculative, but it is an inductive effort to draw some tentative conclusions about change on the basis of limited knowledge. All futurists must do the same—so, without apology, but remembering the tentativeness of it all, let us look at what's happening now.

SOME ALTERNATIVES

There is little evidence to suggest that in the foreseeable future, most people will not continue to opt for the conventional styles of marriage—that is, monogamy as usual, often with other people in clandestine relationships involved here and there. There is evidence, however, that a large (though as yet undetermined) number of people are opting for some alternative(s) to this older model. The reasons for this have been described elsewhere.[1] Extrapolating from current social trends, the following seem likely choices for significant numbers of people in the future—that is, as long as favorable political and economic conditions continue.

---

*By permission of Consensus Publishers, Inc.

Modified Open Marriage

Since its publication, the O'Neills' *Open Marriage* has become a best seller—possibly because many North American marriages are in some kind of semi-desperate straits.[2] Instead of giving up totally on marriage, many people are attempting to work out some kind of nonrestrictive relationship that would enable both partners to have something (such as more autonomy, freedom, time, privacy, and the like) each sees as desirable without totally breaking up the relationship. Attempts in this direction can be seen as a fairly straightforward extension of other North American values and habits. At this time it appears to be extremely difficult for most married people to extend the idea of non-exclusiveness in an open-ended relationship as far as the area of sexuality—a fact attested to by the O'Neills. But is a relationship genuinely open if one can have tennis and cocktails with someone who is a non-spouse, but one must stop short of sexual involvement with a non-spouse? As this problem now stands, it is a gray area, remaining undefined and ambivalently handled by many couples attempting to work out modified open marriages. Jealousy, although partly a result of cultural conditioning which can be modified, is still deeply related to the insecurities felt by almost everyone. Therefore, jealousy remains one of the areas in which it will take more effort to lessen the disparity between intellectual-normative commitment and the ability to follow through in actions and feelings the sense of commitment to new norms, such as non-jealousy.[3]

It is probably true as Jessie Bernard indicates in her recent work on women and marriage that women tend to be the losers in agreements made for open-ended marriages.[4] As women become better able to defend themselves from male put-downs, chauvinism, and manipulation, more true equality in working out satisfactory terms for such arrangements will become a possibility. In the meantime, many more couples will attempt to work out their own set of ground-rules governing their relationships. In the absence of older and more conventional guidelines (such as the Bible, local folklore, and the like) and of social control agencies, marriage in the immediate future is bound to become more difficult and problematic than ever before. Since the church, extended family, and the community no longer count on the old ways to keep us on to narrow paths, we will have to deal with our relationships on a more ad hoc basis.[5] On the negative side, this trend does lead inevitably to more ill-considered experimentation and probably to more disruption, but it also lends itself to innovation, creativity, and openness—values that are strongly held in this culture. It's a pity that we cannot get all this excitement, change, and suspense and keep the comfort of placid stability as well (a combination most of us long for), but unfortunately things don't seem to work out that way. Modified open type marriages which struggle with sets of rules to govern the relationships in some non-standard ways will probably become more of a modal response of younger marriages. How much success they will have in developing an ethic of sexuality in openness with others that still recognizes and supports the continued primacy of the original pair bond remains to be seen.

Post-Marital Singlehood

Increasing numbers of people are joining the ranks of the world of the formerly married.[6] Larger numbers of people are (mostly inadvertently) taking the advice of Bertrand Russell who suggested "get your divorce while you are young." Although there is little evidence as yet that large numbers of these individuals will not be returnees to the sea of matrimony, much more caution is now being exercised by those who married young, have undertaken divorces, and are not quite ready for another go at it. As the literature of women's liberation continues in its impact, as new freedom is experienced by more women (and some more men), marriage as an option becomes less appealing. A trend first described (at least in such detail and so vividly) by Toffler as "rentalism" may now be creeping into the people-specialization arena. Toffler described some of the current trends as ad hoc-ery, rentalism, transience, and novelty. All of these goals and adaptations can be seen in the lives of many young people who do not see how they could become committed to the older and more stable forms of marriage and family life that seem so dreadfully monotonous to them. As a result, many young and some not-so-young people engage in a lifestyle that puts them in touch with a fairly large coterie of friends who can be called upon for a variety of experiences, depending on the need of the moment. One recently divorced young person recently related:

> *Now, as a single female in my own apartment, I can organize my own life in ways that formerly were impossible with my husband—if I want sex now, I know exactly how to get it (and only when the mood is right), if I want good dinnertime conversation or to talk about intellectual things, I know who to call for this. The only problem is at times the hectic nature of life, as all these things do not work out so neatly as with one—but I am enjoying my freedom and ability to organize my life immensely and have no desire to go back to marriage. At some time in the future I may feel differently, but now the positives by far outweigh the negative things. My friends all respect my freedom and understand my needs. If life sometimes feels a bit fractionized, it is a small price to pay for the good things I am getting now as compared to the restrictive nature of marriage.*

What is expressed most clearly here is the fact that this person feels that pair-bonding in monogamy is highly restrictive and that freedom to be oneself can be fully obtained only in the unmarried state. Others have explained to me how they feel that the options open to a pair in marriage—or even in an open-ended relationship—are always constrictive. Fairly obviously, the strength of freedom needs versus security needs will be an important factor in determining who chooses which of these two life styles—an open marriage or post-married singlehood.* In any case, it is predictable that large numbers will opt for one or the other of these two life-styles as they are the simplest extensions of available possibilities of life as we now know it.

Extended Intimate Networks

When these occur without extramarital sexual involvement, they will probably be like those described by Stoller.[7] These networks of non-kin intimates will often include activities involving children and weekend recreational activities. They will sometimes be concerned with cooperative ventures intended to solve some of the economic problems of families, and in some cases may include common housing. More clearly, families with common problems with children, problems involving a lack of clear sense of community, and some sense of need to cooperate with others outside of the nuclear family unit will be most likely to try out this kind of alternative. This is an area that has been investigated pretty much in terms of child-care services and some recreational patterns. There are not as many widespread adaptations designed for sharing of some household goods, cars, and other goods and services not commonly shared between members of nuclear families. Neither the extent nor the direction of this trend is well understood and its implications for more radical forms of family sharing are unclear. There is a clear potential to consider this as a radical alternative if families share cars, TV's, vacations, and other commodities formerly held to be in the domain of the single nuclear family. The implications for sexual sharing are certainly present in any arrangement which involves intimacy and sharing of so many *other* aspects of one's personal life. However, this kind of arrangement must necessarily involve so many factors and be so complex, it may be unrealistic to view this as a viable alternative for very many families.

Swinging

Swinging can probably be dismissed as a non-radical activity in North American society since it does not affect the nuclear structure of the family in any real way.[8] Children are usually brought up conventionally in families of

---

*See typology in summary.

swingers, thus the implications for change—at least as the term is now understood—are minimal. The fears of becoming affectionately involved, if continued as a norm of swinging, do not enhance the probability of creating true alternatives to the conventional marriage. It tends instead to simply translate the old-fashioned ephemeral affair into a game for everyone.

Triad and Group Marriages

This topic has been covered to date best in the work of the Constantines.[9] To date, the amount of talk about the formation of group marriages far exceeds the number of steps taken toward making the commitment to actually doing it. Some group marriages have survived for a considerable length of time, but these have involved only a select minority of the total population. This does not mean that the implications of group marriage for the future are unimportant, for the fact that there is now talk on a large scale appears to indicate a willingness to accept new ideas, and perhaps at some point in the future to consider some kind of alternate venture for oneself. The most important implication is probably for the development of a truly democratic set of alternate possibilities in terms of sex, marriage, and family styles. Legitimizing freedom to try something other than conventional monogamy must be seen as a radical change in North American culture. As a realistic option for a large segment of the population, restrictions of past socialization will make the choice an extremely difficult one for most people. Thus, until the system becomes more open, true group marriages will likely be a statistically unimportant development in the future. Simple recognition of urban sex ratios, when coupled with an emergent norm of non-jealousy, will create a tremendously enhanced potential for triadal arrangements as an alternate life-style.

Rural Subsistence Communes

This form is probably the most subversive alternate life-style of all, even though it calls for something approximating some old-fashioned virtues—especially those of making it on your own and getting by because of your own labour. The rejection, sometimes nearly total, of the technology and consumer package held out as desirable for urbanites must be seen as revolutionary.[10] The adaptation of the work ethic in subsistence farm communes likewise is radical. What seems to be lacking is a rational formula that would describe the optimum ratio of numbers of people (with some requisite skills), the minimum numbers of acres for survival, and the minimum level of technology needed to make it effectively as subsistence farmers. To the extent that some communes have worked some of these problems out and are still operating, this form can be termed to be a limited success. Their goals are very much at odds with the dominant culture's mores of acquisition, consumption, and the never-ending search for status accompanied with the gadgetry of a productive society. Work (if defined as less-than-pleasant tasks) is simply something to be done (celebrated) as a symbolic gesture of man's cooperation with the land. It only helps one survive—then leisure, recreation, crafts, music, dancing, and sex become celebrated as normal events. Although the life-style is romantic and holds a great attraction for large numbers of escapists who hold some kind of idyllic dream of returning to nature, few have enough of a sense of commitment to endure for long a return to the primitive condition required by most of the farm returnees. Thus, as a viable life-style alternate, it must remain for most in an unimportant realm of reverie and daydream. We are, at least most of us, so urbanized and used to technology that few can resist the temptation of the life of "ease," even though it is often accompanied with dis-ease.

Since the rural commune denies many of the major values necessary to the maintenance of corporate capitalism, it is probably the most destructive to it. The fact that the rural subsistence farm commune is pretty much ignored as an aberration probably means that few establishment-types take the movement seriously, or that they have not as yet figured out how to co-opt it. Since in its extreme form, the rural commune denies traditional norms of sexual behavior, child-rearing, consumption, religious practice, and occupational rules of conduct, the establishment may think it safer to ignore than to confront. In terms of current or prospective numbers, it is not likely to become a major social movement.

CHANGING GROUND RULES

Some evidence suggests that there are a number of specific areas of intimate relationships which are undergoing restructuring.[11] Among the important norms that are changing, the following are more likely than some others to have an impact that creates greater awareness of alternate life-styles and possibly supports the trial of them.

Love

As an empathic response, the meaning of a sense of loving relation between individuals is dramatically changing. No longer do so many people believe in lifetime monogamous true-love as a possibility, even though it may be held out as desirable. Many feel that love by its very nature tends to be impermanent but life-giving and so should be enjoyed on those terms. Increasing numbers also feel that love can be shared and that it is possible to love any number of people simultaneously.

Jealousy

As a culturally-induced problem, jealousy tends to be regarded as purely the problem of the person experiencing the feeling, not the person who presumably produced the state. In marriage, if a husband and wife have agreed to a non-exclusive relationship, the problem of jealousy is one which each of them must grapple with and work through essentially alone. No longer is jealousy automatically seen as reasonable and as a sign that one partner loves the other. Jealousy more frequently is seen as a reaction to one's own immaturity and insecurity. Thus it is a problem to work out the best way one can; it less often means the "offending spouse" stops doing whatever it was that produced the jealous state (perhaps a distortion of the psychoanalytic view which holds that it is more often one's emotions that are out of line rather than the environment—or other people—who are provocative or destructive).

Sex

More often these days, sex is seen as an occasion to celebrate one's aliveness with another with whom one shares a loving relationship or at least has an understood sense of common attraction in which exploitation and gamesmanship have been minimized. Its central importance is receding and the symbolic meanings once attached to it appear to be diminishing. As the meanings change, the threat so often associated with sexual activity changes as well. The overall effect is to tend to make sexual activity a celebrated commonplace, much like eating, which can have many social connotations and varieties of expression. It (sex) is somehow becoming legitimized in the face of a still harshly punitive and repressed society. This may be due as much to the prurient interests of the majority and to the voyeurism of "the conventionals" as to the efforts of youth to construct new norms and new meanings surrounding sexuality. At least some of the implications of the changed attitudes on sex for marriage are rather obvious, as sex becomes something less than that magic which either makes or breaks a relationship in its total sense. When it is just one more lovely and loving activity that people do, and insofar as it becomes detached from the old order, humans stand to become enlarged as people.

If we could conceptualize extramarital sex (EMS) as a problem to be understood from the vantage point of role analysis, it might be clearer that more, not less, EMS should be expected in this kind of society. Looking at the respective roles of legal marriage partners as contrasted with lovers (extramaritally), it immediately can be seen that the content of the roles carries with it some relatively powerful portion of the explanation of the glamour of EMS activity (at least in the early stages of the development of EMS relationships).

At the onset of an EMS relationship, there is a flirting period in which all the romance and flashy verve of youth is recaptured, if even for a brief moment before the episode is either consummated or short-circuited. This initial encounter takes people back to more romantic days of their lives to situations replayed that are often forgotten or downplayed in the daily rituals of living as husband and wife. The role expectations for lovers are very similar to the situations in premarriage dating, in which topics of conversation, activities, and body preparations are the sort that tend to heighten romanticism and escape from boring daily realities. Thus it is likely that, given current North American values on newness and experience-seeking, we will continue to see a rise in EMS activity as long as opportunity structures remain open for participants.

After settling into marriage, wives less often have the opportunity (or may not as often make opportunity) to be shown off with husbands under the above described circumstances. Thus, in some combination of forces that impel males and females to stray from the conjugal bed, the following may be among the more important to understand: Given some doubts about current norms (or feelings of anomia—which means a sense that the rules do not apply to oneself or have no meaning), open opportunity, intelligence enough to engage in moral relativism, and a need for new experience (also aided by the contrast of daily dull routines), people are likely to seek EMS experiences more frequently. If this listing of predisposing factors is any indication, it is likely that many more North Americans may be at some level ready to consider the game.

A general hypothesis which may be tested by research also involves the changing nature of touching experiences in marriage. There is probably a decrease over the span of the marriage cycle of frequency of touching, fondling, and general caressing of partners; it may be that this is what people miss in relationships and are searching for in sexual situations. The basic content and meanings sought in EMS may then be sensual rather than sexual. However, due to our strong *expectations* of sexuality, much sexual interaction might occur as a substitute for sensuality. After all, in this culture it would almost be an affront to personal identity to engage in all the processes of beginning an 'affair' and then only engage in petting or body fondling: meanings get sexualized beyond their ordinary significance in the life of this kind of sex-obsessed culture and sexual acting-out is one result.

It is a growing norm that wives and husbands are not so much better or worse than each other, but simply different, and it is enough to experience the difference. However, since we are all extremely well conditioned to exercise a competitive framework in most of our activities, it will probably be some time before this emergent norm about the relative differences in people takes real effect. As siblings in families, we are compared favorably or unfavorably—not thought of simply as different human beings. Thus wives and husbands are similarly compared unfavorably (but apparently on second thought more often favorably) with paramours. Probably adopting such a norm would be extremely humanizing to all social contacts, but its acceptability is made less likely by the fact that it runs counter to what all North Americans seem to use as a perceptual base of experience—namely that there are good guys and bad guys out there and one's task is to simply sort them out, attach labels, then act on the premise that these categories *are* reality. Perhaps the norm is in part changing in response to a need of so many to avoid the bad-guy label for engaging in EMS. If so, the change must be welcomed as a more sophisticated reaction to all people, finally abandoning the witch-hunt process which separates people in favor of a more positive approach which enhances human interaction.

Children

Offspring are no longer seen as an unalloyed blessing to create the fabric of a solid marriage. They are less often seen as extensions of parents, as status objects, or as things to manipulate and control to our own liking. Children are, in counterculture families, less often prisoners of the family, are more likely to be treated as autonomous persons much earlier and kept in positions of dependence less long.[12] As both men and women take responsibility for contraception, both marriage and children will continue to be redefined in terms of the ecological and economic strategies felt to be appropriate for the coming world. Clearly, the meaning of having and rearing children is not the same as in times past.

Privacy

Jessie Bernard has shown that when people marry, there is a marriage that is *his* and one that is *hers*.[13] Quite obviously, if a woman's work is taken at all seriously (and it must be, given its level of professionalism) we might conclude that women will soon be demanding something like equal opportunity. This notion will no doubt extend to cover such exigencies as *her* study, *her* conventions attended, *her* own private sphere in which she can act with impunity and freedom as an agent of her own free will. This does not mean that home and family, husband-wife, and mother-child relationships will be non-existent. It simply means that wives and mothers will probably gain the same (or nearly the same) freedoms to pursue their own private and personal interests in much the same way as men have done for some time. Sports, corner-tavern drinking, and extended liberty from home as privacy spheres will no longer likely be the sole province of men. The future in this area looks as though it will become as good for women as for men—and a reasoned analysis should suggest no reason why this should not be.

SUMMARY

Some alternatives to conventional monogamous marriage have been discussed in the light of changes now occurring in North American society. The

two adaptations held to be most prevalent as potential alternatives to monogamy in its usual sense are modified open marriages and post-marriage single-hood. These are viewed as most probable in terms of the extensions of values and structures now available as options today. Open sexuality remains problematic in the near future for large numbers of people in male-female relationships. Although the norms governing jealousy are changing, some difficulties remain in closing the gap between stated ideals (intellectual commitment to a norm of non-jealous behavior) and actual behavior. Other adaptations such as extended intimate networks, swinging or comarital sex, triad and group marriages, and rural communes were discussed as having a lesser potential as viable options for many people. Changing male-female relationship ground rules involving love, jealousy, sex, children, and privacy were discussed as real changes having a potential effect on all men and women.

Earlier in the paper, it was suggested that people will opt for alternate life-styles in terms of a balance of their needs for freedom and autonomy as related to their sense of personal security or needs to be succored and emotionally supported constantly by one significant other. The following over-simple typology depicts these relationships and provides some suggestive hypotheses for research on the problem. In general, it is hypothesized that in cases of high personal security and high need for freedom, persons would be more likely to either resist marriage in the first place or wind up in the post-marriage single portion of the typology. If high security is found to coexist with a low freedom need, the result may be an expected outcome of marriage, possibly an open-ended style of relationship. Given a low sense of security and a

Marriage Orientations as an Outcome of the Relationship Between Sense of Personal Security and Need for Freedom and Autonomy

Sense of Personal Security*	*Need for Freedom and Autonomy*	
	High	*Low*
High	A. Singles or open-ended marriage	B. Variously open or modified open marriage
Low	C. Deeply ambivalent (but married)	D. Conventional marriage

Rank order of probability of occurrence of cases in cells:
(from highest or most frequent to least-often occurring)

C. Ambivalents
D. Conventionals
B. Modified open marriages
A. Singles and open-marriages

*Security, as used here, might be indicated by any or all of the following: Ability to be alone, To make decisions easily, Feeling good about oneself while alone, Feeling complete when alone, Not needing to compulsively seek company, Ability to face life cheerfully without need to scapegoat or blame others, i.e. accepting responsibility.

high need for freedom, one would expect to find the usual condition of men in marriage today—that is a deep sense of ambivalence and commitment to the idea of marriage.* This is probably the case in which marriage is most disparaged and most participated in by the average married man. It is probable that many married men want the security and good aspects of marriage but still prefer the freedom of singlehood. In the last case, given both low security and low need for freedom, one would expect more conventional marriages in this cell. There are, of course, many implications other than these to be drawn from such an exercise in typologizing, but it is instructive as a means of beginning to look at these relationships anew. There would probably be sex and age differences in the frequency in which each of the cells would locate the indicated responses. Other variables may be of equal or greater importance. Such a typology can be defended if it produces either thinking or research actions leading to verification, substitution, or alteration in terms of the purported realities.

*This is not meant to imply that were women provided with an equivalent structure of freedom and equal opportunity to express autonomy in their socialization experience that they would not be very similar to men in this respect.

References

1. R. Whitehurst, "Violence Potential in Extramarital Sexual Responses" *Journal of Marriage and the Family* (1971), 683–91.
2. N. O'Neill and G. O'Neill, *Open Marriage* (New York: M. Evans Co., 1972).
3. R. Whitehurst, "Jealous Wives and Adaptation Potential" to be published in 1972 by *Medical Aspects of Sexuality.*
4. J. Bernard, *The Future of Marriage* (New York: Grune and Stratton, 1971).
5. A. Toffler, *Future Shock* (New York: Random House, 1970).
6. M. Hunt, *The World of the Formerly Married* (New York: McGraw-Hill, 1966).
7. F. Stoller, "The Intimate Network of Families as a New Structure" in *The Family in Search of a Future*, H. Otto, eds. (New York: Merideth Corp., 1970), 145–60.
8. R. Whitehurst, "Swinging into the Future: Some Problems and Prospects for Marriage" presented at the Midwest Sociological Society, 1972.
9. L. Constantine and J. Constantine, "The Group Marriage" in *The Nuclear Family in Crisis*, Michael Gordon, ed. (New York: Harper and Row, 1972), 204–22.
10. R. Whitehurst, "Back to the Land: The Search for Freedom and Utopia in Ontario" presented at the Canadian Sociological and Anthropological annual meetings, Montreal, P.Q., 1972.
11. R. Whitehurst and B. Plant, "A Comparison of Canadian and American Reference Groups, Alienation, and Attitudes toward Marriage" *International Journal of Sociology of the Family*, I (1971), 1–8.
12. D. Smith and J. Sternfield, "Natural Childbirth and Cooperative Childrearing in Psychedelic Communes" in *The Nuclear Family in Crisis*, Michael Gordon, ed. (New York: Harper and Row, 1972), 196–203. Also, see Berger, et al., in *The Family in Transition*, Skolnick and Skolnick, eds. (Boston: Little Brown and Co., 1971).
13. J. Bernard, *Ms.* Magazine (1972), 46–9.

HEALTHY AND DISTURBED REASONS
FOR HAVING EXTRAMARITAL RELATIONS*

Albert Ellis

Psychologists and sociologists, as Whitehurst points out . . . tend to look upon extramarital relations as an unusual or deviant form of behavior and to seek for disturbed motivations on the part of husbands and wives who engage in adulterous affairs. Although there is considerable clinical evidence that would seem to confirm this view, there are also studies—such as those of Kinsey and his associates and of Cuber and Harroff—which throw considerable doubt on it.[1][2][3] In my own observations of quite unusual adulterers—unusual in the sense that both partners to the marriage agreed upon and carried out extramarital affairs and in many instances actually engaged in wife-swapping—I have found that there are usually both good and bad, healthy and unhealthy reasons for this type of highly unconventional behavior and if this is true in these extreme cases, it is almost certainly equally true or truer about the usual kind of secret adulterous affairs that are much more common in this country.[4]

Let me now briefly review what I consider to be some of the main healthy and disturbed reasons for extramarital unions. My material for the following analysis comes from two main sources: clinical interviews with individuals with whom I have had psychotherapy and marriage and family counseling sessions; unofficial talks with scores of non-patients and non-counselees whom I have encountered in many parts of this country and who are presumably a fairly random sample of well-educated middle-class adults, most of whom have been married for five years or more.[5][6] Although the first group of my interviewees included a high percentage of individuals whose marriages were far from ideal and were in many cases quite rocky, the second group consisted largely of individuals who had average or above-average marriages and who were, at the time I spoke to them, in no danger of separation or divorce.

From my talks with these individuals—some of which were relatively brief and some of which took, over a series of time, scores of hours—I am inclined to hypothesize the following healthy reasons for husbands and wives, even when they are happily married and want to continue their marital relationships, strongly wanting and doing their best to discreetly carry on extramarital affairs:

Sexual varietism. Almost the entire history of mankind demonstrates that man is not, biologically, a truly monogamous animal; that he tends to be

---

Extramarital Relations, edited by Gerhard Neubeck, copyright 1969.

more monogynous than monogamic, desiring one woman at a time rather than a single woman for a lifetime, and that even when he acts monogynously he craves strongly occasional adulterous affairs in addition to his regular marital sex. The female of the human species seems to be less strongly motivated toward plural sexuality than is the male; but she, too, when she can have varietistic outlets with social impunity, quite frequently takes advantage of them.[7]

A healthy married individual in our society is usually able to enjoy steady sex relations with his spouse; but he frequently tends to have *less* marital satisfaction after several years than he had for the first months or years after his wedding. He lusts after innumerable women besides his wife, particularly those who are younger and prettier than she is; he quite often enhances his marital sex enjoyment by thinking about these other women when copulating with his spouse; he enjoys mild or heavy petting with other females at office parties, social gatherings, and other suitable occasions; and he actually engages in adulterous affairs from time to time, especially when he and his wife are temporarily parted or when he can otherwise discreetly have a little fling with impunity, knowing that his spouse is not likely to discover what he is doing and that his extramarital affair will not seriously interfere with his marriage and family life. The man who resides in a large urban area and who never once, during thirty or more years of married life, is sorely tempted to engage in adultery for purposes of sexual variety is to be suspected of being indeed biologically and/or psychologically abnormal; and he who frequently has such desires and who occasionally and unobtrusively carries them into practice is well within the normal healthy range.

Love Enhancement.   Healthy human beings are generally capable of loving pluralistically, on both a serial and a simultaneous basis. Although conjugal or familial love tends to remain alive, and even to deepen, over a long period of years, romantic love generally wanes in from three to five years—particularly when the lovers live under the same roof and share numerous unromantic exigencies of life. Because romantic love, in spite of its palpable disadvantages, is a uniquely exciting and enlivening feeling and has many splendid repercussions on one's whole life, a great number of sensible and stable married individuals fall in love with someone other than their spouses and find, on some level, a mutual expression of their amative feelings with these others. To be incapable of further romantic attachments is in some respects to be dead; and both in imagination and in practice hordes of healthy husbands and wives, including those who continue to have a real fondness for their mates, become involved in romantic extramarital affairs. Although some of these affairs do not lead to any real sexual actualization, many of them do. The result is a great number of divorces and remarriages; but, in all probability, the result is an even greater number of adulterous love affairs that, for one reason or another, do not lead to legal separation from the original mate but which are carried on simultaneously with the marriage.

Experiential Drives.   Loving, courting, going to bed with, and maintaining an ongoing relationship with a member of the other sex are all interesting and gratifying experiences, not only because of the elements of sex and love that are involved in these happenings but also because the sex-love partners learn a great many things about themselves and their chosen ones, and because they experience thoughts, feelings, and interchanges that would otherwise probably never come their way. To live, to a large degree, is to relate: and in our society intimate relationships usually reach their acme in sex-love affairs. The healthy, experience-hungry married individual, therefore, will be quite motivated, at least at times during his conjugal life, to add to the experience which he is likely to obtain through marriage itself, and often to return to some of the high levels of relating with members of the other sex which he may have known before he met his spouse. His desires to experiment or to re-experience in these respects may easily prejudice him in favor of adultery—especially with the kinds of members of the other sex who are quite different from his mate, and with whom he is not too likely to become closely related outside of his having an extramarital liaison.

Adventure Seeking.   Most people today lead routinized, fairly dull, unadventurous lives; and their chances of fighting the Indians, hunting big game in Africa, or even trying a new job after working the same one for a decade or more are reasonably slim. One of the few remaining areas in which they can frequently find real excitement and novelty of a general as well as a specifically sexual nature is in the area of sex-love affairs. Once this area is temporarily closed by marriage, child-rearing, and the fairly scheduled pursuits that tend to accompany domestic life, the healthy and still adventure-seeking person frequently looks longingly for some other outlets; and he or she is likely to find such outlets in extramarital relationships. This does not mean that all life-loving mates must eventually try to jazz up their humdrum existences with adulterous affairs; but it does mean that a certain percentage of creative, adventure-seeking individuals will and that they will do so for reasonably sensible motives.

Sexual Curiosity.   Although an increasing number of people today have premarital sex experiences and a good number also have sex affairs between the time their first marriage ends by death or divorce and their next marriage begins, there are still many Americans, especially females, who reach the age of forty or fifty and have had a total of only one or two sex partners in their entire lives. Such individuals, even when they have had fairly satisfactory sex relations with their spouses, are often quite curious about what it would be like to try one or more other partners; and eventually a good number of them do experiment in this regard. Other individuals, including many who are happily married, are driven by their sex curiosity to try extramarital affairs because they would like to bring back new techniques to their own marriage bed, because they want to have at least one orgiastic experience before they die, or because some other aspect of their healthy information-seeking in sexual areas cannot very well be satisfied if they continue to have purely monogamous relations.

Social and Cultural Inducements.   Literally millions of average Americans occasionally or frequently engage in adultery because it is the approved social thing to do at various times and in certain settings which are a regular part of their lives. Thus, normally monogamous males will think nothing of resorting to prostitutes or to easily available non-prostitutes at business parties, at men's club meetings, or at conventions. And very sedate women will take off their girdles and either pet to orgasm or have extramarital intercourse at wild drinking parties, on yacht or boat cruises, at vacation resorts, and at various other kinds of social affairs where adulterous behavior is not only permitted but is even expected. Although Americans rarely engage in the regular or periodic kinds of sex orgies which many primitive peoples permit themselves in the course of their married lives, they do fairly frequently engage in occasional orgiastic-like parties where extramarital affairs are encouraged and sometimes become the rule. This may not be the healthiest kind of adulterous behavior but it is well within the range of social normality and it often does seem to satisfy, in a socially approved way, some of the underlying sensible desires for sexual experience, adventure, and varietism that might otherwise be very difficult to fulfill in our society.

Sexual Deprivation.   Many husbands and wives are acutely sexually deprived, either on a temporary or permanent basis. They may be separated from each other for reasons beyond their control—as when the husband goes off on a long business trip, is inducted into the armed forces, or is in poor physical health. Or they may live together and be theoretically sexually available to each other, but one of them may have a much lower sex drive than the other, may be sexually incompetent, or may otherwise be an unsatisfying bed partner even though he or she is perfectly adequate in the other aspects of marital life. Under such circumstances, the deprived mate can very healthfully long for and from time to time seek out extramarital affairs; and in many such instances this mate's marriage may actually be benefited by the having of such affairs, since otherwise acute and chronic sexual deprivation in the marriage may encourage hostilities that could easily disrupt the relationship.

The foregoing reasons for engaging in extramarital affairs would all seem to be reasonably healthy, though of course they can be mixed in with various neurotic reasons, too. Nor do these reasons exhaust the list of sane motivations that would induce many or most married individuals to strongly desire, and at times actually to have, adulterous liaisons. On the other side of the fence, however, there are several self-defeating or emotionally disturbed impulses behind adultery. These include the following:

Low Frustration Tolerance.   While almost every healthy married person at times desires extramarital affairs, he does not truly need to have them, and he can usually tolerate (if not thoroughly enjoy) life very well without them, especially if his marriage is relatively good. The neurotic individual, however, frequently convinces himself that he needs what he wants and that his preferences are necessities. Consequently, he makes himself so desperately unhappy when he is sexually monogamous that he literally drives himself into extramarital affairs. Being a demander rather than a preferrer, he then usually finds something intolerable about his adulterous involvements, too; and he often winds up by becoming still more frustrated, unhappier, and even downright miserable and depressed. It is not marriage and its inevitable frustrations that "bug" him; it is his unreasonable expectation that marriage should not be frustrating.

Hostility to One's Spouse.   Low frustration tolerance or unrealistic demandingness leads innumerable spouses to dislike their partner's behavior and to insist that the partner therefore ought not be the way he or she is. This childish insistence results in hostility; and once a married person becomes hostile, he frequently refuses to face the fact that he is making himself angry. He vindictively wants to punish his mate, he shies away from having sex with her (or encourages her to shy away from having sex with anyone who is as angry at her as he is), and he finds it much easier to have satisfactory social-sexual relations with another woman than with his wife. He usually "solves" his problem only temporarily by this method, since as long as he remains anger-prone, the chances are that he will later become hostile toward his adulterous inamorata, and that the same kind of vicious circle will occur with his relations with her.

Self-deprecation.   A great number of spouses are so perfectionistic in their demands on themselves, and so self-castigating when they do not live up to these demands, that they cannot bear to keep facing their mates (who are in the best positions to see their inadequacies). Because they condemn themselves for not being excellent economic providers, housekeepers, parents, sex partners, etc., they look for outside affairs in which fewer demands will be made on them or where they will not expect themselves to act so perfectly; and they feel more "comfortable," at least temporarily, while having such affairs, even though the much more logical solution to their problem would often be to work things out in their marriages while learning not to be so self-flagellating.

Ego-bolstering.   Many married men feel that they are not really men and many married women feel that they are not really women unless they are continually proving that they are by winning the approval of members of the other sex. Some of them also feel that unless they can be seen in public with a particularly desirable sex partner, no one will really respect them. Consequently, they continually seek for conquests and have adulterous affairs to bolster their own low self-esteem rather than for sexual or companionship purposes.

Escapism.   Most married individuals have serious enough problems to face in life, either at home, in their work, in their social affairs, or in their attitudes toward themselves. Rather than face and probably work through these problems, a number of these spouses find it much easier to run to some diverting affairs, such as those that adultery may offer. Wives who are poor mothers or who are in continual squabbles with their parents or their in-laws can find many distracting times in motel rooms or in some bachelor's apartment. Husbands who won't face their problems with their partners or with their employees can forget themselves, at least for an afternoon or an evening, in some mistress's more than willing arms. Both husbands and wives who have no vital absorbing interests in life, and who refuse to work at finding for themselves some major goal which would give more meaning to their days, can immerse themselves in adulterous involvements of a promiscuous or long-term nature and can almost forget about the aimlessness of their existences. Naturally, extramarital affairs that are started for these reasons themselves tend to be meaningless and are not vitally absorbing. But surely they are more interesting than mah-jongg and television!

Marital Escapism.   Most marriages in many respects leave much to be desired; and some are obviously completely "blah" and sterile and would better be brought to an end. Rather than face their marital and family problems, however, and rather than courageously arrange for a separation or a divorce, many couples prefer to avoid such difficult issues and to occupy themselves, instead, in extramarital liaisons, which at least sometimes render their marriages slightly more tolerable.

Sexual Disturbances.   Sexual disturbances are rather widespread in our society—particularly in the form of impotence or frigidity of husbands and wives. Instead of trying to understand the philosophic core of such disturbances, and changing the irrational and self-defeating value systems that usually cause them, many husbands and wives follow the line of least resistance, decide to live with their sexual neuroses, and consequently seek out nonmarital partners with whom they can more comfortably retain these aberrations.[8][9][10][11][12][13][14] Thus, frigid wives, instead of working out their sexual incompatibilities with their husbands, sometimes pick a lover or a series of lovers with whom they are somewhat less frigid or who can more easily tolerate their sexual inadequacies. Impotent husbands or those who are fixated on some form of sex deviation, rather than get to the source of their difficulties and overcoming them in their relations with their wives, find prostitutes, mistresses, or homosexual partners with whom they can remain "comfortably" deviant. In many instances, in fact, the spouse of the sexually disturbed individual is severely blamed for his or her anomaly, when little or no attempt has been made to correct this anomaly by working sexually with this spouse.

Excitement Needs.   Where the healthy married person, as shown previously in this paper, has a distinct desire for adventure, novelty, and some degree of excitement in life and may therefore be motivated to have some extramarital affairs, the disturbed individual frequently has an inordinate need for excitation. He makes himself, for various reasons, so jaded with almost every aspect of his life that he can only temporarily enjoy himself by some form of thrill-seeking such as wild parties, bouts of drunkenness, compulsive moving around from place to place or job to job, or drug-taking. One of the modes of excitement-seeking which this kind of a disturbed person may take is that of incessantly searching for extramarital affairs. This will not cure his basic jadedness, but will give him surcease from pain for at least a period of time—as do, too, the alcohol and drugs that such individuals are prone to use.

If the thesis of this paper is correct, and there are both healthy and unhealthy reasons for an individual's engaging in extramarital sex relations, how can any given person's motives for adultery be objectively assessed? If Mrs. X, a housewife and mother of two children, or Mr. Y, a business man and father of a teenage son, get together with other single or married individuals and carry on adulterously, how are we to say if one is or both are driven by sane or senseless motives? The answer is that we would have to judge each case individually, on the basis of much psychological and sociological information, to determine what the person's true impulses are and how neurotic or psychotic they seem to be. To make such judgments, however, some kind of criteria have to be drawn up; and although this is difficult to do at present, partly because of our still limited knowledge of healthy individuals and social norms, I shall take a flyer and hazard an educated guess as to what these criteria might possibly be. Judging from my own personal, clinical, and research experience, I would say that the following standards of healthy adulterous behavior might be fairly valid:

1. The healthy adulterer is non-demanding and non-compulsive. He prefers but he does not need extramarital affairs. He believes that he can live better with than without them, and therefore he tries to arrange to have them from time to time. But he is also able to have a happy general and marital life if no such affairs are practicable.

2. The undisturbed adulterer usually manages to carry on his extramarital affairs without unduly disturbing his marriage and family relationships nor his general existence. He is sufficiently discreet about his adultery, on the one hand, and appropriately frank and honest about it with his close associates, on the other hand, so that most people he intimately knows are able to tolerate his affairs and not get too upset about them.

3. He fully accepts his own extramarital desires and acts and never condemns himself or punishes himself because of them, even though he may sometimes decide that they are unwise and may make specific attempts to bring them to a halt.

4. He faces his specific problems with his wife and family as well as his general life difficulties and does not use his adulterous relationships as a means of avoiding any of his serious problems.

5. He is usually tolerant of himself when he acts poorly or makes errors; he is minimally hostile when his wife and family members behave in a less than desirable manner; and he fully accepts the fact that the world is rough and life is often grim, but that there is no reason why it *must* be otherwise and that he can live happily even when conditions around him are not great. Consequently, he does not drive himself to adultery because of self-deprecation, self-pity, or hostility to others.

6. He is sexually adequate with his spouse as well as with others and therefore has extramarital affairs out of sex interest rather than for sex therapy.

Although the adulterer who lives up to these criteria may have still other emotional disturbances and may be having extramarital affairs for various neurotic reasons other than those outlined in this paper, there is also a good chance that this is not true. The good Judeo-Christian moralists may never believe it, but it would appear that healthy adultery, even in our supposedly monogynous society, *is* possible. Just how often our millions of adulterers practice extramarital relations for good and how often for bad reasons is an interesting question. It is hoped that future research in this area may be somewhat helped by some of the considerations pointed out in the present paper.

References

1. A. Kinsey, *et al., Sexual Behavior in the Human Male* (Philadelphia: W. B. Saunders, 1948).
2. A. Kinsey, *et al., Sexual Behavior in the Human Female* (Philadelphia: W. B. Saunders, 1953).
3. J. Cuber and P. Harroff, *The Significant Americans* (New York: Appleton-Century-Crofts, Inc. 1965).
4. A. Ellis, *Suppressed: Seven Key Essays Publishers Dared Not Print* (Chicago: New Classic House, 1965).
5. Cuber and Harroff, *op. cit.*
6. A. Ellis, *Reason and Emotion in Psychotherapy* (New York: Lyle Stuart, 1962).
7. A. Ellis, *The Case for Sexual Liberty* (Tucson: Seymour Press, 1965).
8. A. Ellis, 1962, *op. cit.*
9. A. Ellis, *The Art and Science of Love* (New York: Lyle Stuart and Bantam Books, 1969).
10. A. Ellis, *Sex Without Guilt* (New York: Lyle Stuart and Grove Press, 1966).
11. A. Ellis, *The Search for Sexual Enjoyment* (New York: Macfadden-Bartell, 1966).
12. A. Ellis, *If This Be Sexual Heresy* (New York: Lyle Stuart and Tower Publications, 1966).
13. A. Ellis and R. Harper, *Creative Marriage* (New York: Lyle Stuart and Tower Publications 1966).
14. A. Ellis and R. Harper, *A Guide to Rational Living* (Englewood Cliffs, N.J.: Prentice-Hall, Inc. 1967, and Hollywood: Wilshire Books. 1967).

NORTH AMERICAN MARRIAGE: 1990[*]

Leo Davids

As a preamble for this attempt to predict the options and regulations defining marriage and family life in North America a generation from now, let us
consider some of the powerful long-term trends in this area which can be dis-
cerned either at work already, or coming very soon. These provide the casual
principles that will be extrapolated here to provide a scientific indication of
what the mating and parenthood situation is going to look like in another two
decades. The remainder of the paper is essentially a working-out of this predic-
tion exercise so that an account of the new situation is built up, which is the
best way we have to predict the nature of marriage in 1990.

"PARENTHOOD IS FUN"
MYTH WILL DIE

1. The foundation of almost everything else that is occurring in the sphere
of marriage and family life today is a process which will go right ahead in the
next decade or two, and will continue to have a vast effect on people's thinking
and their behavior. This process is what Max Weber called the *entzäuberung*,
the "demystification" or "disenchantment" of human life, which is a hallmark
of the modern orientation. Young people, especially, are continually becoming
more sophisticated—due to television, modern education, peergroup frankness
about all spheres of life, etc.—and they are no longer accepting the myths, the
conventional folklore, upon which ordinary social interaction has been based
during the past few decades. Thus, for instance, young people are gradually
rejecting the myth of "parenthood is fun," realizing that parenthood is a very
serious business and one which ought to be undertaken only when people are
ready to plunge in and do a good job.

Another grand complex of myths that is gradually being rejected is that of
romantic love, under which it is perfectly acceptable to meet a person, form a
sudden emotional attachment to that person without any logic or contemplation, and to marry that person on no other basis than the existence of this
cathexis. Similarly, the whole institution of "shot-gun weddings," in which an
unwanted unintended pregnancy (usually occurring with a lower class girl)
leads to what is called "necessary" marriage, is going to become a quaint

[*]Reprinted from: *The Futurist*, A Journal of Forecasts, Trends and Ideas About the Future.
Published by: World Future Society, An Association for the Study of Alternative Futures, 4916 St.
Elmo Avenue, Washington, D.C. 20014 U.S.A., (301) 656–8274.

piece of history which will be considered with the same glee that modern readers feel when they read about "bundling" in Colonial America. With young men and women who are all fully-informed about reproduction and what can be done to prevent it, such things will occur very rarely; romantic mate-selection, likewise, is going to continue only among the impoverished and marginally-educated segment of society.

Insofar as family life remains almost the only area of modern behavior that has not yet become rational and calculated but is approached with unexamined, time-honored myths, we can expect that this area is "ripe" for fundamental change. When serious, critical examination of all this really gets moving, very great changes will come about in quite a short time.

PROCREATION CAN BE SUBJECT TO COMMUNAL CONTROL

2. The second independent variable leading to the developments that we are discussing is the total control of human fertility which advances in medical technique have made possible. There is no need here to discuss the pill, intra-uterine device (IUD), and the many other ways that are in use already to separate sex from reproduction, and therefore to free relations between men and women from the fear or risk of begetting children who would be a by-product, an unintended side-effect of fulfilling quite other needs. This control of human fertility means that what procreation does occur in the future is going to be by choice, not by accident. Both illegitimacy and venereal disease will be almost extinct, too, in 20 years. It also means that reproduction and child rearing can henceforth be subjected to communal control, will be potentially regulable by society at large. Without contraception, all the rest of these trends and changes would not be occurring at all.

HUSBAND-WIFE EQUALIZATION IS "INEVITABLE"

3. Women's Liberation, I believe, is not a fad or a current mass hysteria but is here to stay. Once the schools had instituted co-education, male dominance was doomed. Let us rephrase that term for present purposes, calling it Husband-Wife Equalization, as a general name for certain tendencies that have been evident for many years and are continuing today. We all know that marriage has shifted, to borrow a phrase, from institution to companionship. Indeed, through the demystification-sophistication of young women, their employment in full-status work, and because of the control over reproduction that has now become a reality, the equalization (in regard to decision-making) of

wives with their husbands has become inevitable. The implications of this are already being voiced, to some extent, in the platforms and proposals of women's rights organizations, and some points will be touched upon herein.

It must be remembered that there will remain in the foreseeable future, a traditionalist minority even in the most advanced and change-prone societies. This segment will expend much effort to maintain patterns of marriage and family living that they feel are right, and which are consistent with the patterns they experienced when they were children. This traditionalist minority will certainly not be gone, or vanished to insignificant numbers, in the short span of one generation; therefore, any predictions we make must take into account not only what the "new wave" pattern is going to be, but also the fact that there will be a considerable number of people who elect to maintain the familiar value system that they were socialized with, and to which they are deeply commited.

LAW WILL ACCEPT ABORTION AND NEW FORMS OF MARRIAGE

4. Another trend which is already at work and which, we may assume, is going to accelerate in the future is that legislatures no longer attempt to shape or create family behavior by statute, but are, and increasingly will be, prepared to adapt the law to actual practice, so that it accepts the general viewpoint that public opinion has consensus on. I think that ever since Prohibition, legislators have been forced to agree that sooner or later legal reform must narrow the gap between law on the books and what is really happening in society. It is likely that this reforming and correlation is going to be speeded up in the next few decades, so that the extent to which there is an uncomfortable and problematic contradiction between the law in force and what people are really doing will be virtually eliminated. Thus, all of the ongoing changes with regard to contraception, abortion, new types of marriage contract, etc., will—it is here assumed—be accepted and in a sense ratified by the Law, as the old-style moralists who can still be found in our agencies of social control cease to fight a rear-guard action against the new norms that are, whether they like them or not, emerging. All modes of birth control will become medical problems, free of any statutory limitation.

5. An important consequence of widespread social-science knowledge among young people today, which is coupled with a greater use of principles drawn from sociology and anthropology in the process of law reform, will be the recognition that continuity or consistency for each person or married couple is necessary, in regard to the larger questions at least, for a particular marriage system to work well in the long run. If the agreements entered into, whatever their content, involve major inconsistency, if people seem to be

changing the fundamental norms between them in midstream or giving much more than they receive, then obviously the community has unwisely allowed these people to enter a situation which must lead to disorganization and conflict sooner or later. This realization from our functionalist understanding of how marriage—or any continuing relationship—operates, will lead to acceptance of the clear necessity for such predictability and fairness in every particular case.

So much for the preamble. What are the consequences? Two major principles underlying our model of marriage in 1990 emerge from the forces and trends listed above. They are: (a) the freedom to personally and explicitly contract the type of marriage one wishes; and (b) formal public or communal control over parenthood.

What is meant by the word "marriage," here? To include the newer forms, we require a looser, broader definition than would suffice in the 1950s. Marriage should therefore be understood to refer to a publicly-registered, lasting commitment to a particular person, which generally includes certain sexual or other rights and obligations between these people (that would not be recognized by their community without such married status).

Free choice of the sort of marriage one wishes does not mean that a man and woman (or two men or two women?) will write their own original contract incorporating any combination of rules and arrangements that they like. The reason that such freedom would be beyond that envisioned in our thinking, as argued above, is that they would be able to invent a contract that has severe internal inconsistencies or flights of self-delusion, and which therefore sets up strains for their relationship from the outset. The sophistication which anthropological functionalism has brought to us will lead society to channel the choice of marriage into a selection from among a number of recognized types, each of which has been carefully thought through so that it is tenable in the long run. Thus, people will select from among various ways of being married, each of which makes sense by itself and will enable them to function on a long-run basis once they have had this choice. Neither monogamy nor indefinite permanence are important in this respect, so they will not be required. However, the agreed-upon choice will be explicit and recorded so there's no question of deception or misunderstanding, as well as to provide statistical information, and official registration of this choice is an element of marriage which will remain a matter of public concern.

PEOPLE UNFIT TO BE PARENTS WILL BE SCREENED OUT

The right of society to control parenthood is something that can be predicted from a number of things we already know. For one thing, the rising incidence of battered and neglected children, and our almost total inability to really cope with the battered child's problem except after the fact, will certainly lead legislators to planning how those people who can be discovered, in advance, to be unfit for parenthood may be screened out and prevented from begetting offspring who will be the wretched target of their parents' emotional inadequacies. Furthermore, increasing awareness of the early-childhood roots of serious crime and delinquency will also lead to an attempt to prevent major deviance by seeing to it that early socialization occurs under favorable circumstances. It does not appear that there will be many other really effective ways in which rising crime rates could eventually be reversed. This, however, will again mean that those who raise children will have to be evaluated for this purpose in some way, so that only those parents who are likely to do a respectable job of early socialization will be licensed to release new members of society into the open community. If such testing and selection is not done, we have no way to protect ourselves from large numbers of young people who have been raised in a way that almost inevitably will have them providing the murderers, rapists and robbers of the next generation. Since we now begin to have the technology and the knowledge to prevent this, we may confidently expect that parent-licensing is going to come into force soon.

One other trend, perhaps phrased from the negative side, must also be mentioned here as we try to describe the norms that will probably circumscribe marriage in another generation. This trend is the decline of informal, personal social control over married couples which was formerly exercised by kinsmen and neighbours. It would not make sense to anticipate massive changes in the law and explicit contractual entry into marriage as the normal way to shape married life, if mate selection and the interactions between husband and wife were still under the regulation of custom, vigilantly enforced by aunts, grandfathers or brothers-in-law. It is precisely because the vast mobility of modern living has led, along with other factors, to the isolation of the nuclear family—which is the source of so many problems in the family sphere today—that this new kind of regulation will be called into force and accepted as necessary and proper. The recognition that marriage has left the sphere of *Gemeinschaft* will help to bring about a consensus that the regulation of this area of life will have to be handled like any other kind of socially-important interpersonal behavior in today's *Gesellschaft* civilization.

COURTSHIP MAY BE "DUTCH TREAT"

What will courtship be like in about twenty years? We can assume that courtship will, as it does currently, serve as a testing ground for the kind of marriage that people have in their minds, perhaps even dimly or unconsciously. Thus, insofar as particular young men or women may have begun to feel that the type of marriage they would like is Type A rather than Type B, their courtship would be of the sort that normally leads to Type A, and in a sense tests their readiness to build their relationship along those lines. Only the traditionalist couples will keep up such classic patriarchal customs as the male holding doors, assisting with a coat, or paying for both meals when a couple dines out together. The egalitarians would go "Dutch treat," i.e., each paying for himself, during this spouse research period. Thus, courtship will be of several kinds corresponding to the kinds of marriage that we are about to describe, with the conventional acts and phases in the courtship signalling the present intention of the parties involved to head toward that kind of marriage. Thus, pre-marriage and marriage will exhibit a psycho-social continuity, the early marriage centering on the basic interpersonal stance that is already represented in courtship.

Of course, courtship will serve this testing and assessing function after people have been approximately matched through computer mate-finding methods. Random dating and hopeless courtships will have been largely prevented through the provision of basic categoric information which people can use to screen possible spouses, such as total years of schooling completed, aptitude and IQ scores, major subjects (which are related to intellectual interests in a very direct way), religiosity, leisure and recreation preferences, and similar things.

For remarriage suitors, data on wealth or credit and occupation would also be used, along with some indication of attitudes concerning home life and procreation. Since homogamy (similarity between spouses) is recognized as an important indicator of marital success, such information will be systematically gathered and made available to cut down on the wasteful chance element in mate selection. It is only when people are continuing their search for a spouse within the appropriate "pool," defined in terms of those who are at the right point with regard to these variables, that courtship as a series of informal but direct experiments in relationship-building will come into play.

CELIBACY WILL BE LEGITIMIZED

Explicit choice of the kind of marriage one enters into is, of course, an effect not only of the emancipation of women but of men as well. What will some of the major options be? With the insurance functions that were formerly secured by having children (who would provide during one's old age) being completely taken over by the government (assisted by unions, pension funds and the like), there will be little reason to warn those who choose childlessness against this course. With celibacy no bar to sexual satisfaction, society will accept the idea that some segments of the population can obtain whatever intimate satisfactions they require in a series of casual, short-term "affairs" (as we call them today), and will never enter any publicly-registered marriage. With celibacy or spinsterhood fully legitimized, and with no fear of destitution when one has retired from the labor force, there will undoubtedly be a sizeable number of people who decide not to enter into a marriage of any sort on any terms.

TRIAL MARRIAGE FOR
THREE OR FIVE YEARS

Another not-unfamiliar option in this regard will be the renewable trial marriage, in which people explicitly contract for a childless union which is to be comprehensively evaluated after three years or five years, at which point either a completely new decision can be reached or the same arrangement can be renewed for another term of three or five years. This would not be, then, a question of divorce; it is simply a matter of a definite arrangement having expired. The contract having been for a limited term, both parties are perfectly free to decide not to renew it when that term is over. This would be a normal, perhaps minor, part of one's "marital career."

A third option, which introduces very few complications, is the permanent childless marriage; the arrangement between the two adults is of indefinite duration, but they have agreed in advance that there will be no offspring, and of course, there is no question but that medical technology will make it possible for them to live up to that part of the arrangement. Some will choose sterilization, others will use contraceptive methods which can be abandoned if one changes his mind and is authorized to procreate.

Compound marriages will also be allowed, whether they be polygamous, polyandrous or group marriages. However, these communes will not be free of the same obligations that any marriage entails, such as formally registering the terms of the agreement among the members; any significant change in the arrangements among members of such a familial commune will have to be recorded in the appropriate public place in the same way as marriages and divorces which involve only one husband and one wife. There will be great freedom with regard to the number of people in the commune, but internal consistency concerning the give-and-take among the members, their privileges and obligations, will be required. The functional, pragmatic ethics emerging in today's youth culture will be strictly adhered to, some years hence, not as moral absolutes, not because people have come to the belief that these represent the true right and wrong, but in order to prevent serious conflict.

LESS THAN THIRD OF MARRIAGES
WILL PRODUCE CHILDREN

With the majority of young people in society choosing one of the foregoing patterns, the number of marriages in which children are expected will be rela-

tively small; perhaps 25% to 30% of the population will be so serious about having children that they will be prepared to undergo the rigorous training and careful evaluation that will be necessary for them to obtain the requisite licenses. The marriages intended to produce children will usually be classic familistic marriages, in which the general pattern of interaction between husband and wife, as well as the relationship between parent and child, may be fairly similar to the contemporary upper middle-class marriage that we know in 1970. However, three-generation households will probably increase. I see no reason to believe that all of childrearing will be done in a collective way, as in an Israeli kibbutz or in the communes which have been set up in some Communist countries; infant care may gravitate in the direction of day nurseries, however, while school children will live at home, as now.

WOULD-BE PARENTS WILL HAVE TO PROVE THEIR SUITABILITY

The familial pattern, then, explicitly chosen by some men and women to perpetuate the classic familistic marriage, will be intended to provide a home atmosphere approximately similar to that which can be found in those middle class families of today's society that have the best socio-emotional climate. The community will be assured that this home atmosphere is, in fact, most probable, since it has been prepared for, rather than left to an accident of kind fate and to happenstance talents that people bring to parenthood nowadays. All those who desire to become parents, and therefore to exercise a public responsibility in an extremely important and sensitive area of personal functioning, will have to prove that they are indeed the right people to serve as society's agents of socialization. Just as those who wish to adopt a child, nowadays, are subjected to intensive interviewing which aims at discovering the healthiness of the relationship between husband and wife and of the motivation for parenthood, the suitability that the man or woman displays for coping with the stresses of parenthood, as well as the physical and material conditions that the adopted child will be enjoying, the evaluation of mother and father applicants in future will be done by a team of professionals who have to reach the judgement that this particular individual or couple have the background to become professionals themselves: that is, recognized and certified parents.

PARENT-TRAINING WILL BE INTENSE

The course of study for parenthood will include such subjects as: human reproduction and gestation; infant care; developmental physiology and psychology; theories of socialization; and educational psychology. Starting with a foundation of systematic but abstract scientific knowledge, the practical and applied courses in hygienic, nutritional, emotional and perceptual-aesthetic care of children will follow, in the same way as training for medicine and other professions. In addition to the subject matter referred to above, prospective parents will be required to achieve some clarity concerning values and philosophy of life, in which they will be guided by humanistic scholars, and will also be required to attain a clear understanding of the mass media, their impact on children, and how to manage mass media consumption as an important part of socialization in the modern urban environment. One side effect of such parent training may be a sharp drop in the power of the peer group, as parents do more and with greater self-confidence.

Suitable examinations will be devised, and only those who achieve adequate grades in these areas will be given a parenthood license. Some young men and women are likely to take the parenthood curriculum "just in case"; that is, although they have not yet thought through the type of marriage that they desire or the kind of spouse they are looking for, they may continue their education by entering parenthood studies and obtaining the diploma, should it turn out that they elect a classic, child-rearing marriage later on. Possibly, fathers will be prohibited from full-time employment outside the home while they have pre-school children, or if their children have extra needs shown by poor conduct or other symptoms of psychic distress.

One of the more striking areas of change, which can serve as an indicator of how different things will be then from what they are now, is age. Age of marriage now is in the early 20's, and child bearing typically occurs when women are in their middle twenties. Also, husbands today are usually about three to four years older than their wives. In another generation, the age of child bearing will probably be considerably advanced, as people who have decided upon parenthood will either be enjoying themselves during an extended childless period before they undertake the burdens and responsibilities of child rearing, or completing the course of study for certification to undertake parenthood. It is probable that women will bear children when they are in their middle and late thirties, so that they will have enjoyed a decade or a decade and a half of companionate marriage in which there was full opportunity to travel, to read, or just to relax before they have to spend 24 hours a day caring for a small child. As to the age difference between husbands and wives, which is essentially based on the patriarchal tradition that the man is the "senior" in the home, it will probably disappear in the case of all forms of marriage other than the classic familistic one; there, where people have explicitly decided that the kind of marriage they want is the same as their parents had back in the medievaloid 1970s, or the ancient 1960s, the husband will continue to be a few years older than his wife.

This picture of the marriage situation in 1990 leaves open various questions and problems, which should be touched upon briefly in conclusion. One of the difficulties in this scenario is the question of what authority will make the necessary decisions: What sorts of committees will be in charge of devising the various internally-consistent kinds of marriage, working out the parent education courses, and, certifying people for parenthood? There are, after all, political implications to controlling marriage and parenthood in this way, and the general public will have to be satisfied that those who exercise authority in this area are, in fact, competent as well as impartial.

Another problem is that of securing complete and valid information: (a) for those who are preparing to locate suitable mates through computer matching, or who are preparing to make a commitment in some specific form of marriage; and (b) concerning those who apply for the parenthood course and later for the license to practice parenthood. Unless we can be sure that the inputs used for making such judgements contain information which is adequate in quantity and true as well, these new systems will not be able to function without a great deal of deviance, and might easily engender problems which are worse than those which we confront today.

WILL CHILDLESSNESS LEAD TO
LESS LONG-RANGE INVESTMENT?

A third issue is that of parenthood having tied people to the community, and given them a commitment to the environment: What will childlessness do to one's motivation for planning/preserving; will it de-motivate all long-range investment? Research on this could start now, comparing parents with the childless.

Finally, we have assumed that marriage is going to continue, in some way. That is based on the belief that people will continue to desire a secure partnership with another person or small group, and that youth will feel it is better to institutionally buttress their sharing of life, in general, by setting up a marriage of some kind. This depends, in fact, on the interpersonal climate in communities, and the extent to which people feel isolation and unmet needs that marriage will solve. When marriage is not desired, then we will have discovered new forms of warm, dependable primary association replacing the old institution which has supplied psychological support to people through the millennia.

FATHER'S FIFTH TALK—
THE TRUE YOUNG KNIGHT*

T. W. Shannon

THE TRUE YOUNG KNIGHT

A true young knight is a boy, or young man, who is strong, brave, ambitious, intelligent, gallant and pure. The knights of the Middle Ages were strong men. They practiced athletics, took their outdoor sports and were proud of their physical strength. In those days, one with a weak, defective body could not be a knight. They were also brave men. They would die for what they believed to be right. They were very gallant toward women. They would offer every courtesy and respect to girlhood, womanhood, wifehood and motherhood. They had to be pure men to be strong, brave, gallant and manly. A knight would die in defense of womanhood.

The purpose of this chapter is to inspire you to become a true knight in your social relations with girls and ladies. The proper social relations of boys and girls, men and women, is one of the best ways of developing the social side of our lives, of improving the mind and strengthening our moral natures. God has made us social beings. He want us to enjoy life.

TREAT ALL GIRLS AS YOU WOULD
HAVE BOYS TREAT YOUR SISTER

Until girls are sixteen and boys are eighteen, when thrown together, it is wisest and best for them to engage in plays and games as children without any thought of being sweethearts. Small boys could learn that it is not manly for them to squeeze the hand of a girl, tease, pinch or pull a girl's hair and he should not think of such an ungentlemanly thing as to try to kiss a girl. The reason for this advice is, these relations tend to create in the mind thoughts that a true knight will not entertain. You would not want a boy to treat your sister in this way. A boy who would treat another boy's sister as he would not want her brother to treat his sister, is not a true knight. Nature and God teach that man is woman's protector.

---

*T. W. Shannon, *Self Knowledge,* 1913.

THE TRUEST BRAVERY

The boy who would expose himself to danger and death to save a girl from drowning or being crushed by a street car, is brave and deserves much praise. But he is not as brave and does not deserve as much praise, as does the boy who defends the honor and purity of a girl, not his sister. To positively refuse to allow a boy to talk about a girl in your presence in a way that you would not allow him to speak to your sister, is the courage of a knight. The good name of a girl is worth more to her than money, houses, and lands. It is so easy for boys, who engage in obscene language about girls, to invent and tell some story about some girl who is perfectly innocent, and, in this way, start others to talking about her. This is called slander. It is one of the most unmanly and cowardly deeds a boy can be guilty of. This is a very common sin among a class of boys. A boy cannot become a true knight who allows himself to have wrong thoughts about girls, much less to talk about them. All vulgar men were once vulgar boys. If you will cultivate a hatred for vulgarity while are a boy, you will hate it when you're a man.

BAD COMPANY

When hundreds of prisoners were asked, "What brought you to this?" they replied, "Bad company brought us to this." No doubt that more boys go wrong through bad company than through any other agency. When a boy keeps bad company, it will be very hard for him not to do as they do. Many times he will do wrong rather than be called "baby." A true knight will be interested in helping a bad boy to overcome his temptations, but he cannot run the risk of being injured by making a bad boy his companion. If he associates with the rude, listens to vulgarity long, he will become rude and vulgar.

BOYS SHOULD PROTECT GIRLS

The very thought of a boy's insulting your sister causes a feeling of great hatred to rise in your breast. Why is this? Girls are not as strong as boys. They need protection. That feeling comes to you because you know that you are your sister's protector. This is bravery. But the knightliest young knight is the boy who will not speak an unmanly word about another boy's sister and will bravely and kindly rebuke the boy who does.

THE TRUE KNIGHT HAS
ONE STANDARD OF MORALS

No young knight would play and associate with a girl who uses cigarettes, vulgarity or swears. Then, if he is brave, a true knight, he will not ask for better company than he is willing to give. The true knight of the twentieth century will have but one standard of morals. Ever since the days of savagery, when man could sway, exchange or sell his daughters in the same way that he could his property, society has been accustomed to a double standard of morals—purity and temperance for woman, do as you please for boys and men. In the days of savagery, the value of a girl on the marriage market was determined by her being pure. If she had been impure, no man wanted to buy her to become his wife, but she was stoned to death or forced to become a slave. Man was free. No one owned him. He could live just as he pleased. Woman could not do as she pleased. Her very life, the privilege of becoming a wife and mother all depended on her being pure. Is it not strange that people have allowed this relic of savagery to pass down the centuries without correcting it? People take what is customary to be right. They do not try to decide whether a custom is fair, just and right or not. It is hard to rid our minds of this old custom. If you should see a girl or woman walking along the street of a city smoking you would condemn her as a bad woman. But there goes a man doing the same thing. Is he as bad as the woman? We judge that he is not. Unless we know him as a gentleman. On a street corner or in a hotel you hear a girl or woman swearing and using the most obscene language. You do not hesitate to believe that she is bad. You would frown upon her in society. You would scorn her association. Even the guilty man would not respect such a woman. This is because custom has biased our very thinking. The very best people are unfair to the girl and the woman. They forgive in man what they condemn in the girl and woman.

WILL YOU ENLIST IN THE NEW KNIGHTHOOD

There was never an organized effort to break down and destroy the double standard of morals until some twenty years ago. In England there are several hundred organizations of young men, in some of these are several hundred members, and they have pledged themselves to live as pure lives as the girls they expect some day to marry. Every one of these boys and young men is a knight. These organizations are being formed throughout Canada, and there are some being formed in the United States. The world has never offered such a grand and great opportunity for boys to become knights as it does in this century. In the days of chivalry, the young man who gave his life to protect the honor of a lady was a truer knight than the man who gave his life on the battlefield to protect his country. It takes a higher form of bravery and manhood to protect the virtue of girlhood and womanhood than it does to face whizzing bullets, booming cannons, and exploding shells. The great purity movement of this age, with its ever-increasing army of brave, determined and self-sacrificing authors and lecturers, is enlisting and marshalling an army of knights destined to overthrow this monster of savagery. All over this country thousands of brave boys and men are enlisting. This great twentieth century crusade against vice is summoning to its ranks every chivalrous boy and man and every good girl and woman. Here is the chance to be a true knight. Will you enlist? We invite you. We welcome you to become a true knight.

X: A FABULOUS CHILD'S STORY*

Lois Gould

Once upon a time, a baby named X was born. This baby was named X so that nobody could tell whether it was a boy or a girl. Its parents could tell, of course, but they couldn't tell anybody else. They couldn't even tell Baby X, at first.

You see, it was all part of a very important Secret Scientific Xperiment, known officially as Project Baby X. The smartest scientists had set up this Xperiment at a cost of Xactly 23 billion dollars and 72 cents, which might seem like a lot for just one baby, even a very important Xperimental baby. But when you remember the prices of things like strained carrots and stuffed bunnies, and popcorn for the movies and booster shots for camp, let alone 28 shiny quarters from the tooth fairy, you begin to see how it adds up.

Also, long before Baby X was born, all those scientists had to be paid to work out the details of the Xperiment, and to write the *Official Instruction Manual* for Baby X's parents and, most important of all, to find the right set of parents to bring up Baby X. These parents had to be selected very carefully. Thousands of volunteers had to take thousands of tests and answer thousands of tricky questions. Almost everybody failed because, it turned out, almost everybody really wanted either a baby boy or a baby girl, and not Baby X at all. Also, almost everybody was afraid that a Baby X would be a lot more trouble than a boy or a girl. (They were probably right, the scientists admitted, but Baby X needed parents who wouldn't *mind* the Xtra trouble.)

There were families with grandparents named Milton and Agatha, who didn't see why the baby couldn't be named Milton or Agatha instead of X, even if it *was* an X. There were families with aunts who insisted on knitting tiny dresses and uncles who insisted on sending tiny baseball mitts. Worst of all, there were families that already had other children who couldn't be trusted to keep the secret. Certainly not if they knew the secret was worth 23 billion dollars and 72 cents—and all you had to do was take one little peek at Baby X in the bathtub to know if it was a boy or a girl.

But, finally, the scientists found the Joneses, who really wanted to raise an X more than any other kind of baby—no matter how much trouble it would be. Ms. and Mr. Jones had to promise they would take equal turns caring for X, and feeding it, and singing it lullabies. And they had to promise never to hire any baby-sitters. The government scientists knew perfectly well that a baby-sitter would probably peek at X in the bathtub, too.

---

*Reprinted by permission of International Creative Management. Copyright 1972 © by Lois Gould. First printed in *Ms. Magazine*.

The day the Joneses brought their baby home, lots of friends and relatives came over to see it. None of them knew about the secret Xperiment, though. So the first thing they asked was what kind of a baby X was. When the Joneses smiled and said, "It's an X!" nobody knew what to say. They couldn't say, "Look at her cute dimples!" And they couldn't say, "Look at his husky little biceps!" And they couldn't even say just plain "kitchy-coo." In fact, they all thought the Joneses were playing some kind of rude joke.

But, of course, the Joneses were not joking. "It's an X" was absolutely all they would say. And that made the friends and relatives very angry. The relatives all felt embarrassed about having an X in the family. "People will think there's something wrong with it!" some of them whispered. "There *is* something wrong with it!" others whispered back.

"Nonsense!" the Joneses told them all cheerfully. "What could possibly be wrong with this perfectly adorable X?"

Nobody could answer that, except Baby X, who had just finished his bottle. Baby X's answer was a loud, satisfied burp.

Clearly, nothing at all was wrong. Nevertheless, none of the relatives felt comfortable about buying a present for a Baby X. The cousins who sent the baby a tiny football helmet would not come and visit any more. And the neigh-

bors who sent a pink-flowered romper suit pulled their shades down when the Joneses passed their house.

The *Official Instruction Manual* had warned the new parents that this would happen, so they didn't fret about it. Besides, they were too busy with Baby X and the hundreds of different Xercises for treating it properly.

Ms. and Mrs. Jones had to be Xtra careful about how they played with little X. They knew that if they kept bouncing it up in the air and saying how *strong* and *active* it was, they'd be treating it more like a boy than an X. But if all they did was cuddle it and kiss it and tell it how *sweet* and *dainty* it was, they'd be treating it more like a girl than an X.

On page 1,654 of the *Official Instruction Manual*, the scientists prescribed: "plenty of bouncing and plenty of cuddling, *both*. X ought to be strong and sweet and active. Forget about *dainty* altogether."

Meanwhile, the Joneses were worrying about other problems. Toys, for instance. And clothes. On his first shopping trip, Mr. Jones told the store clerk, "I need some clothes and toys for my new baby." The clerk smiled and said, "Well, now, is it a boy or a girl?" "It's an X," Mr. Jones said, smiling back. But the clerk got all red in the face and said huffily, "In *that* case, I'm afraid I can't help you, sir." So Mr. Jones wandered helplessly up and down the aisles trying to find what X needed. But everything in the store was piled up in sections marked "Boys" or "Girls." There were "Boys' Pajamas" and "Girls' Underwear" and "Boys' Fire Engines" and "Girls' Housekeeping Sets." Mr. Jones went home without buying anything for X. That night he and Ms. Jones consulted page 2,326 of the *Official Instruction Manual*. "Buy plenty of everything!" it said firmly.

So they bought plenty of sturdy blue pajamas in the Boys' Department and cheerful flowered underwear in the Girls' Department. And they bought all kinds of toys. A boy doll that made pee-pee and cried, "Pa-pa." And a girl doll that talked in three languages and said, "I am the Pres-i-dent of Gen-er-al Motors." They also bought a storybook about a brave princess who rescued a handsome prince from his ivory tower, and another one about a sister and brother who grew up to be a baseball star and a ballet star, and you had to guess which was which.

The head scientists of Project Baby X checked all their purchases and told them to keep up the good work. They also reminded the Joneses to see page 4,629 of the *Manual*, where it said, "Never make Baby X feel *embarrassed* or *ashamed* about what it wants to play with. And if X gets dirty climbing rocks, never say 'Nice little Xes don't get dirty climbing rocks.' "

Likewise, it said, "If X falls down and cries, never say 'Brave little Xes don't cry.' Because, of course, nice little Xes *do* get dirty, and brave little Xes *do* cry. No matter how dirty X gets or how hard it cries, don't worry. It's all part of the Xperiment."

Whenever the Joneses pushed Baby X's stroller in the park, smiling strangers would come over and coo: "Is that a boy or a girl?" The Joneses would smile back and say, "It's an X." The strangers would stop smiling then, and often snarl something nasty—as if the Joneses had snarled at *them*.

By the time X grew big enough to play with other children, the Joneses' troubles had grown bigger, too. Once a little girl grabbed X's shovel in the sandbox, and zonked X on the head with it. "Now, now, Tracy," the little girl's mother began to scold, "little girls mustn't hit little—" and she turned to ask X, "Are you a little boy or a little girl, dear?"

Mr. Jones, who was sitting near the sandbox, held his breath and crossed his fingers.

X smiled politely at the lady, even though X's head had never been zonked so hard in its life. "I'm a little X," X replied.

"You're a *what*?" the lady exclaimed angrily. "You're a little b-r-a-t, you mean!"

"But little girls mustn't hit little Xes, either!" said X, retrieving the shovel with another polite smile. "What good does hitting do, anyway?"

X's father, who was still holding his breath, finally let it out, uncrossed his fingers, and grinned back at X.

And at their next secret Project Baby X meeting, the scientists grinned, too. Baby X was doing fine.

But then it was time for X to start school. The Joneses were really worried about this, because school was even more full of rules for boys and girls, and there were no rules for Xes. The teacher would tell boys to form one line, and girls to form another line. There would be boys' games and girls' games, and boys' secrets and girls' secrets. The school library would have a list of recommended books for girls, and a different list of recommended books for boys. There would even be a bathroom marked BOYS and another one marked GIRLS. Pretty soon boys and girls would hardly talk to each other. What would happen to poor little X?

The Joneses spent weeks consulting their *Instruction Manual* (there were 249½ pages of advice under "First Day of School"), and attending urgent special conferences with the smart scientists of Project Baby X.

The scientists had to make sure that X's mother had taught X how to throw and catch a ball properly, and that X's father had been sure to teach X what to serve at a doll's tea party. X had to know how to shoot marbles and how to jump rope and, most of all, what to say when the Other Children asked whether X was a Boy or a Girl.

Finally, X was ready. The Joneses helped X button on a nice new pair of red-and-white checked overalls, and sharpened six pencils for X's nice new pencilbox, and marked X's name clearly on all the books in its nice new bookbag. X brushed its teeth and combed its hair, which just about covered its ears, and remembered to put a napkin in its lunchbox.

The Joneses had asked X's teacher if the class could line up alphabetically, instead of forming separate lines for boys and girls. And they had asked if X could use the principal's bathroom, because it wasn't marked anything except BATHROOM. X's teacher promised to take care of all those problems. But nobody could help X with the biggest problem of all—Other Children.

Nobody in X's class had ever known an X before. What would they think? How would X make friends?

You couldn't tell what X was by studying its clothes—overalls don't even button right-to-left, like girls' clothes, or left-to-right, like boys' clothes. And you couldn't guess whether X had a girl's short haircut or a boy's long haircut. And it was very hard to tell by the games X liked to play. Either X played ball very well for a girl, or else X played house very well for a boy.

Some of the children tried to find out by asking X tricky questions, like "Who's your favorite sports star?" That was easy. X had two favorite sports stars: a girl jockey named Robyn Smith and a boy archery champion named Robin Hood. Then they asked, "What's your favorite TV program?" And that was even easier. X's favorite TV program was "Lassie," which stars a girl dog played by a boy dog.

When X said that its favorite toy was a doll, everyone decided that X must be a girl. But then X said that the doll was really a robot, and that X had computerized it, and that it was programmed to bake fudge brownies and then clean up the kitchen. After X told them that, the other children gave up guessing what X was. All they knew was they'd sure like to see X's doll.

After school, X wanted to play with the other children. "How about shooting some baskets in the gym?" X asked the girls. But all they did was make faces and giggle behind X's back.

"How about weaving some baskets in the arts and crafts room?" X asked the boys. But they all made faces and giggled behind X's back, too.

That night, Ms. and Mr. Jones asked X how things had gone at school. X told them sadly that the lessons were okay, but otherwise school was a terrible place for an X. It seemed as if Other Children would never want an X for a friend.

Once more, the Joneses reached for their *Instruction Manual.* Under "Other Children," they found the following message: "What did you Xpect? *Other Children* have to obey all the silly boy-girl rules, because their parents taught them to. Lucky X—you don't have to stick to the rules at all! All you have to do is be yourself. P.S. We're not saying it'll be easy."

X liked being itself. But X cried a lot that night, partly because it felt afraid. So X's father held X tight, and cuddled it, and couldn't help crying a little, too. And X's mother cheered them both up by reading an Xciting story about an enchanted prince called Sleeping Handsome, who woke up when Princess Charming kissed him.

The next morning, they all felt much better, and little X went back to school with a brave smile and a clean pair of red-and-white checked overalls.

There was a seven-letter-word spelling bee in class that day. And a seven-lap boys' relay race in the gym. And a seven-layer-cake baking contest in the girls' kitchen corner. X won the spelling bee. X also won the relay race. And X almost won the baking contest, except it forgot to light the oven. Which only proves that nobody's perfect.

One of the Other Children noticed something else, too. He said: "Winning or losing doesn't seem to count to X. X seems to have fun being good at boys' skills *and* girls' skills."

"Come to think of it," said another one of the Other Children, "maybe X is having twice as much fun as we are!"

So after school that day, the girl who beat X at the baking contest gave X a big slice of her prizewinning cake. And the boy X beat in the relay race asked X to race him home.

From then on, some really funny things began to happen. Susie, who sat next to X in class, suddenly refused to wear pink dresses to school any more. She insisted on wearing red-and-white checked overalls—just like X's. Overalls, she told her parents, were much better for climbing monkey bars.

Then Jim, the class football nut, started wheeling his little sister's doll carriage around the football field. He'd put on his entire football uniform, except for the helmet. Then he'd put the helmet *in* the carriage, lovingly tucked under an old set of shoulder pads. Then he'd start jogging around the field, pushing the carriage and singing "Rockabye Baby" to his football helmet. He told his family that X did the same thing, so it must be okay. After all, X was now the team's star quarterback.

Susie's parents were horrified by her behavior, and Jim's parents were worried sick about his. But the worst came when the twins, Joe and Peggy, decided to share everything with each other. Peggy used Joe's hockey skates, and his microscope, and took half his newspaper route. Joe used Peggy's needlepoint kit, and her cookbooks, and took two of her three baby-sitting jobs. Peggy started running the lawn mower, and Joe started running the vacuum cleaner.

Their parents weren't one bit pleased with Peggy's wonderful biology experiments, or with Joe's terrific needlepoint pillows. They didn't care that Peggy mowed the lawn better, and that Joe vacuumed the carpet better. In fact, they were furious. It's all that little X's fault they agreed. Just because X doesn't know what it is, or what it's supposed to be, it wants to get everybody *else* mixed up, too!

Peggy and Joe were forbidden to play with X any more. So was Susie, and then Jim, and then *all* the Other Children. But it was too late; the Other Children stayed mixed up and happy and free, and refused to go back to the way they'd been before X.

Finally, Joe and Peggy's parents decided to call an emergency meeting of the school's Parent's Association, to discuss "The X Problem." They sent a report to the principal stating that X was a "disruptive influence." They demanded immediate action. The Joneses, they said, should be *forced* to tell whether X was a boy or a girl. And then X should be *forced* to behave like whichever it was. If the Joneses refused to tell, the Parents' Association said, then X must take an Xamination. The school psychiatrist must Xamine it physically and mentally, and issue a full report. If X's test showed it was a boy, it would have to obey all the boys' rules. If it proved to be a girl, X would have to obey all the girls' rules.

And if X turned out to be some kind of mixed-up misfit, then X should be Xpelled from the school. Immediately!

The principal was very upset. Disruptive influence? Mixed-up misfit? But X was an Xcellent student. All the teachers said it was a delight to have X in their classes. X was president of the student council. X had won first prize in the talent show, and second prize in the art show, and honorable mention in the science fair, and six athletic events on field day, including the potato race.

Nevertheless, insisted the Parents' Association, X is a Problem Child. X is the Biggest Problem Child we have ever seen!

So the principal reluctantly notified X's parents that numerous complaints about X's behavior had come to the school's attention. And that after the psychiatrist's Xamination, the school would decide what to do about X.

The Joneses reported this at once to the scientists, who referred them to page 85,759 of the *Instruction Manual*. "Sooner or later," it said, "X will have to be Xamined by a psychiatrist. This may be the only way any of us will know for sure whether X is mixed up—or whether everyone else is."

The night before X was to be Xamined, the Joneses tried not to let X see how worried they were. "What if—?" Mr. Jones would say. And Ms. Jones would reply, "No use worrying." Then a few minutes later, Ms. Jones would say, "What if—?" and Mr. Jones would reply, "No use worrying."

X just smiled at them both, and hugged them hard and didn't say much of anything. X was thinking, What if—? And then X thought: No use worrying.

At Xactly 9 o'clock the next day, X reported to the school psychiatrist's office. The principal, along with a committee from the Parents' Association, X's teacher, X's classmates, and Ms. and Mr. Jones, waited in the hall outside. Nobody knew the details of the tests X was to be given, but everybody knew they'd be very hard, and that they'd reveal Xactly what everyone wanted to know about X, but were afraid to ask.

It was terribly quiet in the hall. Almost spooky. Once in a while, they would hear a strange noise inside the room. There were buzzes. And a beep or two. And several bells. An occasional light would flash under the door. The Joneses thought it was a white light, but the principal thought it was blue. Two or three children swore it was either yellow or green. And the Parents' Committee missed it completely.

Through it all, you could hear the psychiatrist's low voice, asking hundreds of questions, and X's higher voice, answering hundreds of answers.

The whole thing took so long that everyone knew it must be the most complete Xamination anyone had ever had to take. Poor X, the Joneses thought. Serves X right, the Parents' Committee thought. I wouldn't like to be in X's overalls right now, the children thought.

At last, the door opened. Everyone crowded around to hear the results. X didn't look any different; in fact, X was smiling. But the psychiatrist looked terrible. He looked as if he was crying! "What happened?" everyone began shouting. Had X done something disgraceful? "I wouldn't be a bit surprised!" muttered Peggy and Joe's parents. "Did X flunk the *whole* test?" cried Susie's parents. "Or just the most important part?" yelled Jim's parents.

"Oh dear," sighed Mr. Jones.

"Oh dear," sighed Ms. Jones.

"Sssh," ssshed the principal. "The psychiatrist is trying to speak."

Wiping his eyes and clearing his throat, the psychiatrist began, in a hoarse whisper. "In my opinion," he whispered—you could tell he must be very upset—"in my opinion, young X here—"

"Yes? Yes?" shouted a parent impatiently.

"*Sssh!*" ssshed the principal.

"Young *Sssh* here, I mean young X," said the doctor, frowning, "is just about—"

"Just about *what?* Let's have it!" shouted another parent.

". . . just about the *least* mixed-up child I've ever Xamined!" said the psychiatrist.

"Yay for X!" yelled one of the children. And then the others began yelling, too. Clapping and cheering and jumping up and down.

"*SSSH!*" SSShed the principal, but nobody did.

The Parents' Committee was angry and bewildered. How *could* X have passed the whole Xamination? Didn't X have an *identity* problem? Wasn't X mixed up at *all?* Wasn't X *any* kind of a misfit? How could it *not* be, when it didn't even *know* what it was? And why was the psychiatrist crying?

Actually, he had stopped crying and was smiling politely through his tears. "Don't you see?" he said. "I'm crying because it's wonderful! X has absolutely no identity problem! X isn't one bit mixed up! As for being a misfit—ridiculous! X knows perfectly well what it is! Don't you, X?" The doctor winked. X winked back.

"But what *is* X?" shrieked Peggy and Joe's parents. "*We* still want to know what it is!"

"Ah, yes," said the doctor, winking again. "Well, don't worry. You'll all know one of these days. And you won't need me to tell you."

"What? What does he mean?" some of the parents grumbled suspiciously.

Susie and Peggy and Joe all answered at once. "He means that by the time X's sex matters, it won't be a secret any more!"

With that, the doctor began to push through the crowd toward X's parents. "How do you do," he said, somewhat stiffly. And then he reached out to hug them both. "If I ever have an X of my own," he whispered, "I sure hope you'll lend me your instruction manual."

Needless to say, the Joneses were very happy. The Project Baby X scientists were rather pleased, too. So were Susie, Jim, Peggy, Joe, and all the Other Children. The Parents' Association wasn't, but they had promised to accept the

Later that day, all X's friends put on their red-and-white checked overalls and went over to see X. They found X in the back yard, playing with a very tiny baby that none of them had ever seen before. The baby was wearing very tiny red-and-white checked overalls.

"How do you like our new baby?" X asked the Other Children proudly.

"It's got cute dimples," said Jim.

"It's got husky biceps, too," said Susie.

"What kind of baby is it?" asked Joe and Peggy.

X frowned at them. "Can't you tell?" Then X broke into a big mischievous grin. *"It's a Y!"*

THE DREAM OF SPIRITUAL MARRIAGE*

Morton Hunt

In the second and third centuries A.D. the Roman Empire, despite its infirmities, still gave the appearance of greatness and glory; indeed, in the great cities life continued to be as sybaritic and elegant as ever, and some of the greatest extravagances of construction and entertainment occurred in this very period. Yet in the midst of these glories, certain citizens were beginning to act in a bizarre and un-Roman fashion: in a world that offered them unprecedented luxuries and pleasures, they were unaccountably attracted to a new religion called Christianity which scorned the former and castigated the latter. Some of the patricians whose philosophy had long been based on the value of power, wealth, and practicality were succumbing to a new philosophy that stressed meekness, poverty, and mysticism. Although they lived in a society that was confirmed in the practice of Ovidian love and the indulgence of desire, they were inexplicably drawn to a faith that denied them the right to worldly love or sensuous enjoyments, and promised them instead a disembodied eternity.

One of these people was a young man named Ammon, who grew up in the latter part of the third century in Alexandria. Despite the buffeting the Empire had taken from civil wars and barbarian attacks for the previous fifty years, that city was still opulent, extravagant, and gorgeous during Ammon's youth; it was the Roman Empire's finest metropolis in the East, and combined the graces and sophistication of Hellenic culture with the pomp and pageantry of Rome. Most of its inhabitants lived just as Alexandrians had for the past two centuries, but a few, including Ammon, had begun to shun luxury and comfort in favor of poverty and pain, and in the very midst of life seemed to long for death.

What Ammon looked like or how he spent his boyhood and youth we do not know; all we are told by historians is that his parents were wealthy, and died when he was young, leaving him in the guardianship of an uncle. He evidently, however, lived in a fine house, was surrounded by servants, and had access to fine food, the baths, the games, the theater, and, of course, women. But Ammon was a Christian, and a devout one; at some point in his youth, taking seriously the words of Saint Paul and the early Fathers of the Church, he decided to remain chaste and to prepare himself for eternity.

The uncle held no such somber views, however, and having selected a proper bride for Ammon, he forced the youth to submit to a wedding. It was celebrated in the traditional Hellenic fashion by a joyous gathering of both families, followed by the usual banquet and then the procession to the nuptial chamber. Here the friends and relatives undoubtedly uttered all the worn amiable jokes, wished the bridegroom well with hearty platitudes, and finally left the two alone. Ammon closed and bolted the door, and turned to his bride, who was lying on the nuptial couch. There followed a remarkable scene, according to the account given by the fifth-century ecclesiastical historian, Socrates Scholasticus:

> He took a book containing the epistles of the apostles and read to his wife Paul's Epistle to the Corinthians, explaining to her the apostle's admonitions to married persons. [1 Corinthians vii: 1–9 are the particularly relevant verses, and include such crucial ideas as: "It is good for a man not to touch a woman. Nevertheless, to avoid fornication, let every man have his own wife, and let every woman have her own husband. . . . I would that all men were even as I myself. . . . I say therefore to the unmarried and widows, it is good for them if they abide even as I. But if they cannot contain, let them marry: for it is better to marry than to burn."] Adducing many external considerations besides, he descanted on the inconveniences and discomforts attending matrimonial intercourse, the pangs of child-bearing, and the trouble and anxiety connected with rearing a family. He contrasted with all this the advantages of chastity; described the liberty and immaculate purity of a life of continence, and affirmed that virginity places persons in the nearest relation to the Deity.[1]

Ammon's young bride—her name was not recorded by Socrates—listened to this harangue with what very likely began as astonishment, but, according to the historian, ended as conviction. She and Ammon forthwith purified their marital union by jointly renouncing the world and taking a vow of celibacy. The last laugh was on the wedding guests.

The young couple lived as brother and sister, devoting themselves to contemplation and to the adoration of God, but after a while they realized that their life in Alexandria, surrounded as it was with fleshly comforts, was out of keeping with their aims. Abandoning all comforts, they moved south of Alexandria to Mount Nitria in the Egyptian desert country, installed themselves there in a rude hut, and took up an ascetic existence. Yet Ammon's wife, considering their way of life, found even this still too close to worldly ways. "It is unsuitable," she said to him one day, "for you who practice chastity to look upon a

woman in so confined a dwelling; if it is agreeable to you, let us live apart."
Ammon thought it a meritorious suggestion; they lived thenceforth in two huts,
near enough for occasional visits, and observed identical rules of self-mortifi-
cation, using neither oil nor wine, eating nothing but dry bread and water, and
often fasting one, two, or three days at a time.

Even so, Ammon sensed that temptation lay always in wait for him. Considering that the sight of his own body involved danger, he took a resolve never
to remove his clothing. "It becomes not a monk," he said, "to see even his own
person exposed." Once he wished to cross a river, but was as unwilling to get
his clothes wet as to remove them. In this dilemma, he besought the help of God;
if one may believe the devout historian, He must not have considered the matter beneath His notice, for an angel promptly appeared, picked Ammon up, and
deposited him on the other side, both dry and virtuous.

The fame of Ammon and his wife spread rapidly; not only did five thousand monks (according to the possibly wishful estimate of Palladius) gather
about them within a few years to emulate their asceticism, but continent marriage became a Christian dream for several centuries thereafter. If it was never dominant statistically, it surely was intellectually. For centuries, while
Christianity struggled against the flesh, continent marriage was praised as the
highest form of union between man and woman. Genuine data do not exist, but
innumerable allusions to cases of continent marriage appear in the patristic
writings and ecclesiastical histories; even if we allow for the adverse effect of
piety upon accuracy, it would seem that it existed with some frequency and
was talked about to the point of obsession.

To be sure, one may doubt that many of the reported cases were altogether successful; even those ecclesiastics who most praise continent marriage admit its fragility, and tell of instances of failure. Saint Jerome, writing from
Palestine in A.D. 408 to a wealthy young man named Rusticus in one of the out-
lying provinces, revealed just such a story. "Your former wife," he said, "who
is now your sister and fellow servant in Christ, has told me that, acting on the
apostolic precept, you and she lived apart by consent that you might give your-
selves to prayer, but that after a time your feet sank beneath you as if resting
on water and indeed—to speak plainly—gave way altogether." For Rusticus
and his wife had moved together again and sunk back into wedded pollution;
then, overwhelmed by a sense of guilt, the wife journeyed to Palestine to do
penance, while Rusticus promised to follow as soon as he could settle his affairs, which were in tangled condition due to a threatened barbarian invasion.
Time passed, but he did not arrive. So Jerome wrote him, urging him to come,
but whether he ever did is not known; he may have feared the misery of continent marriage as much as life under barbarian masters. Yet even though Rusticus failed in his attempt to lead this purified kind of married life, the very fact
that he and his wife tried to do so indicates the power of the new ideal; had he
and his wife lived two centuries earlier, they would have regarded any such
notion with derision and incredulity.

For several centuries—those very centuries when the once-firm structure of the Empire was weakening, and at least disintegrating—continent marriage was celebrated by Christians as a state scarcely less noble than dedicated celibacy; it seemed, indeed, to be one form of Christian reaction to the doom and destruction that first lowered, and then broke, upon the Roman world. Cases of it were reported and celebrated throughout the disintegrating Empire from its most civilized redoubts to its lost colonies, from indolent, decadent Alexandria to semibarbaric Gaul.

It was from Gaul, in fact, that there came one tale of continent marriage that sounded a new and important theme—that of chaste romance. Gregory, Bishop of Tours in the sixth century, told in Book One of his *History of the Franks* the story of Injuriosus, a wealthy young man of senatorial rank who had lived in Auvergne in southern Gaul in the early part of the previous century. Though the Visigothic invasions had disturbed and disrupted life in many parts of the Western Empire, Auvergne was relatively tranquil, and Injuriosus lived in a fine mansion, as befitted a Roman patrician, and got his income from his vast inherited domains. When he reached manhood, he paid a sizable price to obtain a bride of good senatorial stock, and married her. But when they retired that evening, his bride turned her face to the wall as soon as she got into bed, and began weeping bitterly. Injuriosus gently asked why she was crying. According to Bishop Gregory, she explained: "I had resolved to keep my poor body for Christ, pure from the contact of man. But woe is me, who am in such wise forsaken of Him that I availed not to carry out my desire." In place of unfading roses, she added, there would now be disfigurement and corruption. Would that she had died as a child! She abhorred the things of this world, including—for she was specific about it—Injuriosus' fine mansion and great estate.

The young man replied mildly that she was, like him, an only child, and that both their families would be made happy by the continuation of each line. This appeal fell flat; the world and its vanities, she argued at considerable length, were worthless, and the only real bliss lay in the eternal life. Injuriosus, having listened to her long harangue, at last found himself strangely freed of his desires and uplifted in spirit. "Through thy sweetest eloquence," he said, "eternal light hath shone upon me, as it were a mighty radiance." To her great delight, he thereupon vowed to abstain from fleshly desires; husband and wife then made a solemn pact of virginity, clasped hands, and at once fell asleep peacefully.

For many years they slept chastely in the same bed and led a good life, managing their property and serving God. When both of them died, the servants built tombs for them against different walls of the building, but in the middle of the night the tombs moved together until they rested side by side. "Which thing shows," concluded Gregory, "that when two are united in heaven, the tomb that holds their bodies buried may not keep them asunder. The people of that place have chosen to call these twain 'The Two Lovers' until this day." He was much impressed, as always, by a physical miracle; the modern reader may think the emotional miracle by far more impressive.

Even stranger than continent marriage was a somewhat similar arrangement between men and women known as spritual marriage that existed in the early days of the Church. Unmarried virgins known as *agapetae* (from the Greek, *agape*, spiritual love) would become spiritual sisters or spiritual wives (the two terms being used almost interchangeably) of the clergy, with whom they lived in household intimacy. Their relationship ostensibly involved no unchastity, but they had not even the tie of marriage to excuse them from sin in case their feet (to borrow Jerome's phrase) were to sink beneath them. The agapetae must have been numerous and widespread from the second through the sixth century. Tertullian and Hermas, among other early writers, praised them; what is more significant, such ecclesiastical writers as Irenaeus, Jerome, Saint John Chrysostom, Epiphanius, and Eusebius all complained about them, and, at least from the historian's point of view, one complaint is better evidence of their prevalence than ten hosannahs.

Many of the religious leaders and sects which permitted agapetae and spiritual marriage later came to be regarded as heretical. Perhaps the Church was wise to recognize that the arrangement would fail in the long run. Only in a disintegrating society, when men and women were transfigured by their search for an eternal and better world, might they be able to maintain such a relationship, and even then it was often suspect. Paul of Samosata, Bishop of Antioch at the end of the third century, was sharply scolded by a group of fellow bishops for having two "blooming and beautiful" spiritual sisters who traveled everywhere with him. Other heretical clerics such as Alexander the Montanist and Apelles the Marcionite maintained companionships they claimed were pure, but the orthodox doubted the wisdom of their efforts and the truth of their claims. Since the orthodox destroyed the writings of most of the heretics, one can hardly come to an impartial conclusion on the question.

But agapetae were also found within unimpeachably correct churches as well. No diaries or letters of these women or their male friends have survived, but one can glean some vivid details about the companionship from the outraged polemics of the righteous. "From what source has this plague of 'dearly beloved sisters' found its way into the church?" fumed Jerome in A.D. 408. "They live in the same house with their male friends; they occupy the same room, often the same bed; yet they call us suspicious if we think that anything is wrong." The early Christians were, after all, Romans; they tried to carry out the tenets of a new faith within a framework of old customs. Even a celibate cleric and his spiritual sister might still wear senatorial garments and live in a mansion; similarly their sexual patterns might be a composite of old and new, confusing to observers and themselves alike. In the search for chastity, for instance, they evidently arrived at a kind of compromise that consisted of intimate love play stopping short of actual sexual connection; such is the picture one gets from a troubled letter written in A.D. 249 by Cyprian, Bishop of Carthage, to a fellow church-leader who had consulted him on the subject.

*We have read, dearest brother, your letter which
you sent to Paconius, our brother, asking and desiring us to write again to you and say what we thought
of those virgins who, after having once determined to
continue in that condition and firmly to maintain
their continency, have afterwards been found to
have remained in the same bed side by side with men
(of whom you say that one is a deacon); and yet that
the same virgins declare that they are chaste . . . We
must interfere at once with such as these, that they
may be separated while yet they can be separated in
innocence, because by and by they will have become
firmly joined by a guilty conscience. . . .*

    *And do not let any of them think to defend her-
self by saying that she may be examined and proven
a virgin, for both the hands and the eyes of the mid-
wives are often deceived, and even if she be found to
be a virgin in that particular in which a woman may
be so, yet she may have sinned in some other part of
her body which may be corrupted and yet cannot be
examined. Assuredly the mere lying together, the
mere embracing, the very talking together, and the
act of kissing, and the disgraceful and foul slumber
of two persons lying together, how much of dishonor
and crime does it confess![2]*

Some of the more earnest practitioners of this relationship considered that
great merit lay in this "trial of chastity," and sought to expose themselves to
the maximum of temptation so as to gain virtue by resisting it. According to the
legend recorded by a medieval scholiast, a certain Irish holy man of the sixth
century named Scuthin always slept in bed with two beautiful virgins. When
Saint Brendan the Navigator chided him for taking such risks, Scuthin challenged him to prove himself equally capable of virtue. Brendan tried it and
managed to resist temptation; he found himself, however, quite unable to sleep,
and cut the experiment short.

    By diligent opposition, The Church slowly eradicated agapetism. It per-
sisted longest in monastic life; in the Irish Church, for instance, monks and
nuns shared monastic houses until late in the sixth century. "They did not
scorn to administer and live together with women," wrote an old ecclesiastical
historian, "because being founded upon the rock, they did not fear the wind of
temptation." But the church felt the rock could stand some buttressing, and the
practice was condemned by the sixth-century Irish Rules and Penitentials. In
Spain, three separate synods in A.D. 589, 590, and 633 recognized the inability
of conscience permanently to master such temptation, and ordered the house-

keepers and female companions of the clergy to be sold as slaves. As for the central Church itself, from the Council of Nicaea on (A.D., 325), the clergy were forbidden to have women in their houses; the custom must have been difficult to stamp out, for the penalties grew ever stricter as time passed. Leontius, Bishop of Antioch, gave the only convincing answer to those who doubted that a man and his agapeta could be wholly blameless: faced with an order to rid himself of his female companion, he castrated himself and kept her. It was not an answer most men cared to give.

References

1. Socrates: *Ecclesiastical History*, iv, 23. The story was also told, with minor variations, by another fifth-century historian, Palladius, in his *Historia Lausiaca*, 8.
2. Cyprian: *Epistle lxi* in the Ante-Nicene Library edition; same as *Epistle iv* in Oxford edition.

EPILOGUE

Vicarious experience is no adequate substitute for working through a situation. Further reading about family dramas is not the same as encountering those realities. Some of the readers of this book will already have met and resolved to their satisfaction many of the crucial issues presented here; others will not have worked out adequate solutions. None will have escaped all of the concerns up to their present age and stage.

Although no substitute, reading about and studying family realities can provide understanding of the past and facilitate preparation for the future. This has been our hope for *Encounter With Family Realities*.

*

NAME INDEX

*

SUBJECT INDEX

†